History of Central Africa
THE CONTEMPORARY YEARS
since 1960

edited by
David Birmingham and Phyllis M. Martin

Longman
London and New York

Addison Wesley Longman Limited
Edinburgh Gate,
Harlow, Essex CM20 2JE, United Kingdom
and Associated Companies throughout the world.

Published in the United States of America by Addison Wesley Longman, New York.

First published 1998

ISBN 0–582–27608–X CSD
ISBN 0–582–27607–1 PPR

British Library Cataloguing in Publication Data

A catalogue entry for this title is available from the British Library

Library of Congress Cataloging-in-Publication Data

History of Central Africa : the contemporary years since 1960 /
  edited by David Birmingham and Phyllis M. Martin.
      p.   cm.
  Includes bibliographical references and index.
  ISBN 0–582–27608–X (csd). — ISBN 0–582–27607–1 (ppr)
  1. Africa, Central—Politics and government—1960– 2. Africa,
Southern—Politics and government. I. Birmingham, David.
II. Martin, Phyllis.
DT352.8.H57 1998
967.03′2—dc21   97–25419
                                                                  CIP

Set by 35 in 10/12pt Bembo
Produced by Longman Singapore Publishers (Pte) Ltd.
Printed in Singapore

Contents

List of maps

List of tables

Preface

The contemporary history of Central Africa began with rapid political transformation throughout the region. In 1960 France granted independence to its
four equatorial territories, and to Cameroun which it had administered on
behalf of the United Nations. Belgium handed power even more precipitately
to the new politicians of the Congo, though after a brief civil war, and an
armed intervention by the United Nations, the civilians were replaced by
the army, which renamed the country Zaire. The Portuguese faced serious
peasant rebellions in both Mozambique and Angola, though they held on to
government for another fifteen years by dint of military effort. When the
Portuguese left Central Africa the strategic vacuum was partially filled by the
Cold War superpowers, the United States and the Soviet Union. Finally in
British Central Africa a colonial federation collapsed in 1959, eventually leaving African civilians in command of Zambia and Malawi, and heavily armed
settlers in temporary control of Rhodesia which became the internationally
recognised republic of Zimbabwe in 1980.

In the mid-1990s the states of Central Africa still retained the frontiers they
had inherited from their colonial rulers and had in some respects acquired the
attributes of nations with patriotic cultural identities and capital cities bursting
with the economic initiative needed for survival. In each case, however, government had been unable to meet some basic aspirations of their citizens.
They were weakened by civil war or rebellion in the cases of Angola and
Zaire, taken over by self-serving soldiers in Congo and Chad, isolated from
their people by accumulated wealth in Gabon and Malawi, subordinated to
the interests of South Africa in Zimbabwe and Mozambique, dependent on
the neo-colonial influence of France in Cameroun and the Central African
Republic, shackled to the world price of copper in the case of Zambia. Many
of the writers in this book speak of the weakness of the state, the decline of
the state, even the deconstruction of the state. And yet the nations survive,
their schoolrooms are packed with children learning in French, in Portuguese

or in English, their churches and mosques are bursting with worshippers, their markets are thronged with farmers, fishwives and every kind of merchant, their bars beat out the latest popular music by the best new bands.

In the mid-1990s, also, problems in neighbouring regions spilled into eastern Central Africa. The history of Zaire became intimately involved with the politics of the East African highlands. The ancient mountain kingdoms of Rwanda and Burundi had formed part of German East Africa in the early colonial period and had then been governed on behalf of the League of Nations and United Nations by Belgium in the later colonial period. In 1962 they had become independent republics on the eastern border of Zaire. Demographic pressures, land shortages, class rivalry and potent new concepts of ethnicity made the politics of both states very turbulent. As shown in chapters five and ten these disruptions spread into Zaire with dramatic consequences, and a particularly acute rivalry developed over Rwanda between the United States and France. In 1994, Rwanda was taken over by an army trained in Uganda and largely composed of returning refugees who had fled their homeland on the eve of independence. Over two years hundreds of thousands of refugees fled out of Rwanda into the eastern part of Zaire. Those who had survived appalling conditions in refugee camps were later forced to return to Rwanda where competition for land continued and made unlikely a lasting solution to the country's problems. At the same time, in 1996–7, the Rwanda army discreetly supported forces in Zaire which ended the long-running dictatorship of General Mobutu. When Mobutu fell the new president, Laurent Kabila, changed the name of Zaire back to the 'Democratic Republic of Congo' and it seemed likely that provincial names might also change.

Central African historians of the late twentieth century have documented the decline of the state, the crises caused by population growth, the flight from the countryside to the towns, the conspicuous expenditure of the wealth derived from the Atlantic coast oilwells, and the survival of the poor in neglected villages and provinces. They have also observed the suffering wrought by foreign intervention, but as the twentieth century ended hope was again fuelled by democratic elections and by a new development climate. Some observers hoped that Central Africa might cease to be the world's backwater where local people have exclusively to rely on their own resources and skills to recover from a century which has often been filled with pain, exploitation and uncertainty.

David Birmingham, Canterbury
Phyllis M. Martin, Bloomington
April 1997

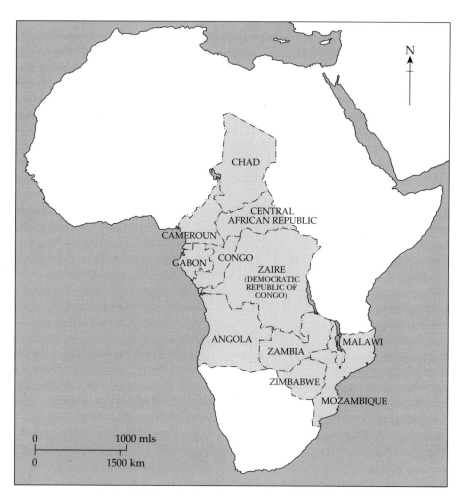

Map 1.1   Central Africa

CHAPTER 1

Beyond independence

PHYLLIS M. MARTIN

1960 is celebrated as a turning point in the grand narrative of African nation-alism. In that year seventeen countries achieved independence and took their seats at the United Nations. In Central Africa, liberation from colonial rule was celebrated throughout the francophone states of Chad, Cameroun, the Central African Republic, Gabon, Congo-Brazzaville (later the Republic of Congo), and Congo-Léopoldville (Zaire) and these developments accelerated the process of decolonisation in regions to the south. By 1964 Nyasaland (Malawi) and Northern Rhodesia (Zambia) had prised themselves loose from British settler domination. Portugal, itself a dictatorship, was reluctant even to consider steps towards decolonisation, yet sustained resistance by guerrilla fighters in Angola and Mozambique, brought an overthrow of colonialism in these countries in 1975. In Southern Rhodesia (Zimbabwe) 1960 was a middle point in the nationalist struggle. An attempt by settlers to retain power by joining in a federated government with Nyasaland and Northern Rhodesia was about to collapse, but in 1965 Rhodesia's white rulers tried to hold back the tide of black nationalism with their own illegal, unilateral declaration of independence. It took fifteen years of armed liberation struggle before white politicians could be forced to negotiate a democratic settlement and the inter-national community recognised the independent state of Zimbabwe under non-racial black majority rule.

The drama of independence was widely reported in newsreels and in the international press. Reports told of scenes of pageantry in which new flags were raised, new anthems sung and new leaders sworn in. In Central African capitals and in remote villages, people marched in victory parades, held street-parties and wore specially designed cloths with heroic images of leaders who had guided the struggle and established modern political parties. In 1960, African exuberance was carried from Kinshasa to Europe by Joseph Kabasele and his 'African Jazz' band which performed its 'Independence Cha-Cha' to excited crowds in Brussels and Paris.[1] While euphoria was high anything

1 Sylvain Bemba, *50 Ans de Musique du Congo-Zaïre*, Présence Africaine, Paris, 1984, p.112.

seemed possible, but realism also crept in. Independence might bring an end to the everyday humiliation of life under colonialism and launch new African governments, but it could not obliterate the colonial past. A large and frequently unfavourable legacy confronted new governments. Furthermore, those who had fought for independence were often bitterly divided over postcolonial agendas, whether national or personal.

Before embarking on a study of the last four decades of the twentieth century in Central Africa, it seems relevant to consider the late colonial context out of which the new nations evolved. The decolonisation process reached many countries very rapidly and these circumstances affected their histories in the last decades of the twentieth century. The late colonial years and the coming of independence were variously experienced by different population groups, often in local and personal contexts rather than on a countrywide scale. Beyond the broad decolonisation narrative lies a host of conflicting stories which derive from the experiences of ordinary people. Only an overview can be given in this introduction but many of these issues are taken up more extensively in the individual chapters which follow.

DECOLONISATION NARRATIVE

Historical explanations for decolonisation after the Second World War have been many and varied.[2] The word decolonisation has been criticised as implying a political process initiated by the great powers and global forces. In Central Africa, suspicion and cynicism towards Europeans and resistance to their ongoing military occupation persisted, despite apparent accommodation to colonial circumstances. Uprisings by peasants and demonstrations by urban workers, petitions and the formation of political parties by élites were landmark events in the long narrative of decolonisation. Peasants rebelled in 1913 in northern Angola and in 1917 in Zambezia; thousands of workers called strikes on the Copperbelt in 1935 and 1940, leaving several protesters dead and many wounded due to police reaction; vocal opposition by nationalist associations and parties grew in the 1940s and 1950s; and guerrilla resistance to the French broke out in Cameroun in 1956.[3] Resistance and survival were sustained by new forms of religion, by popular songs and art that ridiculed the oppressor, by novels that satirised white people, and by the tales of elders who remembered the early days of colonial occupation.[4] In the workplace

2 Useful surveys of African decolonisation which raise some of these issues are J. D. Hargreaves, *Decolonization in Africa*, Longman, Harlow, 1988; and David Birmingham, *The Decolonization of Africa*, UCL Press, London, 1995. See also, the more detailed Prosser Gifford and William Roger Louis (eds), *The Transfer of Power in Africa: Decolonization, 1940–1960*, Yale University Press, New Haven, 1982; and essays in the UNESCO and Cambridge Histories of Africa.
3 For other examples, see the chapters in David Birmingham and Phyllis M. Martin (eds), *History of Central Africa*, vol.2, Longman, Harlow, 1983.
4 For example, for Zaire, Bogumil Jewsiewicki, *Art Pictural Zaïrois*, Editions du Septentrion, Sillery, Quebec, 1992; Jean-Luc Vellut, 'Matériaux pour une image du blanc dans la société coloniale du Congo Belge,' in Jean Pirotte (ed.), *Stéréotypes nationaux et préjugés raciaux aux 19e et 20e siècles*, Editions Nauwelaerts, Louvain, 1982, pp.91–116; for Mozambique, see Leroy Vail

lines of authority were clearly drawn, but the distance that Europeans maintained through segregated residential areas and leisure time created space in which local people could develop their autonomous culture and elaborate new networks of support.[5] The 'confidential' files of security police now stored in colonial archives bear witness to the success of underground 'agitators' who posed threats in the official mind. In the Zimbabwe guerrilla struggle spirit mediums empowered peasants and fighters alike by facilitating collaboration between the living and the dead.[6]

As the costs of maintaining a colonial presence in Africa mounted, governments in Europe began to review their options. Left-wing associations such as the Popular Front in France and the Fabian Society in Britain had begun to consider the liberalisation of colonial rule, though the British colonial secretary noted in 1938 that 'it would take generations, even centuries for the people in some parts of the colonial empire to achieve self-government'.[7] The Second World War accelerated decolonisation, however, by creating economic and social conditions which nationalist leaders could exploit. The international climate also changed since the new superpowers, the United States and the Soviet Union, had no African colonies to protect and were critical of old-style colonialism. African aspirations for some form of self-government seemed to have been legitimised by the signing of the Atlantic Charter and by the founding of the United Nations. The emerging forces of African nationalism also won endorsement from pan-Africanists in the worldwide diaspora, and the winning of independence by Asian peoples in the subcontinents of Indo-China and India also gave encouragement to the forces of liberation in Africa.

In Central Africa, the Second World War created harsh conditions for many. Families lost the labour of men conscripted to fight in foreign wars. Peasants were compelled to grow food and cash crops with little remuneration and often with negative impacts on household economies. Townspeople were caught in a net of inflation as colonial powers restricted the flow of imported goods. The dislocation of rural economies and the hope of finding work and security in towns resulted in large-scale immigration from the countryside to

---

and Landeg White, 'Forms of resistance: songs and perceptions of power in colonial Mozambique', *American Historical Review* 88, 4 (1983), pp.883–919, and Allen Isaacman, *Peasants, Work and Rural Struggle in Colonial Mozambique, 1938–1961*, Heinemann, Portsmouth, NH, 1996. In Cameroun writers pioneered the satirising of the colonial situation; for example, the novels of Mongo Beti and Ferdinand Oyono. See Richard Bjornson, *The African Quest for Freedom and Identity: Cameroonian Writing and the National Experience*, Indiana University Press, Bloomington, 1991.

5 For example, Terence Ranger, *Dance and Society in Eastern Africa, 1890–1970: the Beni Ngoma*, Heinemann, London, 1973; Frederick Cooper (ed.), *Struggle for the City: Migrant Labor, Capital and the State*, Sage, Berkeley, CA, 1983; and Phyllis M. Martin, *Leisure and Society in Colonial Brazzaville*, Cambridge University Press, Cambridge, 1995.

6 David Lan, *Guns and Rain: Guerrillas and Spirit Mediums in Zimbabwe*, James Currey, London, 1985; also, Terence Ranger, *Peasant Consciousness and Guerrilla War in Zimbabwe*, James Currey, London, 1985; and Ngwabi Bhebe and Terence Ranger (eds), *Society in Zimbabwe's Liberation War*, James Currey, London, 1996.

7 Quoted in Michael Crowder, 'Introduction', *Cambridge History of Africa, Volume 8 from c.1940 to c.1975*, Cambridge University Press, Cambridge, 1984, p.4.

urban areas during the war years. The population of Kinshasa increased from 44,000 in 1939 to 96,000 in 1945 and to 222,000 five years later. Although this was the most rapid urban growth in the region, other capitals and commercial centres also increased dramatically in size. Between 1940 and 1950 Lusaka's population quadrupled, and those of Douala, Brazzaville and Zomba doubled.[8] After the war, unemployment, low wages and poor living conditions made urban populations a fertile recruiting ground for new political parties which set forth agendas for change. Such programmes might start in moderation but often outpaced postwar commitments to reform and 'controlled participation' offered by colonial governors. Responses to the struggle for change could differ considerably, even within and between groups that might appear homogeneous. The role of Second World War veterans, generally perceived to have supported nationalist movements, turns out to have been more varied. The Zimbabwean nationalist Ndabaningi Sithole, wrote of the 'revolutionising psychological impact' of war service on veterans, which resulted in their taking up radical positions in the nationalist struggle.[9] Elsewhere, former soldiers in imperial armies played a minimal role in the politics of decolonisation. On returning home they lost ground economically and socially to school-leavers and became so marginalised that they were not considered a political threat by the authorities.[10]

In the four cultural and political zones that made up colonial Central Africa, each European power had its own reasons for seeking a political settlement with its African antagonists. Britain was converted to the concept of African decolonisation by West African intellectuals, war veterans and trade unionists and this led to the landmark independence of Ghana in 1957. Imperial power had been further challenged by guerrillas in Kenya in 1952 and by North African nationalists in Egypt in 1956. In 1960 the Conservative prime minister, Harold Macmillan, flew to Cape Town and warned the white population that they would have to moderate their racist inequities in order to survive the 'winds of change' that were blowing through Africa. His reception was icy and the resolution of the police state in its policy towards African nationalism was shown when sixty-nine anti-pass law demonstrators were killed and hundreds of others wounded at Sharpeville. The tragedy strengthened the resolve of nationalists in English-speaking Central Africa to insist on majority rule.

About ten years before Sharpeville, a plan for a union of Southern Rhodesia with Northern Rhodesia and Nyasaland had been promoted by settlers and

8 Emmanuel Cappelle, *La Cité Indigène de Léopoldville*, Centre d'Etudes Sociales Africain, Léopoldville, 1947; Donald George Morrison et al., *Black Africa: a Comparative Handbook*, The Free Press, New York, 1972.

9 Ndabaningi Sithole, *African Nationalism*, Oxford University Press, London, 1959, p.19, quoted by Michael Crowder, 'The Second World War: prelude to decolonisation in Africa', in Michael Crowder (ed.), *Cambridge History of Africa: Volume 8 from c.1940 to c.1975*, Cambridge University Press, Cambridge, 1984, p.32; for an account of a former soldier, see Johannes Fabian, *History from Below: the 'Vocabulary of Elisabethville' by André Yav*, John Benjamins Publishing Company, Amsterdam, 1990, pp.75 ff.

10 For example, for Gabon and Moyen-Congo, see Florence Bernault, *Démocraties Ambiguës en Afrique Centrale: Congo-Brazzaville, Gabon, 1940–1965*, Karthala, Paris, 1996, pp.75–9.

supported by the British government. From an imperial perspective it made economic sense to link Northern Rhodesia's technical expertise in mining and Southern Rhodesia's settlers' expertise in agriculture with African labour in Nyasaland. For African nationalists and some white liberals both within and outside the region, this was a plan to restrain nationalist aspirations and enhance settler power. Politically conscious African workers, with experience of job reservations, pay discrimination and grossly inadequate living conditions on the Copperbelt and in South Africa, feared an extension of white supremacy throughout the proposed federation. Any benefit that might trickle down to the African population would be minimal and the tentacles of apartheid might expand northwards. In spite of the resistance, the British Colonial Office approved the establishment of the Federation of Rhodesia and Nyasaland in 1953. The African élite was offered the possibility of admission to University College in Salisbury, but few concessions were made on key issues such as land reform, wage differentials, and social segregation. In the compromise the few African representatives in the Federation and territorial parliaments lost the confidence of their local constituencies which had become aware of the real devolution of power in other parts of the continent. While strikes and demonstrations kept up local pressure for reform, leaders such as Hastings Kamuzu Banda and Kenneth Kaunda, the future presidents of Malawi and Zambia, took the campaign for independence to Britain and other parts of Africa. After attending the All-African People's Conference in Accra in 1958, both men were jailed. It became evident to the British Colonial Office that intransigent white voters in Central Africa would not tolerate black majority rule, nor would African nationalists back down in their demands. The break-up of the Federation thus became likely.[11] Leaders in Malawi and Zambia negotiated independence under majority rule, while the struggle continued in Zimbabwe in 'a long search for independence' not finally resolved until many had died in the cause of revolution.[12]

In equatorial Africa, successive French governments responded slowly to their critics. A formula for perpetuating a reformed colonial relationship within a French Union was worked out at Brazzaville in 1944 during a meeting of representatives of de Gaulle's Free France at which some African observers were present. In these arrangements, some of the worst colonial abuses such as forced labour and the African legal code, the *indigénat*, were abolished. A small number of those most tied to colonial structures, mostly appointed chiefs and *notables*, were allowed to vote in an electoral college that sent a few representatives to the National Assembly in Paris. The rest of the population remained effectively debarred from political participation, however.[13] Disillusionment became rampant and the granting of universal suffrage for local

11 On the Federation of Rhodesia and Nyasaland, see chapter by Megan Vaughan in this book. Also, in Birmingham and Martin (eds), *History of Central Africa*, Vol.2, see the chapter by Leroy Vail.
12 See the title and theme of Terence Ranger's chapter in this book.
13 Bernault, *Démocraties Ambiguës*, pp.72–92, 207–13.

assembly elections in 1955 did little to establish faith in a political process associated with fraud, patronage, and racism by the European electorate in equatorial Africa and by the French advisers of African leaders. A postwar economic package of aid and loans for the colonies[14] did little to calm urban unrest. Although it created short-term jobs building infrastructure, it brought scant hope of long-term employment for those with a little schooling who now swelled the ranks of urban youth. Nor was the situation improved by the growing number of Europeans seeking jobs in French Equatorial Africa. In Moyen-Congo and Gabon their number quadrupled between 1936 and 1960, as political and technical advisors, businessmen, and lower-class whites took advantage of emigration incentives to escape from the unemployment in postwar France.[15] While radical leaders demanded an end to European inter- ference in politics, the social élite resented continued discrimination, and the urban workers feared that the new arrivals, especially white women, would provide competition for scarce employment. In this highly charged situation, African leaders were able to combine 'traditional' symbols and beliefs with new political strategies, mobilised mass support and took over power in the early independence years.[16] In equatorial Africa, the end of colonial rule was as much associated with events outside Central Africa as with the internal nationalist struggle. Defeat in Indo-China in 1954 and high death-rates among conscripts in Algeria after 1956 persuaded the French to give Charles de Gaulle special powers to devise a new association with the African colonies. Guinea, which in 1958 was the only French African colony to vote in favour of complete independence rather than continued association with a French- dominated union, acted as a catalyst for independence elsewhere and in 1960 Cameroun and the French Equatorial African colonies also became independent. A large measure of military and financial power remained in French hands, however, and cultural ties continued to draw African élites to Paris. More than elsewhere in Central Africa, this was a 'qualified independence'.[17]

In Belgian Congo, the largest and strategically most important colony in Central Africa, independence, when it came, was abrupt and unexpected. If the French and British had opted for gradual reform after the Second World War, Belgium had no such thoughts. By 1959, however, the impending withdrawal of Britain and France from neighbouring colonies, a growing debt, and rising unrest which had led to rioting in Kinshasa, persuaded the Brussels government to take decolonisation seriously. They hastily called African leaders to a round-table conference in Brussels in January 1960 and in the space of two weeks negotiated a plan for independence six months later.[18]

14 On the 'development' package, FIDES, see the chapter by Austen and Headrick in Birming- ham and Martin (eds), *History of Central Africa*, Vol.2; also, Hargreaves, *Decolonization*, pp.95–7.
15 Bernault, *Démocraties Ambiguës*, pp.40–51. See also Rita Cruise O'Brien, *White Society in Black Africa: the French of Senegal*, Northwestern University Press, Evanston, IL, 1972.
16 Bernault, *Démocraties Ambiguës*, p.215; also, see chapter by Elikia M'Bokolo in this book.
17 Crowder, 'The Second World War', 1984, p.51.
18 See chapter by Crawford Young in this book.

Instead of civil servants inheriting a centralised authority, competing regional leaders, trained in the army, trade unions and business, sought to take on the mantle hastily dropped by the Brussels government. Each regional faction looked abroad for support, not only from Belgium, but also from the United States and the Soviet Union, as the Cold War was making itself felt in the heart of Africa. There were, moreover, few trained to move into top civil service or military positions since Belgium had opted for a colonial educational policy that precluded the training of an administrative élite but rather focused on primary school education for the masses. The situation at independence was a recipe for disaster.

In Portuguese Africa, as in settler Zimbabwe, independence was still many years away in 1960 and liberation was only to be achieved after an armed struggle that cost many lives. While francophone Central Africans were celebrating independence, social tensions reached boiling point in Angola and Mozambique. Forced labour, land alienation, compulsory crop cultivation, low prices for produce, legalised discrimination, and religious persecution were a potent combination of grievances. As in francophone Central Africa, the arrival of white immigrants, who took land and jobs from local people and who were granted privileges denied to the small African élite, exacerbated the situation.[19] The Portuguese dictatorship of António Salazar, far from lifting any measures of repression, introduced a tough security police in Angola and Mozambique after the Second World War and escalated the surveillance of nationalists so that individuals who seemed dangerous to the government could be imprisoned and tortured. After 1961 nationalist parties in exile and leaders of local rebellions mobilised armed resistance. Portugal therefore turned to the United States to provide the military and financial support needed to resist change and to retain control of Angola and Mozambique until 1975. As a consequence, the leading nationalist parties of both countries became protégés of the Soviet Union.[20]

UNRAVELLING DECOLONISATION

Political narratives of decolonisation constructed by historians, published in textbooks, and embroidered in popular memory are a central element in national histories, both those of weak states in search of nationhood and strong nations celebrating their genesis. Yet political narratives, like most narratives, can only be partial, even if significant, interpretations of the past. And they may not be helpful in understanding the present. In the case of Central Africa, moving beyond the theme of independence and broadening the context in which decolonisation struggles occurred seems essential to an understanding of the complexities that followed.

19 See chapter by Gervase Clarence-Smith on Angola in Birmingham and Martin (eds), *History of Central Africa*, Vol.2.
20 See chapters by Messiant and Penvenne in this book; also, David Birmingham, *Frontline Nationalism in Angola and Mozambique*, James Currey, London, 1992.

Phyllis M. Martin

The coming of independence in many countries was full of ambiguities which reflected deep social divisions in African societies in the late colonial years. In some cases, independence itself could be unwelcome and even contested. In Chad, one Muslim northerner wrote to the French saying that more time was needed for 'northerners' to catch up with 'southerners' in terms of access to western education and civil service positions. In this view, it might have been better for Chad to delay full independence and become an overseas territory of France.[21] In the Central African Republic, events were overshadowed by the death of Barthélémy Boganda and by the popular view that white *colons* might have been to blame.[22] In Cameroun, *maquis* resistance had been severely repressed by French troops, but guerrilla fighters remained in the forests.[23] In Gabon, the ruling party initially declined the offer of immediate independence and also suggested that it remain an overseas *département* of France.[24] In Congo, 1959 saw a hundred people killed in Brazzaville as rival groups mobilised around a highly politicised ethnic power struggle. Thirty years were to pass before a debate concerning the meaning of these events, or the role of specific individuals, could be openly engaged in by historians.[25] Nowhere were the implications of independence more difficult to ascertain than in Zaire, where euphoria at the ending of colonial oppression was high, but where independence day was 'heavy with uncertainty'.[26]

In popular memory even the notion of ambiguity does not adequately capture the meaning of independence in a local context. A collection of life histories, which gives the testimonies of eight Zairois, confirms the diversity of experience. These individuals lived in different regions and came from different social groups. One was born in the late nineteenth century, the rest in the 1920s and 1930s, and all lived through colonialism and decolonisation. Their accounts raise pertinent questions about the grand themes of history and how they relate to remembered daily life.[27] Living in a colonial context impinged on individuals in different ways, sometimes overtly but often indirectly. It brought opportunities for a catechist or railway worker or low-level bureaucrat, but it was also remembered as an 'unending stream of restrictions and aggression', from corporal punishment to forced cultivation, and from laws against hunting to the confiscation of 'traditional objects'. In the testimonies,

21 See the chapter by Robert Buijtenhuijs in this book. Having decided that independence for its African colonies was in its best interests, France was not prepared to entertain such views by 1960.
22 See the chapter by Austen and Headrick in Birmingham and Martin (eds), *History of Central Africa*, Vol.2 and the chapter by M'Bokolo in this book.
23 See chapter by Headrick and Austen in Birmingham and Martin (eds), *History of Central Africa*, Vol.2 and the chapter by Andreas Mehler in this book.
24 See chapter by M'Bokolo in this book.
25 *Ibid.*
26 The phrase is taken from the chapter by Crawford Young in this book.
27 Bogumil Jewsiewicki, *Naître et Mourir au Zaïre: un Demi-Siècle d'Histoire au Quotidien*, Karthala, Paris, 1993. See also the chapters in this book on Malawi and Zambia and on Mozambique which skilfully show the creative tension between life histories and larger issues in the remembering and telling of the past.

the 'special political moment [the coming of independence] is only evoked in an incidental manner and is buried in the mundanity of the passing days'.[28] For two men, the years between 1959 and 1962 were particularly marked by the attainment of professional goals. In the testimony of one woman, living in an African district of Kinshasa, independence was not mentioned and the years immediately before and after it were remembered as a time of personal tragedy during which her husband died. Others remembered the early independence years as a time of troubles when people fled from their villages, some to take refuge in the forest. For these ordinary people trying to survive and to move ahead, the year 1960 was hardly a 'turning point', for they continued to struggle and they continued to be subject to others more powerful than themselves.[29]

The 'decentring' of decolonisation, both the moment and the process, in life histories draws attention to the problem of viewing the colonial past in dichotomies, whether 'resistance' and 'collaboration', or 'nationalism' and 'accommodation'. Such dichotomies, as an article reviewing the historiography of the colonial period noted, 'risk flattening the complex lives of people living in colonies and underestimate the possibility that African . . . action might actually alter the boundaries of subordination within a seemingly powerful colonial regime'.[30] Politics and social struggles in a colony, the writer suggests, cannot be reduced to 'anti-colonial politics' or to 'nationalism', since the communities that Africans 'imagined' were 'both larger and smaller than the nation'.[31] Thus a worker on strike might be engaged in an anti-colonial demonstration, or in trying to obtain better wages to pay a child's school fees, or might be making a statement to his or her kin about the seriousness of family responsibility.

Most people experienced the nationalist struggle in their own local context and in local societies where a wide range of interests was present. While inequalities of class, gender, ethnicity and age might be partially put aside in the push to end colonial rule, deep social divisions were likely to re-emerge under the new regimes of independent nation-states.

In many societies class distinctions were accentuated in the last years of colonialism. The postwar 'development' and 'social welfare' policies of Britain and France benefited some workers who found jobs on the railways, in mining or in professions such as teaching. This emerging African middle class shared aspirations for material possessions, respectability and social status. In Congo and Gabon bureacratic élites engaged in conspicuous consumption, gave parties where imported liquor and expensive food were served, and enjoyed luxuries beyond the wildest dreams of ordinary people. At the same time, all over Central Africa rural populations flowed to town in search of

28 Jewsiewicki, *Naître et Mourir*, introduction by Elikia M'Bokolo, p.32.
29 *Ibid.*, pp.19–22.
30 Frederick Cooper, 'Conflict and connection: rethinking colonial African history', *American Historical Review* 99 (December 1994), p.1517.
31 *Ibid.*, p.1519.

jobs which were often in short supply. Unemployment created a mass of discontented young people with a little education but no prospects and a growing number of urban poor.[32] Disparities in wealth and opportunity also affected rural populations during the 1950s, for example in Nyasaland and Northern Rhodesia where social differentiation increased as a distinct group of rich peasants benefited from government incentives.[33] In his famous book *How Europe Underdeveloped Africa*, which emphasised the external reasons for Africa's problems in the postcolonial period, Walter Rodney wrote that 'the vast majority of Africans went into colonialism with a hoe and came out with a hoe'.[34] The thought of colonial exploitation, so graphically expressed, caught the attention of Rodney's readers, but the first part of the statement acknowledged the minority who did quite well under colonialism. At independence and beyond, a few – usually men – drove lorries or tractors, worked in offices, owned shops, or carried guns. Africans were not equal when they encountered Europeans, nor were they when colonialism ended, although the basis and shape of inequality might have changed.

Tensions relating to the changing roles of women were also evident as the colonial period drew to an end and these, too, continued beyond independence. Many women were economically disadvantaged, since boys had better opportunities for education than girls and women had less chance of earning wages in the cash economy than men. Female farmers tended to grow subsistence crops rather than crops for export. Women had problems establishing themselves in new towns unless they were incorporated into a male-headed household, and 'traditional' authorities such as chiefs and elders used their direct influence with male colonial administrators to negotiate favourable 'customary marriage' and property rights.[35] On the other hand, some women – traders, farmers, professional women, and the wives of successful men – did well. The diversity of experience is too complex to accommodate a unidirectional view of change. In southern Cameroun female farmers responded innovatively over three generations to maintain their position in the food economy and preserve adequate nutrition for household members.[36] On the Copperbelt and in Brazzaville after the Second World War some élite women

32 Georges Balandier, *Sociologie des Brazzavilles Noires*, Presses de la Fondation Nationale des Sciences Politiques, Paris, 2nd edn., 1985; Roland Devauges, *Le Chômage à Brazzaville en 1957*, ORSTOM, Paris, 1958; Martin, *Leisure and Society*, pp.50–1.
33 See chapter by Vaughan in this book.
34 Walter Rodney, *How Europe Underdeveloped Africa*, Bogle-L'Ouverture Publications, London, 1972, p.239.
35 This generalised statement cannot do justice to the recent work on African women's history and gender relations. For an excellent collection of introductory essays, see Margaret Jean Hay and Sharon Stichter (eds), *African Women South of the Sahara*, Longman, Harlow, 2nd edn., 1994, and for overviews of changing directions in the field, see Nancy Rose Hunt, 'Placing African women's history and locating gender', *Social History* 14, 3 (1989), pp.359–79, and the same author's introduction to the special issue of *Gender and History* 8, 3 (November 1996) on 'Gendered colonialisms in African History'.
36 See Jane Guyer, *Family and Farm in Southern Cameroon*, Boston University African Studies Center, Boston, paper no.15, 1984.

chose to attend clubs run by churches and social service agencies in order to learn skills and etiquette that would demonstrate their standing in urban society. Crafts, childcare and nutrition likely resonated with local values in women's household responsibilities, and élite women who learnt to manage a home on a European model promoted their position as 'inventors' of new upper-class traditions.[37] In Kinshasa and in Brazzaville relations between independent young women who married late and the men who outnumbered them were expressed in the songs which young men sang in bars and dance halls accompanied by guitar bands.[38]

In the evolving structure and membership of 'nationalist' parties tensions relating to different agendas had to be resolved, at least temporarily, so that a successful struggle could be waged. According to one writer, 'Africans in Nyasaland had a confusing variety of anti-colonial grievances' and 'anger could be expressed in very local terms'. It was opposition to the Central African Federation rather than a broad sense of national identity that unified competing interests in the last years of colonialism.[39] The old view that the language and agendas of élite leaders resonated throughout non-literate communities in town and countryside was clearly too simple. Rather people were mobilised as their local needs resonated with the larger struggle. Multiple levels of enthusiasm had to be considered.[40] In Northern Rhodesia and Nyasaland, tension between trade union leaders and political leaders in the 1950s over relations to employers and colonial administrators were common. Workers who enjoyed a good standard of living might baulk at joining militants who might jeopardise their jobs. More radical groups, on the other hand, might view political leaders as being too conservative in their social and economic agendas.[41]

The importance of appreciating nationalist movements within their local social and economic context was shown by incidents during the 1956 Salisbury Bus Boycott organised by the male-led City Youth League, which was part of the larger nationalist movement in Southern Rhodesia. Some

---

37 Jane L. Parpart, 'The household and the mine shaft: gender and class struggles on the Zambian copperbelt, 1926–64', *Journal of Southern African Studies* 13, 1 (October 1986), pp.49–50; Nancy Rose Hunt, 'Domesticity and colonialism in Belgian Africa: Usumbura's *Foyer social*, 1946–1960', *Signs* 15, 3 (spring 1990), pp.447–74; Dagmar Engels and Shula Marks, *Contesting Colonial Hegemony: State and Society in Africa and India*, British Academy Press, London, 1994, p.4, suggest that 'the successful acceptance of colonial ideology and politics as natural and legitimate depended on their being rooted in the worlds of both rulers and subjects alike'.
38 Balandier, *Sociologie des Brazzavilles Noires*; C. Didier Gondola, *Villes Miroirs: Migrations et Identités Urbaines à Kinshasa et Brazzaville, 1930–1970*, L'Harmattan, Paris, 1996; Martin, *Leisure and Society*, chapter 5.
39 Landeg White, *Magomero: Portrait of an African Village*, Cambridge University Press, Cambridge, 1989, p.218.
40 For Malawi, see, O. J. N. Kalinga, 'Resistance, politics of protest and mass nationalism in colonial Malawi, 1950–1960: a reconsideration', *Cahiers d'Etudes Africaines* 143, 36–3 (1996), pp.443–54; and in general, see Allen F. Isaacman, 'Peasant and social protest in Africa', *African Studies Review* 33, 2 (1990), especially p.49.
41 For example, Parpart, 'The household and the mine shaft', pp.53–5; Tony Woods, '"Bread with freedom and peace . . .": rail workers in Malawi, 1954–1975', *Journal of Southern African Studies* 18, 4 (December 1992), pp.729–30; also, see the chapter by Vaughan in this book.

11

independent women travelling to work refused to join in the boycott and a group of young men took the law into their own hands and decided to 'discipline' the women by instigating a violent attack on the women's hostel. The resulting rapes and injuries represented a male backlash against the success of independent women who had successfully established themselves in the formal economy at a time when the job market was tight. Housing, equal wages, competition for employment and recognition of independent women living in towns had escalated gender tensions in the months before the attack. The result of the incident was the sidelining of women in African politics and the setting up of Women's Leagues as branches of political parties. These organisations usually dealt with 'women's problems' while the political mainstream was masculinised.[42]

Among the mobile and shifting identities that influenced the formation of nationalist politics none was more potent or more malleable in the hands of political leaders than ethnicity. An article in the *New York Times* describing the violence between city youths and armed militias that rocked some neighbourhoods of Brazzaville in 1994 attributed the problem to 'ancient tribal animosities' perpetuated in modern political parties.[43] The writer was, knowingly or unknowingly, only reiterating the opinion of a French observer who, on the eve of independence, had also attributed politicised violence to 'traditional rivalries between the North and South'.[44] Yet, both assessments represented the way outsiders 'imagined' Central Africa rather than the reality. The 'ancient tribalism' claimed for Congo politics was in fact a new ethnicity using old symbols and loyalties creatively for new ends, namely wrestling for position in postindependence politics.[45]

It was especially in colonial towns that ethnicity became a key element in emerging social identities. Together with other social identities of class, gender, and age it burst forth in moments of crisis to express and mobilise particular interests. The new ethnicity was partially shaped by European perceptions but it was amplified by the variety of African perspectives. In the early colonial period, Europeans had arrived with notions of 'tribe' that were used to categorise, order, count, map, administer and tax local populations which had fluid identities. In new colonial towns urban planners often laid out 'ethnic' neighbourhoods not only to divide and rule, but also to replicate in town the 'ancient' order which they thought they perceived in the countryside. In fact, they were often structuring bounded loyalties that were previously nonexistent or much more localised. Townspeople, however, were quick to

42 Timothy Scarnecchia, 'Poor women and nationalist politics: alliances and fissures in the formation of nationalist political movements in Salisbury, Rhodesia, 1950–6', *Journal of African History* 37, 2 (1996), pp.283–310.
43 'Democracy brings turmoil in Congo', *New York Times*, 31 January 1994.
44 Jean-Michel Wagret, *Histoire et Sociologie Politiques de la République du Congo (Brazzaville)*, R. Pichon and R. Durand-Auzias, Paris, 1963, p.61.
45 Bernault, *Démocraties Ambiguës*, chapters 5, 6, 7; Martin, *Leisure and Society*, pp.199–200. See the complex interrelations of class and ethnicity in Angola in the chapter by Christine Messiant in this book.

appropriate administrative categories and reinterpret them in local terms.[46] Migrants from the countryside gravitated to districts of the town where others from their own region lived. Settling together helped to humanise the strange environment and protect communities against the weight of colonial authority. Elements of the rural past were creatively incorporated into social relations, into religious and secular celebrations, into mutual-aid associations, into a burgeoning popular culture, and into nascent political parties. Thus, the new ethnicity became an inseparable part of town life and of the volatile politics of the late colonial years. The 'nation' was the category which African politicians and European administrators recognised as the defining basis for independence, but in popular experience other loyalties were at least as powerful. The power of new ethnic identity had already shown itself under colonial regimes in army mutinies in the Belgian Congo, crowd violence at football matches against supporters of opposing teams in French Congo, attacks by coffee plantation workers on migrant labour in northern Angola, and in the emergence of new forms of religion which incorporated elements of Christianity with beliefs and symbols from specific regions.[47] These strong, emerging loyalties were not legitimised in 'nationalist' politics, however, or in negotiations for independence.[48] Yet far from fading, ethnic identity became a salient and demarcated feature of the late twentieth century, and nowhere more than in African towns which experienced unprecedented growth. (See Tables 1.1 and 1.2.)

Beyond independence there lay, therefore, a complex mix of problems which new governments had to confront. At the time many outsiders only understood the generalised political narrative of decolonisation which highlighted imperial perspectives, watershed events and African nationalist leaders. Yet these narratives often lacked local roots. The same outside observers tended to assume that hastily imported democratic institutions from the West would provide Central African governments with the stability to address the pressing social and economic problems of ordinary citizens. Their failure to do so seems less surprising when the conflicting interests and aspirations of people in a local context are taken into account. The fragility of political institutions, and the attraction of authoritative 'solutions' then seem more predictable.

Colonial rule, itself, had been authoritarian. European administrations left virtually no tradition of democracy, nor had they allowed African politicians to gain much experience in government. In the British sphere, the judge who inquired into the 1959 uprisings in Nyasaland and the subsequent state of

46 See Terence Ranger, 'The invention of tradition revisited: the case of colonial Africa', in Terence Ranger and Olufemi Vaughan (eds), *Legitimacy and the State in 20th Century Africa: Essays in Honour of A. H. M. Kirk-Greene*, Macmillan, London, 1993, pp.62–111; and Leroy Vail (ed.), *The Creation of Tribalism in Southern Africa*, James Currey, London, 1989.
47 See the chapter by Jean-Vellut in Birmingham and Martin (eds), *History of Central Africa*, Vol.2; Martin, *Leisure and Society*, pp.124–5; Birmingham, *Frontline Nationalism*, pp.41–2; Wyatt MacGaffey, *Modern Kongo Prophets: Religion in a Plural Society*, Indiana University Press, Bloomington, IN, 1983; Benault, *Démocraties Ambiguës*, chapters 5, 6, 7.
48 Cooper, 'Conflict and connection', p.1537.

Phyllis M. Martin

TABLE 1.1
POPULATION 1960 AND 1994

| Country | 1960 | | |
	Country population	Urban population	Urban population as % total
Angola	4,816,000	503,000	10
Cameroun	5,296,000	734,000	14
Central African Republic	1,534,000	348,000	23
Chad	3,064,000	209,000	7
Congo	988,000	315,000	32
Gabon	486,000	85,000	17
Malawi	3,529,000	155,000	4
Mozambique	7,461,000	274,000	4
Zaire	15,333,000	3,420,000	22
Zambia	3,141,000	541,000	17
Zimbabwe	3,812,000	481,000	13

| Country | 1994 | | |
	Country population	Urban population	Urban population as % total
Angola	11,072,000	3,569,000	32
Cameroun	13,233,000	5,938,000	45
Central African Republic	3,315,000	1,301,000	39
Chad	6,361,000	1,362,000	21
Congo	2,590,000	1,523,000	59
Gabon	1,320,000	660,000	50
Malawi	11,129,000	1,505,000	13
Mozambique	16,004,000	5,481,000	34
Zaire	43,901,000	12,766,000	29
Zambia	9,456,000	4,071,000	43
Zimbabwe	11,261,000	3,619,000	32

Source: Department for Economic and Social Information and Policy Analysis Population Division, *World Urbanization Prospects: The 1994 Revision*, United Nations, New York, 1995, 86–87, 102–103.

14

TABLE 1.2

CITY POPULATIONS 1960 AND 1990

City	1960	1990
Bangui	90,000[1]	474,000
Brazzaville	251,000	793,000
Bulawayo	190,000[2]	621,742[3]
Douala	172,000	1,001,000
Harare	183,000	854,000
Kinshasa	451,000	3,455,000
Kitwe	144,000[4]	338,207[5]
Libreville	28,000[6]	286,000
Lilongwe	★★★	310,000
Luanda	219,000	1,642,000
Lubumbashi	183,711[7]	564,830[8]
Lusaka	88,000	979,000
Maputo	181,000	1,561,000
Ndjaména	80,000[9]	613,000
Pointe-Noire	79,000[10]	298,014[11]
Port-Gentil	30,000[12]	164,000[13]
Yaoundé	99,000	823,000

[1] Donald George Morrison et al. *Black Africa: A Comparative Handbook*, The Free Press, New York, 1972, p.201.
[2] 1959 population. Statistical Office of the United Nations. *1962 Demographic Yearbook*, United Nations, New York, 1962, p.318.
[3] 1992 population. Department for Economic and Social Information and Policy Analysis. *1994 Demographic Yearbook*, United Nations, New York, 1996, p.264.
[4] 1966 population. Morrison, *Black Africa*, p.379.
[5] Department for Economic and Social Information and Policy Analysis. *1994 Demographic Yearbook*, p.264.
[6] Morrison, *Black Africa*, p.243.
[7] 1959 population. Statistical Office of the United Nations. *1962 Demographic Yearbook*, p.316.
[8] 1984 population. Department for Economic and Social Information and Policy Analysis. *1994 Demographic Yearbook*, p.263.
[9] Morrison, *Black Africa*, p.206.
[10] c.1966 population. Morrison, *Black Africa*, p.212.
[11] 1984 population. Department for Economic and Social Information and Policy Analysis. *1994 Demographic Yearbook*, p.260.
[12] c.1966 population. Morrison, *Black Africa*, p.243.
[13] 1988 population. *Africa South of the Sahara 1997*, Europa Publications Limited, London, 1996, p.418.
Source: Unless otherwise footnoted, information is from Department for Economic and Social Information and Policy Analysis Population Division, *World Urbanization Prospects: The 1994 Revision*, pp.132–42.

emergency found the colony to be a 'police state'.[49] Throughout Central Africa, colonial governments employed outsiders from other colonies as militia to impose control on those who protested at the injustices of colonial rule. In Congo, these agents earned the title of '*mboulou-mboulou*' (Lingala, jackal).[50]

49 Devlin Commission report quoted in A. J. Wills, *An Introduction to the History of Central Africa*, Oxford University Press, London, 1964, p.340.
50 Martin, *Leisure and Society*, p.84.

In Cameroun, the French army moved in to crush the radical movement demanding independence.[51] The Portuguese dictatorship dispensed with even a façade of democracy when crushing popular resistance and nascent political mobilisation after the Second World War. In Belgian Africa the colonial army had played a central role in government, and at independence army officers quickly seized power as the 'national government' collapsed.[52]

Although the colonial powers relinquished political control, they nonetheless retained powerful influence across the region. Fragile governments and politicians eager to maintain their position were willing to sustain neocolonial relations through formal linkages and personal friendship with civil servants and politicians in Europe. Nowhere was this more the case than in the close relations that persisted between France and its former colonies.[53] In 1959 a central bank for the former French Equatorial African states was established at Brazzaville to control the CFA currency of the region and the value of the equatorial African franc was pegged to the French franc.[54] Military bases were maintained throughout the former French colonies and enabled France to intervene quickly in Central African affairs. In 1964 paratroopers arrived to restore the government of Léon M'Ba, Gabon's first 'independent' president, when he had been removed from office by a military coup. Leading African politicians nurtured close personal ties with France also, and the African élite travelled frequently to Europe for business and pleasure.

One new external force which influenced Central African affairs in the postcolonial years was the Cold War. As Zaire erupted in violence in the early years of independence the regional factions looked abroad for support, both to the former colonial power, Belgium, and also to the United States and the Soviet Union. They received covert financial and military assistance as Cold War rivalries played themselves out in the affairs of independent Africa. In Angola and Mozambique Cold War intervention by the great powers was experienced in the use of surrogate troops from Cuba and South Africa.

Internal instability and external pressure left little space for the new states to create independent nations. The lack of roots in the precolonial past, volatile urban populations, weak and dependent economies, rising demographic pressures and diminishing resources all compounded the political problem. The ongoing struggle of ordinary people to make sense of contrasting adversity and prosperity shaped the larger society. Popular strategies and options included economic innovations, social networks, and an array of religious and ideological inspiration ranging from imported socialism to African Christianity and empowerment by traditional healers and priests. Daily struggles,

51 See chapter by Mehler in this book.
52 See chapters by Messiant, Penvenne and Young in this book.
53 This is a persistent theme that runs through the chapters by Mehler, Buijtenhuijs, and M'Bokolo in this book.
54 The CFA franc referred to the *Colonies Françaises d'Afrique* when the term came into existence in 1946. The common acronym was preserved at independence by changing the reference to *Communauté Financière Africaine*. See Patrick Manning, *Francophone Sub-Saharan Africa, 1980– 1985*, Cambridge University Press, Cambridge, 1988, pp.125, 192.

structural problems, foreign intervention and the tragedy of war are at the heart of the contemporary history of Central Africa.

Writing the contemporary history of Central Africa is in some respects qualitatively different from writing about earlier history, though the methodology of the historian remains much the same. The sources for contemporary history offer both advantages and disadvantages. Their richness can open up a wide array of approaches but their weight and diversity can be 'copiously numbing'.[55] Some sources can be quite fragmentary and others await 'discovery' by future generations of scholars. Good analysis involves a sensitivity to 'long-term', 'middle-range' and 'immediate' history, yet, as one contributor to a 1996 workshop on this History of Central Africa succinctly put it, discerning what is of transitory relevance from what forms part of the *longue durée* is difficult when living so close to the recent past.[56] Nowhere is this point more dramatically made than in recent events in Zaire. As this book went to press, a civil war hardly discernible six months previously had engulfed the country. Rebel forces threatened the capital and the long-standing dictatorship of Mobutu. It will be for future historians to analyse the long-term implications of these 'immediate' events.

Within Central African history, work on some problems is much more advanced than on others and the state of historical research also varies from country to country. For some areas, sub-fields such as women's history, health or popular culture are quite well established, elsewhere these same topics of research have hardly opened up. The state of historical research overall also varies between countries and regions according to research conditions. In all areas conditions of research for local scholars are extremely difficult as they have to deal with lack of resources, lack of publishing opportunities, and adverse material conditions in which to support their families. In some areas insecure and unpredictable conditions make travel impossible for both local and foreign researchers. In spite of these constraints, however, visits to Central African universities and research institutes show continuing lively debate expressed in student theses, unpublished papers, and important seminars and conferences.

The contemporary period of history is also the research ground of scholars whose methods of analysis are rooted in other disciplines although their work may be set in an historical context. The six historians, one sociologist and

55 The words of the historian of modern Britain, Arthur Marwick, in an article on the writing of social history and on other types of writing, especially postmodernism, in the *Journal of Contemporary History* 20, 1 (1995), pp.1–25. For a discussion of 'contemporary history', see the first issue of this journal (1, 1, 1966), the editorial note and the article by Llewellyn Woodward, 'The Study of Contemporary History', pp.1–13, although it should be noted that the field of study for this journal is noted as 'Europe in the 20th century'.
56 Comment by Robin Palmer at a workshop at Saint Antony's College, Oxford, July 1996.

three political scientists who have contributed to this book represent a wide range of interests and perspectives which influence the choice of lens through which they view contemporary history. They have constructed their essays around questions which seem of major importance in their region of specialisation. In four cases (Chad, Cameroun, Zaire and Angola) the fragility of the state and the resultant pressures on ordinary lives lie at the heart of the analysis. In the case of Zimbabwe it is the genesis of independence through war and the ongoing search for land reform, industrial development and political transformation that are presented as key issues. Violence intensified by foreign intervention was also a common experience. In the case of Chad, Angola and Mozambique a complicated narrative of conflict and civil war runs through each chapter. In other countries, despite tensions and competing claims to resources, the state has continued to mediate conflict, albeit not without some violent episodes of civil strife. The discussion of Gabon, Congo and the Central African Republic skilfully compares and contrasts the drama of political change, the nature of economic resources (including oil), high levels of urbanisation, and the vibrancy of popular culture. The chapter which combines a consideration of Zambian and Malawian history looks at issues of contemporary history through the prism of gender and the experience of rural population. Women are also significant actors in the analysis of the contemporary history of Mozambique.

This consideration of contemporary Central African history is largely structured along national lines. In spite of civil war and a highly politicised ethnicity, nations are a fundamental fact of life in modern Central Africa. A sense of 'national' identity may be less well developed than elsewhere but 'nationhood' cannot be written off for it is still an evolving reality and a popular aspiration for many.[57] Scholars are increasingly reflecting on comparative and global history but their research, their empirical knowledge and their technical skills still tend to be rooted in particular countries.

The chapters that follow also demonstrate, however, that Central African history cannot be contained within national frontiers, for people spill across such political barriers in the activities of daily life. Mobility, movement and the permeability of borders have been a key feature of Central African history from the distant past to the present, sometimes as a matter of choice and sometimes when local circumstances compel people to flee across frontiers. Borderlands may set limits but they also provide opportunity. Refugees fled across colonial frontiers to escape colonial oppression, and they have sadly been forced to cross national frontiers to avoid violence and war in recent times. Crossing borders in search of work and economic opportunity has also been a continuous feature of Central African history. For centuries, the Congo river was an essential waterway in regional trade and in colonial times people

57 For the debate on African nation-states, see Basil Davidson, *The Black Man's Burden: Africa and the Curse of the Nation-State*, James Currey, London, 1992; Jean-François Bayart, *The State in Africa: the Politics of the Belly*, Longman, London, 1992; Colin Leys, 'Confronting the African Tragedy', *New Left Review* 204 (1994), pp.33–47; and a special issue of *Politique Africaine* on the 'Besoin d'Etat', 61 (March 1996).

took ferries across the river to seek work, trade or entertainment or to visit friends and family. Statistics from both capitals show a large migrant population over many decades, with intensification of population flows from Kinshasa to Brazzaville in the late twentieth century.[58] The opportunities created by borders were both legal and illegal. Smugglers took cattle from Chad to Nigeria, diamonds from Angola to Zaire, and gold from Zaire to Rwanda. Popular culture was likewise not confined by frontiers and, starting in the late colonial period when a recording industry was established in Central Africa, the export of recorded music became a lucrative business. Lingala, once spread as a trade language along the Congo river, is now commonly spoken in Gabon and the Central African Republic through the influence of popular song. The spread of Swahili as a lingua franca in eastern Central Africa is also evidence of the movement of populations, ideas and culture over a long period of time.[59]

The transparent nature of frontiers is also evident in the boundaries of Central Africa, both in the experience of those who live there and in the minds of scholars. The 'large' Central Africa which is the focus of this book grew out of the study of precolonial history when the region of modern-day Cameroun was important in the early history of Bantu-speaking populations and from the study of colonial history when French Equatorial Africa included Chad and British Central Africa stretched to the Limpopo. In the late twentieth century the boundaries of Central Africa seem even more open than in past centuries. Chad has been increasingly drawn into the affairs of Libya and Sudan and its history is less attached to regions to the south than in the colonial period. The tragic events in Rwanda have dramatically spilled across the Great Lakes into Zaire. The expanding influence of South Africa is paralleled by a contemporary 'southern Africa' that extends northwards into Angola, Zambia and southern Zaire. 'Central Africa' may sometimes seem like a mirage to those who try to 'imagine' it as a place. The people are the reality and this is their contemporary history.

58 For the precolonial period, see for example, Robert Harms, *River of Wealth, River of Sorrow: the Central Zaire Basin in the Era of the Slave and Ivory Trade, 1500–1891*, Yale University Press, New Haven, 1981, and Jan Vansina, *The Tio Kingdom of the Middle Congo, 1880–1892*, Oxford University Press, London, 1973; for the colonial period, see Martin, *Leisure and Society in Colonial Brazzaville*, and C. Didier Gondola, *Villes Miroirs*.
59 See chapter by Elikia M'Bokolo in this book; on the spread of Lingala, see William Samarin, 'The origins of Kituba and Lingala', *Journal of African Languages and Linguistics* 12, 1 (September 1991), pp.47–77, and for Swahili, Johannes Fabian, *Language and Colonial Power: the Appropriation of Swahili in the former Belgian Congo, 1880–1938*, Cambridge University Press, Cambridge, 1986.

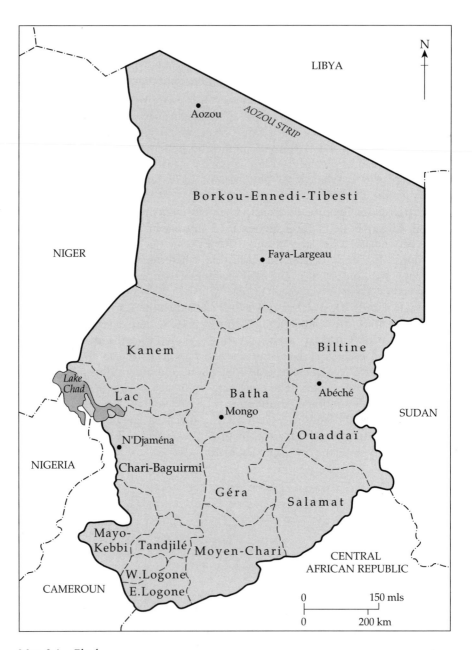

Map 2.1   Chad

CHAPTER 2

Chad in the age of the warlords

ROBERT BUIJTENHUIJS

Since Chad gained its independence in August 1960, the country's history has been marked by a civil war which started towards the end of 1965 and has continued intermittently to this day. The horror and destruction have not been on the scale of experiences in Liberia, Mozambique, Rwanda or Somalia but the armed struggle has seriously affected all domains of life, be they political, economic or social. Successive armed revolts have uncovered and exacerbated the deep-rooted historical forces at work in postcolonial Chad. They have in particular highlighted the fragility of the nation, although only recently did rebel movements begin to question its legitimacy. The weaknesses of the Chad state, which at times appeared to be on the verge of disappearing in the internal turmoil, have also been revealed. Sustained conflict has furthermore underlined the country's extreme dependency on foreign powers such as its neighbours Libya and Sudan, on France and, more recently, on international financial institutions such as the International Monetary Fund (IMF) and the World Bank.

1965–77: REBELLION IN THE NORTH

The problems started almost immediately after independence when Chad's first president, François (later Ngarta) Tombalbaye, a native of the south, imposed a one-party system. This gave rise to protests, mainly in the north of the country. In September 1963, in N'Djaména, a confrontation between police and partisans of certain Muslim leaders turned into a riot that claimed dozens of lives. Although this event in the capital was not directly linked to the rural uprisings which later shook the country, many Chadians consider this bloody confrontation as marking the beginning of the civil war. The incident clearly highlighted the dangers of instituting a political system which prevented opposition groups from expressing their viewpoints peacefully and democratically and which outlawed dissident voices.

It was the rebellion in the Mangalmé region (Guéra *préfecture*) in October 1965 which actually marked the beginning of the civil war. The uprising was partly due to localised discontent (a chieftaincy dispute) and partly to more general grievances (high taxes, corrupt and contemptuous civil servants, often of southern origin), which many northerners shared.[1] The Chad army launched a campaign of repression against the Guéra rebels but was unable to stamp out the revolt which spread to the Batha, Ouaddaï and Salamat regions. Entire villages took to the bush or spontaneously 'liberated' themselves from the hold of the central administration. At this time, the revolts were still contained within the central and eastern regions and it was only after March 1968 that popular uprisings also broke out in the Borkou-Ennedi-Tibesti (BET) *préfecture* in the north. Here again, the reasons for insurrection stemmed partly from local issues and partly from general grievances; in the beginning at least, there were no direct links between the central, eastern and northern rebels.

In the meantime, in neighbouring Sudan, in June 1966, the politico-military *Front de Libération Nationale du Tchad* (Frolinat) was formed with the aim of coordinating rebels in the field and representing them abroad. It is still difficult to ascertain what Frolinat really stood for. Throughout its existence, the movement not only presented many different faces, but also underwent various transformations. Under its first secretary-general, Ibrahima Abatcha (killed in action in 1968), but also later on, Frolinat claimed to be an anti-imperialist and anti-neo-colonialist movement, with a national programme of Third World inspiration.[2] Yet, in spite of this programme, aimed in principle at the entire nation, recruitment of Frolinat fighters never extended beyond the northern Islamic regions. Even in these areas, Frolinat never achieved unanimous support. The rebellion only spilled over into the western part of the country quite late, in about 1978, while several social strata, such as the sultans and other traditional political leaders, the religious élite and the big business class were long resistant to Frolinat's radical ideology. R. Pascal summed up this situation concisely yet accurately when he wrote that 'all Muslims weren't rebels, but all rebels were Muslim'.[3]

Should it then be concluded that Frolinat's fighters were rebelling as Muslims? This question is difficult to answer. In 1978 reservations of fundamentalists about the rebellion and the absence of any allusions to holy war in the movement's tracts, suggested that for most fighters their adhesion to the Muslim world had a cultural rather than a religious significance. In other words, while the insurrection in Chad was a revolt of Muslims, it was not an Islamic war. In the 1990s, this hypothesis still appeared to hold true but it

1 For a factual and detailed account of the Mangalmé events, see N. Abbo, *Mangalmé 1965: la Révolte des Moubi*, Editions Sépia, Saint-Maur, 1996. In Chadian vocabulary, 'the north' is used for those regions that have been touched by Islam, e.g., the *préfectures* of Kanem, Lac, Chari-Baguirmi, Guéra, Batha, Salamat, Ouaddaï, Biltine and Borkou-Ennedi-Tibesti (BET). This region covers the Saharian and Sahelian parts of the country and represents about three-quarters of the national territory, with about half of the population. By contrast, 'the south' is used for the remaining *préfectures*: Moyen-Chari, Logone Oriental, Logone Occidental, Tandjilé and Mayo-Kebbi.
2 Several political programmes have been developed by Frolinat leaders over the period 1966–74. See R. Buijtenhuijs, *Le Frolinat et les Révoltes Populaires du Tchad, 1965–1976*, Mouton, The Hague, 1978, pp.123–4, 198–200, and 246.
3 R. Pascal, *L'Islam au Tchad*, CHEAM, Paris, 1972, p.9.

deserved some qualification. Publications that explored grass-roots rebels' behaviour and preoccupations in different areas of Chad suggested that militants were acting on more of a Muslim impulse than Frolinat's official publications were willing to admit.[4] Yet, these findings did not show conclusively that Frolinat was, even at the local level, an Islamic movement in a strictly religious sense.

Whatever the ideological interpretation of their insurrection, the Frolinat fighters, after a hesitant beginning, rapidly gained ground. Towards the end of 1968, they managed on several occasions to rout the Chad army's regular units, while the authorities were forced to abandon most of the administrative posts in the central and eastern regions. During the first half of 1969, Frolinat's armed forces closed in on several urban centres, including Mangalmé, Mongo and Abéché. In view of this situation, President Tombalbaye decided to call upon French military support, which was granted by General de Gaulle in April 1969. For the next three years, a French army corps of approximately 2,000 men managed to inflict military defeat on the Frolinat troops, but Tombalbaye's regime proved incapable of turning this military victory into a political one. Discontent in the north continued to simmer and with the end of the French military intervention, war resumed again. Tombalbaye's death in an otherwise fairly bloodless coup d'état in April 1975 did not change the situation. The new regime, led by General Félix Malloum, at least until 1978, proved just as incapable of gathering the rebels back to the fold.

Until 1978, Frolinat's rebellion can be seen primarily as a northern uprising. The revolt was not directed at the southern populations, but rather at an oppressive regime led mainly, in the eyes of Frolinat sympathisers, by southerners. To grasp the nature of the north–south divide, some historical overview is necessary. There is no denying that Chad is a nation made up of two distinct parts sharply distinguished from one another by geographical and human factors. This was summed up by one author:

> Northern Chad, a region of cropped savannah, steppe or desert, propitious to a pastoral way of life . . . where Islam is deeply entrenched; southern Chad, a region of tall wooded savannah, with a focus on agriculture, where animism, still very much alive, is occasionally overlain by Christian influences.[5]

In fact, during the last two centuries, relations between the north and the south, or rather between some of their respective components, have been strained, although the regions have never existed as structured entities. Indeed, until recently, the notions of 'north' and 'south' did not exist in Chadian vocabulary. Over the course of the nineteenth century, however, some of the powerful Muslim sultanates exploited their military superiority to raid their

---

4 P. Doornbos, 'La révolution dérapée: la violence dans l'est du Tchad (1978–1981)', *Politique Africaine* 4 (September 1982); R. Buijtenhuijs, 'Le Frolinat: mouvement islamique ou mouvement de musulmans?', in J.-P. Magnant (ed.), *L'Islam au Tchad*, Centre d'Etude d'Afrique Noire, Bordeaux, 1992; C. Pairault, *Retour au Pays d'Iro: Chronique d'un Village du Tchad*, Karthala, Paris, 1994; and Abbo, *Mangalmé*.
5 A. Le Rouvreur, *Sahéliens et Sahariens du Tchad*, Berger-Levrault, Paris, 1962, p.24.

Robert Buijtenhuijs

southern neighbours for slaves, a practice that had a long-lasting impact on popular memory on both sides of the divide.[6] During the colonial era, however, the north remained attached to its traditional structures, refusing to profit in most domains except trade from the few advantages offered by colonisation. Southerners, by contrast, chose the other option. Certain groups such as the Sara took advantage of colonisation, especially the French educational system, and progressively gained the upper hand. They were active in the fight for independence, and, by the end of the colonial era, found themselves with many more educated people in their group. This accentuated existing divisions. Towards the end of the 1950s, some of the Muslim leaders, realising how far the north had fallen behind in terms of education, and fearing a southern political domination in the future, did everything in their power to gain some time under colonial rule, in order to allow the north to catch up.[7] In 1958, one of these leaders even asked that Chad be given Overseas Territorial status, rather than immediate independence.

This was the context for the first revolts. Overall, the Tombalbaye regime was certainly no more oppressive than most of its counterparts elsewhere in Africa, while in the economic field, it did not do badly. However, from the earliest days of independence, northern rural communities began to feel marginalised within the new nation state. With little exaggeration, it can be argued that independence never really came to the north since French domination was replaced by a regime of southern civil servants, particularly at the local level. In the eyes of the northerners, these civil servants were often as foreign as the colonial regime had been. Some of them despised or did not understand the local populations, others were dishonest and greedy, and the harrassment they inflicted on the northern communities was enough to trigger the rural revolts, in the BET, eastern and central regions.

The north–south divide was not only a reality among grass-roots militants, but also among educated northerners. The insistence that Arabic, the *lingua franca* of the north, be recognised as Chad's second official language formed an integral part of Frolinat's programmes. This was critical for all the young northerners who, from the early 1940s, had enrolled in growing numbers at Arab universities, notably in Cairo and in the Sudan. In view of the exclusive status of French in Chadian public life, these graduates had few chances of finding decent career opportunities upon their return. It is, therefore, not surprising that quite a few members of this 'counter-élite', frustrated and without a future in Chad, joined the ranks of the rebellion, providing Frolinat with a number of its leaders and junior officials. It was this mainly north–south cultural divide which dominated the civil war and supplied the rebellion with recruits in its early phases.

6 For further information on the nineteenth-century history of the region, see Dennis D. Cordell, 'The savanna belt of North-Central Africa', in David Birmingham and Phyllis M. Martin (eds), *History of Central Africa*, 2 vols, Longman, Harlow, 1983, I, pp.30–74.
7 J. Le Cornec, *Histoire politique du Tchad de 1900 à 1962*, R. Pochon and R. Durand-Auzias, Paris, 1963, p.231.

Around 1978 Chad's war fortunes began to change, with important consequences for the scale of fighting and its significance. Libya which had previously been a relatively discreet neighbour made a surprising entry onto Chad's
politico-military scene. By granting substantial military aid to the branch of
Frolinat led by Goukouni Weddeye and formed by men mostly from the
BET, Colonel Khadafi was able to ensure for his protégés the capture of all
the BET garrisons, including Faya-Largeau, the provincial capital. Fearing complete military defeat, General Malloum's regime made contact with another
BET-dominated faction of rebels led by Hissein Habré. In August 1978 negotiations led to an agreement, with the resulting nomination of Hissein Habré
as prime minister, while General Malloum remained president.[8] During the
ensuing confusion, some of Goukouni Weddeye's Frolinat units infiltrated
N'Djaména in the first few weeks of 1979.

The Malloum–Habré coalition very quickly came up against difficulties
since both protagonists aspired to the senior role. In February 1979, war
broke out in N'Djaména itself, with Chad's national army, consisting mainly
of southern soldiers, opposed to Habré's *Forces Armées du Nord* (FAN) which
were soon joined by Goukouni Weddeye's fighters. After a few weeks of combat, the Habré–Weddeye coalition claimed victory, forcing the Chad government troops to abandon the capital and to withdraw to the south. They were
soon followed by almost all of N'Djaména's southern inhabitants.[9]

At that point, Chad was divided in two. In the south, the military and civil
servants, under the leadership of Colonel Kamougué, rapidly organised a
parallel administration, headed by a *comité permanent* with all the attributes of
an actual government except in name and international recognition. For over
two years, the south functioned in complete autonomy, politically as well as
economically. Cotton, its main export, was sold directly through Cameroun
and the Central African Republic. Cameroun also provided banking services,
while most medical centres and primary and secondary schools were kept
functioning with local resources and personnel.

In contrast, the north sank into complete chaos. Victory, instead of uniting
Frolinat, shattered the movement into at least ten different 'tendencies' (to
use the Chadian term), each led by warlords who ruled supreme over their
respective strongholds and waged incessant war against each other. Goukouni
Weddeye, while nominally president from the end of 1979 to June 1982, could
not exert any control over the south, nor could he dominate the northern
regions held by rival warlords, though some eventually joined his alliance
against Hissein Habré, his main adversary. For two years, civil war raged

8 The new constitution elaborated during the Khartoum negotiations recognised Arabic as Chad's
second official language. The more recent Chadian constitutions have all maintained this principle
of bilingualism.
9 For the first time in independent Africa, a rebel movement managed to take power through a
long-lasting guerrilla war. Until then, successful wars of liberation had been fought against a
colonial overlord but not against an independent government.

throughout the northern part of the country, while the south remained free of violence, thanks to the efforts of its *comité permanent*. With the help of a massive intervention by Libyan troops, which temporarily occupied a large part of northern Chad, including N'Djaména, Goukouni Weddeye and his allies (including a rather half-hearted Colonel Kamougué) won the first round against Habré towards the end of 1980. A year later, however, Libyan troops left Chad, probably as a result of incessant pressure from France, and Habré staged a spectacular comeback. Thanks to the remarkable organisation of his armed forces, and with some help from Sudan, Egypt and the United States, he effectively reconquered the land lost and in June 1982 took N'Djaména, forcing Goukouni Weddeye to flee to Libya.

Habré was also able to seize the south, which fell with little resistance, partly because of internal disputes between its military leaders and partly because the *comité permanent* had become unpopular due to its corruption and nepotism. Chad's unity was thus reinstated, but not for long. In 1983, when Libya again provided Weddeye's allied forces with massive military support, war resumed. At this point, Habré was only saved by a new French military intervention ordered by President François Mitterrand to counter Khadafi's expansionist tendencies. The Libyan leader did, however, manage to maintain his troops north of the 16th parallel, regions which Mitterrand considered of little interest and, therefore, refused to protect.[10] It was only in 1987 that the Chadian army, by bold actions, managed to expel the better armed but poorly motivated Libyan troops who were fighting on foreign soil. Only the Aozou strip remained under Libyan occupation[11] and the unity of the Chadian state was thus re-established.

Habré took advantage of French aid, which guaranteed him freedom of action below the 16th parallel, to reorganise and strengthen the political and administrative structures of the country. He had some qualities such as a keen sense of state and indisputable abilities as an organiser and 'manager'[12], which enabled him to put Chad back on track and initiate a modest but noticeable economic recovery. Unfortunately, as a former guerrilla leader, he also had quite a few shortcomings such as authoritarianism, contempt for human rights and clannishness which, in the end, prevailed. Despite commendable attempts, particularly from 1984 to 1986, to become a president to all Chad's people, Habré never managed to rid himself of his habits as a warlord. He only trusted a few close persons belonging to his own ethnic group, which explains why most groups and political leaders who had rallied to him when his political power was at its zenith, later abandoned him when serious problems arose.

Problems were caused by a number of Habré's former friends who had belonged to the *Forces Armées du Nord* since 1980, but who, under the leadership of Colonel Idriss Déby, turned against their old ally. This probably happened because Habré's regime was becoming more authoritarian, and also,

10 J. Attali, *Verbatim I: Chronique des Années 1981–1986*, Fayard, Paris, 1993, pp.462, 484.
11 See below, p.31.
12 Close collaborators of Habré often called him 'the boss', a revealing term.

perhaps, for more personal reasons such as gradual marginalisation within the regime. Whatever the case may be, in April 1989, Déby broke with Habré, fled from N'Djaména and managed to establish a stronghold in Darfur in Sudan's border province. From there, he organised his forces with some military help from Libya. After a few unsuccessful attempts, Déby launched a decisive offensive in November 1990, with the blessing of France, or at least of the French secret service.[13] Contrary to what most observers expected, Habré's regime, and in particular his élite troops, collapsed like a house of cards, and in December, Idriss Déby took N'Djaména. This seizure of power marked the beginning of a new era in the history of Chad. Before dealing with this new development, however, some further analysis of events just described is necessary.

As already pointed out, the Frolinat rebellion before 1977 needs to be seen as an uprising of some northern rural communities against a regime perceived as too exclusively southern. The rebellion was not, however, solely a civil war between the north and south. Indeed, Frolinat's fighters never targeted the southern civilian population. Rather, their actions were aimed at the central administration's representatives, regardless of whether they were from the north or the south.[14] Although the rebellion revealed a strong north–south division within Chad, such an explanation was no longer sufficient to account for the civil war after 1978. Certainly, the split between north and south remained an important element, as was demonstrated in the flight of most southerners from the capital in 1979, but other tensions were also beginning to show. The rupture of Frolinat into ten or so different splinter groups indicated, for instance, that northern Chad was anything but unified. On the contrary, Frolinat's warlords often engaged in bloody wars against each other. The conflict between Goukouni Weddeye and Hissein Habré for over ten years is the best example of these, but there were others. These wars between northerners can partly be explained by political reasons, and more particularly by differing attitudes towards Libya. Some of the warlords such as Hissein Habré were fiercely opposed to Libyan intervention of any kind. Others, such as Goukouni Weddeye, were more inclined to enter into tactical alliances with Colonel Khadafi, although they ultimately lost control. Ethnic differences also influenced development, as in the hostility between Toubous or Goranes and Arabs, while personal rivalries occasionally played a crucial role. Finally, purely materialistic motives underlay all confrontations between northern warlords. During the period of utter anarchy that Chad went through, it was always of vital importance for each faction to control some territory in order to collect tithes from the local rural communities. As P. Doornbos pointed out:

13 C. Silberzahn (with J. Guisnel), *Au Coeur du Secret: 1500 Jours aux Commandes de la DGSE (1989–1993)*, Fayard, Paris, 1995, pp.214–21.
14 There have been a few exceptions, however. In February–March, 1979, on several occasions Habré's FAN selectively killed southern civil servants which led to killings of Muslims in the south. Later on, Habré's conquest of the south in 1982 resulted in victims among the civilians. The same holds true for army actions against southern rebels in 1984–86, and 1993–96.

I have the feeling that the only preoccupations of Chad's eastern rebels since 1978 have been ensuring their day-to-day survival and defending themselves against neighbouring rebels. An attack from the outside can reduce the territory in which they rule over the *masakin*, the common people.[15]

The events of the last few years have revealed that southern Chad is not really much of a structured entity either. Differences between various military leaders allowed for a lightning conquest of the south by Habré's forces in 1982. At a deeper level, regional identities have also emerged. By the end of the 1970s, the people of the Mayo-Kebbi region began to express independent opinions which were voiced by their leaders, and a 'south-west' identity seemed to be developing. Within the rather nebulous Sara ethnic group, which did not exist fifty years ago,[16] subgroups with divergent interests have also begun to express themselves, although not through armed combat.

Certainly since 1978, Chad's civil war can no longer be viewed exclusively in terms of a 'north–south dialectic', and R. Lemarchand is right in suggesting factionalism as another interpretation:

Factions are non-corporate, highly personalised and intensely competitive social aggregates recruited by leaders on the basis of diverse principles. Patron–client relations, kinship ties, segmentary lineages, clan solidarities, friendship networks – all of these and more can serve as the basis of factional groupings . . . 'friend' and 'foe' are terms that have no absolute meaning in the context of factional competition.[17]

This model appears particularly relevant in the case of a Chad ruled by warlords with their 'wars without end' and their fickle alliances that sometimes did not respect the north–south divide, as when Colonel Kamougué allied himself to Goukouni Weddeye against Hissein Habré. However, the opposition between the north and the south is still a crucial dimension in the dissensions which tear Chad apart.

WAR AS AN INDUSTRY AND AS A WAY OF LIFE

Between 1979 and 1982 and in the wake of civil war, Chad completely disintegrated as a state.[18] President Goukouni Weddeye without any hesitation admitted his lack of control over the country during this period, when he said that: 'The GUNT (*Gouvernement d'Union Nationale de Transition*) has neither the power, money, nor local administrative infrastructure to face factions

15 Doornbos, 'La révolution dérapée', p.9.
16 J.-P. Margant, 'La conscience ethnique chez les populations sara', in J.-P. Chrétien and G. Prunier (eds), *Les Ethnies ont une Histoire*, Khartala-ACCT, Paris, 1989.
17 R. Lemarchand, 'The dynamics of factionalism in contemporary Africa,' in Z. Ergas (ed.), *The African State in Transition*, Macmillan, Basingstoke, 1987, pp.149–65.
18 Already in 1978, an article in *Jeune Afrique*, 905 (10 May 1978), carried the title, 'Chad: a state reduced to nought'. This led to protests by the Chad authorities but the authors were not really far off the mark.

which constitute states within the state. The GUNT is a government solely in name'.[19]

By this time Chad no longer had a national army. When Goukouni Weddeye's government 'ruled' Chad, each faction leader disposed of his own troops, and nobody had overall control of the armed forces. It was only in the international arena that Chad remained a legal entity and only in the eyes of foreign governments and international agencies that it still existed as a state. No faction could claim an advantage in this field.

Only the warlords ruled supreme, each in their own stronghold, surrounded by groups of supporters who obeyed them exclusively.[20] These fighters were no longer motivated by Frolinat's early ideology. For the first decade or so of war, a rebel's life was particularly tough. Most often malnourished and inadequately armed, these fighters lacked even the most basic necessities of daily life, as evidenced by a letter, dated May 24, 1971, from Goukouni Weddeye to Abba Sidick, then secretary-general of Frolinat:

At the moment, all three detachments are being fed through collection and by the local population, which as you should know is all rather meagre. One of the detachments has gone eight days without any food (not even dates), drinking water and the dried fruit of the palm tree 'doum'. In such conditions, needless to say, fighting or even defending oneself is out of the question.

At that time, therefore, conviction was necessary to take up service as a rebel since the material gains were slight, even nonexistent.

From 1977 the situation changed radically. At this point, war became an industry, a career, and a way of life, as much for the grass-roots rebels as for their leaders. Writing of the warlords, J.-L. Triaud has noted that: 'Factionalism in Chad has become a full-time occupation which involves only a small part of the population . . . The use of foreign donors on a wide scale supports an entire politico-military class which lives off the war and its dividends. . . . At this level, aspirations to "national reconciliation" are not obvious'.[21]

Even many of the grass-roots fighters had become 'professional' soldiers, embracing the revolution as a career. Such a choice, for lack of other prospects, can be seen primarily in terms of survival, immediate well-being, and future perspective. This happened, however, to the detriment of the rural communities which had to bear the brunt of very oppressive 'revolutionary' fiscal policies. Local populations became the victims of arbitrary acts perpetrated by armed young men with no respect whatsoever for law or for traditional moral standards.[22] Under these circumstances, the magical saying:

19 *Agence France Presse*, 19 May 1981.
20 It is said that some sultans, such as the Alifa of Kanem, have also reaped some advantages from the current chaos in order to re-establish their waning authority, but not much is known about this subject. See, however, E. Conte, *Marriage Patterns, Political Change and the Perpetuation of Social Inequality in South Kanem*, ORSTOM, Paris, 1983.
21 J.-L. Triaud, 'Le refus de l'Etat: l'exemple tchadien', *Esprit* 100 (April 1985), p.21.
22 Doornbos, 'La révolution dérapée', p.7.

'Je suis combattant' (I am a fighter) became a kind of *laissez-passer*, entitling an individual to anything and everything, and excusing all abuses. In August 1991, the staff of the N'Djaména hospital went on strike for three days partly in order to obtain payment of their June and July wages, but also to gain improvement in security arrangements on the premises. One report noted that: 'The strikers claim that armed men, demanding priority for themselves and their families, have on several occasions "threatened, intimidated, jostled and insulted" the nursing staff on the premises'.[23] Gone was the Frolinat of the early days whose demands on local communities were at least supported by revolutionary fervour, and whose men behaved as 'bandits of honour', not as outright gangsters.

THE WEIGHT OF FOREIGN PATRONS

The civil war not only revealed the fragility of Chad as a nation and as a state, but also highlighted its extreme dependency on foreign 'patrons'.[24] This did not mean that Chad's leaders were left with no room for manoeuvre, for, by skilfully playing off its external supporters – especially France and Libya – against each other, they occasionally managed to maintain a certain independence. Goukouni Weddeye, just as much as Hissein Habré, excelled at the game. However, events have shown that this freedom can quickly collide with its own limits.

It is obvious, for example, that to remain in power in N'Djaména without French help or against the wishes of France was difficult. As early as 1969, Tombalbaye had had to call in the French army to repel the threat posed by the Frolinat rebels, while Hissein Habré, in 1983, could probably not have contained Libya's advance without another French intervention. Moreover, those leaders who did oppose French interests did not last long. Such was the case of President Tombalbaye who from 1973 maintained extremely strained relations with France. The military coup which cost him his life in 1975 was not directly orchestrated by France, but it is certain that Paris knew of preparations for the coup and turned a blind eye. Similarly, when Hissein Habré dared to disregard François Mitterrand's advice in favour of democratisation during the summer of 1990, France withdrew its support and opened up the way for his rival, Idriss Déby.[25] According to some authors such as G. Nder, these events may be explained primarily by economic rivalries between France and the United States:

> Oil and the war of influence France and the USA are engaged in, were somehow related to some of Chad's upsets. Tombalbaye's anti-French

23 *Marchés tropicaux et méditerranéens* no. 2390, 30 August 1991.
24 It has to be noted that outside interventions in Chad since independence demonstrate that Chad only marginally belongs to Central Africa. Apart from France, the main interventionists in Chad have been Libya and Sudan, not its southern neighbours. After independence, the *longue durée*, that is, the ties with countries to the north and east again gained the upper hand.
25 Zilberzahn, *Au Coeur du Secret*.

diatribes alone do not explain his downfall and assassination. Many witnesses to his reign are convinced he signed his own death warrant the day he offered exploration permits to an American firm. Hissein Habré's supporters maintain that their leader's refusal to hear the call to democracy or his cruelty were mere pretexts. His pro-American stance, which had a smell of oil, in the end exasperated Paris.[26]

That was the situation with France. Libya, on the other hand, has been a rather problematic neighbour to Chad. Immediately upon Khadafi's rise to power in 1969 problems began. Basing his stance on an unratified Franco-Italian treaty dating back to 1935, he claimed a territory of 114,000 square kilometres in northern Chad, known as the Aozou strip. Helped by unrest in the region stirred up by Frolinat, Libya occupied the town of Aozou in 1973, without, initially, incurring any official protest on the part of Chad.[27] Four years later, Colonel Khadafi played another trump card. By providing Goukouni Weddeye's Frolinat faction with substantial military reinforcements, he effectively helped them to seize the BET area. This marked the beginning of a long series of interventions, which, on several occasions, brought Libyan troops to Faya-Largeau and even as far as N'Djaména and Abéché. In general Colonel Khadafi used the ongoing war between different factions to his advantage.[28] On several occasions in the 1980s, Libya's eruption onto the Chadian scene gave rise to prolonged arm-wrestling between Libya and France as both parties maintained troops on Chad soil. These encounters never led to direct confrontation, however.[29]

Understanding the motives for Khadafi's actions in Chad is difficult due to the multiple complex dimensions of the situation. Libya's minimal requirement was the security of its southern border. From the beginning, Tripoli made it clear that an anti-Libyan government in N'Djaména was unacceptable. Indeed, and not without reason, Libya lived in fear of being closed in by a Cairo–Khartoum–N'Djaména anti-Libyan axis, an axis that barely hid the threat of strangulation by the USA. Sometimes, however, Libya's demands extended much further. Many would agree that: 'Longer term objectives have included the replacement of western practices and influences in Africa with a universal acceptance of Islam and the Jamahiri [Libyan political] system as a means of restoring the pre-colonial sense of Sahelian–Saharan community and culture'.[30] Within the context of rehabilitating a Sahelian–Saharan community, that is, the rallying of 'all those who live under a tent', Colonel Khadafi

26 G. Nder, 'Pétrole: le mythe est devenu réalité', *N'Djaména Hebdo* 68 (23 December 1992). At the present, it is impossible to say whether such hypotheses correspond to reality. It has to be noted that President Tombalbaye, a few weeks before his death, himself suggested that France bore a grudge against him because of the oil-exploration permits; see *N'Djaména Hebdo* 107 (25 November 1993).
27 B. Lanne, *Tchad-Libye: la Querelle des Frontières*, Karthala, Paris, 1982.
28 J. Wright, *Libya, Chad and the Central Sahara*, Hurst and Company, London, 1989, p.143.
29 See Y. Rabier, 'Politique internationale du conflit tchadien (1960–1990): guerre civile et système mondial', Thèse d'état en science politique, University of Paris, 1993.
30 Wright, *Libya, Chad and the Central Sahara*, p.143.

claimed not only the annexation of the Aozou strip but also large parts of northern Chad.

Libya thus represented a real threat to Chad for nearly ten years between 1978 and 1987, and had not the French intervened on several occasions, Libya might have been able to achieve its ends. By the mid-1990s, however, the threat was reduced. In 1987, Hissein Habré's troops managed to drive the Libyan army out from all the fortified posts it occupied, forcing Khadafi to compromise. Weakened financially by a drop in oil prices, giving in to the weariness of the Libyan people, and undermined by military leaders for whom unending conflict cost a high price in loss of men, the guide of the Libyan revolution called an end to all hostilities. He even allowed the case of Aozou to be arbitrated by the International Court of Justice in the Hague. When the verdict was returned in February 1994, the Court sided with Chad and, surprisingly, Libya evacuated Aozou without further trouble. Colonel Khadafi's conciliatory attitude may have been due in part to the fact that President Déby was less anti-Libya than his predecessor, thus lessening the threat on Libya's southern frontier.

Chad, however, had another restless neighbour in Sudan. Although Khartoum had never pressed territorial claims as Libya had, it did play a large part in Chad's civil wars by supporting certain factions and offering them sanctuary in Darfur. Sudanese intervention actually began before Libya's, when, in 1964–65, armed opponents to President Tombalbaye's regime took refuge there and founded Frolinat. Sudan remained Frolinat's main sanctuary until 1972, as it was again from 1980 to 1982 for Hissein Habré and, more recently still, for Idriss Déby. In the last few years, however, Chad's eastern neighbour's priorities have changed. Hassan Al-Tourabi of Sudan made claims that far exceeded those of previous Sudanese regimes. Sudan, through the medium of fundamentalist Islam, sought to bring Chad under its cultural and religious influence, a goal much feared by many Chadians, especially in the south.

Aside from its political dependency, on France and Libya in particular, and to a lesser degree on Sudan,[31] Chad was also economically dependent on foreign powers. As stated in a 1993 United Nations report: 'More than 100% of the state revenue is used to pay the salaries of a very limited fraction of the population . . . , and this to the detriment of other expenditures . . . This has increased Chad's dependency on foreign funds which today cover all public investments and a growing part of day-to-day expenses'.[32] France has always been Chad's main donor, followed by the United States. More recently, N'Djaména has also resorted to very different sponsors with their own set of specific requirements, that is the IMF and the World Bank. In May 1992, the Chad government implemented a draconian plan to rehabilitate the economy, a plan which the minister of finance pointed out had been elaborated on the

31 Chad's other neighbours have been less troublesome, although Nigeria, too, has sometimes intervened in Chadian affairs.
32 *La Situation Économique et Financière au Tchad: Choix et Contraintes en Matière de Finances Publiques*, Bureau du coordinateur résident des Nations Unies, N'Djaména, March 1993, pp.10–11.

basis of IMF guidelines. The proposed measures, which sorely affected civil servants and other workers, sparked off a long series of strikes. After that the IMF intervened on several occasions to remind the Chad authorities of the necessity of certain restrictive measures, even although their negative social consequences were considerable.[33] In the mid-1990s, Chad operated under the supervision of the international monetary institutions which regularly threatened to put a stop to all financial assistance should Chad not prove to be a 'good pupil'. Moreover, the 1994 devaluation of the French Africa franc, which in itself highlighted the limited economic independence of Chad, was decided by France under pressure from the Bretton Woods institutions.

ECONOMIC NON-DEVELOPMENT

In 1960, Chad was extremely poor, and the situation has hardly improved since. According to United Nations statistics, Chad is one of the twelve most underdeveloped countries in the world, whether the criteria used be gross national product per capita or a human development index. This non-development is due in part to causes common to many African countries, unequal terms of trade and a lack of exploitable resources, but also, in the case of Chad, to the civil war which has undeniably aggravated economic difficulties.

First and foremost, the civil war has caused huge human losses. Accurate figures, or even reliable estimates, are lacking, but tens of thousands of people, including civilians, are known to have been killed, and thousands of others are disabled for life. Demographic figures suggest a somewhat paradoxical problem. Provisional results from the April 1993 national census credit Chad with a population of 6,288,261, a number greater than most previous projections.[34] However, this same census established for the whole of Chad a masculinity ratio of 93 men for every 100 women, and an even lower ratio in regions that were particularly hard hit by armed conflict.[35] This ratio probably does reflect the consequences of the war and the flight of thousands of refugees who moved away to neighbouring countries on several occasions. Some refugees settled more or less permanently and hundreds of thousands of Chadians live abroad, particularly in Sudan, but also in Libya and in the Central African Republic.

The civil war has also caused vast material damage, first in the north, the exclusive theatre of operations until 1978, then in N'Djaména, hit by fighting during 1979–80, and finally in the south where, following its occupation by northern troops, guerrilla operations broke out in 1984 and 1985, and again in 1992–96. Again, it is not possible to know precisely the extent of losses, but they were extensive. Roads disappeared, entire villages were abandoned,

33 See G. Bérassidé, 'Le FMI désapprouve le pacte social', *N'Djaména Hebdo* 143 (5 August 1993).
34 *Recensement Général de la Population et de l'Habitat 1993: Résultats Provisoires*, Ministère du Plan et de la Coopération/Ministère de l'Intérieur et de la Sécurité, N'Djaména, 1993, p.3.
35 *Ibid.*, p.8.

hospitals, medical centres and schools were destroyed. The still young university of N'Djaména had to be closed for several years while civil war raged in the capital. Given the general insecurity and the destruction of much infrastructure, many development projects never got beyond the planning stage, while others had to be abandoned along the way. A 1993 report noted that:

> the average per capita income has remained about constant in real terms over the last 15–20 years, and, today, it amounts to a little more than half of the average income in sub-Saharan Africa. . . . In Chad, 210 children out of every 1000 die before the age of 5, as opposed to the African average of 167 out of every 1000; 70% of the population is illiterate compared to 51% over the continent.[36]

The war also weighed heavily on the state's budget, and continued to do so after the conflict subsided. Between 1988 and 1992, military expenses amounted to more than the total budgets allocated to health, education and other social services.[37] This was mainly because Chad had to maintain an army whose numbers had swollen progressively over years of civil war. Many rebels demanded integration into the armed forces as compensation for their rallying to the government, with costly budgetary consequences. With the technical and financial assistance of France, an operation to restructure and deflate the army was embarked on and had results. According to official sources, of the 40,000 men in the army in 1990, 15,000 had been demobilised five years later.[38] These figures may, however, have been somewhat optimistic and the project was far from finished.

Yet, even if Chad had not been subjected to civil war, its economic situation would not have been brilliant. The country's most important export product – at least 60 per cent of all monitored exports and its main source of revenue – was cotton. This has never been a really lucrative product, and for several years, it has been the object of a world slump. The cost price of Chadian cotton-fibre has been, on various occasions, higher than its selling price on the international market. The Cotontchad company, which is in charge of cotton buying, has consequently had trouble surviving and has come close to shutting down. On the other hand, the state has encouraged peasants in areas of poor productivity to abandon cotton cultivation without, apparently, preparing the farming communities to develop alternative crops which would generate revenue.[39] In view of the fact that the cotton industry, directly and indirectly, provided a living for about two million people, this precarious situation did not bode well for the future of Chad.

The other main export, livestock, did not fare any better at bringing in sizeable revenues, and was also the object of a slump. Chad's main market,

36 *La Situation Economique et Financière au Tchad*, p.6.
37 *Ibid.*, p.6.
38 'Idriss Déby rompt le silence', *Africa International* 288 (October 1995).
39 B. Mamout, 'La rechute', *Tchad et Culture* 129 (December 1992), p.3.

Nigeria, had been closed to Chad stockbreeders by successive devaluations of the Nigerian currency, although the devaluation of the French African franc seemed to offer new opportunities. Other potential cattle markets in Africa were eliminated by the introduction of frozen meat from South Africa and the Netherlands at unbeatable prices.[40] Part of the exported livestock crossed the Nigerian and Sudanese border on foot, thus escaping any monitoring by the Chad authorities. The civil war aggravated this smuggling and the state obtained relatively little foreign currency from cattle.

When it comes to food production, Chad has also been through tough times. During 'normal' years, it was self-sufficient in food, but even without war, not all years are normal. Drought is a constant threat which can jeopardise food security. This was the case at the beginning of the 1970s, when thousands died of starvation and livestock was decimated.[41] In 1984 and 1985, famine struck again, affecting some of the southern regions, causing huge human losses, and bringing about mass migration to Sudan and the Central African Republic. Moreover, the economic dislocation which followed each bout of civil war only worsened the effects of drought. Forced population movements caused by fighting often rendered the sowing and harvesting of crops next to impossible. War operations, and the poor maintenance of roads, did not help the supplying of food to disaster victims, even when provisions were available in other areas. In the decade after 1985 Chad did not have another famine, but the threat of drought was always present.

Periods of famine were only the surface manifestation of the much deeper and permanent problem of ecological degradation. The phenomenon is, as yet, under-studied, but it appears that the environment, especially in the Sahelian and Saharian areas, has been gradually eroded over the course of recent years. The long-term consequences could be disastrous. From time to time, the media have given the issue some coverage: 'Three or four decades from now, if nothing is done to try and save it, the second most important lake in Africa could be wiped off the face of the earth. Lake Tchad is seriously endangered'.[42]

Ecological problems have also emerged in the N'Djaména area. The capital, where 10 per cent of Chad's total population lives, uses huge amounts of firewood, so that within a 70-kilometre radius, almost no vegetation is to be found.[43] Elsewhere, particularly in the east, the fauna has been destroyed, partly because the military and the fighters of different armed factions no longer respect the rules set down by the National Parks' administration. All these problems await urgent solutions, but the latent war has not helped the people in charge.

40 S. Abdel Madjid, 'Développement de l'élevage: des handicaps sérieux', *Tchad et Culture* 131 (April 1993).
41 C. Bouquet, 'Le déficit pluviométrique au Tchad et ses principales conséquences', *Cahiers d'Outre-Mer* 27, 107 (July–September 1974).
42 'Sauver le Lac Tchad', *N'Djaména Hebdo* 89 (8 July 1993).
43 Bendjo, '7e journée du CILSS: la gestion des terroirs', *N'Djaména Hebdo* 59 (17 September 1992).

Women have suffered badly from such natural and social disasters. Due to the war, among other factors, their specific problems have never received priority on Chad's political agenda. Their participation in the civil war has been minimal, understandably in a Muslim milieu, although a few individual young women did join the fighting troops of some of Frolinat's branches. One of them was known as 'Ms Bazooka'. This did not help the advancement of women much, and they remained underrepresented in the modern sector. In 1994 women made up only 12 per cent of the public service workforce.[44] Women have, however, begun to emerge on to the political scene. Thus, at the National Sovereign Conference held in early 1993, the women present signed a motion requesting the implementation of a ratio of one women to two men in all the country's higher administrative and political institutions. As of 1996, this demand had not been honoured by any N'Djaména government.

1990—96: TENTATIVE DEMOCRATISATION

In December 1990, when Idriss Déby came to power, having ousted his predecessor by force, his first address to the nation included the following sentence: 'The fighters in the patriotic forces have experienced immense pleasure in having delivered the precious gift that you have been hoping for. This gift is neither gold nor silver: it is freedom!'[45] Coming from a warlord, such a statement surprised many, and most observers immediately expressed their misgivings about the new head of state's sincerity and doubts as to whether he could deliver his promise. From that moment on, however, democratisation actually did get underway. It was a slow and hesitant process along a tortuous route.

In the early days, from December 1990, independent newspapers began to sprout and express their opinions very freely. In January 1992 political parties were allowed and more than sixty different groups were formed. From January to April 1993, the National Sovereign Conference which met in N'Djaména, resulted in the adoption of a provisional constitution and the election of a new prime minister. Although slow, democratisation did make progress. The main documents approved at the Conference marked a considerable advance in political liberties.[46] After the Conference, however, democratisation slowed down. The period of transition, which was supposed to lead up to the first free elections since independence, was only meant to last one year, but delaying tactics by the government, and sometimes also by the opposition parties, resulted in elections being postponed from one year to the next.

44 'Population et développement', *N'Djaména Hebdo* 143 (4 August 1994).
45 'Message à la Nation, prononcé par le colonel Idriss Déby à sa désignation à la présidence du Conseil d'Etat, le 04 décembre 1990', *Actualités Tchadiennes* 1 (March 1991).
46 See R. Buijtenhuijs, *La Conférence Nationale Souveraine du Tchad: un Essai d'Histoire immédiate*, Karthala, Paris, 1993.

It was only in 1996 that a final breakthrough was made, with presidential elections being held in June and July, and parliamentary elections at the beginning of 1997. Unfortunately, these polls did not solve Chad's political problems. It is almost certain that the presidential elections, which led to the victory of the incumbent President Déby, were rigged. Independent observers were inclined to think that Déby would have won without cheating, but the results, especially in the first round of the presidential election, did not reflect the political situation of Chad. Déby was credited with more votes than he deserved while his main opponents were denied their real tally. As a consequence many voters, especially in the south, did not recognise Déby as their legitimate president. He therefore needed to overcome this handicap by a genuine policy of peace and national reconciliation over the five years of his mandate.[47]

Other problems also arose again after 1990. One of them was linked to the north–south divide. In 1978, when Habré became prime minister under General Malloum, Arabic was recognised as Chad's second official language in a rather hasty concession to Frolinat demands. At first, this recognition was only a matter of principle with no real practical consequences. After Déby's accession to power, however, the situation started to change. A restless minority of Arabic-speakers tried with some success to translate the principle of bilingualism into fact. This provoked some passionate responses amongst other groups, particularly in the south. Quite a few political leaders feared, for example, that the implementation of two parallel school systems, as the Arabic-speakers requested, would only deepen the existing division of the country. Others worried that the Arabic language was just a Trojan horse for Islam.

At a local level also the north–south issue took on new dimensions as the southern regions were more and more 'invaded' by northerners. Following successive droughts, and also as a result of the appointment of northern administrative and military representatives to the south, pastoralists from the Sahelian area moved southwards. In the conflicts between the newcomers and the local farmers, northern administrators tended to settle disputes in favour of the herdsmen, causing discontent to southern peasants. Another source of discontent was the rise of a fundamentalist and aggressive Islam. This was mainly Sudanese-inspired and stood in marked contrast to the traditionally much more tolerant and pacific Chadian Islam.[48] This upsurge of a more uncompromising Islam could be observed at both the national and local level. During the National Sovereign Conference, the Imam of the Great Mosque in N'Djaména actually asked for the introduction of *shari'a* law in Chad. In the south some Muslims occasionally behaved in a particularly aggressive

---

47 R. Buijtenhuijs, '"On nous a volé nos voix!" Quelle démocratie pour le Tchad?', *Politique Africaine* 63 (October 1996).
48 On traditional Islam in Chad and its recent evolution, see H. Coudray, 'Chrétiens et musulmans au Tchad', *Islamochristiana* 18 (1992).

manner towards the local population.[49] With a little exaggeration, it can perhaps be argued that the south had become an 'occupied zone', just as the north had been about 1965. This new phase in the north–south dialectic did not really bode well for the future. Its grave consequences included minor rural revolts and demands for the south's secession.

In the past, no politico-military faction ever advocated secession, or even suggested the possibility of a federal state. By the mid-1990s, however, federalism was no longer a taboo subject and several parties openly campaigned for such a solution. According to some authors, southern peasants along with a few city dwellers, had become receptive to separatist slogans.[50] Occasionally, such opinions were even voiced in newspapers.[51] It was not an easy task for the newly elected president to manage such demands, especially since he started his career as a democratically chosen head of state with a severe political handicap. During the second round of the presidential elections he had obtained a victory in the north with 90 per cent of the vote. Most of the southern districts, however, expressed their preference for General Kamougué, who received 85 to 90 per cent of the vote except in the Mayo-Kabbi *préfecture* where Déby gained 59.5 per cent. In other words, Déby did not win a national victory, and he needed to manoeuvre skilfully to overcome his handicap.

Insecurity was another worrying problem for the elected president. It stemmed on the one hand from the indiscipline of some units of the army, which in theory answered directly to the presidency if they answered to anyone. In practice, however, soldiers continued to act as they had during the time of the warlords. These soldiers held captives to ransom and killed and raped with impunity, especially in the south. Insecurity also stemmed from the activities of politico-military factions which had not yet rallied to the regime. They continued to be active in rural areas in the west around Lake Chad and the Logones.[52] In Eastern Logone there had been heavy fighting during the last few years which had provoked mass repression by the security forces and the civilian population which had suffered most.[53] According to W. F. S. Miles:

> the security situation has deteriorated substantially and the state is suffering from a severe lack of authority. Indeed, only habit or convention can justify speaking of 'a' state in Chad. Functionally, there are two of them: that part ... which remains linked, however tenuously, to the government in the

49 R. Buijtenhuijs, 'La situation dans le sud du Tchad', *Afrique Contemporaine* 175 (July–September 1995).
50 J.-P. Magnant, 'Le Tchad', in G. Conac (ed.), *L'Afrique en Transition vers le Pluralisme Politique*, Economica, Paris, 1993.
51 R. Djimtoide, 'Non à la conférence nationale, oui à un référendum sur le fédéralisme ou la partition du Tchad', *N'Djaména Hebdo* 53–4 (18 June 1992).
52 Some of these are offshoots of Idriss Déby's own armed forces whose leaders turned against him when they felt marginalised by the new regime.
53 See *De Vaines Promesses – les Violations des Droits de l'Homme se Poursuivent en Toute Impunité*, Amnesty International, 27 April 1995.

capital; and a second Chad which includes territories and populations, northern and southern, operating beyond the control of N'Djaména.[54]

According to this author, the Chad of the warlords was thus not yet completely a thing of the past. The prevailing insecurity not only overshadowed the democratisation process, it also hung over economic development and, in particular, over the exploitation of oil. Oilfields of some significance had been discovered in the Doba region of Eastern Logone. A consortium of American companies, joined by Elf-Aquitaine, was poised to exploit this oil through a pipeline constructed across Cameroun. This venture, however, was still threatened by the activities of one of the politico-military factions, the *Forces Armées pour la République Fédérale*, which had made it known that oil would not flow from Doba unless a peace agreement was reached with the government. Even if Chad's oil reserves do not come close to equalling those of Kuwait, they nevertheless guarantee the government sizeable revenues, provided the insecurity diminishes.

Thus, Chad's future remained uncertain. In the economic field, Déby's regime did not succeed in improving the situation, quite the contrary. Under his rule, the country's few industrial enterprises ran into trouble and some even shut down, while in the public sector, salary arrears mounted. This led to unending strikes and growing difficulties for the business sector, since money was no longer circulating. There was an implosion of the economy. On the political scene, the 1996 elections did represent a step forward but the elected president still had to fully establish his legitimacy. More alarmingly, many Chadians seemed to have given up all hope of seeing any future for their country, as was illustrated in a series of interviews published by *N'Djaména Hebdo* on the thirty-fourth anniversary of independence.[55] Below are a few representative passages:

> I miss the colonial times. Judging by what we have been through over the last thirty-four years, I prefer colonisation to independence.

> Independence is now regarded as a burden. I remember a statement of a Cameroonian quoted by René Dumont: When will independence end?

> Without wishing to appear pessimistic, I would venture to say that we have no future. We are at point zero.

Facing such a display of negative assessments, it was difficult for the foreign observer to remain optimistic in 1996. Much depended on the manner in which Idriss Déby used his 1996 election victory. Would he remain the prisoner of his politico-military 'clan', as some said he had been, or would he behave as 'the prisoner of his voters', as some political leaders who rallied to

54 W. F. S. Miles, 'Tragic tradeoffs: democracy and security in Chad', *Journal of Modern African Studies* 33, 1 (1995), pp.53–65.
55 '11 août 1960–11 août 1994: le Tchad souffle ses trente-quatre bougies', *N'Djaména Hebdo* 144 (11 August 1994).

his cause hoped? One recent positive occurrence is worth noting. Since the end of 1990, a vibrant and active civil society has progressively been formed and this has played an important role in the fight for true democracy. Will it be in a position to tip the scales over the course of the next few years? Or will democratisation prove to be no more than false currency, as many fear, and that not only for Chad?

Map 3.1 Cameroun

CHAPTER 3

Cameroun and the politics of patronage

ANDREAS MEHLER

The new president of the republic has managed, with normal help from the former metropolitan power, to impose his authority and unshakable wisdom by suspending a sterile multi-party system that has hindered positive action in the country.

Bernard Nanga, *Les chauves-souris*[1]

Nanga's ironic recitation of familiar official phrases reflects two main features of postcolonial development in Cameroun, authoritarianism and the 'French factor'. From its independence in 1960 to the 1980s Cameroun has often been portrayed as an example of political stability and successful capitalist development. In fact, structural economic deficiencies, which had been inherited from the colonial period, could not be remedied and a short-lived boom from 1978 to 1986 only masked gross mistakes resulting from economic mismanagement. Wounds sustained during the colonial period did not heal easily and 'civil society' was hardly given freedom to grow. The potential of Cameroun remained submerged. It was a state in decline whose rulers adopted short-sighted strategies to serve their own interests.

EARLY POLITICAL DEVELOPMENTS: PLURALISM AND THE ONE-PARTY STATE

The central feature of Cameroun politics was the concentration of power in the hands of the president, Ahmadou Ahidjo, which began in the waning years of colonialism and continued into the 1970s. Demands for independence dated back to 1948 when a political party, the *Union des Populations du Cameroun*/Union of the Populations of Cameroun (UPC)[2], was founded in

1 Bernard Nanga, *Les Chauves-Souris*, Présence Africaine, Paris, 1980. Cameroun writers are known for their biting satire and Nanga is a widely-read novelist.
2 See for example, R. Joseph, *Radical Nationalism in Cameroon: Social Origins of the UPC Rebellion*, Oxford University Press, Oxford, 1977; A. Mbembe, *La Naissance du Maquis dans le Sud-Cameroun (1920–1960)*, Karthala, Paris, 1996; and W. Johnson, 'The *Union des Populations du*

43

the French-ruled eastern sector of the colony.[3] Seven years later, when unrest spread to the city of Douala in the French sector, the party was banned and forced to go underground. It created an armed resistance movement, the *maquis*, which operated in several districts and became especially prominent in the Sanaga Maritime and Bamiléké regions. Guerrilla warfare became a seminal feature in the collective memory of Cameroun nationalists. In September 1958 a colonial patrol shot and killed the now-legendary leader of the movement, Um Nyobé, and two years later Moumié, the president of the movement, was poisoned in Geneva by members of the French secret service. Despite this, the guerrilla struggle continued and a significant number of French troops were deployed in the Bamiléké region.[4] Even after independence the rebellion went on.[5] The number of casualties is impossible to ascertain since estimates range widely from 600 to 150,000. Certainly many lives were sacrificed in the name of rebellion and repression.[6]

A tradition of pluralistic politics, that also included less prominent political parties, had barely taken root before independence was declared on 1 January 1960. Already in the previous October, Prime Minister Ahidjo of eastern Cameroun had used continuing *maquis* insurgency to persuade parliament to hand over sweeping emergency powers, including authorisation to rule by decree.[7] A month after independence French civil servants, who continued to wield influence, helped the government to win a referendum for a new constitution. In elections in April Ahidjo's *Union Camerounaise* (UC) party was able to win 51 out of 100 parliamentary seats, a result partly achieved through a convenient division of constituency boundaries. This situation then permitted Ahidjo to become the elected president by means of indirect parliamentary proceedings in May. Hence, the president's rise to absolute power had been a hard-fought battle, determined by tactical manoeuvres and through French influence.[8]

Cameroun in rebellion: the integrative backlash of insurgency', in R. I. Rotberg and A. A. Mazrui (eds), *Protest and Power in Black Africa*, Oxford University Press, New York, 1970, pp.671–92. On the controversial formation of UPC, see A. Eyinga, *L'UPC – Une Révolution Manquée?*, Editions Chaka, Paris, 1991, pp.23–5.

3 The old German colony of Kamerun had been divided under a British and French mandate after the First World War. For this history, see Ralph A. Austen and Rita Headrick, 'Equatorial Africa under colonial rule', in David Birmingham and Phyllis M. Martin (eds), *History of Central Africa* Vol. 2, Longman, Harlow, 1983, pp.27–94, including Map 2.2, p.31.

4 J. Guillemin, 'Les campagnes militaires françaises de la décolonisation en Afrique sud-saharienne', *Le Mois en Afrique* 17, 198–199 (1982), pp.124–41.

5 The public execution of the UPC vice-president, Ernest Ouandié, in January 1971 symbolically marked the end of the rebellion.

6 W. Johnson, *The Cameroon Federation: Political Integration in a Fragmentary Society*, Princeton University Press, Princeton, NJ, 1970, pp.352–3, fn.11; and H. F. Illy, *Politik und Wirtschaft in Kamerun. Bedingungen, Ziele und Strategien der staatlichen Entwicklungspolitik*, Weltforum Verlag, Munich, 1976, p.84.

7 V. T. Le Vine, *The Cameroons from Mandate to Independence*, University of California Press, Berkeley, CA, 1964, pp.186–7; and J.-F. Bayart, *L'Etat au Cameroun*, 2nd edn., Presses de la Fondation Nationale des Sciences Politiques, Paris, 1985, pp.69–72. On 'permanent martial law', see Abel Eyinga, 'Government by state of emergency', in R. Joseph (ed.), *Gaullist Africa: Cameroon under Ahmadou Ahidjo*, Fourth Dimension Publishers, Enugu, 1978, pp.100–10.

8 Bayart, *L'Etat au Cameroun*, p.76.

In the history of decolonisation Cameroun is a peculiar case in that the leading movements in the struggle for national liberation, especially the UPC, were losers after independence. Elsewhere, as in Algeria or Kenya, those who participated in armed struggle had a prominent role in new governments. In Cameroun after independence, France continued to have an influential role in foreign policy, cultural life and the economy. Since the struggle to repress guerrilla opposition continued until 1970, the Ahidjo regime also remained dependent on French military aid. Indeed, the president's room for manoeuvre in foreign policy was so restricted that he was commonly considered as little more than a French puppet. Cooperation and defence treaties concluded between Cameroun and France in November 1960 set tight limits on independent action[9] and, as if it were a matter of course, Cameroun remained a member of the franc zone.

After independence had been established under these difficult conditions, a central issue for the new government concerned the future of the British sectors of Cameroun. In a plebiscite 'Northern Cameroons' decided to amalgamate with Nigeria whereas 'Southern Cameroons' decided to join the Republic of Cameroun. The ensuing constitutional negotiations, which the English-speaking élite conducted with the Ahidjo government in Foumban in July 1961, defined the nature of the federation which came into force in October 1961.[10] The anglophone negotiators could not push through more than a few of their ideas. Although each federal state kept its parliament, the new constitution did not create a real federation. The two regions turned out to be too dissimilar, not only in terms of their political influence but also in their economic potential and demographic make-up. Although West Cameroun's prime minister, John Ngu Foncha of the *Kamerun National Democratic Party* (KNDP) automatically became national vice-president, this turned out to be a 'decorative' role from the perspective of President Ahidjo, who took little interest in the federal arrangements.[11] Each leader was able to appoint his own followers to the central parliament (40 UC and 10 KNDP representatives) for a transitional period until a partly pluralistic election was held in April 1964.[12]

After its difficult birth Cameroun continued to be a country beset by internal conflict. In order to repress its enemies the government built political prisons at Tcholliré, Yoko, Mantoum and elsewhere, and the very mention of such names instilled fear in the population. The country ranked among

9 D. Oyono, *Avec ou sans la France? La Politique Africaine du Cameroun depuis 1960*, L'Harmattan, Paris, 1990.
10 E. Ardener, 'The nature of the Reunification of Cameroun', in A. Hazlewood (ed.), *African Integration and Disintegration*, Oxford University Press, London, 1967, pp.285–337, especially, pp.306–11; Johnson, *The Cameroon Federation*, pp.181–98; Illy, *Politik und Wirtschaft*, pp.99–101; and V. J. Ngoh, *Constitutional Developments in Southern Cameroons, 1946–1961: from Trusteeship to Independence*, Pioneer, Yaoundé, 1990.
11 J. Benjamin, *Les Camerounais Occidentaux: La Minorité dans un Etat Bicommunitaire*, Les Presses de l'Université de Montréal, Montréal, 1972.
12 Representatives to the Federal Assembly were elected in the two legislative parliaments in a system which allowed the UC and KNDP leaders to decide the outcome.

Africa's more oppressive regimes.[13] Freedom of speech was systematically curtailed,[14] and popular protest took the form of covert noncooperation with the government. Discontent and suspicion were expressed in the growth of witchcraft.[15] Special presidential powers, emergency legislation, and the arrest of even moderate parliamentary opponents were common, and political freedoms severely limited. When the election of 1964 was finally held only one constituency in the eastern part of the country fielded opposition candidates.[16] Two years later all political parties were absorbed into the ruling party, the *Union Nationale Camerounaise/Cameroon National Union* (UNC/CNU), and the president picked a cabinet composed exclusively of loyalists.[17] According to propaganda the single party was designed to facilitate nation-building, and *unité nationale* became the political slogan, much reiterated by a regime otherwise devoid of ideology. The party was tightly structured around a politburo, a secretariat, a central committee, a women's organisation, a youth organisation and a trade union wing. The mass membership participated in party cells, which were organised in sections and sub-sections, and an élite school was geared to doctrinal education.[18] The party as the 'political organ of the masses' projected an aura of strength but in practice there were underlying weaknesses and the federal experiment soon came to an abrupt end.[19] In 1967 President Ahidjo engineered the replacement of the West Cameroun prime minister by a more pliant appointee. He did the same in 1970 when he appointed a new vice-president.[20] Two years later he changed the constitution by a sudden referendum which turned the federation into a united republic with seven provinces ruled by governors appointed by the president. Ahidjo was now at the peak of his power at the head of a police state.

FOREIGN POLICY: MODERATE PROGRESS TOWARDS EMANCIPATION

The early foreign policy of Cameroun was deeply affected by a desire to root out government opponents who had been given asylum in Ghana, Guinea,

13 M. W. DeLancey, 'The construction of the Cameroon political system: the Ahidjo years, 1958–1982', *Journal of Contemporary African Studies* 6, 1–2 (1987), pp.3–24, especially p.20.
14 F. Beng Nyamnjoh, 'Contrôle de l'information au Cameroun: implication pour les recherches en communication', *Afrika Spectrum* 28, 1 (1993), pp.93–115.
15 J.-F. Bayart, A. Mbembe, C. Toulabor, *La Politique par le Bas en Afrique Noire: Contributions à une Problématique de la Démocratie*, Karthala, Paris, 1992.
16 Bayart, *L'Etat au Cameroun*, p.117.
17 Ahidjo removed the two ministers who most obviously had ethnic backing as well as most of the open-minded individuals in the UNC hierarchy. See *ibid*, p.121.
18 J.-F. Bayart, 'L'Union Nationale Camerounaise', *Revue Française de Science Politique* 20, 4 (1970), pp.681–718; and J.-F. Médard, 'L'Etat sous-développé au Cameroun', *Année Africaine*, 1977, pp.35–84, especially p.45.
19 A. Mehler, *Kamerun in der Ära Biya. Bedingungen, erste Schritte und Blockaden einer demokratischen Transition*, Institut für Afrika-Kunde, Hamburg, 1993, pp.163–72, using leads provided by F. Sengat Kuoh's speeches. For the party's lack of impact in rural areas, see P. Geschiere, 'Paysans, régime national et recherche hégémonique. L'implantation de l'U(N)C, le "Grand Parti National" dans les villages maka', *Politique Africaine* 22 (1986), 73–100.
20 Bayart, *L'Etat au Cameroun*, p.126.

Egypt and, after the overthrow of Youlou, in Congo.[21] The regime joined the *Organisation commune africaine et malagache*, the organisation of former French colonies in Africa, which established its headquarters in Yaoundé. It also joined the Organization of African Unity (OAU) and, although not a dynamic participant in the organisation's affairs, provided two of its secretaries-general from 1972 to 1978. Cameroun also supported at least verbally the Movement of Non-Aligned states, opposed imperialism and *apartheid*, and in 1971 recognised the People's Republic of China.[22] As early as 1971–72, and against France's wishes, Cameroun suspended its affiliation with *Air Afrique* in order to build its own separate, national airline. Ahidjo also tried to open new commercial and aid relations through a 'flirtation' with Germany; on the other hand, Britain's original influence as the former mandate power in western Cameroun diminished.[23] To some extent Ahidjo, and his successor Biya, did thus succeed in diversifying contacts, especially with potential aid donors.[24]

Regional affairs were at first dominated by the outbreak of the Biafran war of secession and by the civil war in Chad. Relations with Nigeria, the regional giant, had never been easy since the big neighbour was a reference point for Cameroun's English-speaking minority and for the two million Nigerians living in Cameroun. Border disputes between the two countries were another source of tension, for example during the 1980s and in the Bakassi crisis of 1994–96 which almost led to open war, cost lives, and created many refugees.[25] During the Biafran war an estimated 25,000 Igbos sought refuge in Cameroun, though the government supported Nigeria and did not follow the lead of France, which supported Biafra. Border disputes continued even after the Biafran war had been settled and Cameroun took its case to the International Court of Justice in The Hague.

During the civil war in Chad, Cameroun feared the expansion of Libya in Africa's affairs and initially sided with France and the United States in support of Hissein Habré. In 1984, when Libya was suspected of aiding rebels in an attempted coup in Cameroun, Cameroun's support for Habré became more overt.[26] French troops were allowed to cross into Chad and Habré

21 Apart from the countries mentioned above, relations with Sudan, Libya, Morocco, Tunisia and Liberia were strained at certain times.
22 During the 1960s China supported the UPC rebellion. Under Biya excellent relations were maintained and he paid a state visit to Beijing in October 1983.
23 N. Kofele-Kale, 'Cameroon and its foreign relations', *African Affairs* 80, 319 (1981), pp.197–217, especially pp.205–6.
24 After France (1987, 36 per cent), Germany became the second biggest supplier of bilateral foreign aid (26 per cent), followed by the United States (10 per cent) and Canada (6 per cent). With the ongoing crises the donors' faith diminished and in 1992 France was again responsible for supplying the bulk (73 per cent) of bilateral aid. Estimates according to *EIU Country Profile, 1994–95*, p.24.
25 Border disputes were to some extent influenced by competition over fishing grounds, and projected natural gas and oil deposits. In both countries, governments also wanted to distract populations from domestic disputes with a bit of sabre-rattling.
26 D. Oyono, 'Le coup d'état manqué du 6 avril 1984 et les engagements de politique étrangère du Cameroun', *Le Mois en Afrique* 20, 223–224 (1984), pp.48–56.

Andreas Mehler

was allowed asylum in northern Cameroun when he escaped from Chad following his military defeat.

THE SUCCESSION CRISIS

On 4 November 1982 problems of health and weariness caused Ahidjo to resign as head of state, though he retained the party chairmanship.[27] His prime minister, Paul Biya, who had been appointed in 1975, now inherited the presidency. Biya had been chosen partly because his political weakness did not threaten the power of the president, and partly to fulfil the need to have a southerner at a high level in government, even if in a largely symbolic role.[28]

Regional–ethnic differences were usually depicted as east–west or north–south antagonism.[29] One further element in understanding the divisions arises from the fact that Cameroun was, and still is, heterogenous in matters of religion. While the Catholic Church has a large following, mainly in the central province, Islam has spread slowly from the north where it predominates. Although ethnic and religious cleavages overlapped, religion was a meaningful ingredient only in conflicts in northern Cameroun. Under Ahidjo the state promoted the expansion of Islam in the north at the expense of traditional religions which were still powerful belief systems throughout the country. When Biya came to power this official sponsorship of Islam was discontinued.[30]

Ethnicity has also been viewed as a potentially significant source of conflict. Events such as the repression of the postcolonial guerrilla resistance with its identifiable focus in the Bassa-Bamiléké regions, and the attempted coup in 1984, which many observers and participants did not hesitate to attribute to Fulani initiative, were blamed on 'ethnic' animosity. The situation, however, was much more complex. Out of some two hundred small ethnic communities which had once existed there emerged larger groupings shaped by a variety of forces. Political alliances gained ethnic labels such as Kirdi for the non-Fulani groups in the north, Bamiléké in the west and Beti/Bulu in the centre and south. Several medium-sized groups retained at least regional importance, such as the Douala, Bassa, Bafia and Bamoun. Although the anglophone population did not form an ethnic community, it nevertheless constituted a notable minority with shared cultural experiences and a minority

27 P. Gaillard, *Le Cameroun*. 2 vols, L'Harmattan, Paris, 1989, II, pp.93–4. For various interpretations of the succession crisis see N. Ntumazah (UPC) in an interview in *Peuples Noirs, Peuples Africains* 55–58 (1987), pp.198–219, especially p.212. See also, Gaillard, *Le Cameroun*, p.89, Bayart, *L'Etat au Cameroun*, and articles in *Marchés Tropicaux, Jeune Afrique* during September 1983.
28 E. Mbarga, 'La réforme des articles 5 et 7 de la constitution du Cameroun', *Penant* 90, 769 (1980), pp.262–87. Regarding Ahidjo's assessment of Biya see C. Monga, *Cameroun. Quel Avenir?* Silex, Paris, 1986, p.60; and *Le Monde*, 30 August 1983.
29 For example, see J.-P. Fogui, *L'Intégration Politique au Cameroun: Une Analyse Centre-Périphérie*, Librairie Générale de Droit et de Jurisprudence, Paris, 1990, pp.78–102.
30 K. Schilder, 'Etat et Islamisation au Nord-Cameroun (1960–1982)', *Politique Africaine* 41 (1991), pp.144–9. E. A. Schultz, 'From pagan to Pullo; ethnic identity change in northern Cameroon', *Africa* 54, 1 (1984), pp.46–64.

consciousness enhanced by systematic discrimination. Under Ahidjo career opportunities had been divided up regionally, with the Fulani dominating the army and police, the Bamiléké gaining control over commerce, and the Beti having a predominant role in the civil service. Some kind of ethnic proportional representation was attempted in the allocation of scholarships and political posts.[31] Ethnicity was so important in job applications that it was promoted by individuals when advantageous. Thus a new 'tribalism' was 'invented' in modern Cameroun.

Ethnicity, however, was not the most important key to understanding the Cameroun succession crisis. When Biya succeeded to the presidency he took care to honour his 'illustrious' predecessor in his speeches, but found the heavy hand of the founder irksome when Ahidjo continued to take precedence over the new president in matters of protocol. The old president also interfered with decision-making.[32] In August 1983 Biya announced that a conspiracy against his government had been uncovered. When two essential ministers from the north left the government in the course of a cabinet reshuffle, this was interpreted as a sign that northerners had been implicated. Two close collaborators of the old president were also arrested while their patron was absent from the country in France. Ahidjo protested from afar but had to relinquish the party chairmanship to Biya.[33]

A presidential election in January 1984 in which 97.73 per cent of the population was alleged to have voted, 99.98 per cent of whom were said to have supported Biya, bore all the marks of the old-style authoritarian politics. Biya could now claim that he had been elected by popular vote and could dissociate himself from Ahidjo. Ten days after the election he abolished the post of prime minister and thereafter could rule as president unhindered by rivals. The state of Cameroun was now renamed and the United Republic of Cameroun thus became the Republic of Cameroun.

The next move against Ahidjo came in February 1984 with the staging of a treason trial which sentenced the former president to death in his absence, a penalty commuted a few days later to a prison sentence.[34] In April the élite *garde républicaine* revolted and violent fighting raged through the streets of the capital before forces loyal to the government could bring the situation under control. Official estimates cited 70 casualties but others suggested that up to a thousand may have been killed.[35] The confusion opened the way for the settling of old scores and popular acts of revenge against the gendarmerie caused the loss of more lives. According to official statements 1,053 arrests

31 Mehler, *Kamerun in der Ära Biya*, pp.64–5.
32 Monga, *Cameroun. Quel Avenir?*, pp.28, 41–2,43.
33 *Le Monde*, 25 August 1983.
34 For well-known descriptions of the trial, see Monga, *Cameroun. Quel Avenir?* and A. Mbembe, 'Crimes et châtiments au Cameroun: la faillite du mythe de la stabilité', *Le Mois en Afrique* 20, 229–30 (1985), pp.155–66. For an official account of the events of 1983–84, see H. Bandolo, *La Flamme et la Fumée*, SOPECAM, Yaoundé, 1985.
35 Monga, *Cameroun. Quel Avenir?* dismisses the 6,000 estimate of the opposition in exile (UPC); see Woungly-Massaga, *Où va le Kamerun?*, L'Harmattan, Paris, 1984, for the UPC version.

were made, but by May 617 prisoners had allegedly been freed. The government also announced that 46 executions had taken place[36], though Amnesty
International estimated the figure at 120.[37] According to observers the trials
were 'irregular' and prisoners were held without due process of law until
amnesties were granted in 1990–91. Ninety per cent of those condemned were
from the north, or were alleged to be so, and the loyalty of an entire region
of the country was thus put in doubt in the popular memory of the events.
The attempted coup increased the importance of the army since Biya had
survived with the approval of his generals rather than through any well-
regulated political process designed to resolve conflict.[38] The whole succession crisis irritated Cameroun's relations with France, which had shown an
ambivalent attitude towards the attempted coup. As a result Cameroun turned
to Israel as a source of military training and support.

A party congress at Bamenda in 1985 showed that Biya's government was
now firmly established and its power-base secure. The proceedings did not
produce anything new and business as usual prevented the expected show-
down between progressive and conservative forces. The UNC/CNU was
renamed the *Rassemblement Démocratique du Peuple Camerounais/Cameroon
People's Democratic Movement* (RDPC/CPDM) which Biya forged as a united
party and his symbolical instrument of power. Minor attempts to heal the
wounds of the past by belatedly rehabilitating nationalist pioneers also
belonged to the symbolic arena.[39] In public discussion hope for far-reaching
reform still within the parameters of the one-party system was kept alive by
the publication of the president's book, *Pour le libéralisme communitaire (Communal Liberalism)*. Semi-competitive elections held in 1986–88 left their mark
nationally and locally. Competition for power within the single party led to
conflicts between the centre and the regions and to the controlled change of
élites from the old order to the new.[40] Biya maintained most of Ahidjo's
institutions, including the emergency ones of 1962 and 1967. Most of the
political élites survived but personalities were shuffled from one position to
another with even greater regularity and speed than under Ahidjo. Under
Biya 'tribalisation' increased, mafia-style management methods were adopted
without checks or balances, and the president's power of patronage aimed at
creating a broad coterie of supporters.[41] Loyal followers were rewarded with
salaried administrative posts created in 1983 through the restructuring of provinces and *départements*.[42] To sweeten business cooperation captains of industry

36 Monga, *Cameroun. Quel Avenir?*, pp.147–9.
37 M. W. DeLancey, *Cameroon: Dependence and Independence*, Westview Press, Boulder, CO,
1989, p.72; and more recent details in *Le Messager* (Douala), 3 April 1991.
38 Mehler, *Kamerun in der Ära Biya*, pp.132–54.
39 J.-F. Bayart, 'Les fondements sociaux de l'Etat au Cameroun (1982–1988)', in P. Geschiere
and P. Konings (eds), *Proceedings: Conference on the Political Economy of Cameroon – Historical
Perspectives*, African Studies Centre, Leiden, 1989, pp.811–31, esp. p.825.
40 Mehler, *Kamerun in der Ära Biya*, pp.173–229.
41 Médard, 'L'état sous-développé au Cameroun', pp.35–84.
42 On these 'predatory positions' see J.-F. Bayart, *L'Etat en Afrique. La Politique du Ventre*,
Fayard, Paris, 1989, pp.106–7.

were co-opted onto the party's central committee. Military and civilian posts previously held by those implicated in the attempted coup were reallocated to the new president's men. Some evaluations have suggested that out of about 1000 senior positions, 125 vacancies were filled.[43] The grand reshuffle included not only cabinet and central committee seats but also posts in the state security apparatus and ambassadorships.

No major ethnic group was left out in the cabinet appointments, and the important Beti-Bulu association, Biya's own ethnic group, won additional government seats and key military positions.[44] University graduates were hired into public service for the purpose of widening the base of those loyal to the president. Furthermore, Biya encouraged the development of a personality cult. He travelled throughout the country offering highly personalised rewards for loyalty to his regime. While such strategies achieved genuine political success, they resulted in harmful economic consequences.

ECONOMIC DEVELOPMENT FROM BOOM TO CRISIS

Cameroun always had the natural resources to achieve economic success but it could not overcome its structural deficiencies. With independence a unified economic region needed to be created and so the Nigerian currency used in West Cameroun was replaced in 1963 by the CFA franc.[45] The economic development of Cameroun can be divided into three phases. In the 1960s and 1970s a steady but unspectacular growth was achieved through the export of agricultural products, especially coffee, cocoa and cotton.[46] This was paralleled by a state-sponsored programme of industrialisation mapped out in five-year plans.[47] Petroleum exports began in 1978 and made up 45 per cent of state income by 1985. Steeply rising oil revenues enabled the government to expand the manufacturing of import substitutes through parastatal corporations.[48] From 1980 to 1986 the gross national product tripled and by 1985 mining and manufacturing accounted for about one-third of the gross domestic product; however, state enterprises turned out to be increasingly parasitic and any successes were equated to growth without development.

43 V. T. LeVine, 'Leadership and regime changes in perspective', in M. G. Schatzberg and I. W. Zartman (eds), *The Political Economy of Cameroon*, Praeger, New York, 1986, pp.20–52, esp. p.46.
44 See Mehler, *Kamerun in der Ära Biya*, pp.82,84.
45 The CFA franc is the common currency of the *Communauté Financière Africaine* (CFA). Before 1994 this was at the rate of 50 CFA to the French franc but in that year the value was halved to 100:1.
46 World Bank, *Trends in Developing Economics 1995*, Washington, DC, 1995, p.82, shows a yearly growth rate of 7 per cent from 1960 to 1985.
47 For a critique, see J.-C. Willame, 'Cameroun: les avatars d'un libéralisme planifié', *Politique Africaine* 18 (1985), pp.44–70.
48 Under Ahidjo about 160 parastatals had been established although without sufficiently defined goals. Under Biya another 40 were established. See P.-J. M. Tedga, *Entreprises Publiques, Etat et Crise au Cameroun*, L'Harmattan, Paris, 1990, p.200; N. van de Walle, 'The politics of public enterprise reform in Cameroon', in B. Grosh and R. S. Mukandala (eds), *State-Owned Enterprises in Africa*, Lynne Rienner, Boulder, CO, 1994, pp.151–74, esp. p.153. The *Société Nationale d'Investissement* established in 1963 was the most important instrument for funding public enterprises.

Several factors contributed to the crisis which ushered in the third phase of economic change in 1985. A decline in world cocoa and coffee prices was partly to blame, as was an adverse shift in exchange rates relative to the US dollar. Furthermore, oil prices weakened and Cameroun's petroleum reserves dwindled. Between 1985 and 1994 the value of oil revenues dropped by two-thirds to $531 million per annum.[49] The crisis was accentuated by domestic conditions as well as external factors. Poor political decision-making, corruption, embezzlement and the flight of capital all contributed to decline.[50] The crisis was enormous. The gross national product decreased by about 26 per cent between 1983 and 1991, and the national budget had to be pruned by almost a third in an austerity period between 1986 and 1992. Industrial production, which was mainly food processing, aluminium production, wood processing, and chemical production, decreased by about 11 per cent between 1986 and 1988. At the same time the external debt rose from $2.7 million to $6.6 million between 1984 and 1993, or 71.8 per cent of the gross national product.[51] The situation was aggravated by the growth of smuggling in the portion of the import–export sector dominated by local businessmen.[52] Within very few years the successes of the late 1970s were annihilated in the 1980s.

AGRICULTURE AND OIL

Even with a boom in oil production, agriculture remained the backbone of Cameroun's economy. In the 1990s two-thirds of the workforce, including a large majority of women, continued to work in the rural sector.[53] Women were largely engaged in producing for polygynous households and selling their surplus in local markets, while men farmed and marketed produce in the more lucrative export economy. This gender division of labour was already well established in the colonial period and continued into the late twentieth century.

Agriculture varied from region to region according to different climatic zones, with millet, maize and rice dominating in the north and cassava, yams and plantains in the south. Cattle-keeping was common in northern and western regions. The cultivation of grain and of export crops such as cotton, rubber, palm-oil and tea was largely taken over by state or by partly state-owned

49 See World Bank, *Trends*, p.82.
50 See N. van de Walle, 'The politics of non-reform in Cameroon', in Carter Center at Emory University (ed.), *African Governance in the 1990s. Objectives, Resources and Constraints. Working Papers from the Second Annual Seminar of the African Governance Program*, Carter Center, Atlanta, GA, 1990, pp.53–80; Philippe Hugon, 'Sortir de la récession et préparer l'après pétrole: le préalable politique', *Politique Africaine* 62 (1996), pp.35–44; and N. Jua, 'Cameroun: jump-starting an economic crisis', *Africa Insight* 21, 3 (1991), pp.162–70.
51 *EIU Country Profile*, for 1991–92, see pp.25,36, and for 1994–95, see p.37.
52 See J.-P. Warnier, *L'Esprit d'Entreprise au Cameroun*, Karthala, Paris, 1993; and P. Geschiere and P. Konings (eds), *Les Itinéraires de l'Accumulation au Cameroun/Pathways to Accumulation in Cameroon*, Karthala, Paris, 1993.
53 J. K. Henn, 'Food policy, food production and the family farm in Cameroon', in Geschiere and Konings (eds), *Proceedings*, pp.531–53.

corporations as laid out in the country's third development plan for 1971–76.[54] The big agro-industrial complexes were meant to symbolise progress and to serve as a model to smallholders, but they turned out to be unprofitable in the 1985 crisis.[55] On the other hand, small peasant farmers, who used traditional methods to grow food for local consumption and crops such as cocoa and coffee for export, survived the crisis.

In 1973 Ahidjo had declared a 'green revolution' which he said would lead to a higher rate of production. Farming was to benefit from biannual agricultural conventions and from its association with Cameroun's college of agriculture at Dschang. The primary focus of government strategy, however, was expanding exports. Production for national self-sufficiency in food, which was possible in the 1960s in view of the country's rich natural resource base, was now grossly neglected. A growing urban population developed new consumption habits which demanded imported food, especially rice, which was often smuggled into the country.[56] The 'green revolution' also had adverse ecological consequences since increased production for export meant that large new areas were brought under production. Although traditional subsistence practices of slash-and-burn agriculture did have some negative results such as deforestation and a medium-term deterioration of soil quality, the damage wrought by agro-industrial complexes, especially massive lumbering projects, was much worse. Furthermore, using marginal soils to cultivate export crops such as cotton and cocoa encouraged desertification in the north and soil degradation in the south in the 1970s. After the decline of petroleum revenues, the timber industry was further expanded, leading to overexploitation of the rainforests with concomitant major ecological problems. French, Lebanese and Italian concession-holders attacked the country's 22 million hectares of timber reserves, and by 1993 timber exports, which constituted 10.5 per cent of the national total, were second only to oil as an earner of foreign exchange. This was at a huge cost, however, since Cameroun was losing an estimated 175,000 hectares of timber per year.

Demographic growth and urbanisation also contributed to the country's ecological problems. Between 1960 and 1987 the national population had risen from 4 million to 10.5 million, of whom over a third lived in towns, particularly in the major seaport, Douala, with 810,000 inhabitants, and in Yaoundé, the capital, with 650,000.[57] The growth of towns at the expense of rural

54 F. Tchala Abina, 'De l'indépendance à la dépendance: étude de l'évolution des relations sociales de production dans le secteur agricole au Cameroun de 1967–1987', in Geschiere and Konings, (eds), *Proceedings*, esp. pp.253–4.
55 See, J. C. Willame, 'Cameroun: les avatars', and G. Courade, 'Des complexes qui coûtent chers: la priorité agro-industrielle dans l'agriculture camerounaise', *Politique Africaine* 14 (1984), pp.75–91. Also, P. Konings, *Labour Resistance in Cameroon. Managerial Strategies and Labour Resistance in the Agro-Industrial Plantations of the Cameroon Development Corporation*, African Studies Centre, Leiden, 1993.
56 N. van de Walle, 'Rice politics in Cameroon: state commitment, capability, and urban bias', *Journal of Modern African Studies*, 27, 4 (1989), pp.579–99, especially p.594.
57 *Recensement Général de la Population et de l'Habitat 1987*, excerpts published in *Cameroon Tribune*, 21 March 1991.

populations dated back to the colonial period when migration by the Bamiléké from the densely populated western province was especially marked. The arrival of new migrants contributed to a growing ethnic consciousness in urban areas.[58]

Cities held some attractions, initially at least, since they did offer better access to services such as clean water, electricity and medical clinics, than did villages. Social well-being declined, however, when the economic bubble burst in the mid-1980s. Cameroun dropped to number 127 in the world per capita income league. Despite this, life-expectancy rose from 39 to 53.7 years between 1960 and 1990 and infant mortality dropped to 9 per cent. During the postcolonial years hospitals and polio clinics were opened but the slogan of 'health for everyone by the year 2000' could not be realised. Under Biya state-of-the-art hospitals constructed in the two major cities remained closed to the general public, and in the economic crisis of the late 1980s per capita expenditure for health was reduced by 40 per cent, greatly affecting the rural population.

Another reason why towns attracted a growing number of people was that politicians gave preference to city interests. When a government marketing board was established in 1976 to buy rural produce, it offered such low prices, and syphoned off so much revenue into the pockets of urban administrators, that the motivation of farmers declined.[59] When the agency was dissolved in 1991 it owed 75 billion francs to farmers.[60] Even the export sector of farming was neglected and coffee estates were partially abandoned. Some farmers and some market women assumed that, with the economic recession, urban consumers would revert to eating home-grown foodstuffs, and they farsightedly reverted to growing domestic crops. Women continued to dominate the buying and selling of food at a local level, whereas wholesale trade was a predominantly male domain.[61] Despite the crisis, the economy remained export-oriented. In the 1990s the high-quality Cameroun banana became an increasingly important export crop, though the quality of cocoa and coffee did not meet world market standards and exports dropped.

A key feature of Cameroun's economic development was the rise and fall of oil as the major source of revenue. Oil prospecting began modestly with off-shore drilling in the Rio del Rey area, on the border with Nigeria. The French corporations, Elf and Total, were later joined by companies of other nationalities such as the American giants Exxon and Philipps, and by the Italian Petrofina. In 1985, when production reached a peak, 9.16 million tonnes

58 J.-L. Dongmo, *Le Dynamisme Bamiléké (Cameroun)* 2 vols, CEPER, Yaoundé, 1981.
59 P. Dessouane and P. Verre, 'Cameroun: du développement autocentré au national-libéralisme', *Politique Africaine* 22 (1986), pp.111–19.
60 Its replacement by private merchants did not prove to be much more favourable to producers, however. See Pierre Janin, 'Un planteur sans Etat peut-il encore être un planteur?', *Politique Africaine* 62 (1996), pp.45–56.
61 A. van den Berg, '"Playing with two houses". Businesswomen in Bamenda, Cameroon', in S. Ellis and Y. A. Fauré (eds), *Entreprises et Entrepreneurs Africains*, Karthala, Paris, 1995, pp.473–82.

were produced annually. After that production and state income from oil declined. The government stake in the industry was managed by the *Société Nationale d'Hydrocarbures*, a national company run by associates of the president. The group's financial transactions were politically determined and were kept outside the framework of the nation's publicised budget. Revenue could be used to mask losses in the parastatal enterprises and even to make good budget deficits until the 1986 economic collapse. The secrecy surrounding state oil revenues may have been partially justified by the desire to avoid a 'boom mentality' and speculative financial gambles, but if so it failed and rumours concerning the use of profits were leaked to the press. International investors, especially the International Monetary Fund (IMF), finally insisted on disclosure.[62]

Overall, the disadvantages of oil exploitation were as marked as any advantages: the treasury became increasingly dependent on the fast oil money; oil did not create many jobs; there were few linkages to the rest of the economy; and foreign companies were mainly interested in getting their profits out of the country as fast as possible. Ultimately, oil only delayed the painful business of rectifying the economy since foreign investors were content to maintain the *status quo* as long as the political environment favoured their economic interests.

BELATED AND PAINFUL STRUCTURAL ADJUSTMENT

Negotiation over structural adjustment came late to Cameroun and implementation was a painful process. The first World Bank loan for the purpose was negotiated in May 1989 but five years later only two of the three tranches of the loan had been advanced. Reforms had been demanded in banking, in administration, in parastatal enterprises, in agricultural commodity marketing, and in the budget. The IMF was unable to require the country to devalue since it did not have its own currency but was tied to the French franc through the CFA zone. Reform of the parastatals, of banking, and of prices given to producers for cocoa and coffee was implemented cautiously, though the process had been set in motion by 1992.[63]

Reform in personnel in the civil service proceeded slowly for political reasons and before the end of 1992 this delicate matter had not been resolutely addressed. Capital expenditure was cut in preference to current expenditure and overall this resulted in reduced efficiency in the public sector. This, in turn, further inhibited foreign investor confidence. To have reduced the civil service in the capital, Yaoundé, would have eroded President Biya's main

62 J. N. Ngu, 'The political economy of oil in Cameroon', in Geschiere and Konings (eds), *Proceedings*, pp.109–46. See also the optimistic view of N. J. Benjamin and S. Devarajan, 'Oil revenues and Cameroonian economy', in Schatzberg and Zartman (eds), *The Political Economy of Cameroon*, pp.161–88.
63 Van de Walle, 'The politics of public enterprise reform', p.161; A. Mehler, 'Politische Hindernisse der Strukturanpassung in Kamerun', in J. Betz (ed.), *Politische Restriktionen der Strukturanpassung in Entwicklungsländern*, Deutsches Übersee-Institut, Hamburg, 1995, pp.295–307.

political base and been regarded by those in power as politically foolhardy. In 1993, however, the situation compelled him to make cuts in public service salaries, starting with a 20 per cent cut in January, and then in November, recommending further cuts ranging from 6 to 50 per cent. In 1995, he also made a beginning in slimming down the state payroll of 180,000, although not by as much as donors had hoped.

France's decision to devalue the CFA franc by 50 per cent in January 1994 had a huge impact in Cameroun as it did in other francophone African countries. The middle class, accustomed to buying imported goods and already suffering from the pay-cuts introduced to meet IMF demands, now found that its purchasing power was cut in half. Inflation, which came to average 53 per cent per year in the mid-1990s, hit Cameroun's population. Prices for some basic foods such as rice, wheat, palm-oil, tomatoes, beverages and salt shot up by as much as 70 per cent. Peasants benefited somewhat from devaluation since it made prices for agricultural produce more competitive on world markets, but this gain was offset by a rise in the price of imported fertilisers and by an inability to replace obsolete equipment. By 1994 Cameroun was considered to be experiencing a greater problem in coping with devaluation than any other state in francophone Central Africa. A year later the picture seemed brighter though many individuals still suffered severely.[64]

International financial institutions responded to the change by negotiating new letters of intent, and new loans, but still Cameroun was unable to respond sufficiently radically to satisfy them and the agreements lapsed. The combined impact of structural adjustment and devaluation, together with the economic strategies used by the president to preserve his political base, proved too much for the national economy. Individuals therefore turned to their own strategies for economic and social survival. Those who distrusted banks moved to join informal credit and saving associations called *tontines*.[65] In the 1990s three out of four urban workers were employed in the informal sector, and small businesses found themselves in competition with an army of street-vendors whose activities barely assured their own survival.[66]

THE SOCIAL DIMENSION OF THE GATHERING CRISIS

As the economy began to decline after 1985, the gap between rich and poor and between rural and urban populations widened. Many people could not meet their most basic material needs and aspirations. Although social distinctions existed and were legitimate in precolonial and colonial societies[67], those

64 G. Courade and V. Alary, 'Les planteurs camerounais ont-ils été réévalués?', *Politique Africaine* 9 (1995), pp.74–87.
65 See A. Henry, G.-H. Tchente, P. Guillerme-Dieumegard, *Tontines et Banques au Cameroun. Les Principes de la Société des Amis*, Karthala, Paris, 1991.
66 General Agreement on Tariffs and Trade (GATT), *Trade Policy Review. Cameroon 1995*, Geneva, 1995.
67 For precolonial societies, see the special issue of *Paideuma. Mitteilungen zur Kulturkunde* 16 (1995), entitled 'Slavery and slave-dealing in Cameroon in the nineteenth and early twentieth century', edited by B. Chem-Langhëe.

that emerged after independence were greatly accentuated due to differential incomes and to the ability of the ruling élite to cream off a disproportionate share of the country's wealth. A thin layer of civil servants and small businessmen separated this small upper class from the rural and urban masses.[68] The incomes of rural primary producers varied greatly but on average their income was less than a quarter of the national average wage.[69] Furthermore, city dwellers not only had better wages than those who lived in the countryside, they also had greater access to social services such as medical care and education.[70] Poverty was also unequally distributed between the provinces (see Map 3.2).

In some parts of the country the integration of town and country was facilitated by the development of infrastructure. In these areas roads and railways allowed urban wage-earners to visit their home villages regularly, and rural populations to travel to visit relatives in the cities. Although overall infrastructure was neglected by Ahidjo's government, important roads were built from Douala to Tiko in 1969, and west–east communications were helped by a road from Kumba to Loum. On the other hand, several road construction projects were neglected by Ahidjo since they ran through territories of the former UPC rebels, and the extension of two important routes from Yaoundé to Douala and from Yaoundé to Bafoussam was not completed until Biya came to power. In the 1960s the railways were also extended from Mbanga to Kumba, and in 1974 the trans-Cameroun railway joined the capital at Yaoundé to Ngaoundéré in the northern region.[71] In the mid-1980s only 2,500 out of 62,000 kilometres of the country's roads were paved[72], and more emphasis was given to extravagant prestige projects such as the building of expensive airports in presidential home regions.

The new class of successful Camerounians were often the descendents of colonial employees who had risen above the level of ordinary peasant farmers. The father of President Biya was a catechist for example. Only the ruling class had the means and contacts to send their children overseas to study. Others, immediately below them in social ranking, were able to send their children to the country's best schools. Affiliation with Christian communities was also an advantage in access to education.[73] The balance sheet on education in

---

68 N. Rubin, *Cameroun: An African Federation*, Pall Mall Press, London, 1971, p.176; and M. Prouzet, *Le Cameroun*, Librairie Générale de Droit et de Jurisprudence, Paris, 1974, p.81; N. Jua, 'The petty bourgeoisie and the politics of social justice in Cameroon', in Geschiere and Konings (eds), *Proceedings*, p.742.
69 World Bank, *Cameroon Agricultural Sector Report*, Report 7486–CAM (1, Main Report), Washington, DC, 1989, p.19; also, World Bank, *Cameroon, Diversity, Growth, and Poverty Reduction*, Report 13167–CM, Washington, DC, 1996.
70 In 1987, only 23.4 per cent of the economically active urban population over 11 years old were illiterate compared to 64 per cent in the countryside.
71 In 1995 a total of 1173 kilometres of railways existed. For major colonial road and railway construction, see Austen and Headrick, 'Equatorial Africa under colonial rule', in Birmingham and Martin (eds), *History of Central Africa*, Vol.2, especially pp.54–5.
72 DeLancey, *Cameroon, Dependence and Independence*, p.138.
73 This was visible in the building of a Catholic university near Yaoundé in 1991.

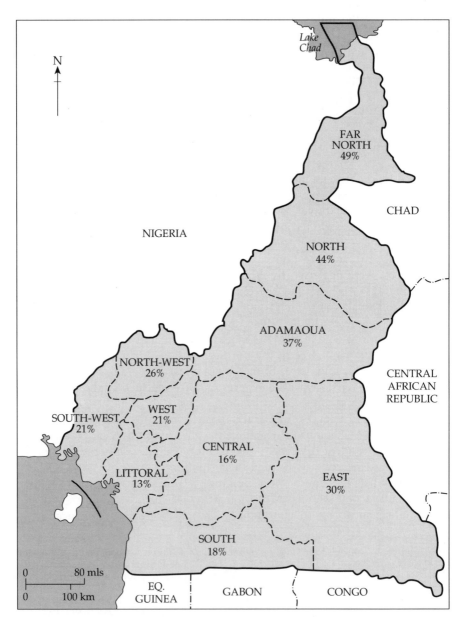

Map 3.2   Cameroun poverty index. Percentages of households in poverty based on housing, illiteracy and malnutrition. Based on the data of the 1987 census and a demography and health survey of 1991

Source: World Bank, *Cameroun. Diversity, Growth and Poverty Reduction* (Report 13167-CM), World Bank, Washington, D.C., 1995.

Cameroun was ambiguous, with the greatest successes being achieved in the 1980s. In 1987 the literacy rate stood at a remarkable 60 per cent, but after 1989 school attendance steadily declined due to lack of revenue and a cut in grants of 50 per cent.[74] Educational budgets were so severely cut in the 1990s that the Ministry of Education was replaced by the Ministry of Defence as the department with the highest allocation from the national budget. Although literacy reached more than half the population, education tended to reproduce, or even enhance, social differentiation.

At the apex of the social system were those, perhaps some one thousand individuals, with direct or indirect access to state resources. Within this group was a smaller inner circle of about two hundred people from which members of the cabinet were generally chosen.[75] This élite was quite self-contained, sharing consumer habits, status symbols, and meeting places such as the Rotary Club or the party central committee.[76] The élite also looked after its own, finding directorships for fallen politicians and vetting the new generations of university graduates who aspired to join the exclusive ranks of the establishment.[77] The University of Yaoundé grew rapidly from 213 students graduating in 1961, to 10,000 in 1982, and 41,000 in 1992[78], though those who graduated found entry to the labour market ever more competitive. When frustrated in their ambition by the closed nature of the upper reaches of society, it was these graduates, together with their teachers and professors, who started to agitate for a process of democratisation. In the 1993–94 academic year there were several strikes and classes met on only 80 out of 250 teaching days. Further grievances were caused by an increase in fees, a reduction in the salaries of university professors, and a withdrawal of job guarantees for graduates. The branches of Yaoundé University in Buéa, Dschang, Ngaoundéré and Douala, meanwhile received enhanced status for reasons of prestige and were declared fully-fledged universities. Yaoundé University itself was divided into two divisions. The government's guarantee of a job for every school leaver graduating from an élite school modelled on French examples (the Ecole Normale Supérieure for instance) was no longer viable.

While students and teachers, like lawyers and journalists, tried to evade state violence and create a civil society, the élite continued to flaunt their ostentatious consumption of luxuries such as champagne, expensive villas and Mercedes cars. One writer noted ironically:

They have built little prisons for themselves in an attempt to imitate fences in Europe! Some of my folks here in Briqueterie might wonder . . . , what

74 UNDP, *Le Développement Humain au Cameroun*, October 1991, pp.34,36,56.
75 P. F. Ngayap, *Cameroun: Qui Gouverne? De Ahidjo à Biya. L'Héritage et l'Enjeu*, L'Harmattan, Paris, 1983, pp.13–14; also, V. T. LeVine, 'Leadership and regime changes', and N. Jua, 'The petty bourgeoisie'.
76 Bayart, *L'Etat au Cameroun*, p.19.
77 Jua, 'The petty bourgeoisie', pp.739–41.
78 E. Mveng, *Histoire du Cameroun* 2 vols, CEPER, Yaoundé, 1985, p.280; and *Cameroon Tribune*, 21 January 1993.

residents of Bastos have done wrong against their people and the rest of the world, that they have chosen to live behind barbed wire, protected by pieces of broken beer and champagne bottles?[79]

But while the wealthy might try to barricade themselves into suburbs for protection against the urban poor, they could not escape the 'sorcery' that sprang from envy and jealousy. Belief in an ideal of equality was incompatible with individual economic success. Occult forces were used as an instrument of accumulation and domination as well as a means of mobilising resistance. In postcolonial Cameroun the old internal contradictions and tensions of egalitarian segmentary societies were alive and well.[80] During the succession crisis, many Camerounians believed that Biya and Ahidjo would mobilise the occult to wage their struggle. When the economy declined accusations of witchcraft increased.[81] New sects proliferated and it was alleged that Biya and many in his inner circle had joined the Rosicrucians. At the same time a number of Catholic intellectuals and clergymen with connections to the government were mysteriously murdered, occurrences which soured relations between the government and the Vatican.[82]

LIBERALISATION: A WEAK REGIME VERSUS A WEAK OPPOSITION

In 1990 pressure from below persuaded the regime that more serious concessions than the half-hearted measures of the mid-1980s must be made. The process began after a former president of the Law Society, Yondo Black, and nine of his associates were accused of planning to set up a new political party. They were charged in a secret trial from which journalists were barred but from which details nonetheless leaked out in the press.[83]

Soon afterwards the move towards a multi-party system was given another impetus by the announcement that a Social Democratic Front (SDF) was about to be established. The new party was launched amidst festivities in the English-speaking stronghold of Bamenda in May 1990 with a speech by John Fru Ndi who claimed to be a simple bookseller. After two decades of repression, the whole nation could share his dream of freedom when he said: 'You must yell because even if you are ignored, your children and your children's children will not be ignored tomorrow . . . You have nothing to lose but the

79 F. Beng Nyamnjoh, *Mind Searching*, Kucena Damian, Awka, 1991, p.73. Bastos is the richest residential area in Yaoundé, and Briqueterie is the neighbouring poor area.
80 See P. Geschiere's subtle depiction in *Sorcellerie et Politique en Afrique. La Viande des Autres*, Karthala, Paris, 1995. The amount of accumulation that is permitted within a society varies from region to region. Individual economic success was generally more socially acceptable in the more hierarchical societies of the western grasslands than in the segmentary societies of the woodlands, which were traditionally suspicious of the accumulation of wealth.
81 E. Ardener, 'Witchcraft, economics and continuity of belief', in Mary Douglas (ed.), *Witchcraft Accusations and Confessions*, Tavistock, London, 1970, pp.141–60; reprinted in E. Ardener, *Kingdom on Mount Cameroon*, Berghahn, Oxford, 1996.
82 Pope John Paul II, nevertheless, paid two visits to Cameroun in 1985 and 1995.
83 A. Mehler, *Presse und politischer Aufbruch in Kamerun. Kommentierte Presseschau für das Jahr 1990*, Institut für Afrika-Kunde, Hamburg, 1991, pp.44–60.

straight-jacket in which you as a free-born citizen have been cast'.[84] The celebrations were broken up by security forces who shot dead six of the demonstrators, although the government claimed that they had been trampled to death. Thus the first martyrs of the multi-party cause had been created. Voices demanding a pluralistic political system could no longer be silenced. Among the supporters of the campaign was the head of the Catholic hierarchy, Cardinal Tumi. At Whitsun his bishops read out in public a pastoral letter which laid some of the responsibility for the country's economic and moral crisis at the door of the government.[85] Biya resisted a few weeks longer before conceding extensive political reforms at a CPDM party convention in June 1990. Censorship of the press was relaxed, travel restrictions eased, and a committee on human rights appointed.

Pressure for reform came not only from local opposition but also from France, where President Mitterrand had indicated in a speech to African leaders at La Baule that in future the allocation of aid would be related to progress in the process of democratisation. Cameroun's reform laws, however, left much to be desired.[86] Although a return to pluralism was decreed, new parties needed authorisation from the Ministry for Territorial Administration before they could function. In January 1991 the first parties were registered and several of them became important protagonists on the political stage. In addition to the CPDM ruling party and the radical SDF opposition party, there was also a socially conservative party, the *Union Nationale pour la Démocratie et le Progrès* (UNDP), a moderate *Union Démocratique du Cameroun* (UDC), various wings of the old opposition UPC, and the *Mouvement pour la Défense de la République* (MDR), which became a coalition partner of the CPDM. Each party had its own ethnic and regional strength but each party also had its own crises and divisions.[87] During this period of reform serious ethnic conflict broke out within the élite. It was caused by the distortions of ethnic proportional representation and by the 'tribalisation' of leadership positions under Biya. Old rivalries between cattle-keepers and arable farmers in well-populated regions with land shortages were now blamed on ethnic tensions, as for example, between the Fulani and the Gbaya in Adamawa province.[88] Long-standing and fierce conflicts between the Kotoko people of the far north and the Choa Arabs erupted over ancient grazing lands. Clashes led a thousand people to flee into Chad and several hundred more escaped to Nigeria

84 Speech delivered by the SDF chairman on 26 May 1990 at Bamenda on the occasion of the launch of the SDF.
85 *Lettre Pastorale de la Conférence Episcopale du Cameroun sur la Crise Economique dont Souffre le Pays*, undated (3 March 1990).
86 For a more positive assessment, see M. Kamto, 'Quelques réflexions sur la transition vers le pluralisme politique au Cameroun', in G. Conac (ed.), *L'Afrique en Transition vers le Pluralisme Politique*, Economica, Paris, 1993, pp.209–36; also on the disappointing press law, see C. Manga Fombad, 'Freedom of expression in the Cameroonian democratic transition', *Journal of Modern African Studies* 33, 2 (1995), pp.211–26.
87 See Mehler, *Kamerun in der Ära Biya*, pp.262–84.
88 Philip Burnham, *The Politics of Cultural Difference in Northern Cameroon*, Edinburgh University Press, Edinburgh, 1996.

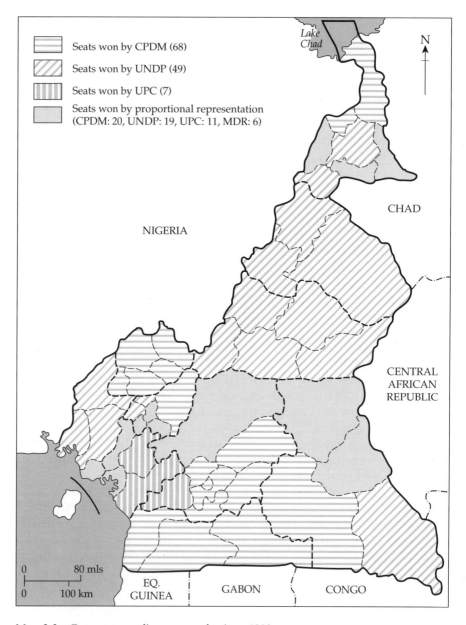

Map 3.3   Cameroun parliamentary election, 1992
Sources: Andreas Mehler, *Kamerun in der Ära Biya. Bedingungen, erste Schritte und Blockaden einer demokratischen Transition*, Institut für Afrika-Kunde, Hamburg, p.401 and Commission nationale de recensement générale des votes, 'Procès-verbal du recensement générale des votes et de la proclamation des résultats des élections législatives du premier mars 1992', in *Cameroon Tribune*, 12 March 1992.

in April 1994. Rival party affiliations and the involvement of mercenaries from Chad and troops from Cameroun caused the conflict to expand. Even more attention was devoted by the media to the long-running rivalry between the Béti and the Bamiléké.

Political conflict in the capital was brought to a head by a celebrated court case. The writer Célestin Monga and the editor of the weekly *Le Messager*, Pius Njawe, who had published an open letter to Biya, were charged with insulting the president, the parliament, and the law courts. Crowds assembled in front of the tribunal in which the case was heard and the accused were fined, given suspended prison sentences of six months, and put on probation. The demonstrations were the start of a protest movement that spread strikes throughout most of the country in April 1991. The objective, known as *opération villes mortes* ('operation dead cities'), was to bring the cities to a standstill. In the ensuing repression the security forces killed two or three hundred demonstrators and placed seven of the country's ten provinces under military control. Only through the loyalty of the security forces did Biya's regime survive the immediate crisis. In October the president ordered his prime minister to organise a meeting with the opposition leaders, most of whom signed an agreement to end the operation.

Following this settlement Biya decreed new parliamentary elections for March 1992 which combined proportional representation with majority rule in such a way as to favour the larger parties. Despite the manipulation of the vote, and a boycott by several important parties such as the SDF, the results turned out surprisingly badly for the ruling party. With the exception of the north-west where the CPDM won owing to the SDF boycott, the regional distribution of votes showed declining support for the regime in most parts of the country (see Map 3.3). For the formation of a new government, Biya had to rely on a coalition partnership with the smallest of four parties represented in the new parliament.

These parliamentary elections were followed in October 1992 by presidential elections on the basis of a relative majority and a single ballot. Had the opposition been able to collaborate it might have been able to bring about change, but the parties fielded five rival candidates, each suffering from extreme egotism and unable to agree on a tactical alliance. Despite the fragmentation of the opposition vote, the ruling party again felt compelled to intervene in order to fraudulently influence the ballot.[89] Even then Biya only defeated John Fru Ndi with 39.98 per cent of the vote against his opponent's 35.97 per cent, at least according to the official results. Fru Ndi won votes well beyond his regional political base[90] and claimed that he was the 'legitimate

---

89 See the final report by the election observers of the National Democratic Institute for International Affairs, *An Assessment of the October 11, 1992 Election in Cameroon*, NDI, Washington, DC, 1993; and Collectif 'Changer le Cameroun', *Le 11 Octobre. Autopsie d'une Election Présidentielle Controversée*, Yaoundé, nd.
90 M. Krieger, 'Cameroon's democratic crossroads, 1990–4', *Journal of Modern African Studies* 32, 4 (1994), pp.605–28, especially p.615.

president'. Following the announcement of the controversial results, riots erupted in the anglophone provinces but no radical challenge could be attempted against the armed capability of the government. In the following two years the opposition was halted by intense arguments, its following disintegrated, its inexperienced supporters were frustrated, and the democracy movement lost momentum.

Foreign criticism of the Cameroun elections was most strongly expressed by the United States. France, on the other hand, after a few words of admonition, remained the regime's most stalwart supporter throughout the crisis. Although Cameroun had absented itself from French–African summits and also, as a bilingual country, from the francophone summits, the 'French factor' remained a strong element throughout Cameroun's modern history. In the late 1980s Biya changed his policy, sent his foreign minister as an observer to the 1989 francophone summit in Dakar, and from 1991 attended summit meetings himself. At the same time he tried to gain admission to the Commonwealth of former British colonies, and Cameroun was given observer status at the meeting held in Cyprus in 1993 and full membership at the New Zealand meeting in 1995, against the wishes of the anglophone separatists and federalists.

Latent discontent on the part of the anglophone minority had surfaced in the 1990s over the question of a return to federalism. The Cameroon Anglophone Movement (CAM) demanded a return to federalism and threatened secession if no action was taken. CAM and the Anglophone Standing Committee called an All-Anglophone Conference with about 5,000 delegates from the north-west and south-west provinces in April 1993 to express their grievances. The final communiqué, in which they presented a slightly exaggerated interpretation of the exploitation suffered in the anglophone regions, demanded a return to federalism.[91] The growing campaign for change enlisted some old political veterans such as Muna and Foncha who attended the first meetings of the Southern Cameroons National Council (SCNC) in December 1994. Demands for autonomy were now clarified and plans made for secession in case matters turned out unfavourably. In July 1995 a SCNC delegation travelled to the United Nations headquarters to claim that the 1972 cancellation of the federal agreement by means of constitutional manipulation had been an illegal action on the part of the Yaoundé government. Since 1991 attempts to introduce a new constitution that would meet the demand for party pluralism had been discussed, mostly by committee meetings behind closed doors. The withdrawal of the anglophone representatives in May 1993 ended this effort to arrive at consensus. President Biya then directed parliament to debate the reform proposals and some changes were agreed. A senate and a constitutional council were novel institutions.[92]

91 See the French copy of the documents in English, 'Déclaration de Buea', *Politique Africaine* 51 (1993), pp.140–51; and P. Konings, 'Le "problème anglophone" au Cameroun dans les années 1990', *Politique Africaine* 62 (1996), pp.25–34.
92 *Le Messager*, 19 December 1994, and *Cameroon Tribune*, 30 November 1995.

With a changing global climate which favoured freedom and democracy, the secret police, although still omnipresent in 1989–90, were no longer able to impose repression with their previous efficiency. Private and foreign newspapers were able to report the persecution of those who supported democracy. Although they still practised violence, and curtailed freedom of speech, the security police could no longer generate fear once their corruption and nepotism had come to light. On the other hand trials for defamation still secured convictions and newspapers still had to be careful lest whole editions be confiscated and their financial security jeopardised.[93]

HOPE FROM BELOW

One of the paradoxes of Ahidjo's attempt to prevent political discussion was the politicising of nonpolitical areas of public life such as sport. The monolithic politics of 'national unity' left a small space in which subcultures with ethnic and local connections could flourish. In the cities whole neighbourhoods remained ethnically homogeneous and their organisations revealed close ties with rural regions of origin. This was where expressions of self-realisation, unconfined by the dominant public sphere, came to be found. In these enclaves of self-awareness the emerging political parties of the 1990s were able to mobilise ethnic and family support. The development of a wider, more self-confident, civil society was slow, however, and was beset by reversals. Thus a weak state, undermined by inefficiency and illegitimacy, was faced by an equally weak society when the radical changes of the 1990s began to stir. And yet marginal segments of society had been politicised. Demonstrators who marched in the streets in 1991–92, calling for a national conference on the model of the one held in Benin, were demanding democratic reforms rather than merely protesting against mass redundancies and arrears in wages.

Cameroun's history abounds in intrigue, violence and oppression. For this reason fundamental distrust sets politicians against each other and divides society from government. The economic crisis further minimised opportunities for Camerounians and yet the government did not try to find a solution, even for the élite. By the mid-1990s coercive government practices had left the community torn into powerless segments. The state, now shorn of its western attributes, was in danger of losing its relevance. Or perhaps it was merely losing its pretentious façade and revealing its quintessential reality. It still continued to exist, however, and it still had an impact on its citizens. The influence of continuities, such as an extraordinary amount of transborder commercial activity, and community-oriented attempts to achieve accountability of local political leaders, may also become clearer in the long term. The disillusionment felt throughout Cameroun in the mid-1990s may have a positive outcome and generate political realism.

93 For new legislation, see *Cameroon Tribune*, 5 January 1996.

Map 4.1 Congo, Gabon and the Central African Republic

CHAPTER 4

Comparisons and contrasts in equatorial Africa: Gabon, Congo and the Central African Republic

ELIKIA M'BOKOLO

When colonialism ended in French Equatorial Africa some key features of the past, including structures, symbols and historic memory faded while others influenced the new era quite deeply.[1] As relations between the four members of the former colonial federation evolved, Chad became more detached and distinctive, while a loose Libreville–Brazzaville–Bangui axis emerged which distinguished the three countries of the Central African Republic, Congo, and Gabon, from their larger neighbours in Cameroun and Zaire. All three were small states, at least in terms of population. The Central African Republic, which in the colonial period had once been the demographic reservoir of French Equatorial Africa, had only 3.3 million people while Congo had 2.5 million and Gabon 1.3 million.[2] If demographic weakness was shared by the three states, more positive similarities derived from common colonial and precolonial experiences which were reclaimed, and celebrated, in public events sponsored by governments, by local authorities and by cultural associations.

A narrative history of recent political events would highlight the growing territorial and national distinctiveness of the three states, but an alternative thematic approach to the history of the region throws up numerous linkages. Without minimising or denying the specific importance of local political developments within individual nations, a transnational and problem-oriented approach provides a broader framework and brings out more clearly important cross-cutting experiences. Such a thematic history revolves around three sets of questions.

1 For the colonial history of French Equatorial Africa (Chad, Gabon, Ubangi-Shari and Moyen-Congo), see the chapter by Ralph Austen and Rita Headrick, 'Equatorial Africa under colonial rule' in David Bimingham and Phyllis M. Martin (eds), *History of Central Africa*, Vol.2, Longman, Harlow, 1983. After independence, Chad and Gabon retained the same names, Ubangi-Shari became the Central African Republic, and Moyen-Congo became Congo.
2 These figures are simple estimates. The usable censuses are old and date from 1981 (Gabon), 1984 (Congo) and 1988 (Central African Republic).

In the first place, it is important to define the nature of the environment, be it ideological, economic, social or political. Particularly striking is the weakness of the structures that emerged from the colonial past and which still constrain political, economic, strategic and intellectual development. Secondly, significant events in the history of the three states turn out to be similar because they derived in a broad sense from shared experiences. Finally, an approach that favours political events is not sufficient and must make way for social history which can reflect the depth and strength of local continuities and changes, and take account of external forces.

A FRAGILE ENVIRONMENT IN THREE EQUATORIAL REPUBLICS

Colonisation of the region took place at different times, relatively early for Gabon and very late for the Central African Republic. The French created Congo in 1886 and then unified the federation in 1910 with common institutions, legislation, judicial practices, transport policies, financial planning and schooling systems. After independence the three states were unable, or reluctant, to maintain the close ties that had been forged under colonialism yet, paradoxically, were active in seeking out other linkages. While remarkably blind to the advantages of drawing closer together, leaders were open to ambitious projects that involved wider types of alliance.

The impulse to wider integration was initiated by Barthélémy Boganda of Ubangi-Shari at the moment of independence.[3] The emancipated social status achieved by this leader inspired other members of the generation born in the first two decades of the twentieth century. They willingly, or unwillingly, became the cultural and social intermediaries that enabled the colonial regime to take root in equatorial Africa. They were constantly torn between their loyalty to France and their equally passionate sense of an African identity. In 1958 Boganda recalled that his only ideal as a student was to become French and Latin, in order that he might serve Ubangi well. As a pupil of the missionaries, and as a seminary student in Brazzaville, in Yaoundé and at Kisantu in the Belgian Congo, he was able to experience colonial cultures of Central Africa distinct from those of Ubangi-Shari. From 1946 Boganda was regularly elected to the French parliament and probably gained an awareness of pan-Africanist ideals from his fellow members. His own distinctive vision focused on Central Africa rather than the whole continent and gave especial attention to 'Latin Africa', a term he used for the Belgian, Portuguese and French spheres. From this grew his project for a 'United States of Latin Africa', which he envisaged in several phases: joining Ubangi-Shari with Chad initially; then joining this nucleus to the two Congos of Brazzaville and Léopoldville; and in a third step spreading from Cameroun and Gabon to

3 P.Kalck, 'Barthélémy Boganda (1910–1959). Tribun et visionnaire de l'Afrique centrale', in C.-A. Julien, M. Morsy, C. Coquery-Vidrovitch and Y. Person (eds), *Les Africains*, Jeune Afrique, Paris, 1977, III, pp.103–37; P. Kalck, *Barthélémy Boganda, 1910–1959*, Ed. Sépia, St Maure-des-Fosses, 1995.

Angola, Rwanda and Burundi. Considered at the time a more credible scheme than the grand pan-African visions of Kwame Nkrumah or Cheikh Anta Diop, the project remained a utopian ideal for Central African intellectuals, for political élites, and for leaders throughout the region. Not only did the scheme never see the light of day, but French Equatorial Africa itself broke into separate territories. Political reality was brutal, with a slow and pervasive nationalism taking hold of the colonially-inspired states regardless of the aspirations of political actors.

Among the individual states, the example of Gabon was perhaps most significant.[4] Proudly dwelling on the fact that their ancestors had been the first French subjects in Central Africa, the Gabon élite frequently expressed their resentment that the capital of French Equatorial Africa had been transferred from Libreville to Brazzaville. These frustrations were later accentuated by economic and political developments. As a producer of *okoumé* wood Gabon was reputed to be the richest of the three colonies and it resented the alienation of its wealth as the milch cow of the otherwise impoverished federation. A land frontier between Gabon and Congo was fixed by the French by 1946 but soon afterwards both uranium and manganese were found in the upper Ogowe basin and the border became a source of discord. A railway to the region was built in 1959–62 to take manganese out through the Congo seaport at Pointe-Noire, but in 1987 Gabon completed its own national railway to enable minerals to be shipped through its port at Libreville. While the new railway aided national integration and enabled Gabon to control the exploitation of its own mineral resources, it simultaneously weakened the planned economic integration with Congo.

The tendency to fragmentation in equatorial Africa was heightened by social tensions as much as by economic ones. The phenomenon of states deciding to expel whole categories of 'aliens' from their territory had wide repercussions that have not yet been adequately analysed. Rich Gabon was particularly prone to expelling non-nationals and to warn against the influx of invading foreigners. Waves of 'nationalist' fever were engineered and these produced new concepts of identity which contrasted with the identities given to groups who were targeted for exclusion. One striking example of cross-frontier ethnic politics concerned the Teke who straddled Congo and Gabon as well as Zaire. The Teke had long-established traditions, real and imagined, of common origins and communal solidarity, and in the colonial period, labour migration from Gabon to Congo and from French Congo to Belgian Congo reinforced these sentiments. It is remarkable how in Teke identity today, there exist 'traditions' which distinguish quite specifically the 'Gabon Teke' from the 'Congo Teke'.[5] These distinctive 'traditions' are visible on both sides of the frontier. On the Gabon side, it is probable that possession of a Teke identity has achieved new prestige during the lengthy presidency of

4 The pioneer work of Roland Pourtier on Gabon has unfortunately no equivalent for other countries. See R. Pourtier, *Le Gabon* 2 vols, L'Harmattan, Paris, 1989.
5 E. M'Bokolo, *L'Epopée Teke au Gabon: Disque et Livret*, GRECHO, Libreville, 1989.

Omar Bongo, who has emphasised his identity as a 'Gabon Teke'. On the Congo side, successive regimes have tried to find legitimacy, at least in symbolic terms, through association with the old Teke ruler, the Makoko. In December 1994, at the National Peace Conference, the Makoko of the Teke and the Maloango ruler of the Vili were presented as the fraternal guarantors of efforts by modern politicians to bring harmony to Congo public life. The symbolism was also designed, however, to appropriate for Congo the power of the Makoko monarchy to which Zaire and Gabon also laid claim, though without the same historic legitimacy.

Territorial fragmentation and ethnic exclusiveness stood in contrast to an opposing set of political trends that created new solidarities, revived old ethnic associations, and founded common political interest groups. The most striking new convergence was the one that brought the former Spanish colony of Equatorial Guinea into such close association with Gabon that it joined the CFA franc zone. The rapprochement may have been facilitated by cultural and kinship ties between Fang peoples on either side of the border. Further north, rivalry between Muslims and non-Muslims was the factor that brought cross-frontier migrations between the Central African Republic and its neighbours, Chad and Sudan. Military insecurity on both borders, and the flow of refugees from war zones, caused politicians to try to maintain good relations with the north.[6] Perhaps the most striking factor promoting integration throughout the region was the legacy of the equatorial African franc which also provided continuing links with France. This fiscal collaboration was matched by a Customs Union and an Economic Community.

In the field of culture, the president of Gabon took the initiative in creating an international study centre on Bantu civilisation (CICIBA). Article four of the charter claimed that the centre would 'protect, promote and preserve the authentic values of Bantu civilisations and the common cultural heritage of the Bantu-speaking peoples north and south of the equator as well as in the lands of the Bantu diaspora'. The striking feature of the project was an attempt to take an academic concept relating to the unity of the Bantu languages and turn it into a social and cultural identity that could be used for political ends. The policy was designed to reach out beyond the internal politics of Gabon and create linkages with other African states. Although the project fell below expectations after its foundation in 1983, it nevertheless received some support from ten states: Gabon, Central African Republic, Congo, Equatorial Guinea, São Tomé and Príncipe, Angola, Zaire, Rwanda, Zambia and the Comoros. Libreville thus became the centre of a network of identities and memories of which the consequences cannot yet be measured.

Another example of the tendency to form larger units of integration was the promotion of certain regional languages of which Lingala was a good example. Initially the lingua franca of diverse populations linked along the great Congo river trading network, the development and expansion of Lin-

6 See chapter by Buijtenhuijs on Chad in this book.

gala continued during and after colonisation. First used in Congo and Zaire, it later spread to Gabon and the Central African Republic. Its popularity was enhanced in local culture when Lingala songs performed by Kinshasa and Brazzaville entertainers were broadcast over the radio or disseminated through tapes to distant corners of equatorial Africa. The language was also carried far afield by migrant workers who returned to their villages having learnt Lingala in the towns of Congo and Zaire. Artisans and petty officials who moved between town and countryside also spread the use of the language.

PERSISTENT ECONOMIC FRAGILITY

The raw statistical data relating to the economies of Central Africa can be both heartening and discouraging, illuminating as well as misleading. In the late 1980s Gabon's national product appeared to make it rich with an average income of $(US)2,689, while the Central African Republic was poor with $275 and Congo lay in between with $1,126.[7] Ten years later, despite some improvement in the position of the Central African Republic, the respective ranking of the three countries had not changed: $4,050 per head in Gabon; $2,430 for Congo; and $1,060 for the Central African Republic.[8] In all three countries attempts at diversification failed and the exploitation of primary materials remained the norm.

In the Central African Republic economic continuity from the colonial period was most marked. The political insecurities of the 1960s led to the withdrawal of some of the great colonial agricultural companies and their replacement by small-scale African farmers. Politicians encouraged the exodus of foreign companies in 1969 by banning the foreign working of diamond fields and regulated diamond production fell to 334,000 carats by 1989–90, a mere 4 per cent of the national income. In the south the production of coffee passed from the great companies to individual farmers so that by the 1970s, 75 per cent of production was in the hands of small planters and marketing was taken over by a parastatal organisation. In the north cotton continued to be grown but, like coffee, it was vulnerable to fluctuations in world prices and was locally subject to damaging droughts. Between them the two great crops provided peasants with only 20 per cent of their overall revenue. The country's land-locked position limited the scope for other forms of extraction such as timber.

In comparison to the Central African Republic, Congo underwent an economic revolution which turned it from farming and forestry to mineral extraction. Until 1973 timber remained the principal export of Congo, which also continued to derive substantial revenues from transport and service, as it had done in the colonial period.[9] As tree felling had followed the path of the

7 Data from 1986.
8 Data for 1993.
9 For the colonial economy of French Equatorial Africa, see chapter by Austen and Headrick, 'Equatorial Africa under colonial rule' in David Birmingham and Phyllis M. Martin (eds), *History of Central Africa*, Vol.2.

railway, and the major colonial arteries, timber was largely exhausted in the south of the country by the time of independence and the stands that did survive were preserved by national politicians for local African entrepreneurs to exploit in conjunction with a state marketing monopoly. Foreign extraction companies were given access to the rich but remote northern forests and continued to export 3.6 million cubic metres of timber a year. Although this revenue remained stable, its importance in the national economy was eclipsed by the spectacular rise in petroleum production. From the first discoveries of offshore petroleum in 1957, the growth of the industry turned the Congolese economy upside down. Between 1969 and 1984 petroleum rose from 5 per cent of export revenue to 90 per cent.

Gabon underwent a similar but even more dramatic transformation. In the last colonial decades *okoumé* wood, together with other less important hardwoods, earned 75 per cent of the national export revenue. With the discovery of petroleum in 1967, however, wood and other agricultural products declined sharply and their importance for state revenues dropped, to 5 per cent in 1990. Yet timber remained important since it still employed 15 per cent of the national labour force, and some fifty foreign concessions still worked in the logging business alongside hundreds of small Gabonese timber-working companies. In farming peasants remained active in the small-scale production of cocoa and coffee.[10] The state did not entirely neglect the agro-timber sectors and authorised a large enterprise to revive rubber production (which had lapsed since the dark days of colonial exploitation) and to establish estates of up to 5,000 hectares.

The difficult postcolonial relations between the independent states and mining companies are not dissimilar to the troubled relations that formerly existed between colonial governments and the early concessionary companies of Central Africa. Oil companies, in particular, overshadowed the sovereignty of any state. In Congo the two major production companies, the French Elf-Congo and the Italian Agip-Recherches, were able to increase the private domination of the industry not only by buying out the 25 per cent interest of the state in export production, but also by privatising the national refining and distributing company which supplied petroleum products within the country. In Congo the state apparently surrendered to international business.

In Gabon the state appeared to hold its own better than in Congo and retained its one-quarter share in each of the largest companies, Elf-Gabon and Shell-Gabon. It also kept a greater national stake in the refining business. The explanation for the greater power of the Gabon politicians may derive from their continuity in office which contrasts with frequent changes of government in Congo. It may also be explained by the greater diversity of mineral resources in Gabon which gave the government a stronger hand to play. In particular Gabon was able to maintain a stake in the uranium mines and the

---

10 Giles Sautter, *De l'Atlantique au Fleuve Congo. Une Géographie du Sous-Peuplement* 2 vols, Moulton, Paris, 1966.

manganese mines and could hold out the prospect of exploration for zinc and lead. The relative success of Gabon in negotiating mineral rights did not, however, lead to any sustained economic development designed to satisfy domestic needs as perceived by ordinary people at a local level.

The prospect for industrialisation seemed better in Congo than in Gabon since Congo had a large hinterland which was a transit zone for goods passing to and from the Central African Republic and Chad. Gabon, on the other hand, had a minute internal market and was relatively isolated compared to Congo. 'Scientific socialism', the official ideology of the Congo government from the 1960s to the 1980s, encouraged the adoption of bold industrialisation projects. These aimed at spending petroleum revenues on infrastructure, agriculture and manufacturing rather than on social amenities, although these might have resulted in more instant political rewards for the politicians. A textile industry was sponsored and one factory opened at Kinsoundi in 1968 and another at Brazzaville in 1969. A cement plant was opened in 1968 to supply demand in nearby Kinshasa as well as markets as far away as Chad. These investments, however, did not produce an adequate return, production remained below capacity, customers were not satisfied with quality, and management was blamed for inefficiency. After 1986 a decline in oil prices exposed the inadequacies of an industrialising policy that had been based on rhetorical ideology unsustained by well-defined objectives.

The shortcomings of the politics of food, and the absence of a sound agricultural policy, were made critical by demographic figures which showed constantly rising populations: 3 per cent per annum in Congo, 2.8 per cent in Gabon and 2.5 per cent in the Central African Republic. The three countries grew the same foodcrops: cassava, maize, yam, sweet potato, banana, plantain, with rice, millet and sorghum grown in addition in the Central Africa Republic. The two oil-producing states virtually abandoned any attempt to monitor domestic food production, and in Congo 'operation cassava', launched in 1971, failed to grow basic food on a system of huge collective farms. Imported food featured large in the Congo economy. Brazzaville came to be fed with produce cultivated in market gardens around Kinshasa and ferried across the river by Zairian traders anxious to earn hard Congo francs when the Zaire currency was subject to high inflation.[11] In Gabon, the situation was still more extreme. Only 0.5 per cent of potential agricultural land was cultivated and production nationwide satisfied only 10 to 15 per cent of food needs. A parastatal company was set up to expand food production in the 1980s but in fact it invested mainly in the production of palm-oil for export.

In the Central African Republic government initiatives had some success in converting commercial agricultural land back to food production. The project was given a loan by the World Bank to help market-gardening and stock-raising, but this was less successful than the efforts of local farmers who turned

11 'L'approvisionnement', *Journées d'Etude sur Brazzaville. Actes du Colloque*, Brazzaville, 25–28 avril 1986, Mission Française de Coopération et d'Action Culturelle, Brazzaville, 1987, pp.213–71.

Elikia M'Bokolo

to food crops when disillusioned by the returns to be gained from cotton and coffee. Farming was also improved by the return to the land of youths who had failed to make good in the towns. By the late 1980s the republic was again self-sufficient and no longer needed to spend 10 per cent of its revenue on imported food as it had done in the 1970s.

FRANCO-AFRICAN RELATIONS: A PRIVILEGED 'PARTNERSHIP'?

Since independence relations of the three equatorial republics with France have been especially complex and intense. Based on treaties of cooperation that were signed in the early days of independence when the new states still had little diplomatic maturity, the nature of these relations resembled those of other francophone states. The relationship was orchestrated by an 'African cell' in the presidential secretariat in Paris and by a ministry for cooperation staffed by ex-colonial bureaucrats who were rarely susceptible to innovation and who maintained networks of affiliation that were subject to improper influence.[12] French influence was also reinforced by the growth of the French presence on the ground in Africa and by the material, political and symbolic power of the financial chain forged by the CFA franc which bound francophone Africa to the former colonial power.

Military intervention was the ultimate sanction that permitted France to dictate policy in the three republics of equatorial Africa. The most decisive action took place in Gabon, when in February 1964 a parachute regiment landed in Libreville. It was the first French intervention of this magnitude, publicly based on defence treaties signed four years previously at the time of independence. The aim was to restore the president, Léon M'Ba, who had been removed in a military putsch, and to ensure a continued French presence in a region where French companies had huge mineral interests. The invasion was sufficiently effective to reassure France's client presidents throughout the region that, although Paris had not intervened to protect the Congo government from revolution in 1963, it was able and willing to restore its friends to power when necessary. In Gabon parachute troops were again called on in 1990 to protect the government from the hostility of its own people and to protect French oil workers from an uprising in the installations at Port-Gentil.

French military interventions came later to the Central African Republic than they did to oil-rich Gabon but there, too, they fundamentally affected the course of political events. In 1979, when popular demonstrations against the 'emperor' Bokassa I were rocking the city of Bangui, French troops landed, marginalised the radical politicians, and paved the way for the return to power of David Dacko, a reputed friend of French interests. In 1996 a series of

---

12 The best sources are the reports and investigations of journalists such as Pierre Péan, *Affaires Africaines*, Fayard, Paris, 1983; *L'Homme de l'Ombre. Eléments d'Enquête autour de Jacques Foccart, l'Homme le Plus Mystérieux et le Plus Puissant de la Ve République*, Fayard, Paris, 1990; and Claude Wauthier, *Quatre Présidents et l'Afrique. De Gaulle, Pompidou, Giscard d'Estaing, Mitterrand. Quarante Ans de Politique Africaine*, Le Seuil, Paris, 1995.

74

mutinies in the republic's army brought a return of French military forces in support of a president who had been 'democratically' elected according to the norms imposed on Central Africa by external interests. These French interventions were only the most spectacular aspect of a structural military control that purported to maintain 'security' in the region. This so-called security had the twin aims of preventing outbreaks of violent conflict between Central African countries and of repressing those within each state who sought to change the team of politicians in power without the approbation of France. Permanent military bases in Gabon and the Central African Republic, and military rights in Congo, also enabled France to intervene in Chad and Zaire when metropolitan interests so required.

The networks of French influence in the three equatorial republics, as in the rest of former French Africa, have thus been complex and varied as they competed, cooperated or supplanted one another. The Gaullist networks were controlled by the enigmatic 'shadow man' Jacques Foccart, while the Giscard fraternities linked his presidency to a compromising association with the dictator Bokassa. The Mitterrand chain of command in Africa was run by his son Jean-Christophe, dubbed 'papa says' by the wits of Libreville and other capitals. Other powerful political and financial networks were managed by the great French trading houses. A few dozen key figures, 'Messers Africa', facilitated or impeded decisions that related to francophone Africa's affairs.[13] Some were placed in the senior civil service of France, some in the private commercial sector, some were visible in public life and others hidden in the most opaque branches of the secret service. The historical analysis of the role of such networks is perplexing since the fragmentary record shows them as exclusively French-dominated and presents Africans only in stereotypical roles as victims, accomplices or intransigent adversaries. Yet within the three republics able statesmen were able to reverse the workings of institutions that had been created without their consent and against their interests and draw benefit from the French connection. President Bongo of Gabon described the semi-voluntary, semi-imposed relationship vividly in the statement that Gabon without France is like a gallon of petrol without a car, while France without Gabon is like a run-down car without any fuel. In the 1960s some Gabon leaders were concerned to escape from the influence of exclusive French masonic lodges which allegedly played an influential role in the postcolonial networks. They set up their own African masonic lodges in order to capture power and patronage and counterbalance French initiative. The future president of Gabon, Bongo, established the lodge of the Grand Equatorial Rite while his colleague George Rawiri set up the Grand National Lodge with close ties to British masonic lodges. These African lodges did admit Frenchmen, including the highly influential Pierre Prouteau, who had broad links to both the right wing and the left wing of French politics. Prouteau was a minister

13 S. Smith and A. Glaser, *Ces Messieurs Afrique. Le Paris-Village du Continent Noir*, Calmann Lévy, Paris, 1992.

in the Barre government of France, a former grand-master of the Grand Orient lodge of France, and was known as the 'patron of the patrons of Africa'.

Afro–French relations in the equatorial republics were regularly enhanced by the fostering of historic myths. Well before independence colonial mythology had found in equatorial African history personalities whom memory cherished. Pierre Savorgnan de Brazza was portrayed as the architect of 'peaceful conquest' in French Congo, while the West Indian Felix Eboué, the first black governor-general in the French colonies, was presented as the friend of the 'natives' and the symbol of racial harmony. During the Second World War, while Eboué ruled French Equatorial Africa, General de Gaulle emerged as another epic figure of African colonial mythology.[14] During the 1970s Africans appropriated to themselves the myths of colonial history and organised ceremonies of commemoration that suited their own political agendas. At the same time successive French governments presented the Gaullist decolonisation as a golden legend designed to prove both the continuity of French benevolence and the responsiveness of France to necessary change. The rhetoric changed, however, in July 1996 when President Chirac visited Brazzaville. He condemned the tradition of Afro-pessimism but recognised that Africa had not finished paying its tribute to history. The slave trade, he acknowledged, had carried off the most vigorous young men and 'launched the continent on the long era of under-development whose scars [had] not yet healed'. Such a thesis might appear banal to scholars, but on a political scene where many real and imaginary rivals operated, France had recognised the need for fresh arguments capable of seducing Africans into partnership.[15]

International competition had had a particularly long history in the case of Congo and Gabon. French fear of rivals dated back to their earliest trading settlements in the mid-nineteenth century and focused on an obsessive antagonism to the United States.[16] Such anxieties were reactivated during the Second World War as African leaders in Brazzaville expressed ambiguous loyalties and so heightened French concern.[17] When US Steel won the 1959 contract to build a Gabon railway, French fear of American encroachment increased yet further.[18] It resurfaced again even more dramatically in the attempted 1964 Gabon coup d'état which French networks perceived as an American plot. American influence, which was politically discreet but culturally demonstrative, was especially active in the economic sphere when the United States became the principle trading partner in oil. By 1990 more than 41 per cent of Gabon's petroleum exports went to the United States, and from

14 F. Bernault, *Démocraties Ambiguës en Afrique Centrale. Congo-Brazzaville, Gabon, 1940–1965*, Karthala, Paris, 1996, pp.135–46.
15 'L'appel de Brazzaville', *Jeune Afrique Economie* 223 (5 Aug. 1996), pp.52–5.
16 E. M'Bokolo, *Noirs et Blancs en Afrique Equatoriale. Les Sociétés Côtières et la Pénétration Française (c.1820–1874)*, Mouton-Editions de l'EHESS, Paris, 1981.
17 P. Gifford and W. Roger Louis (eds), *The Transfer of Power in Africa. Decolonization, 1940–1960*, Yale University Press, New Haven, CT, 1982.
18 R.-Ph. Rey, *Colonialisme, Néo-colonialisme et Transition au Capitalisme. Exemple de la 'Comilog' au Congo Brazzaville*, Maspéro, Paris, 1971, pp.468–75.

Congo the figure was above 37 per cent. Other countries were also active in economic ventures. For oil the main American competitors were Italy, Britain and the Netherlands. Meanwhile Japan entered the scene as a major buyer of timber. By contrast, the Soviet Union had little cultural, strategic or economic influence in the region, despite all the Marxist-Leninist rhetoric of the political leaders in Congo.

Since the early 1980s, the most intrusive external influences which disturbed French hegemony came from international financial agencies. In the Central African Republic the soldiers who came to power in 1982 uncovered such a catastrophic financial situation that they turned to the International Monetary Fund (IMF) for help. A structural adjustment plan was devised which demanded the introduction of classic measures to reduce public expenditure by cutting back salaries and employee numbers in the civil service, the army and the police. The ensuing social malaise was disastrous and the political equilibrium was upset. Part of the opposition attempted to turn the situation to its advantage with an attempted coup d'état led by Ange-Félix Patassé. This forced a postponement of structural adjustment until 1987. The new plan insisted on economic 'liberalisation', the privatisation of public companies, the auditing of public finances, and the encouragement of private enterprise for a three-year period. Further measures dictated by the IMF in 1990 were hampered by the fall in coffee and cotton prices. By 1994 the financial crisis was so acute that Patassé, now the elected president, was compelled to make further concessions to the Fund and thereby brought on new social and political unrest and a series of army mutinies.

THE POLITICAL TURBULENCE OF INDEPENDENCE

The political history of the three equatorial republics may be understood from three different angles. It can be seen as the progressive evolution of a political culture that might or might not be described as 'national'. Alternatively, it can be described as the creation of personalised systems, some ephemeral and some durable, built around men of ability or authority. In yet another light it can be interpreted as an evolving struggle between antagonistic socio-political groupings. Each of the three facets intersects with the others in ways so complex that only the salient points of transition can be identified.

Independence had long been the dream of men and women in French Equatorial Africa and when it came it was rich in colour and aura, in tone and expectation. The word 'independence' was launched on the public in 1958 and rapidly took root in the popular imagination before becoming a constitutional reality in 1960. Within five years the fathers of the nations had disappeared, or been forced from the scene, and by 1968 the new states had adopted directions that were entirely unexpected. The long first decade of independence contrasted sharply with the same period in much of the rest of Africa. It was marked by seminal events that were disruptive in the short term and significant in their long-term impact on posterity. At first independence seemed to be a painless and peaceful revolution but soon an inverted reality took hold and change imposed by a French timetable brought much sadness. In Ubangi-Shari change seemed to come too late, in Gabon too early, and in Congo the transition brought drama that challenged the very concept of nationhood that independence was intended to consolidate.

In Ubangi-Shari the leader, Boganda, was killed in an accident on 29 March 1959 even before independence was achieved. Popular opinion held that he had been assassinated by settlers and unrest erupted at the death of a man whose political agenda was now threatened. Settlers who had been dismayed at Boganda's intrepid bid for independence, in what they perceived as Africa's most backward colony, saw his death as a quasi-divine sign of revenge. Boganda, however, was not a lone prophet as the settlers claimed, but had belonged since the 1930s to an active educated élite which admired the 'true' France which stood for the rights of man and fraternity between equal peoples. These colleagues tried to carry the torch he had lit into the 1990s[19] but power eluded them owing to a convergence of interests between neo-colonial forces and their local ethno-regional clients. These groups supported the leadership bid of a 'kinsman' of Boganda, David Dacko, who was astute enough to seize and reformulate the policies of his predecessor. He pragmatically negotiated an 'amicable' separation with colonial France, but it was a quite different France from the one that Boganda and the intellectuals had admired for its ideological support of basic human rights and social emancipation.

In Congo the march towards independence was marked by a collective drama with a massacre in the streets of Brazzaville in February 1959. For three years, verbal and physical confrontation had become commonplace and in the minds of European observers political killings were reduced to 'traditional rivalries'. The conflict between the two parties, the *Union Démocratique pour la Défense des Intérêts Africains* (UDDIA) and the *Mouvement Socialiste Africain* (MSA) was presented as Balali–M'Bochi rivalry.[20] Such a simple 'tribal' analysis did not, however, comprehend the complexity of the political interests at stake. Violence followed in the wake of inflammatory action by the UDDIA leader, Abbé Fulbert Youlou who violated a 1956 agreement to form a two-party joint government. The elimination of MSA politicians from political and parliamentary activity in November 1958, and a crucial constitutional vote to transfer the Moyen-Congo capital from Pointe-Noire to Brazzaville, led to retaliatory calls for civil war by the MSA. As rumour circulated that militia units were being mobilised, the government tried to eliminate the opposition. The tension culminated in the killing of a hundred people and the wounding of two hundred more. The transfer of sovereignty in Congo thus took place in an atmosphere of repression and sadness. For the next thirty years discussion of the drama surrounding the birth of the nation was a taboo

19 One thinks in particular of the Central African Republic political veteran, Abel Goumba.
20 J.-M. Wagret, *Histoire et sociologie politique de la République du Congo (Brazzaville)*, Librairie Générale de Droit et de Jurisprudence, Paris, 1963, p.85.

subject among Congo politicians and historians.[21] The idea thus took shape that Congo had been, and remained, split into two competing camps. The north, speaking Lingala and largely M'Bochi, lived in the Brazzaville suburb of Poto-Poto, while the south, speaking Kikongo and largely of Lari origins, was focused on the capital's Bacongo suburb.[22]

The independence of Gabon was not overshadowed by tragic conflicts such as those which deprived both Congo and the Central African Republic of popular rejoicing. Unlike most countries of Africa, however, Gabon did not celebrate its independence with panache. The leaders were unashamedly francophile and parliament chose 9 February as Gabon's national day, the date on which the original treaty with France had been signed by Denis Rapontchombo and Bouët-Willaumez in 1839. They desired to celebrate the uniqueness of the Gabonese and their very long French connection in contrast to other Africans of French Equatorial Africa. In 1960 the ruling party in the Gabon parliament even went further and declined the offer of immediate independence, protesting that they would prefer to become an overseas department of metropolitan France.[23] Jacques Foccart was tempted by the prospect of turning Gabon into a West Indian-style dependency and De Gaulle recognised the Gabon leader, Léon M'Ba, as 'a model of fidelity' in his attachment to France. Gabon was nevertheless forced, all protests notwithstanding, to accept independence at the same time as its equatorial neighbours.

The sombre coming of independence to the three equatorial states gave the political parties, the management teams and the leading personalities of each country the authority to install precociously despotic governments. In some other parts of Africa the postcolonial regimes gradually hardened into dictatorships only after independence, but in equatorial Africa dictatorships were effectively in power before independence. In the Central African Republic the huge popularity of Boganda's *Mouvement d'Evolution Sociale de l'Afrique Noire* (MESAN), which had won 97.5 per cent of the vote in 1957, was used by David Dacko as an excuse to abolish other parties and declare the republic a single-party state. In Gabon, which had started with several parties, Léon M'ba's *Bloc Démocratique Gabonais* (BDG) quickly emerged as the dominant party, and won strong majorities in the elections of 1957 and 1960. When faced with demonstrations organised by the opposition in 1958, the president persuaded parliament to pass laws that enabled the government to maintain 'order'. He also coopted Jean-Hilaire Aubame, the leader of the opposition *Union Démocratique et Sociale du Gabon* (UDSG), into the government as minister of foreign affairs. Displays of debonair paternalism, however, were belied by the maintenance of colonial instruments of repression. Gabon was

21 E. M'Bokolo, 'Histoire, mémoire et patrimoine: contribution à une politique volontier de construction de l'Etat de droit', in P. Yengo (ed.), *Identités et Démocratie en Afrique*, L'Harmattan, Paris, 1996.
22 Bernault, *Démocraties Ambiguës*, pp.288–91.
23 The 1958 constitution had allowed three options for France's African colonies: the status quo, independence, or becoming a French *département*. See L. Sanmarco, *Le Colonisateur Colonisé*, ABC, Paris, 1983, pp.210–11.

carpeted with a network of police informers recruited from among bureaucrats, chiefs, businessmen, white settlers, women's leaders, sports organisers, and others layers of society. Fear of opposition politics continued to preoccupy the ruling party despite the tightly-knit instruments of repression. In 1963 M'Ba distanced himself from Jean-Hilaire Aubame, removed him from his ministerial post but retained him on the government payroll as president of the supreme court. In Congo the trend towards authoritarianism was also accentuated in 1958. President Youlou declared himself to be equatorial Africa's first line of defence against communism and introduced legislation in 1960 that restricted individual and collective freedoms and enabled him to arrest trade unionists and youth leaders accused of 'communist' plots. As in Gabon, the president coopted the opposition leader, Jean Opangault, into his government and subsequently won 97.5 per cent of the 1961 vote. Two years later parliament accepted the creation of a single-party state and Congo appeared set to become a stable despotism like its neighbours. Congo politics, however, remained a fragile edifice exposed to the converging forces of opposition.

Among the leading sources of opposition to the new regimes, 'youths' were a sociological rather than a biological category. This mixed-age group included townsmen and farmers, school-leavers and illiterates, élites who had been to Europe and students who were training in Africa. They had all become allergic to the city politicians and district chiefs with whom they had associated in the colonial past. Youths were organised through territorial and metropolitan student bodies often imbued with Marxism. Those who had been in France were subject to especially intense surveillance on their return to Africa. Fulbert Youlou obliged returnees to stay in Congo for two years before they again became eligible to travel. Compulsory public service in work deemed socially useful was also imposed on youths aged 18–23 by the Congo state.

A widespread and popular display of public expression that escaped the control of political parties and of government agents took the form of songs and dances. In the rural areas villagers demonstrated their opposition through the medium of 'traditional' songs and dances, while in the towns 'modern' songs provided an outlet for popular discontent. Performers expressed satirical views about absentee members of parliament, bemoaned the oppression of little people by power-brokers, showed the derision that many felt towards the still numerous whites in their midst, and above all evoked the fear of the remote state and the hatred of arbitrary power. In all three equatorial countries the symbolic or material benefits which the state's representatives could bestow were limited to privileged regions. Opposition grew in the neglected regions, removed from access to government services.

Organised forms of opposition emerged in trade unions, in churches and among the military. Trade unions had significant weight among company employees and civil servants in the cities of Pointe-Noire, Libreville and Brazzaville. At the time of independence, one quarter of Gabon's 100,000 salaried state workers belonged to unions linked to metropolitan France, though the political profile of the unions remained discreet. In Congo the three main trade unions were much more militant, especially after 1957 when they organised themselves to combat rising unemployment. Congo unions thrived in the complex, diversified, late-colonial economy near the political nerve-centre of the territory. Soldiers formed a distinctive part of the colonial workforce, and had gained a certain prestige from their role in the Second World War and from their association with the mystique surrounding the French resistance to the Nazi occupation of France. Colonial soldiers, mainly from Chad and the Central African Republic, had also helped the French to fight their colonial wars in Indochina and Algeria. On their return home some of the soldiers' leaders, such as Jean-Bedel Bokassa, became political strongmen in an army culture which was marked by an aversion to civilian politicians.

The challenges faced by the early leaders of the equatorial republics were so great and so numerous that they could not overcome them, despite their undoubted abilities and the advantages which they had inherited from retiring colonial administrations. Their days in power were thus numbered. Their initial strength had been based on the urban vote and on the support of white settlers. Both Youlou of Congo and M'Ba of Gabon had also allegedly used the occult to inspire a mass following. Many of their admirers believed that the dominance of such big men could only be explained by their ability to control African witchcraft and white magic. But the construction of despotic structures could not keep pace with the rising tide of popular discontent. This tide culminated in massive popular demonstrations, some of which were covertly supported by members of parliament and by France.

The first regime to fall was that of Fulbert Youlou of Congo who on the 13–15 August 1963 was toppled in 'Three Glorious Days', a phrase borrowed from revolutionary France.[24] The key to the Congo revolution was a trade union movement which the regime had tried to ban, only to cause a general strike. Youlou, 'Monsieur l'Abbé' to the masses because of his background as a Catholic priest, immediately blamed international communism in general, and China in particular, for the fall of his government. For whatever reason, France did not send in troops to protect the falling dictator from the wrath of the masses but allowed the revolution to take its course and throw up another experienced politician, Massemba-Debat, as the new president. Less than a year later it was the turn of Gabon to experience revolution. Young military officers seized the Gabon government palace and forced President M'Ba to resign in a radio broadcast and make way, as in Congo, for another old-guard politician, Aubame, deemed acceptable to France. In the case of Gabon, however, France declined to accept the transfer of power to Aubame and intervened to restore M'Ba. In both countries the situation remained uncertain. In Congo a new constitution, the election of Massemba-Debat as president, and

---

24 See Georges Duveau, *1848*, Gallimard, Paris, 1965. The vocabulary of the élites in French Equatorial Africa, especially in Congo, was heavily influenced by the political history of France.

Elikia M'Bokolo

the creation of a new Marxist-Leninist party, the *Mouvement National de la Révolution* (MNR) which proclaimed a one-party state in 1964, did not resolve the basic contradictions in society. A deep social malaise continued to fuel trade union activity and heighten the impatience of youth, expressed in the party youth movement. The army, hitherto absent from the political scene, emerged as the alternative means of restoring order. In 1968 a young military leader, Marien Ngouabi, who was a foreign-educated intellectual rather than a colonial recruit, seized power in a coup d'état.

In Gabon the change of guard took a different course. President M'Ba, the anti-hero of independence, had lost his credibility as leader and in 1967 fell ill and died. Thereupon, the neo-colonial networks looked for legitimate ways to bring to power a leader who was young, politically competent, internationally experienced in management, and above all totally loyal to France. The ruling BDG party that had won the fear-ridden elections of 1964 set about creating a single-party regime by alternatively threatening and bribing its opponents until it succeeded in gaining a monopoly of parliamentary power in 1967. As the new president it appointed the then vice-president, Albert-Bernard Bongo, although he had attained his post by appointment rather than through an election process. The new president quickly proclaimed a one-party state and in March founded his own party, the *Parti Démocratique Gabonais* (PDG). In both Gabon and Congo, the flow of events had led to the firmly entrenched establishment of single-party authoritarianism.

In the Central African Republic the crises which affected Gabon and Congo were absent, but the country also ended up in the hands of autocratic governments. Although not directly challenged by opponents, the regime of President Dacko proved to be both despotic and powerless. The country's problems were summed up by a Protestant-educated reformer, François-Sylvestre Sana, when he noted that the Central African Republic was suffering from five sicknesses: bureaucratisation, professional incompetence, *tabagisme*, alcohol and diamonds. During the 1960s diamond production rose tenfold to 600,000 carats and the revenue generated an unbridled climate of opportunism and corruption. In three years no less than twenty district commissioners were arrested for embezzlement and overworked state inspectors were forced to abandon prosecutions relating to cases worth less than a quarter of a million francs. The impoverished state was compelled to reduce both civil and military salaries and thereby drove public employees into freelance diamond prospecting. On New Year's Eve 1965 several senior army officers attempted to overthrow the regime and in the ensuing confusion Jean-Bedel Bokassa was able to turn the disorder to his own benefit and capture the power of the state. His success heralded two long decades of despotism in all three equatorial republics.

ONE-PARTY DICTATORSHIP: A FALSE SHOWCASE

For some twenty years the societies of the three equatorial republics tolerated as best they could the oppressive, often extreme, measures imposed by the

82

authoritarian power of the state. Actual experience can be grouped into two types. The stability of the regime and the continuity of the ruling personnel in Gabon contrasted sharply with the structural uncertainties and volatile politics of Congo and the Central African Republic.

The stability of the Gabon regime was due to the convergence of several factors: a favourable economy, the skill of the politicians in power, and the hesitations of an opposition which was also deeply divided. From 1965–80 the country experienced a remarkable economic growth rate of 9.5 per cent. Gabon, in particular, benefited from the 1973 rise in oil prices and two years later it joined the Organization of Petroleum Exporting Countries. The president adopted Islam, made the pilgrimage to Mecca, and took the title of Al-Hajj Omar Bongo. Rising oil revenues not only enriched the oligarchy of politicians and civil servants but also permitted a consolidation of the social base of the regime by incorporating into the salaried work force migrants who were fleeing the neglected countryside to find prosperity in the city. High salaries were also used to satisfy the aspirations of a new generation of university graduates who might otherwise have been prone to organise protests. As migrant labour arrived from other parts of Africa such as Biafra, Cameroun, Benin, Equatorial Guinea and Congo, the media and the highest government officials cleverly exploited the situation. Public opinion was favourably impressed by the image of Gabon as the Kuwait of Africa, able to absorb foreign workers without creating anxieties in the national workforce. But economic success was not the only factor which enabled Bongo to concentrate power and win successive elections with 99 per cent of the vote. His political skill in opening dialogues with potential opponents enabled him to bring back to Gabon qualified personnel who had been working abroad but who now offered their services to their country and took part in policy debates within the confines of the single ruling party.

When petroleum prices began to fall Gabon's economy grew by less than one per cent per annum between 1980 and 1992 and opposition started to gather strength. From 1986 the government was forced to undertake structural adjustments which had a serious impact on social programmes. Opposition among radical students, some of them in Gabon and others in France, had previously existed but in 1981 the first opposition party came into existence in Gabon itself. This was the *Mouvement de Redressement National* (MORENA) established by a priest, Father Paul M'Ba Abessole. The party attempted unsuccessfully to field an opposition candidate against Omar Bongo in the elections of 1986. Two years later austerity caused the government to cut public sector salaries and MORENA sponsored strikes by civil servants. President Bongo, however, was able to divide his opponents through political and financial bargains and by 1990 the opposition party was split between one faction dominated by timber workers led by Abessole, and another, MORENA *Original*, which proclaimed the purity of its ideological opposition to the regime. The stability of Gabon was particularly impressive when compared to developments in the two neighbouring countries.

The Central African Republic, in contrast to Gabon, went through four political phases between the coup of 1965 and the so-called democratisation process of the 1990s. Bokassa ruled as a republican president between 1966 and 1977, then as a self-declared 'emperor' from 1977 to 1979; Dacko returned to power between 1979 and 1981; and General Kolingba ruled from 1981 to 1993. These were merely changes of name, however. Real change of both structure and personnel was limited and France played a determining role in preserving some kind of continuity in the midst of extremely fragmented political and social forces. After his seizure of power Bokassa imposed a forced march towards dictatorship. He declared himself president for life and in 1974 took the military rank of field marshall. In 1976 Bokassa proclaimed 'the revolution', with a council made up of leaders who included Ange-Félix Patassé, appointed as prime minister, and David Dacko, now special adviser to the president. The council had hardly been installed, however, before Bokassa dissolved it and the revolution gave way to an 'empire'. The official cere-monies, involving a lavish coronation, squandered one quarter of the national export revenue for 1977.

Before 1977 political leaders had largely been recruited from the old olig-archy. They now became concerned at the autocratic actions of a new regime which arrested several ministers and former ministers and accused them of plotting against the government. The opposition gained new vitality and recruited personnel from the provinces, where leaders were uncontaminated by earlier collaboration. The most distinctive of these new opponents of the regime were pupils enrolled in both primary and secondary schools. Some of these youthful opponents were killed by the security forces, allegedly on the order of the 'emperor' himself. Old-guard politicians such as Patassé tried to use the student disturbances to regroup the political and military leadership in opposition to Bokassa. The French, however, decided to support the old veteran, David Dacko, when in 1979 they sent troops to Bangui to overthrow Bokassa. The chosen leader convinced no one of his independent credentials. Despite serious attempts to manipulate the polls in 1981 he had great difficulty in getting his version of the constitution, and his own candidacy for the presidency, accepted by the voters. A cycle of events similar to that which followed independence began to unfold. Political parties were banned, elec-tions rigged, and human rights violated. The new socialist government of France decided not to tolerate a new round of dictatorial hardening and per-suaded Dacko to give way to military rule under the army commander-in-chief, General Kolingba.

Kolingba had no more success than his predecessors in holding the Central African Republic together. He remained dependent on French economic and fiscal assistance and faced the continued opposition both of old-style leaders from the Boganda era and of new leaders emerging from the French univer-sities. Rivalry and factionalism split the political scene and insurrection con-stantly threatened. Opponents of government were regularly convicted of treasonable activities and given heavy sentences, only to be pardoned later. As a façade of legality, the military organised presidential elections which gave Kolingba over 91 per cent of the vote in 1986. The following year, in the first parliamentary elections since independence, all the candidates were from the president's *Rassemblement Démocratique Centrafricain* (RDC). The only notable occurrence in this long period of authoritarian rule was perhaps the unexpected return of Bokassa from exile in France in 1986. His trial for crimes against the people allowed the country to lift the taboo on the discussion of the terrible years endured under the old dictator and gave insights into the harsher aspects of despotic repression. The emperor was sentenced to death, though his sentence was gradually reduced on appeal and, finally, ten years later, he was able to walk free.

In Congo similar instability seemed to reign, though in fact the presidency was held by only three men, all of them from the *Parti Congolais du Travail* (PCT), or Congo Labour Party, which was founded in 1969 as the only political party. The years of Marien Ngouabi between 1968 and 1977 were filled with drama as the party leaders struggled over personal agendas, acceptable ideological lines, and a set of policies to deal with the economy, ethnic tensions and the mobilisation of political support. After several attempted coups were foiled, Ngouabi finally fell to assassins in March 1977. The 'northerners' who were from the same region as Ngouabi blamed the people of the 'south' and avenged their leader by murdering the former president, Massamba-Debat, and the archbishop of Brazzaville, Cardinal Biayenda.

For the next two years power was held by Colonel Yhombi-Opango who then passed it to a provisional committee of the PCT chaired by Denis Sassou-Nguesso, the much-feared head of the security services. He was able to hold the balance between the rhetoric of Marxist-Leninism and the pragmatism of a pro-western political economy based on oil exports. Although regularly elected president and head of state by the leaders of the single party, he did face opposition both from right-wing soldiers and from left-wing trade unionists. The most serious rebellion was one in the north in 1987 led by Pierre Anga, but after a year of conflict Anga was killed by the security forces. Although economic troubles increased, the PCT maintained a façade of power and popularity and in the September 1989 elections for the legislature won over 99 per cent of the vote. By this date, however, the process known as 'democratisation' was already underway in Congo, as it was in the Central African Republic and Gabon.

THE AMBIVALENCE OF DEMOCRATISATION

The democratisation that overtook the equatorial republics in 1989 did not arrive like a bolt from the blue. Those who had been cut out of public life, and critics within each single party, had continually tried to influence public affairs through negotiation or by violence. Within the three countries those in power had attempted to control the pressures but seemed to lose the political initiative and merely follow events and ratify decisions driven by other forces. Far from being bestowed from above, democratisation was manipulated from below.

In March 1990 those in power in Gabon, the first equatorial country to organise a National Conference, categorically rejected the opposition's demands for a multi-party system. Instead the government invoked fears that a multi-party system would aggravate ethnic conflict and compromise economic development. Opposition pressures, especially from trade unions and students, nonetheless obliged the PDG to set up a 'Special Committee for Democracy' which convened a National Conference. This gathering thwarted the president's plan for a slow transition to a multi-party system and insisted that it be established immediately and unconditionally.

In Congo the first moves in favour of democracy took place in 1989, the year of the triumphant re-election of Sassou-Nguesso as head of the single party and head of state. At first those in power only released political prisoners but in the parliamentary elections of September 1989 they ceded some seats to candidates from outside the ruling PCT. These included representatives of trade unions, women's associations, youth movements and religious groups. Matters came to a head in 1990 when the Congo Trade Union Federation detached itself from the party and forced the PCT to lift restrictions on independent parties and to call a National Conference. In 1991 this conference confirmed the end of the single-party state and the beginning of 'democracy'.

Political change was most problematic in the Central African Republic. A small turn-out of only 50 per cent of registered voters at the 1987 parliamentary election, the first in twenty years, demonstrated the appeal of opposition parties which had urged voters to stay away from the poll. Feeling the wind of change, the leaders of the RDC allowed multiple candidates supported by the party to stand for office in the municipal election of 1988. They also authorised the return of political exiles who were offered senior jobs in finance, business and administration. At the same time, however, those who refused to cooperate met with tough repression of even their mildest demonstrations, while strikes and public gatherings were made illegal. By July 1991 the government had accepted the principle of multi-partyism, but emphasised that this would not meet the political and economic needs of the country and that the measures were the result of foreign pressure. It also opposed the idea of a National Conference as demanded in a petition signed by two hundred and fifty national celebrities. The government proposed instead a 'great national debate' which it would tightly control. In August 1992, without the participation of the principal opposition parties or of the powerful Catholic Church, a gathering gave birth to new legislation which was at once undermined by those in power. Although President Kolingba did everything to derail subsequent elections, they finally took place in 1993 and resulted in his own defeat and the coming to power of Patassé and his *Mouvement de Libération du Peuple Centrafricain.*

Explanations of these moves towards democratisation in equatorial Africa have often tended to emphasise the role of external forces, especially French influence and the fall of the communist dictatorships in eastern Europe. Although the evidence suggests that political transformation in equatorial Africa was part of a global movement, external factors should not be overemphasised. At the La Baule conference in June 1990 François Mitterrand accelerated the process of democratisation, but did not initiate it. Only in the Central African Republic did French intervention and French threats to suspend financial aid determine the direction of change. France could not play the same economic role in Congo and Gabon with their rich mineral resources. In Gabon, indeed, the intervention of French paratroopers at Port-Gentil in May 1990 appeared to save rather than liberalise the threatened regime of President Bongo. Less publicised, but nevertheless influential, were the activities of the United States, the United Nations and international financial organisations. These involved giving nominal support to campaigns for human rights and for elections or even, as in the case of Congo, supporting one of the political movements. But the actions of international organisations were full of ambiguities. On the one hand 'good government' demanded honest and rigorous management and multiple political movements; on the other, structural adjustment lowered wages, cut public sector jobs, stirred social discontent and weakened the foundations of new regimes.

Economic troubles gave impetus to old opposition movements and to open revolt. Loss of external revenue, especially for Congo and Gabon which experienced a fall in petroleum prices, increased external debt and the weight of servicing it, and a 50 per cent devaluation of the CFA franc in January 1994 all led to the lowering or stopping of wages. Civil servants, business employees and students with grants were most affected and led the struggle for political change. Trade unions, both those with a solid tradition of struggle in Congo and the newer and less experienced ones in Gabon, also lent their weight to the demands for change. These movements were essentially urban, except in central and southern Gabon where rural populations took part. In the countryside voters nevertheless supported leaders of urban movements without necessarily holding identical views or proclaiming the same slogans.

Among the influential organisations which promoted moves towards a more democratic society was the Catholic Church. In the Central African Republic the Catholic Church never ceased to denounce the delaying tactics of President Kolingba. In Congo the long church resistance to the official Marxist-Leninist ideology of the PCT allowed the bishop of Owando, Monsignor Ernest N'Kombo, to be elected president of the National Conference and president of the High Council of the Republic. The army also played an unexpected role in the struggle for democracy. In Gabon, where those in power had kept the military in check by using the threat of French military intervention, the army had maintained a long silence. In Congo, on the other hand, the army, although deeply divided, showed itself on several occasions in favour of change. It was the army that contributed to the calming of political fever in December 1992 following the break-up of key political alliances and the dissolution of the National Assembly by President Lissouba.

The Congo army threatened a military coup d'état if the politicians failed to find a compromise. In the Central African Republic popular disillusionment was fomented by soldiers whose repeated mutinies in 1996 benefited from the sympathy of the population of Bangui.

Although all three countries held a National Conference to work out a basis for a new democracy, each gathering took a different form and had a differing agenda. In Gabon, in March 1990, the conference was gradually mastered by the president and the election which followed confirmed his power. The conference lasted much longer in Congo, from February to June 1991 and confirmed itself as being a sovereign body. Those assembled put the Congo regime on trial and this led to the defeat of Sassou-Nguesso in the legislative and presidential elections of 1992. In the Central African Republic President Kolingba's refusal to organise a National Conference, and his staging of an alternative 'great national debate', created instability as his opponents continued to demand a National Conference.

If a process of institutional change was clearly underway at the beginning of the 1990s, it was otherwise with social change. The 'democratisation' process had brought to power individuals whose political careers dated back to the colonial period. Occupying positions as administrators, teachers, clergymen, military officers and trade unionists, they shared a training in colonial institutions. The new generation, especially graduates of universities and military academies, had been absorbed into the ranks of this bourgeoisie. The rapid advance and enrichment of this privileged group had been at the expense of the masses who were denied access to power. Their disillusion was quite evident by the mid-1990s. Opportunities for new leadership remained limited but support shifted as new geo-political groups came into existence. Parties received support from 'ethnic' groups whose loyalty was sealed with favours and privileges bestowed by political leaders. In Congo there was a proliferation of political action groups when 104 associations and 77 political parties sent representatives to the National Conference. Their recruitment and discourse were deeply marked by ethnic and regional allegiance.

Developments in the 1990s showed how those prominent in national politics acquired legitimacy. Their strategy was much as it had been at the time of independence, rewarding supporters, acquiring foreign backing, especially from France, exploiting ethnicity, and projecting a strong image of political success through secret protection from magical or religious forces. New requirements were added to this political heritage. In reaction to bad management by successive regimes, approval by international organisations became a criterion for success. New men at the top were financial experts with experience in pan-African organisations, United Nations agencies or the World Bank. Many former administrators still influential in politics were converted to democracy with help from religion. The Congolese Bernard Kolélas[25] had

---

25 See especially R. Bazenguissa, 'Histoire sociale du champ politique congolaise, 1946–1991', Ph.D. thesis, EHESS, Paris, 1995; M.-E. Gruénais, F. Mouanda Mbambi, and J. Tonda, 'Messies, fétiches et lutte de pouvoirs entre les "grands hommes" du Congo démocratique', *Cahiers d'Etudes*

been secretary-general of Youlou's UDDIA before independence, and then became Youlou's minister for foreign affairs. He then joined Congo's Marxist regime but was later accused of conspiracy and forced into exile in 1969. Thereafter he referred to his 'way of the cross' and presented himself as a martyr, following 'the living God of our ancestors' and the God of the Christians. He succeeded in winning support through these claims, and favourable newspapers saw in him the rich legacy of three heroic, historic, and religious figures from Congo's past: Kimpa Vita, Simon Kimbangu and Fulbert Youlou. As a politician in the 1990s he evoked the party symbols of Youlou's UDDIA.

URBANISATION, SOCIAL CHANGE AND SOCIAL DIVISION

The rapid and sustained growth of cities has been an important aspect of equatorial Africa's social history. The cities had different origins as precolonial trading centres or colonial administrative and economic capitals, but whatever their beginnings, all experienced remarkable growth starting in the last two decades of colonialism. The annual urban growth rate for the three countries of equatorial Africa was 5.4 per cent in 1970–80, higher than the 4.95 per cent of Africa as a whole. In 1994 the percentage of citizens living in towns was 61 per cent for Congo, 49 per cent for Gabon and 39 per cent for the Central African Republic. Congo has tellingly been called 'the suburb of Brazzaville'.[26] Congo is very far from what has been called 'village Africa' where townspeople constitute less than 10 per cent of the population, as they do in Rwanda or Burundi, or less than 15 per cent as in Niger, Uganda, Ethiopia and Malawi.[27] Uneven concentrations of populations in equatorial Africa are especially marked because people tend to live near towns, as they do along the railway line from Pointe-Noire to Brazzaville, in the Ogowé and Wolem-Ntem valley in Gabon, and in the southern Central African Republic.

Whatever their colonial history, the distinctions between urban environments in the three countries have become blurred since independence as all governments have followed development policies that have led to uncontrolled urban growth. The priority given to the state and administration, low investment in agriculture, free and compulsory education in the towns and the prevailing notion that salaried employment was prestigious, all encouraged a drift to the towns. The model of social success rested on the tripartite requirement of schooling, a professional job, and living in a town. This was the myth underlying rural exodus. In Brazzaville only 54 per cent of the 1984 inhabitants were born in the city while 32 per cent were immigrants from rural areas. The rest came from small towns or from foreign countries.

Africaines 137 (1995), pp.163–93; F. R. Weissman, *Election Présidentielle de 1992 au Congo: Entreprise Politique et Mobilisation Electorale*, Centre d'Etudes d'Afrique Noire, Université de Bordeaux I, 1993.
26 The title of a special issue of *Politique Africaine* 31 (October 1988).
27 E. M'Bokolo, *Villes d'Afrique: Tendances, Problèmes et Perspectives*, UNESCO, Paris, 1996.

In Congo the majority of foreign immigrants were from Zaire. In Gabon, most came from Equatorial Guinea, Cameroun, Benin, 'Biafra' during the Nigerian civil war, Zaire and Congo. There were also West African Muslims known as 'Sénégalais'. In the Central African Republic, a large number of immigrants arrived from Chad, fleeing from civil war and poverty. Foreigners tended to concentrate in specific areas of each town and enlivened its cosmopolitan atmosphere. Nationals aspired to the prestigious wage-earning jobs, but foreigners often had specialised skills, set up small-scale businesses as artisans, and engaged in profitable informal commerce.

The bright lights of the town proved to be treacherous, however. Unemployment grew to 20 per cent in Brazzaville in the 1980s and provoked conflict, trade union agitation, political confrontation, accusations of witchcraft, and a search for 'traditional' protection and therapeutic cures.[28] The problem of town life was expressed in the discourse of survival and by metaphors that conveyed crisis and *'conjunctures'*. The layout of Brazzaville particularly accentuated conflict and social unrest. Property disputes were common, with 'traditional' chiefs of districts claiming ancient rights, landowners ruined by multiple claims to their property, and people with small property claims fighting with each other and with speculators who drove up prices. Overcrowding in the inner city led to promiscuity and many who were forced to live in distant suburbs found transport to work a nightmare. The number of waged employees was small in relation to the size of Brazzaville's population, but the numbers of dependents, children, students, and unemployed or old people increased. In this potent mix social conflict was endemic, as it was in other equatorial African towns.

THE SHAPING OF IDENTITIES

Individuals and social groups took on multiple identities in which contradiction and fluidity led to antagonism in local and in national life. The theme of 'constructing the nation' was at the centre of the political discourse of successive regimes in all three countries. As a utopian ideal, nationalism was used by those in power for their own ends. A real sense of emerging national identity was nevertheless discernible.

Evidence of nationalism was demonstrated through xenophobia. In underpopulated Gabon a deeply-rooted fear of foreigners was expressed by the infamous stereotyping of strangers, particularly 'Biafrans', and 'Equatorians'. In Congo hostility was directed at Zairians. Hostilities sometimes exploded out of small incidents such as disputed football matches and ended in the massive expulsion of foreigners. The economic crises of the 1980s and 1990s led to accusations that foreigners had come to steal the national wealth, a charge which seemed confirmed by high unemployment figures among nationals.

28 See the pioneering works of R. Devauges, *Le Chômage à Brazzaville en 1957: Etude Sociologique*, ORSTOM, Paris, 1959, and *L'Oncle, le Ndoki et l'Entrepreneur: la Petite Entreprise Congolaise à Brazzaville*, ORSTOM, Paris, 1977.

In 1974, unemployment in Brazzaville was 20 per cent among nationals, former wage-earners and victims of economic down-sizing, but only 9 per cent among foreigners, almost all self-employed and better able to survive the crisis in the formal economy.

None of the three equatorial countries experienced a serious separatist movement, even among groups such as the Teke and Kongo which straddled frontiers. Historical events were kept alive in the popular memory[29], encouraged by the state in order to add to a sense of national integration. In the Central African Republic Barthélémy Boganda's tragic death in 1959 was commemorated annually in a day of public mourning. In spite of his drawn-out trial, Jean-Bedel Bokassa was given a national funeral. Such episodes in a country's past were harnessed to the cause of national identity. In Gabon the construction of national identity was linked to both a French culture and a Bantu one. The Gabon emphasis on an early French presence was not related to any notion of dependence, but rather to pride in a colonial past which distinguished it from its neighbours.[30]

In the case of Congo the quest for a national identity took a different turn. In spite of the diversity of successive regimes, there was a remarkable continuity in popular identification with common glories and misfortunes. Youlou used the anti-colonial resistance of Matswa, the prestige of the Teke Makoko, the status of Pierre Savorgnana de Brazza, and the position of Brazzaville as the one-time capital of Free France, to shape his new nation. Although subsequent socialist regimes proclaimed the 'internationalism of the proletariat' they also enhanced national identity with countrywide youth movements. In obliterating territorial units based on 'ethnic' lines they banned identification by 'tribe' in the 1984 census. School textbooks were revised to emphasise socio-economic and regional factors, and broad civilisations rather than rival kingdoms. Successive regimes also gave prominence to the national holiday on 15 August, the date of independence, but also the third day of the 'Glorious revolution' of 1963, and the day when reconciliation marked the birth of a new democratic regime in 1993. A special mass confirming the place of the Catholic Church in Congo history was held in the National Assembly building, which was associated with the period of the Marxist state. Thus, a building associated with the rule of a specific regime was transformed into a national monument.

The affirmation of national identity went hand in hand, paradoxically, with the growth of a politicised ethnicity which at times exploded in urban violence. Ethnicity was the focus of political life in Gabon and Congo but ethnic divisions were much less marked in the Central African Republic. In Gabon the troubles of 1990 in Libreville and Port-Gentil were marked by attacks on Teke citizens considered to be the accomplices of 'brother' Bongo and the principal beneficiaries of his regime. After this violence recruitment of party

---

29 See Pierre Nora, *Les Lieux de la Mémoire*, Vol.1 *La République*, Gallimard, Paris, 1984.
30 B. Weinstein, 'Léon M'Ba: the ideology of dependence', *Genève-Afrique* 6, 1 (1967), pp.49–62.

members and the mobilisation of voters at elections followed ethnic and regional lines.

The association of ethnicity and politics was even more dramatic in Congo where the divisions that existed between 'northerners' and 'southerners' under Youlou hardened even more under the socialist regimes that followed. The opposition was identified with 'southerners' such as Kolélas. The National Conference and the election which followed were interpreted as a victory for 'southerners', notably the new president, Pascal Lissouba, and his supporters. Although the different parties carefully chose national names, public opinion identified them quite clearly with the ethnic homelands of their leaders. The *Mouvement Congolais pour le Développement et la Démocratie Intégrale* (MCDDI) belonged to Kolélas and the Lari. The *Rassemblement pour la Démocratie et le Progrès Social* was associated with Jean-Pierre Thystère-Tchicaya and the Vili; the *Union Pan-Africaine de la Démocratie Sociale* (UPADS) and Lissouba were rooted in the 'Nibolek' region of Niari, Bouenza, and Lékoumou; and the PCT of Sassou-Ngouesso was the party of the 'people of the north'. Election results confirmed the association of ethnicity and politics and frequent elections in 1992 and 1993 caused controversies, changing alliances, and a civil war in Brazzaville. The parties recruited their militias along ethnic lines and the armed groups divided up the residential zones of the capital between the *Ninja* (MCDDI), the *Cobras* (PCT) and the *Zoulous* (UPADS). The confrontation sent refugees fleeing across the capital to join the 'camp' where they would feel safe. This new ethnicity was unrelated to any ancient, authentic or African identity. Rather such identities were short-term political phenomena instantly affecting large numbers of people.[31]

CELEBRATION AND SUFFERING, CULTURE AND SOCIABILITY

From Brazzaville to Libreville and from Pointe-Noire to Bangui, the second half of the twentieth century was marked by a remarkable effervescence in popular culture which could not be contained within national boundaries. Music, fashion, social life and popular religion associated all three countries with each other and with Zaire in all essential aspects of daily life, especially town life.

Concepts of leisure and music rooted in the colonial period remained beyond the reach of political forces.[32] The proliferation of orchestras, the growth of the entertainment business, and the power of popular music were enhanced by a rich use of local language.[33] During the early years of independence and revolution, artists such as Franklin Boukaka and famous groups such as the

31 R. Bazenguissa-Ganga, *Milices Politiques et Bandes Armées à Brazzaville: Enquête sur la Violence Politique et Sociale des Jeunes Déclassés*, CERI, Fondation Nationale de Sciences Politiques, Paris, 1996.
32 See S. Bemba, *50 Ans de Musique du Congo-Zaïre*, Présence Africaine, Paris, 1984; P. Martin, *Leisure and Society in Colonial Brazzaville*, Cambridge University Press, Cambridge, 1995.
33 See especially the analysis of J. Berque, *Langages Arabes du Présent*, Gallimard, Paris, 1978.

'Bantous' expressed themselves in political songs which praised solidarity, work, the new women and men, and themes supported by the regime. In opposition to government political songs often flourished on the margins of power, using scorn and cryptic criticism rather than frontal attack. The festive quality of modern music was dazzling. Singing and dancing enlivened private parties and public bars with music full of social commentary. The songs dealt with affairs of the heart, with professional adventures and misadventures, and with the conflict of generations. The experience of urban life, individual emancipation, lovers and rivals, and Saturday night fever were all celebrated. Despite the significance of emerging local identities the language of song adopted by singers everywhere was Lingala, the language of Kinshasa. Musicians emphasised transnational relations for commercial reasons and wrote songs such as the pioneering composition of Franklin Boukaka, 'Bridge Over the Congo'.

Fashion, and the display of elegance, was another means of mediating the tensions of city life.[34] The use of clothing as a sign of distinction between the sexes, age-groups and classes had deep roots in the precolonial past. Colonialism had enriched this panoply of costume and the subtle distinctions that it could convey. In the towns the pursuit of elegance and of high fashion was especially marked. The Bacongo district of Brazzaville, which was already known in the 1930s for the number of its tailors, became famous for the association dedicated to the pursuit of fashion called the *Société des Ambianceurs et des Personnes Elégantes*, and popularly known as SAPE. After the fall of Youlou, and the assassination of Massemba-Debat, the Bacongo suburb became a centre of political opposition, where young men of this sartorial society were often poor, unemployed, school drop-outs. Their SAPE association took on new meaning with the second petroleum price rise in 1979 when those with political power amassed new wealth and relations between youth and the party were ambiguous. The government ordered the Ministry of Youth and the party's youth movement to challenge the *sapeurs*, branding them as 'delinquents', as 'lazy' and as 'bad examples'. Top political leaders nevertheless took the young men under their wing and employed them to organise their own social calendars. In turn the elegant young men complimented statesmen such as Sassou-Nguessou and Omar Bongo on their sense of high fashion.

In the 1950s common interest groups were one of the most characteristic phenomena of the urban milieu.[35] Townspeople began to join associations and clubs that were no longer associated with family, ethnicity and region. Recreation groups met in bars and dance-halls that could be either public space or

---

34 The study of fashion was once left to anthropologists and sociologists, see for example, J.-D. Gandoulou, *Dandies à Bacongo: le Culte de l'Elégance dans la Société Congolaise Contemporaine*, L'Harmattan, Paris, 1989, but is now claiming the attention of historians, see for example, Martin, *Leisure and Society*, pp.154–72.
35 G. Balandier, *Sociologie des Brazzavilles Noires*, 2nd edn., Presses de la Fondation Nationale des Sciences Politiques, Paris, 1985, p.143.

exclusive to the interests of those involved. These establishments mimicked European models and carried names such as 'Pigalle', 'Elysée Bar', 'Lolita', 'Dollar', 'Violette et Elégance' or 'Diamant'. Only European-style drinks were served, especially beer produced locally by affiliates of Heineken and Kronenbourg. The bars reflected the vigour of African urban initiative and served many subtle social functions.[36] Most were established by élite members of the civil service, by clerks, domestic servants, and scouts, or catechists who served as social and cultural intermediaries in the colonial system. Bars were chiefly recreational, depending on their tripartite association with drinking, women, and dancing. They also had a political role, however, and political parties regularly held public meetings in them. It was a gathering at the 'Beauté-Brazza' that installed Fulbert Youlou as party leader before he won election as mayor of Brazzaville in 1956.

From Brazzaville, and from Kinshasa, recreational facilities spread rapidly into expanding suburbs and became targets of political surveillance. After the assassination of Marien Ngouabi in 1977, the Congo government ordered a year-long curfew, banned meetings of more than five persons, and limited the hours when drinks could be sold. To get around the vigilance of the authorities, places of illegal drinking and secret trading sprouted up in private homes where the owner could reserve the right of entry. These new *nganda* bars reflected the social differentiation that came to mark equatorial African towns. The *nganda* catered for the upwardly mobile while bars were patronised by the population at large. The *nganda* sold imported beer rather than the less expensive local varieties. Their expensive intimacy and discreet location made them ideal places for amorous encounters and for the political and financial dealings of the upper class.

Another complex area of daily life which experienced great effervescence after independence was religion. This was shown both by the forceful revival of the Catholic Church and by the popularity of syncretic and prophetic movements. Although long identified with colonial power, Catholicism gained credibility and influence under single-party regimes, both as a source of political resistance and as a substitute for the state which failed to provide adequate social services. In both Gabon and Congo the National Conferences demonstrated the renewed power of the Catholic Church. Even more influential was the proliferation of syncretic movements, which continually increased in strength and number. In the 1980s about a hundred were known in Congo, half of them in Brazzaville, and several dozen flourished in Gabon and the Central African Republic. Some were offshoots of long-established sects such as the Kimbanguists and Matswaists. Others were more recent off-shoots from the Catholic or Protestant Churches. Some of the newer groups were inspired by philosophical and mystical traditions from Europe such as the freemasons and the Rosicrucians, and some had Asian roots. Unlike some

36 C.-D. Gondola, 'Musique moderne et identités citadines, le cas du Congo-Zaïre', *Afrique Contemporaine* 168 (October–December, 1993), pp.155–68; also, see his *Villes Miroirs: Migrations et Identités Urbaines à Kinshasa et Brazzaville, 1930–1970*, L'Harmattan, Paris, 1996.

religious movements of the colonial period many sects were not overtly political, although their solidarity as social groups could lead them to joint political action. In consolidating their religious base the sects developed institutional strength. They also provided therapeutic services which competed with modern medicine as 'magicians' and *féticheurs* sought cures to combat the spread of ancient diseases and new afflictions such as AIDS.

Map 5.1   Zaire

CHAPTER 5

Zaire: the anatomy of a failed state

CRAWFORD YOUNG

The state does not exist or no longer exists in Zaire. It is no more than a skeleton which sustains the illusion.

Buana Kabue, 1978[1]

The balance sheet of . . . the last quarter-century is globally negative.

Zairian Prime Minister Mulumba Lukoji, 1991[2]

To say that Zaire has a government today would be a gross exaggeration.

Herman Cohen, former United States Assistant Secretary of State for African Affairs, 1993[3]

In 1978 the judgement of a former supporter of the Mobutu regime was still a rhetorical exaggeration. In the years that followed, a downward spiral of decay transformed opposition hyperbole into unhappy prophecy. By 1995 Mulumba and Cohen were understating their points. Zaire, a vast country richly endowed with natural resources, more fully approximated the description of 'collapsed state'.[4] Yet Mobutu Sese Seko (Joseph), who had mainly resided in recent years in his remote gilded palace in Gbadolite over a thousand kilometres from the capital, or in Europe, celebrated his thirtieth anniversary as president. He ruled over a fictive domain, boasting to his intimates that he might ultimately become known as the late president, but never as the former president.[5] Among the fifty-three African heads of state only Hassan

1 Buana Kabue, *Citoyen Président: Lettre ouverte au Président Mobutu Sese Seko . . . et aux autres*, L'Harmattan, Paris, 1978, p.23.
2 Crawford Young, *The African Colonial State in Comparative Perspective*, Yale University Press, New Haven, CT, 1994, p.282.
3 Cited in Herbert Weiss, 'Collapsed society, surviving state, future polity', in I. William Zartman (ed.), *Collapsed States: The Disintegration and Restoration of Legitimate Authority*, Lynn Rienner, Boulder, CO, 1995, p.157.
4 *Ibid.*
5 This statement was cited by various participants at a conference of Zairian intellectuals in the United States, convened in Lexington, Kentucky, 4–5 April 1996. The statement was to seem prophetic soon after, when Mobutu required surgery in Switzerland for an apparently fatal prostate cancer, though he actually lived until September 1997.

II of Morocco had ruled longer.[6] But the then prime minister, Mulumba, delivered a verdict of laconic candour on the Mobutu era from which few Zairian citizens would dissent.

A postcolonial history of Zaire[7] necessarily becomes a narrative of state decline. Analysis is shaped by the permanent crisis which afflicted the public realm after the mid-1970s. Civil society, however, developed survival responses to the progressive erosion of formal public institutions. Although state decline carried in its wake a large part of the formal economy, parallel processes of regeneration through local and regional initiative took root. In the silent but ongoing transformation of state–society relationships, the balance of initiatives shifted to the people. A reworking of economic relationships unfolded on a broad front and became an elusive but important element in the historical chronicle.

For analytical purposes the postindependence period can be divided into four phases. The First Republic, from 1960 to 1965, began with the achievement of independence. Its suddenness was wholly unanticipated, and it was almost immediately followed by a breakdown in the fragile formula for the transfer of power. After a brief moment of apparent revival this first epoch ended with a wave of rebellions which engulfed one-third of the country during 1963–65. The second period opened with a military seizure of power on 24 November 1965 which installed Mobutu in office. During the first decade of his rule the unity and authority of state institutions were restored but the personalisation of power by Mobutu reached dizzying heights. Under this autocratic state, redolent of the potent colonial regime but with an additional patrimonial overlay, a moment of seeming economic prosperity and expansion occurred. Retrospectively, however, the restoration was largely illusory. In the third period, beginning in 1974–75, rapid decline set in. State institutions progressively lost their capacity to transform public resources into accustomed services. An increasingly pervasive venality invaded the public realm at all levels. To the subject the state became not just the alien oppressor of colonial memory but a simple predator, at best irrelevant to the daily needs of the citizen. In the quest for survival society was on its own with the crumbling state at best an occasional impediment. Finally, in 1990, a fourth phase opened with a call for democratisation. For a brief moment the possibility of a transition to a new political order seemed open. However, Mobutu and his ruling clique soon fatally shattered this moment of renewed hope

6 Hassan II ascended the throne in 1961, on the death of his father, Mohammed V.
7 Terminological difficulties arise with respect to names of places and persons because of changing nomenclature over the years. Mobutu rebaptised the former Congo as Zaire in 1971. Provincial and many urban names were also Africanised at the same time or, in a few instances, earlier. In the same year all Zairians were required in the name of 'authenticity' to drop forenames of European provenance, and to take on African postnames. In recent years, the rigours of authenticity have slackened, and a number have reclaimed their earlier first names. In this chapter, we shall use 1971–1996 place-names throughout, providing the colonial designations on first encounter. For persons, we will employ the usual current form, with former first names also provided once in parentheses if known. In May 1997, when Laurent Kabila seized power, he restored to the country its former name of 'Democratic Republic of the Congo'.

with a series of manoeuvres designed to retain their grip on power. The consequence was accelerating decay in the remnants of the public realm and the formal economy, a prelude to the far-reaching crisis of 1996.

The Belgian colonial state, at its apogee, had a remarkable architecture of domination. It was metaphorically represented in the popular imagination as 'Bula Matari', the crusher of rocks. The Belgian apparatus of subjugation stood out in tropical Africa for the density of its white occupation, the scale of evangelising mission enterprises, and the reach of capitalist investment in enterprises and infrastructure. Authority, on the eve of independence, remained almost exclusively in the hands of Europeans, who included 10,000 civil servants, 1,000 military officers, 6,000 Catholic missionaries, and several thousand managers of colonial corporations.[8] Until 1959 there was no provision for African entry into the top three executive grades of the civil service, nor into the officer ranks of the army. At the beginning of 1960, only three of the top 4,500 functionaries, and no army officers, were Zairian.[9]

Intoxicated with the apparent success of their supervision and the extraordinary prosperity generated by the postwar commodity boom, the colonial state managers did not hasten to promote change. Until the late 1950s they imagined that a gradual incorporation of Zairians into shared responsibility over decades could occur in partnership with Belgium and the substantial community of 110,000 Europeans in the country. Not until 1956 did a Zairian voice challenging this leisurely timetable become audible.[10]

Belgian expectation of gradual change based on metropolitan blueprints was shattered in January 1959 when order in the capital, Kinshasa (Léopoldville), dissolved in several days of urban rioting. In the immediate aftermath of this seismic, if leaderless, event which shook the colonial state to its foundations, King Baudouin uttered a fateful pledge of independence 'without undue precipitation, but without fruitless delays'. In the turbulent months that followed, the colonial state lost control over key districts, particularly in lower Zaire, Kwilu and Maniema.

In the newly opening political space nationalist movements sprang up across the country, reaching out both from Kinshasa and from the six provincial capitals. In their struggle to reach an audience, audacity and intransigence became the currency of competition.[11] Political parties were strongly marked by a battle for ethnic constituencies, especially those associated with social competition in Kinshasa and the regional capitals.

8 For detail on the colonial state, see Crawford Young, *Politics in the Congo*, Princeton University Press, Princeton, NJ, 1965, and literature cited therein.
9 *Ibid.*, p.402.
10 For a collection of the basic texts of Zairian nationalism in the terminal colonial period, the documentary yearbook of the Centre de Recherche et d'Information Socio-Politiques, *Congo 1959*, CRISP, Brussels, 1960, remains invaluable.
11 For detailed treatment of terminal colonial nationalism, the key early works have not been supplanted; see in particular Herbert Weiss, *Political Protest in the Congo*, Princeton University Press, Princeton, NJ, 1967; René Lemarchand, *Political Awakening in the Congo: The Politics of Fragmentation*, University of California Press, Berkeley, CA, 1964; Benoît Verhaegen and Jules Gérard-Libois, *Congo 1960* 2 vols, CRISP, Brussels, 1961.

The once-monolithic colonial superstructure cracked in many places. The Catholic hierarchy began to disengage from its formerly resolute support for 'Bula Matari' in 1956. Belgian trade union federations sponsored affiliates in the colony, while political parties and their clienteles manoeuvred for colonial advantage. As events spun out of control on the ground, the rapid political evolution of British and French colonies cast a growing shadow and the Cold War superpowers sought potential allies.

Belgium, acutely aware of its weakness and mesmerised by the agonies of France in its calamitous colonial war in Algeria, faced narrowing options as 1960 dawned. Uncertainty grew over the reliability of the colonial constabulary, the *Force Publique*, in containing nationalist agitation. The immediate economic prospects in the colony were also sombre; budget surpluses ended in 1957, and by 1960 the Belgian Congo had accumulated an external debt of one billion dollars.

In a desperate effort to regain the initiative, Belgium invited the leaders of the Congo political parties to a round-table conference in Brussels in January 1960 to discuss the terms and timetable for independence. This remarkable assembly, which prefigured the wave of 'sovereign national conferences' in francophone Africa in the early 1990s, brought together eleven Zairian and three Belgian parties. The Zairian parties at once pledged themselves to a common front and insisted that the conference decisions should be binding. On the Belgian side a decisive factor was the inclusion of the opposition Socialist Party as a participant, thereby transferring negotiating authority from the government to the political parties.[12]

The united Zairian delegates insisted that the conference begin by agreeing to immediate independence. Even the parties most sympathetic to the Belgian perspective, the administration's own *Parti National du Progrès* (PNP) and Moise Tshombe's *Confédération des Associations Tribales du Katanga* (Conakat) supported independence and the Belgian negotiators had no room for manoeuvre. They thus took a gamble, the '*pari congolais*'. In it they conceded to the nationalist demand for an immediate transfer of power. In so doing they assumed that the actual transition to Zairian rule would occur after independence rather than before.

The essence of the 1960 deal was that a political superstructure would be rapidly created. Provincial and national elections would be organised in May and provincial and national ministries would assume political responsibility. But the core of the colonial state – the bureaucracy and the army – would remain under Belgian command. The economy would continue in the hands of the colonial corporations. Of the great institutions of the colonial system only the Catholic Church had begun to Africanise, though the top hierarchy remained Belgian. The jubilant nationalist leaders had nevertheless gained far

12 On this extraordinary conclave, see Georges H. Dumont, *La Table Ronde Belgo-Congolaise*, Editions Universitaires, Paris, 1961; Verhaegen and Gérard-Libois, *Congo 1960*, I, pp.15–69; Pierre de Vos, *La Décolonisation: les Evénements du Congo de 1959 à 1967*, Editions ABC, Brussels, 1967, pp.47–76.

more than they had anticipated, that is, the winning of immediate independence. The Belgians calculated that the goodwill they had purchased would satisfy the politicians with the trappings of power and make a long period of informal postcolonial tutelage feasible. They also hoped that the 'moderate' parties would fare well in the election, due to the residual influence of the colonial administration and its rural chiefs.

In retrospect, Belgian reasoning seems fatuous, at best, yet the circumstances of the time offered little real choice. Nearly four decades later, the judgement of the most authoritative account of the transition still stands: 'The chance of succeeding was slight, but still one must prove it was not the only one. The failed decolonisation of the Belgian Congo was perhaps inevitable'.[13]

Electoral discourse was dominated by those politicians most forceful in exposing the iniquities of the colonial system. 'Moderation' on the hustings was scarce and the PNP quickly proved a weak vessel for Belgian hopes. In the mood of exhilaration and sense of limitless possibilities offered by universal electoral competition, there were two kinds of appeal, one an aggressive nationalism and the other an appeal to ethnic and regional audiences.

Three crucial Zairian figures who emerged from the independence struggle were Patrice Lumumba, Joseph Kasavubu and Moise Tshombe. Through his subsequent martyrdom, Lumumba eclipsed the other two as an historical icon.[14] In 1958 he participated in the creation of what became the most important nationalist party, the *Mouvement National Congolais* (MNC). When the party split in 1959 the MNC-Lumumba faction retained its national audience. Mercurial, charismatic, endowed with matchless oratorical skills in three vehicular languages, Lumumba commanded a following among young urban intellectuals and radical nationalists throughout the country. In addition to his passionate anti-colonial nationalism Lumumba also enjoyed an ethno-regional constituency which stretched beyond the confines of his own small Tetela group to include similar populations in Maniema and the Mongo groups of the central Congo basin. In the city of Kisangani he appealed also to migrants from the rural hinterlands.[15] Overseas, the captivating force of Lumumba's personality reached the minister of colonies, Auguste Buisseret, who had extensive contact with him on a 1954 visit. Lumumba also had two royal audiences with King Baudouin during the latter's tour of the colony in 1955.[16]

13 Verhaegen and Gérard-Libois, *Congo 1960*, I, p.8.
14 Born in eastern Kasai, Lumumba achieved visibility in the *évolué* ranks in Kisangani (Stanleyville) in the middle 1950s, as a postal clerk maintaining a febrile activity in a range of *évolué* associations. In 1957, he became promotion agent of a major beer firm in Kinshasa.
15 By far the best evaluation of Lumumba is provided by Jean-Claude Willame, *Patrice Lumumba: La Crise Congolaise Revisitée*, Karthala, Paris, 1990. See also Thomas Kanza, *The Rise and Fall of P. Lumumba: Conflict in the Congo*, Rex Collins, London, 1978; J. van Lierde, *La Pensée Politique de Patrice Lumumba*, Présence Africaine, Paris, 1963; Pierre de Vos, *Vie et Mort de Lumumba*, Calmann-Lévy, Paris, 1961.
16 Willame, *Patrice Lumumba*, pp.30-1. At this time, the nationalist doctrines of Lumumba had not yet taken clear form, and he continued to extol the achievements of the coloniser, while advocating greater rights for the subject and a partnership for the *évolué* class. See his posthumously published manuscript, written in 1956, Patrice Lumumba, *Le Congo, Terre d'Avenir*,

Particularly influential for Lumumba was his attendance at the 1958 pan-African conference in Accra, where he met Kwame Nkrumah and Sekou Touré. Their vision of a radical mass single party as the motor of African liberation profoundly marked his political perspectives.

Kasavubu, by contrast, spent his entire career in Kinshasa and his native lower Zaire region. He was enigmatic and passive, and his political prominence came through the leadership of the *Alliance des Bakongo* (Abako), an ethnic association which became a political party. In 1956, before such bold language became common, the Abako included 'immediate independence' among its demands during the first municipal elections. As independence neared, the Abako struggle for Kongo rights, particularly in the contested terrain of Kinshasa, evolved into a claim for a federal structure for the new state.[17] Although Kasavubu had appeared the most intransigent challenger to the colonial state in 1956, by 1960 his opposition to a unitary nationalist agenda created the impression, particularly in Belgium and the West, that he was a suitable foil for Lumumba.

The ascent of Tshombe found an explanation in his strategic location at the heart of the Copperbelt, the most important centre of mineral wealth and the source of half the state's revenue and foreign exchange. Affable, malleable and ambitious, Tshombe emerged as leader of a political movement, Conakat, which expressed the resentment of southern Shaba (Katanga) over the domination of the Copperbelt towns by immigrants from neighbouring Kasai.[18] Tshombe, who was connected by marriage to the Lunda royal house, was the son of one of the rare Zairian merchants prosperous enough to own a motor car before the Second World War. He formed alliances with the European settler population in Shaba and with the powerful mining giant, *Union Minière du Haut-Katanga* (UMHK), thereby deeply staining his nationalist image in the country, in Africa, and in progressive circles abroad.

The 1960 elections, whose integrity was not disputed, inevitably reflected the political fragmentation of the country, the strong influence of ethnic and regional votes and the short time to mount electoral campaigns. The parties had only had the weeks between the round-table conference in February and elections in May to mount their campaigns and few were organised outside the urban centres. In the voting no party gained a majority but the psychological

---

Est-Il Menacé?, Office de Publicité, Brussels, 1961, and Jean-Marie Mutamba Makombo, 'Patrice Lumumba correspondent de presse (1948–1956)', *Cahiers Africains* 3 (1993). The collection of his letters appearing in the colonial press confirms that the general tenor of the ideas expressed in the book, contested by some as a distortion, did reflect the drift of his thought at an earlier stage, tailored to conform to officially tolerated forms of expression.

17 This was probably untrue; a persuasive dissent to the secessionist suspicions is provided by Loka ne Kongo, 'La pensée politique de Kasa-vubu', Mémoire de licence, Université Nationale du Zaire, Lubumbashi, 1974. For biographic details, see Charles-André Gilis, *Kasa-vubu au Coeur du Drame Congolais*, Editions Europe-Afrique, Brussels, 1964, and the account by his sometime mentor and advisor, A. A. J. Van Bilsen, *L'Indépendance du Congo*, Casterman, Paris, 1962.

18 On the Shaba background, see especially Jules Gérard-Libois, *Sécession au Katanga*, CRISP, Brussels, 1963, and Crawford Young, 'The politics of separatism: Katanga 1960–63', in Gwendolyn M. Carter (ed.), *Politics in Africa: 7 Cases*, Prentice-Hall, New York, 1966, pp.167–208.

triumph went to the unitary nationalist parties. The Lumumba party won 33 of the 137 seats, mainly in the Kisangani hinterland, but also gained one national seat in each of the six provinces. Together with his allies Lumumba held 41 seats compared to only 15 for the conservative nationalist PNP. The regional parties which supported a unitary state had 30 seats and their alliance gave Lumumba a narrow majority.[19]

Creating a viable government was difficult. Belgium hoped for a moderate alliance around Kasavubu to circumscribe Lumumba.[20] The swirling under-current of hidden advisers influenced the bargaining between the shifting parties, their factions and individuals. In a fragile compromise Lumumba accepted the post of prime minister, rather than that of president. A week before independence he won narrow approval in the Chamber of Represent-atives with 74 votes out of 137. The agenda for a unitary state was even more ominously threatened by a plot to declare the Shaba province independent. This was blocked by the colonial administration on the eve of independence.

THE FIRST REPUBLIC, 1960–65

Independence day on 30 June 1960 was heavy with uncertainty. No one could imagine what independence would be like. For Zairians there was mingled exhilaration and apprehension, soaring hope among the young, nourished on extravagant political promises, but also diffuse fear of the unknown. For the Europeans, bewildered by the suddenness of the loss of domination, appre-hensions ran much higher.

The precarious formula for independence dissolved in less than a week. The trigger of change came from an unexpected direction when a mutiny of the *Force Publique* on 5 July rapidly spread across the country. Within three days the now embattled Lumumba announced a nearly complete Africanisation of the army officer corps and the departure of the majority of Belgian officers. On 11 July the wealthiest province, Shaba, declared its secession from the new state and Belgian forces intervened to give the secession an opportunity to consolidate itself. Panic swept through the European population and exag-gerated reports of rape and assault by mutinous soldiers seemed to confirm their fears. On 12 July Belgian functionaries were given permission to flee the country in view of the insecurity and were offered guarantees of civil service careers in Belgium. Those in the rebel province of Shaba, however, were instructed to remain at their posts. Even more provocatively, Belgian troops were dispatched to Zaire to protect European lives and property, a move which proved highly inflammatory. Within a fortnight of independence,

19 The *Parti Solidaire Africain* in Kwilu, the *Centre de Régroupement Africain* in Kivu, and the *Cartel Katangais* in north Shaba.
20 See the documentary account of his mission by Belgian Resident Minister W.J. Ganshof van der Meersch, *Fin de la Souveraineté Belge au Congo*, Institut Royal des Relations Internationales, Brussels, 1963.

the Lumumba government had thus lost control over its army, seen its administration stripped of its top cadres, found a revolt in its richest province being protected by the former colonisers, and witnessed the return of Belgian troops to a number of its major towns.

The crisis became international and drew in an array of global forces which helped shape the first phase of Zairian independence. A war of rival visions overlay the struggle for power in a state deflated by the loss of control over its army. The contest magnified the differences separating the contenders and sustained an illusion of coherence amongst the shifting protagonists of nationalism and federalism. In Africa the more radical states perceived the struggle as pitting African liberation against imperial subjugation. Cold War protagonists projected upon the conflict their own interpretive vocabulary of global competition, 'communist penetration' and 'Western imperialism'. The United Nations, whose secretary-general, Dag Hammarskjold, nursed large ambitions for the organisation to become a protector of newly independent countries, envisaged a neutral role. Yet its decision-making structures and operating staff had to incorporate the conflicting ambitions of the major powers. The multiple prisms of perception both simplified and distorted the unfolding realities as the magnitude of international involvement in Zaire grew.[21]

United Nations involvement began in mid-July with the arrival of the first international contingents of troops, whose mission was to restore order and replace Belgian units. From the outset there was a fundamental misunderstanding between Lumumba and Hammarskjold over the United Nations' role. For the former, the international body was obligated to uphold and enforce the authority of his government, while for the United Nations Secretariat the task was to insulate the country from unilateral international interventions. This misunderstanding deepened by August when key United Nations officials came to share the American and Belgian judgement that Lumumba was too erratic and irrational to be trusted, while Lumumba concluded that restoration of his legitimate authority would require support from radical African states and the Soviet Union.

On 5 September, President Kasavubu announced that he was 'revoking' the prime minister's appointment, an act urged upon him by the American, British and French ambassadors as well as by the Catholic hierarchy and opposition parties. There were indications that Lumumba had intended to end the

21 The 'Congo crisis' has attracted a literature commensurate with its amplitude. In addition to the CRISP documentary yearbooks, published from 1959 through to 1967, particular mention should be made of Madeleine G. Kalb, *The Congo Cables: The Cold War in Africa from Eisenhower to Kennedy*, Macmillan, New York, 1982; Richard D. Mahoney, *JFK: Ordeal in Africa*, Oxford University Press, New York, 1983, both of which made extensive use of declassified American diplomatic documents; Stephen R. Weissman, *American Policy in the Congo*, Cornell University Press, Ithaca, NY, 1974. Various former United Nations officials contributed autobiographical accounts: Conor Cruise O'Brien, *To Katanga and Back: A UN Case History*, Hutchinson, London, 1962; Rajeshwar Dayal, *Mission for Hammarskjold: The Congo Crisis*, Princeton University Press, Princeton, NJ, 1976; Indar Jit Rikhye, *Military Adviser to the Secretary General: U.N. Peacekeeping and the Congo Crisis*, Hurst and Company, London, 1993, among others.

uncertainty with a bid for full powers for himself. The legality of Kasavuba's 'revocation' was debatable, but the United Nations, in close cooperation with the United States, chose to accept its validity and prevented an effective Lumumba response.

Kasavubu named Joseph Ileo as prime minister, but there was no possibility of a parliamentary confirmation and Lumumba won a large majority in both chambers in favour of cancelling his dismissal by Kasavubu. A week later, the young colonel serving as chief of staff, Mobutu Sese Seko (Joseph), announced that the army had seized power, neutralised both Kasavubu and Lumumba, and installed a provisional government of university students.

The institutional breakdown meant that the struggle for internal power now occurred outside the framework of legal process. Kasavubu, Mobutu, and the youthful interim government enjoyed decisive support from the population of Kinshasa, which was heavily dominated by ethnic groups opposed to Lumumba. Key United Nations officials were reserved, if not downright hostile to Lumumba and were thus disposed to interpret Security Council mandates in a manner favourable to Kasavubu. Colonel Mobutu, initially a Lumumba ally, had changed sides, and developed links with the American Central Intelligence Agency (CIA) and anti-Lumumba elements among the United Nations staff. He was able to gain relative control over factions of the national army located in and near Kinshasa. Finally, Western, especially American, capacity for diplomatic and covert action far exceeded that of the Soviet Union. In contrast to the Angolan crisis fifteen years later, the Soviet Union at the time lacked the capability for a rapid projection of its power into a crisis arena as distant from its homeland as Zaire.

In September 1960 Lumumba found himself under house arrest, his residence surrounded by Ghanaian troops, who in turn were surrounded by the Zairian army. In a daring bid to recover the initiative, Lumumba managed to elude his captors, and sought to make his way overland to Kisangani about a thousand miles away. He was, however, captured at midpoint on this odyssey, and confined to a military prison in lower Zaire beyond United Nations surveillance. Already far larger than life, particularly in progressive African and radical anti-imperialist circles, no incarceration could remove Lumumba from the political equation. The CIA therefore engaged in its notorious schemes to assassinate Lumumba.[22] The actual assassination was carried out near Lubumbashi (Elizabethville) on 17 January 1961. The assassins were Zairians acting with Belgian complicity.[23]

Once martyred, Lumumba became a myth larger than life in Africa's collective memory. His complex persona and extraordinary charisma were flawed

22 Kalb, *Congo Cables*, pp.129–52.
23 Thomas Kanza, who though closely linked to Lumumba is a generally reliable source, lists among those involved to some degree Fernand Kazadi, Jonas Mukamba, Victor Nendaka Bika, Justin Bomboko Lokumba, Damien Kandolo, Albert Delvaux, Mobutu, Kasavubu and Ileo; *The Rise and Fall of Lumumba*, pp.346–47; Tshombe and Godefroid Munongo also belong on the list.

by an impulsive judgement and an autocratic disposition. His dream of an integral state[24] harnessing the institutional force of 'Bula Matari' to the vision of African liberation, became a symbol of Africa's struggles. His assassination marked the nadir of Zaire's initial postcolonial crisis. Lumumbist forces regrouped in Kisangani and proclaimed themselves the custodians of legality under deputy-premier Antoine Gizenga who was backed by the Soviet bloc and radical Afro-Asian states. When the assassination of Lumumba became known in February 1961, the international furore badly tarnished the image of the Kinshasa regime. It also placed Zaire's western supporters on the defensive.

In the months that followed efforts were made to restore credible authority in Kinshasa, and to bring back into the fold the rebel provinces of South Kasai, Shaba and Kisangani. An appearance of constitutional legality was restored in August 1961, when a new government headed by the trade unionist Cyrille Adoula won an overwhelming vote of confidence in a parliament attended by all except Tshombe's Conakat party.[25] The Adoula investiture brought to an end the initial crisis, and for a time seemed to promise an era of relative stability. In most of the country, the private sector, only briefly disrupted in 1960, resumed full operation. The South Kasai and the Kisangani dissidence ended, although the latter resumed again the following year, and political attention shifted to ending the Shaba secession. In January 1963 the mainly-Indian United Nations forces crushed the Tshombe gendarmerie and Zaire was reunited.[26]

This moment of optimism did not last long. Members of the former Lumumbist coalition, believing they had been outmanoeuvred at the Lovanium parliament and marginalised by Adoula, mounted an armed challenge to the regime. In January 1964, the first skirmishes broke out in the Kwilu region, under the leadership of Lumumba's former education minister, Pierre Mulele. Mulele, a particularly intransigent radical, had left the country after Lumumba's overthrow, travelled widely, studied guerrilla warfare in China, and returned to Zaire in July 1963 to organise an underground *maquis* in his native Kwilu district. In his forest camps he instructed his partisans in simple revolutionary ideas resembling Maoism but with a particular Mulelist gloss. The Mulelist bands, fortified by the belief that ritual protection provided supernatural invulnerability to the bullets of the national army, carried out a series of assaults on such symbols of government as mission stations, business installations and

24 Crawford Young, 'Zaire: the shattered illusion of the integral state', *Journal of Modern African Studies* 32, 2 (1994), 247–64. An integral state is a system of perfected hegemony and comprehensive domination.
25 The vote of confidence was not won by merit alone. The parliamentarians were isolated on the University of Kinshasa (then Lovanium) campus, then well outside Kinshasa, quarantined by UN detachments. The CIA discovered sewers penetrating into the campus, providing access to wavering delegates by cash-bearing emissaries.
26 For detail, see Gérard-Libois, *Sécession au Katanga*; O'Brien, *To Katanga and Back*; Young, 'Katanga'.

administrative outposts.[27] After initial successes, the excesses of the insurgents, and their narrow ethnic base, limited their impact and by mid-1964 the national army had regained the initiative.

After the repression of the Kwilu rebellion a second, eastern rebellion opened up in northern Shaba. The leaders were radical exiles from Brazzaville with an external sanctuary in Burundi. Under Gaston Soumialot and Nicolas Olenga the insurgent forces swept from Maniema into Kisangani in early August 1964, then reached Lisala in Equateur, Lodja in Sankuru, and drove the central authority out of most of Kivu and all of Haut-Zaire (Orientale). On 5 September 1964 Lumumba's ally, Christophe Gbenye, proclaimed a revolutionary government in Kisangani.

After the high-water mark of the rebellion factional struggle broke out among the leaders. The rebels committed atrocities by indiscriminately killing thousands of white-collar workers whom they accused of supporting the central government. Their excesses cast doubt on the nature of the revolution. At the same time rebel expansion reached the outer limits of the region where the invocation of Lumumba provided an effective revolutionary symbol. In quelling the rebellion the Kinshasa central government reinforced its army with several hundred foreign mercenaries and some units of the former Shaba gendarmerie. Mercenary-led columns, enjoying Belgian and American intelligence support, advanced on Kisangani as insurgents retreated, taking a thousand European and American captives with them as a 'white shield' to protect them against Kinshasa attack. On 24 November, Belgian paratroopers, transported by American planes, seized Kisangani, rescued the hostages, and struck a fatal blow at the rebels.[28]

A supply of arms from Algeria, Egypt, Sudan, Uganda and Tanzania arrived too late to alter the course of events. Also too late was the appearance in 1965 of the legendary Latin American organiser of world revolution, Ernesto 'Che' Guevara, with a few hundred Cuban followers. After several discouraging months in Zaire, Guevara concluded that revolutionary consciousness was insufficiently developed to permit his mission to bear fruit, and he quietly departed in November 1965.[29]

Although the disruptive impact of the rebellions was substantially greater than the disorders of 1960, economic life did soon recover. The lasting impact

27 On the rebellions, see especially the magisterial documentary and interpretive history, *Rébellions au Congo* 2 vols, CRISP, Brussels, 1966, 1969. See also Crawford Young, 'Rebellions and the Congo', in Robert I. Rotberg and Ali A. Mazrui (eds), *Protest and Power in Black Africa*, Oxford University Press, New York, 1970, pp.969–1011; Catherine Coquery-Vidrovitch, Alain Forest and Herbert Weiss (eds), *Rébellions-Révolution au Zaire 1963–1965*, 2 vols, L'Harmattan, Paris, 1987.
28 For detail on American involvement in the defeat of the rebels, see Sean Kelly, *America's Tyrant: The CIA and Mobutu of Zaire*, American University Press, Washington, 1993, pp.133–72. Kelly, a retired United States Information Service officer, scoured the presidential libraries and other government documentary sources, as well as interviewing many of the American participants in this episode.
29 Jules Gérard-Libois and Benoît Verhaegen are completing a monograph on the bizarre episode of the Guevara band and its failed effort to re-energise the rebellions. See also Daniel James, *Che Guevara: A Biography*, Stein and Day, New York, 1969, pp.131–60.

Crawford Young

Map 5.2   The rebellions of 1964

of the rebellion was psychological. The high levels of violence experienced had been traumatising for a large section of the population. Many people had hidden in the forests for weeks to escape from the rebel or national army. A powerful craving for peace and security provided support for a strong government at the time of the 1965 Mobutu coup. Three decades later the fear of violence persisted in vivid folk memories. Herbert Weiss estimated that the two rebellions took a million lives. Deep-rooted fear made militant mobilisation of the masses against a now discredited Mobutu regime seem impossible before the 1990s.[30]

Despite the rebellions a semblance of attachment to legal forms persisted during the First Republic. The six colonial provinces were reconstituted as twenty-one, loosely patterned along lines of ethnic self-determination, and shaped largely by the old colonial districts. In 1964 a constitutional commission produced a revised constitution which was approved by a fairly conducted referendum. In an astonishing political comeback the defeated premier of secessionist Shaba, Tshombe, resurfaced in 1964, this time on the national political scene. He disarmed his critics by promising to reduce American influence and to negotiate an end to the rebellions. Kasavubu appointed him as prime minister of a transitional government in July 1964. A year later parliamentary elections were fairly conducted in spite of the disruptive impact of the rebellions. Some 223 parties coalesced into loose-knit pro- or anti-Tshombe blocs. Tshombe created an extensive national alliance of forty-nine parties to support his bid for the presidency. The anti-Tshombe group absorbed most of the former Lumumba bloc. When the new parliament convened in October 1965 Kasavubu, in a surprise gambit, announced that Tshombe's transitional mission was complete. He named Evariste Kimba, another Shaba politician, as prime minister. The proposed Kimba cabinet, however, failed by thirteen votes to obtain parliamentary approval.

The impasse over the appointment of a prime minister set the stage for the Mobutu coup. The seizure of power does not appear to have been planned but rather took advantage of the stalemate in the political arena. At the October 1965 Organization of African Unity summit in Accra, Kasavubu had earned praise for his sacking of Tshombe and his pledge to dismiss his white mercenaries. This perceived leftward drift unsettled the American embassy. Lawrence Devlin, the Central Intelligence Agency station chief, and McMurtrie Godley, the American ambassador, urged Mobutu to act. Although the actual coup was not orchestrated by American intelligence – Devlin learned of it by the radio – the encouragement provided to Mobutu doubtless reinforced his own inclination.[31]

---

30 Weiss, 'Zaire', in Zartman (ed.), *Collapsed States*, pp.166–7. When I was teaching in Zaire a decade after the events, in 1973–75, the profound impact of the rebellions, and the deep fears of a recurrence of such a trauma, were encountered in innumerable conversations.
31 Kelly, *America's Tyrant*, pp.166–70. The Kelly account is based on his own observation as a correspondent in Kinshasa at the time, as well as interviews with Devlin.

THE MOBUTU REGIME ASCENDANT, 1965–75

The Mobutu seizure of power was greeted with surprising equanimity both within the country and elsewhere in Africa. Within Zaire the discredited political class, trapped in a demeaning impasse and fearful of the return of insecurity, helped win acceptance of the coup. Outside Zaire several African countries such as Ghana, Nigeria, the Central African Republic, Algeria and Benin, were installing military governments, while radical African governments accepted a regime that removed Tshombe from the scene. The Zaire parliamentarians, summoned into session the day of the coup, 25 November 1965, gave their approval to Mobutu by acclamation after receiving a promise, subsequently revoked, that they would continue to receive their salaries. The initial Mobutu cabinet contained representatives from each province and a well-respected army officer, Mulamba Nyunyi (Leonard), as prime minister.

Mobutu, whose durability demonstrated his versatility and cunning, was not in the front rank of the pre-independence figures; he won his position through strategic networks rather than nationalist agitation. An unruly youth, he was expelled from several schools, then incorporated into the army as a disciplinary measure. His excellent command of French and evident intelligence soon brought him to the notice of his Belgian officers, and he was assigned to a staff position at the non-commissioned officers' school in Kananga (Luluabourg). This posting proved a critical strategic resource in ways that could not have been anticipated. The most promising non-commissioned elements of the colonial army attended training courses there. In later years these cadres who had known Mobutu were suddenly promoted when Belgian officers fled following the July 1960 mutiny. After his release from the army in 1956, Mobutu, who enjoyed the sponsorship of some anti-clerical Belgian army officers, settled in Kinshasa as a journalist. In 1959, with the abrupt opening of a crash training programme in Belgium for the évolué class, Mobutu was sent to a training institute for journalists in Brussels where he stayed until the eve of independence. Here he formed critical links with a network of American and Belgian intelligence services. He also participated in radical nationalist politics on the basis of which Lumumba appointed him his chief-of-staff after the July 1960 mutiny. At this critical point Mobutu was thus in a position to gain a decisive control over the greater part of the post-mutiny army, particularly in the western half of the country. During the First Republic, he had been a key member of the shadowy 'Binza Group', an informal caucus around Adoula and Kasavubu which also kept in touch with Western embassies and the Central Intelligence Agency which provided it with resources and services.

In 1965 Mobutu claimed extra-constitutional legislative powers for a five-year period, and appropriated full legislative authority. Political parties were swept away. He abolished elected provincial institutions soon after and, in a major recentralisation of power, reduced the number of provinces from twenty-one to eight, plus the capital district. He developed a potent text of legitimation

by imposing on the First Republic an interpretive grid of 'chaos'. The 'very
existence of the Nation has been threatened', he lamented. 'The social, economic, and financial situation of the country is catastrophic.' His perception
of the 'disorderly shambles' created by his predecessors contributed a degrad-
ing new French word, 'Congolisation'.[32] Mobutu's therapy for this malady
of 'Congolisation' was a return to the robust state tradition of 'Bula Matari'.
His administration would radiate downward and outward from a single presidential centre and recapture the citizen as a compliant subject. This revived
state doctrine was articulated in forthright terms by Engulu Baanga Mpongo
(Leon) in a 1974 speech to the Makanda Kabobi Institute for party ideological
instruction:

> The administrative organisation of the Colony, the hierarchical military
> type, was a heritage of the structure established by Leopold II for the
> occupation of Zaire. It was founded on the principle of unity of command,
> which means that, for whatever action, an official receives his orders only
> from one chief. Wishing to create and maintain in the administration, as
> among the people, a unity of views and action, Belgium entrusted complete
> responsibility for the colonial enterprise to a single cadre: the territorial
> service. The real motivation for concentration of function in the territorial
> cadre was political. It was necessary to indicate to the population that
> authority was one and indivisible.

Mobutu soon adopted fear and intimidation as a weapon in the consolidation of his power. In May 1966 four former ministers of the First Republic,
Kimba, Jerome Anany, Emmanuel Bamba and Alexandre Mahamba, were
arrested on conspiracy charges, tried for treason by a military tribunal, and
publicly hanged before 50,000 spectators. In justifying these arbitrary executions, Mobutu spoke bluntly: 'One had to strike by a spectacular example,
and create the conditions for a disciplined regime. When a chief takes a decision, he decides, full stop'.[33] In the following year, the former rebel leader
Mulele was lured across the river from his exile in Brazzaville by a promise
of amnesty. Once returned he was immediately arrested, tried by a military
tribunal, and executed. Mobutu was anxious to extinguish any residual claims
to First Republic legitimacy and Kasavubu, who had retired penniless to his
home village in lower Zaire, died in 1969 without being given access to
medical assistance. It was widely rumoured that he had been poisoned.[34]

Another potential claimant to legitimacy, who had been scheming to make
a comeback from exile in Spain, was Tshombe. By taking a belligerent stance
towards Tshombe, Mobutu bolstered the legitimation of his regime and in
March 1967 Tshombe was tried in absentia for treason, and condemned to

32 Mobutu Sese Seko, *Mobutu: Discours, Allocutions et Messages, 1965–1975*, Editions J. A., Paris, 1975, I, pp.20–1.
33 Kamitatu, *La Grande Mystification*, Maspéro, Paris, 1971, p.176.
34 Monguya Mebenge (Daniel), *Histoire Secrète du Zaire*, Editions de l'Espérance, Brussels, 1977, p.147.

death. Tshombe had maintained some contacts in Belgian financial milieux, and was surrounded by a doubtful assortment of adventurers. In 1967 one of these lured him aboard a small plane which was then hijacked to Algiers, where the authorities obligingly imprisoned him. Two years later his death was announced, officially of a heart attack, although other explanations were whispered in Zaire.[35]

With the remnants of the First Republic swept away by the end of 1966, Mobutu was ready to formalise a new institutional order. A constitution was drafted, confirming in judicial prose the recentralisation of state power and its concentration in the hands of the president. At the same time, a new political party was launched, the *Mouvement Populaire de la Révolution* (MPR), as an instrument of political monopoly. The regime had by now erased its military origins, and presented itself with a political public face modelled on the mass single-party formula then ascendant in Africa. 'Bula Matari' was back, but with a political superstructure above its autocratic bureaucracy.

The ascendancy of the Mobutu regime was well-nigh complete. Fear and intimidation certainly played a part, as they had in the colonial state. But so also did relief experienced by the population at the end of the period of disorder; the new regime was able to claim legitimacy by contrasting discipline and order with 'Congolisation' and rebellion. The runaway inflation of the late First Republic was staunched and a new, initially stable currency introduced. Most of the political class, in return for submission and loyalty, found rewarding positions in the restored state. Promising careers were available for virtually all the university students beginning to graduate in significant numbers. Zaire was fully rehabilitated as a member of the African family of nations, as symbolised by the choice of Kinshasa as the venue for the 1967 Summit Conference of the Organization of African Unity.

The following eight years were a period of political and economic expansion during the flood tide of the Mobutu regime. The personalisation of power was reinforced and the political class was transformed into a service class as key personalities from the First Republic with significant regional followings were assigned to foreign ambassadorships, relegated to minor ministries, retired to profitable private mercantile pursuits or imprisoned. The power of patronage was perfected by granting positions in the political bureau of the MPR, and by rotating membership of the council of ministers with its opportunities for winning personal wealth. In the first decade of Mobutu rule, some 212 persons held positions on one or other of these two bodies though only 41 served as long as five years and only Mobutu served continuously. Threats as well as rewards were important in sustaining loyalty and 29 of the 212 went directly from office to prison while another 26 were removed on charges of

35 On Tshombe, see the admiring biography by Ian Colvin, *The Rise and Fall of Moise Tshombe*, Leslie Frewin, London, 1968, and his own memoire on his brief reign, Moise Tshombe, *Quinze Mois du Gouvernement au Congo*, Table Ronde, Paris, 1966. For a résumé of the various theses concerning his kidnapping, see Crawford Young and Thomas Turner, *The Rise and Decline of the Zairian State*, University of Wisconsin Press, Madison, WI, 1985, pp.419–20.

disloyalty or dishonesty. Disgrace and prison seldom lasted long, however, and could be followed by rehabilitation, a return to favour, or help in finding a commercial career.[36]

Patronage and personalised power led to an obligatory personality cult and presidential adulation reached amazing levels of fawning sycophancy. Public references to the president were accompanied by praise-names such as 'guide of the Zairian revolution', 'helmsman', 'father of the nation' and 'founding president'. Spokesmen invoked the analogy of a village, the nation writ small, whose people recognised in their chief an ancestral embodiment, a nurturing protective father, a firm and unquestionable authority entitled to obedience. The hagiographic character of public discourse in the personality cult was captured by then-minister of the interior, Engulu:

> In our religion we have our own theologians. In all religions, and at all times, there are prophets. Why not today? God has sent a great prophet, our prestigious Guide Mobutu – this prophet is our liberator, our Messiah. Our Church is the MPR. Its chief is Mobutu, we respect him like one respects a Pope. Our gospel is Mobutism. This is why the crucifixes must be replaced by the image of our Messiah. And party militants will want to place at its side his glorious mother, Mama Yemo, who gave birth to such a son.[37]

The complete concentration and personalisation of power was embodied in the 1974 constitution. Mobutu was vested with the power to name all members of the council of ministers, national legislature, supreme court, and party political bureau. 'Mobutism' was declared a constitutional doctrine, and 'deviationism' was a high crime. For one brief period the press was even forbidden to mention any official other than Mobutu by name and identified them by their office titles only.[38]

The expanding ambition and changing character of the regime found reflection in the ideological realm as well. In a first version, the regime characterised its doctrine as 'authentic Zairian nationalism', the primacy of the territorial nation over ethnic identities, the supremacy of African rights over European, the jealous defence of sovereignty. Only socialism was missing from the mainstream discourse of African nationalism current at the time and authentic Zairian nationalism was deemed 'neither left nor right' but vaguely progressive through its 'revolutionary' content. In 1971, the official doctrine was redefined as 'authenticity', a programme of cultural self-assertion. It was inspired by Senghor's *négritude* and enacted a sweeping Africanisation of place-names and a replacement of 'Christian' or, as Mobutu sometimes said, 'Jewish' first names with Zairian postnames. Clothing of European derivation

36 Young and Turner, *The Rise and Decline*, pp.167–8.
37 *Zaire-Afrique* 91 (January 1975), 25.
38 These attributes won for Mobutu a place of choice in the influential study by Robert H. Jackson and Carl G. Rosberg, *Personal Rule in Black Africa*, University of California Press, Berkeley, CA, 1982.

was banned in favour of the collarless suits of loosely Maoist sartorial style
called 'abacos' meaning '*à bas les costumes*' ('down with suits'). Full-length
African cloth replaced dresses for women. Then, in 1974, 'authenticity' gave
way to 'Mobutism', which emphasised the words, spoken or written, of the
president. As the regime tilted into permanent decline after 1975, however,
ideological discourse gradually faded from the scene.

Nationalist zeal, patrimonial practice, and personalised style intertwined
with economic policies during the expansion of the Mobutu regime. The
abruptness of decolonisation had left unresolved the often outrageous claims
of colonial corporations towards the Zairian state. In response, the Bakajika
Law of July 1966 stipulated that all public land belonged to the state, and that
all land-grants and concessionary powers delegated to colonial corporations
by the Belgian colonial state were to be annulled. The corporations were
given one month to file claims for holdings they actually exploited. These
claims were generally confirmed, but huge stakes in territories held in reserve
were not. According to the leading Belgian financial journal, 48 per cent of
the total land surface of Zaire had been pre-emptively claimed by one or
another concessionary company but these reserves were now forfeited.[39]

The major target of the new concession legislation was the mineral giant
Union Minière du Haut Katanga (UMHK) which, in 1965, produced 300,000
tons of copper, nearly 10,000 tons of cobalt (then half the internationally
traded total), 174,000 tons of zinc concentrates, and smaller amounts of various precious metals. In addition to its mineral operations, UMHK controlled
an array of subsidiaries in Shaba. Its assets were valued at $430 million and it
provided 50 per cent of Zaire's state revenue, and 70 per cent of its foreign
exchange.[40] Within three months of Mobutu's 1965 coup his advisers decided,
in a private meeting, that some form of takeover of UMHK was indispensable. Kamitatu, in a dissertation on the subject, puts his finger on the core
motivation:

> The decision to nationalize UMHK was a political act, deliberately and
> carefully prepared. Its objective was less, for the decider [Mobutu], the
> recovery of the economic independence of the Nation, than the consolida-
> tion of presidential power, the budgetary underpinning of which was basic-
> ally constituted by fiscal levies on UMHK . . . The second political aspect
> of nationalization was the presidential determination to remove from UMHK
> the capacity to offer financial backing to potential political opponents of the
> regime, in particular Moise Tshombe, considered to be the protégé and
> secular instrument of UMHK.[41]

39 *Echo de la Bourse*, 24 August 1970.
40 Jules Gérard-Libois, 'L'affaire de l'UMHK', *Etudes Congolaises* 10, 2 (March–April 1967),
pp.1–4; Pierre Joye and Rosina Lewin, *Les Trusts au Congo*, Société Populaire d'Editions Politiques
de Paris, Brussels, 1961, pp.217–22.
41 Kamitatu Massamba, 'Problématique et rationalité dans le processus de nationalisation du
cuivre en Afrique Centrale: Zaire (1967) et Zambie (1969)', Ph.D. dissertation, Institut d'Etudes
Politiques de Paris, 1976, p.181.

114

A titanic struggle ensued, with Zaire demanding that UMHK register as a purely Zairian corporation and the company threatening to withdraw its expatriate personnel and block the sale of Zairian copper. Zaire feverishly sought other corporate partners willing to take on mine management before a compromise was reached in February 1967 whereby the Zairian operations of UMHK were turned over to a state corporation, the *Générale des Carrières et des Mines* (Gécamines). The terms proved very fruitful for UMHK which created a sister company to take on a management contract for the mining operations under the giant Belgian holding company, the *Société Générale de Belgique*.[42]

A series of grandiose development projects was launched in the expanding years of the Mobutu regime, with a steel mill at Maluku near Kinshasa; a giant dam on the lower reaches of the Zaire River at Inga; a long-distance power line from Inga to Shaba; an ambitious new copper mining project; an array of infrastructure projects; and a number of multinational manufacturing plants. The outcome of these superficially impressive but often poorly conceived ventures and visions, which were driven by Mobutu's 'inflexible will to transform the equatorial forest into a terrestrial paradise' according to one publicist, was economic decline.[43]

The zenith of the regime's expansion in the economic sphere was a set of measures known as 'Zairianisation'. This 'radicalisation of the revolution', was crafted by Mobutu in solitary reflection in 1973 and 1974. These surrealistic edicts, which swiftly led to catastrophe, confiscated the assets of foreign residents in the commercial and plantation sectors and allocated them in a patrimonial distribution mostly to leading political figures and their clientele. In the following year, Mobutu announced a 'war on the bourgeoisie' and proclaimed a state takeover of private ventures along with what remained of the colonial business sector. The predictable dislocation of large sectors of the domestic economy forced a humiliating retreat in 1976, but the damage inflicted on the economy was a major factor in triggering national decline.[44]

One feature of the regime's expansion had been its international dimension. Zaire had a vocation of *grandeur*, of leadership in Africa and beyond, which would be commensurate with its geographic dimensions and resource endowments. In the extravaganza which celebrated the sixth anniversary of his coup, Mobutu proclaimed the goal of making Zaire 'a great international power'.[45]

42 Young and Turner, *The Rise and Decline*, pp.289–95. At the end of the 1980s, Belgium itself experienced a profound cultural shock when the SGB, the core symbol of Belgian capitalism with some 1,261 subsidiaries, and large holdings by the monarchy itself, was taken over by the Groupe Suez of France; Renée C. Fox, *In the Belgian Chateau: The Spirit and Culture of a European Society in an Age of Change*, Ivan R. Dee, Chicago, 1994, p.21.
43 Manwana Mungongo, *La Général Mobutu Sese Seko Parle du Nationalisme Zairois Authentique*, Editions Okapi, Kinshasa, n.d. (1972?), p.116.
44 For detail, see Young and Turner, *The Rise and Decline*, pp.326–62; Michael G. Schatzberg, *Politics and Class in Zaire: Bureaucracy, Business and Beer in Lisala*, Africana Publishing Company, New York, 1980, pp.121–74; David J. Gould, *Bureaucratic Corruption and Underdevelopment in the Third World: The Case of Zaire*, Pergamon Press, New York, 1980, pp.50–60.
45 *Africa Contemporary Record, 1971–72*, p.B540.

He masterminded an active African diplomacy, serving for a time as patron and mentor of smaller African states, such as Rwanda, the Central African Republic, Chad, and Togo. He also sponsored one of the main Angolan insurgent movements, the *Frente Nacional de Libertação de Angola* (FNLA). In 1970 he visited ten other African states and in 1973 spent as many as 150 days outside Zaire. He sought privileged relationships with China and North Korea, as well as with the United States and France. On 4 October 1973, in an address of astonishing audacity to the United Nations General Assembly, he declared that, 'between a brother and a friend, the choice is clear', and that he was therefore breaking off relations with Israel. A cascade of similar actions followed in Africa and his spectacular gesture was rewarded by an invitation to attend an Arab state summit as the sole non-Arab participant.

STATE DECLINE 1975–90

The turn of Zaire from expansion to accelerating decline began in 1974–75. The process of decay was not immediately visible, however, since an aura of strength surrounded the regime and there was little sign of internal opposition. The small coteries of Mobutu's exiled opponents had little audience and one by one they were brought home with promises of posts. The regime was visibly reliant upon citizens from Equateur province, especially from Mobutu's own Ngbandi group, for sensitive posts as in the security apparatus and the presidency. Undercurrents of disaffection were detected in groups such as Kongo and Luba-Kasai which believed themselves disfavoured, though numerically they were reasonably represented in the top ranks of the political élite. Intellectuals were privately critical but their public views were carefully dissimulated. Zaire in 1975 had the appearance of a leviathan state, a cunningly crafted design of perfected hegemony. All Zairians were party members by birth, and party pins bearing the Mobutu effigy were worn on formal occasions. Even university students felt it necessary to turn out for the frequent support marches, harangues by dignitaries, and ritual celebrations of deference to state power.[46]

The appearance of solidity, however, was deceptive. Callaghy astutely characterised the country as a 'lame leviathan'.[47] The cost of management by patronage was now exorbitant and state power was vulnerable to an economic downturn. Corrosive venality was now on a scale which attracted unwelcome notice. The state could no longer assure promising careers to the swelling number of university graduates. Managerial weakness in the parastatal sector was exposed. The armed forces, which had performed respectably in limited

46 One may note that two major inquiries into Zairian politics, separately initiated in 1973, both addressed the theme of the plenitude of regime hegemony. Thomas M. Callaghy, in his masterful study, *The State–Society Struggle: Zaire in Comparative Perspective*, Columbia University Press, New York, 1984, began with a comparison of the construction of absolutism in the France of Louis XIV and in Zaire. My co-author, Thomas Turner, and I began our research with authoritarianism as the primary focus.
47 Callaghy, *The State–Society Struggle*, passim.

116

engagements during the first Mobutu decade, were now much weaker.[48] The mood of the citizenry at large was now resigned rather than moderately supportive of Mobutu as had been the case in his early years in office.

The first signs of downward drift occurred in 1974 when prices fell on the copper market after a long favourable period, and by the next year this decline was taking a heavy toll of export revenues and tax flows. The New York price fell from a record high of $1.40 per pound in April 1974 to 53 cents per pound in early 1975, and by 1977 reached an all-time low. In 1975 Zaire exports were worth only half their 1970 value and negative growth rates became persistent. The first public sign of impending bankruptcy was the suspension of export insurance guarantees by the Belgian *Office Décroire* in April 1975. On 20 October 1975, the *Wall Street Journal* revealed the Zairian failure in debt repayments. By that time, Mobutu, after exploring all other avenues, found himself compelled to initiate discussions with the International Monetary Fund (IMF), thus beginning a two-decade charade of external debt management. Once international financial representatives began prowling through state financial records, information concerning cases of embezzlement multiplied.

The Angola fiasco of 1975 was another major blow to Mobutu. At the time of the Portuguese coup d'état in April 1974, Mobutu appeared to hold trump cards concerning Angola's future, and perhaps hoped to secure a share of Angola's oil by laying claim to the Angolan enclave of Cabinda. The FNLA, operating under Mobutu's tutelage from Zairian bases, had Angola's largest guerrilla force and Mobutu also exercised substantial leverage over one of Cabinda's political factions. Both the United States and China joined Zaire in backing the FNLA. The main rival, the *Movimento Popular de Libertação de Angola* (MPLA), was at the time badly splintered.[49] The end game, however, proved disastrous for Mobutu as the MPLA overcame its divisions, received large-scale Soviet and Cuban support, and emerged triumphant. Not only did the FNLA guerrillas perform poorly, but Zairian army units sent to attack Luanda in September 1975 broke rank and fled. The intervention of South African forces, the exposure of the CIA involvement in the Angolan campaign, and the subsequent defeat of the invasion, placed Mobutu in a damaging light.[50] By participating in such an unholy alliance, Mobutu undid much of his careful African diplomacy. His regime never regained the standing it had hitherto enjoyed and was henceforth embattled externally, economically and politically.

The economic decline never ceased, though there were moments of remission in the late 1970s and in the mid-1980s. Stretched resources and aggravated

48 Young and Turner, *The Rise and Decline*, pp.248–75. The primary engagements were against the weak remaining pockets of rebel resistance, a Shaba gendarme mutiny in 1965, and a mercenary revolt in 1967. Closely inspected, each of these cases revealed significant weaknesses.
49 See the chapter on Angola in this book.
50 For confessional details, see John Stockwell, *In Search of Enemies: A CIA Story*, W. W. Norton and Company, New York, 1978. The best account of the Angolan civil war remains John Marcum, *The Angolan Revolution* 2 vols, MIT Press, Cambridge, MA, 1969, 1978.

debt crises meant that maintenance of state infrastructure steadily declined. The debt had risen to $3 billion by 1975. Zaire received an initial loan from the IMF in 1976 and managed an initial round of rescheduling agreements with private and public creditors. Thereafter, Mobutu engaged in an unending dance with his creditors. In the words of one scholar, Zaire exhibited an 'amazing ability to consistently circumvent reform efforts'.[51] By the early 1990s, the international financial institutions had severed their relationships with Zaire. The external debt had reached $10.3 billion; this figure was 445 per cent of recorded exports, and 141 per cent of Gross National Product (GNP).[52] By 1995 the debt was $12.3 billion, and payments were $5.5 billion in arrears in 1994.[53] There was no possibility of repayment and the process whereby the debt could be written off remained a mystery.

Hyperinflation was another mark of decline. The reformed Zairian currency, introduced at a rate of two 'zaires' to the dollar in 1967, held its value until 1974. Accelerating inflation set in thereafter and the exchange rate reached seven million 'zaires' to the dollar by 1993. At that time a 'new zaire' was introduced, with a nominal exchange value of three million old 'zaires' for one 'new zaire'. By 1995, the value of Zairian money in terms of the original currency had sunk to 21,072,000,000 per dollar.[54] Zaire had become the undisputed world champion with inflation rates of 2,155 per cent in 1991, 4,129 per cent in 1992, 1,890 per cent in 1993, 23,770 per cent in 1994, and a mere 542 per cent in 1995.[55] The frequent need to introduce new and larger denomination bank notes became a major source of revenue for Mobutu.

During the Mobutu era, from 1965 to 1990, the average annual growth rate in GNP per capita, according to World Bank data, was –2.2 per cent. There was a strongly positive growth until 1974, but decline thereafter, with a disastrous deterioration to a negative growth of –8.42 per cent annually between 1990 and 1995.[56] By 1995 the Economist Intelligence Unit estimated the per capita income at $125, making Zaire the fourth poorest country in the world.[57] There can be no doubt that the economic standing of the great bulk of the population was far below that achieved on the eve of independence.

An important factor in plunging the economy into decline was the diversion of resources into the private enrichment of Mobutu and his entourage. Exceptional amounts of the official budget, as much as 20 per cent, were allocated to the presidency by the 1970s. Outlays from these funds were not subject to any financial control. In addition, the Bank of Zaire was frequently

51 Winsome J. Leslie, *The World Bank & Structural Transformation in Developing Countries: The Case of Zaire*, Lynne Rienner, Boulder, CO, 1987, p.156. The Leslie study is a useful summary of the debt negotiation saga.
52 World Bank, *World Development Report 1992*, OUP, New York, 1992, pp.258,264.
53 I am indebted to Pierre Englebert, author of the Zaire Economist Intelligence Unit reports, for these figures.
54 Economist Intelligence Unit, 'Zaire Country Profile, 1995–96'.
55 Pierre Englebert, personal communication.
56 World Bank, *World Development Report 1996*, p.218.
57 *Ibid.*

ordered to turn over large amounts of foreign exchange to the president. Nguza Karl-i-Bond, in one of his moments of defection from being a Mobutu henchman, testified to an American Congressional hearing, Bank of Zaire documents in hand, that between 1977 and 1979 personal expenditure by the Mobutu family, financed by foreign exchange diverted from the central bank, totalled $150 million annually.[58] Mobutu was also a major beneficiary of the Zairianisation measures and most of his properties were exempted from retrocession.[59] Another frequent practice was to divert shipments of copper, cobalt or diamonds from the state mining corporations to his personal account. The presidential fortune has been estimated to total $5 billion at its peak but a precise figure is impossible to document.[60]

Corruption became an instrument of control permeating the state apparatus. Mobutu himself stigmatised the practice in a speech to the 1977 MPR Congress:

> In a word, everything is for sale, anything can be bought in our country. And in this flow, he who holds the slightest cover of public authority uses it illegally to acquire money, goods, prestige, or to avoid all kinds of obligations.
>
> Even worse, the citizen who simply asks for his most legitimate rights to be respected is subjected to an invisible tax, which is then openly pocketed by officials.[61]

The unrelenting economic decline from 1975 threw into sharp relief the calamitous miscalculations in the gigantic development projects launched in the early 1970s, which were the source of most of the Zairian debt. The Inga dam merits particular attention, as the largest and most damaging of these schemes. Between a quarter and a half of the national debt was attributable to this project, which had two phases of hydroelectric dam construction, the steel mill, and the Inga–Shaba 1,800 kilometre direct current transmission power line.

There were indeed phenomenal energy possibilities amounting to 13 per cent of the world's unexploited hydroelectric potential in the 300-metre drop in the Zaire river between Kinshasa and Matadi. A series of parallel dry valleys into which the river could be diverted and dammed added to the attractions. The Belgians had made tentative plans for tapping these energy resources as early as the 1920s, but had set the project aside as uneconomic. The first 300-megawatt phase of the Inga project was to service Kinshasa, but one of its major anticipated customers, the Maluku steel mill, proved a costly fiasco.

58 Nguza Karl-i-Bond, *Mobutu ou l'Incarnation du Mal Zairois*, Rex Collings, London, 1982, p.127.
59 For detail, see Young and Turner, *The Rise and Decline*, pp.179–81.
60 The American television programme 'Sixty Minutes' advanced the $5 billion figure in a 4 March 1984 segment on Zaire; some diplomats have argued that this figure is too high. It has probably shrunk significantly in recent years; the decaying Zairian economy no longer provides the possibilities of diversion that existed in the 1970s, and the costs of purchasing the loyalty of key military units and a critical minimum of political figures remains high.
61 Gould, *Bureaucratic Corruption*, p.49.

The mill was constructed by Italian and German contractors at a cost of $250 million. The feasibility study, which had been carried out by a firm tied to the eventual Italian contractors, had presumed that iron ore deposits would be developed using immense Zairian state investments and offered inaccurate projections of both market prospects and production costs. The mill's theoretical capacity of 250,000 tons of steel per year was four times Zaire's requirements. After the mill was opened in 1975, actual production peaked early at 25,000 tons and never exceeded 10,000 tons after 1978, until the plant was closed in 1986. The machinery was limited in the kinds of steel it produced. It had operated with imported or local scrap iron to produce low-grade steel at eight times the cost of better-quality imported steel.[62]

An even greater disaster awaited Inga II and the Inga–Shaba power line. The only market for the new 1200-megawatt capacity of Inga II was the Shaba mining complex. The second phase of the dam was begun in 1973 and became operational in 1977 at a reported cost of $260 million. The Inga–Shaba power line was the object of intense competition between contractors and eventually cost close to $1 billion, four times the initial estimates. Americans won the lion's share of the contract with muscular backing from the American embassy. Work began in 1973 and was only completed in 1982, six years behind schedule and well after loan repayments should have begun. By the time the project was finished, changed market conditions led the company, which had intended to exploit rich copper deposits in *Union Minière's* reserves, to abandon new mining although it had sunk $250 million into the project. By the 1990s Gécamines, the state holding company was in acute distress, starved of foreign exchange to maintain its infrastructure, and subjected to frequent presidential diversion of its products. Copper output, which had peaked at 471,000 tons in 1985, dropped to 35,000 tons in 1994.[63] Only 18 per cent of the Inga II hydroelectric capacity was used and about 20 per cent of the Inga–Shaba line.

There were alternative energy possibilities in Shaba which could have been developed at a fraction of the cost of Inga. The logic of the actual choice thus requires closer examination. Political motivations are part of the explanation. In the years of expansion, the Mobutu regime's claim to legitimacy rested in part on grandiose development aspirations. Politics rather than development lay behind the Inga–Shaba scheme, however, and ensured that the formerly secessionist province of Shaba would become dependent on Kinshasa for its energy. Any revival of the secessionist claim of 1960 could henceforth be extinguished by the throw of an electric switch. Another perverse logic also underlay the scheme. Key participants such as foreign contractors, lenders, embassies, and the president, all had short-term interests in concluding a deal which would immediately benefit them, while shifting the long-term risks to

62 This section is based upon Jean-Claude Willame, *Zaire: L'Epopée d'Inga: Chronique d'une Prédation Industrielle*, L'Harmattan, Paris, 1986, and Young and Turner, *The Rise and Decline*, pp.296–309, and sources cited in the latter work.
63 Economist Intelligence Unit, 'Zaire Country Profile', 4th quarter 1995 and 3rd quarter 1996.

the Zairian state and ultimately to Zaire's citizens. No external capital was interested in any of these projects. Foreign contractors were bidding to participate in a lucrative contract without incurring any liability for the viability of the project. International bank lenders assumed that rich mineral deposits would be collateral, and that the international financial institutions would police Zairian loan repayments. The competing American, British, German, French and Italian contractors enlisted the support of their embassies. Successful ambassadors won credit for winning business for their national firms and were serving elsewhere (or retired) when the bills came due. On the Zairian side the contracts carried very large sub rosa commissions. Overall this package of projects involved $2 billion. In comparative perspective, and translated to the scale of the United States economy, such a family of ventures would cost $4 trillion.

One major shortcoming in a direct current transmission line was the cost of building transformer substations to serve cities in its path. Initially, the line went direct from Inga to Kolwezi in Shaba. Subsequently, the line was tapped for branches to Mbandaka and Bandundu. Some surplus power was also sold to Zambia. Hallucinatory schemes surfaced at times to help pay the loan, as when Zaire and Egypt announced plans to build a branch, the 'Mobutu–Mubarak' line, to Egypt at a cost of $28 billion and passing through the endemic civil war zones in Sudan.[64]

The mystique of invincibility of the Mobutu regime was punctured by the 'Katanga gendarme' incursions of 1977 and 1978. Remnants of the former Tshombe gendarmerie had taken refuge in Angola where they were joined by young opponents of the regime from Shaba who were victims of repression aimed at those accused of sympathising with the former secession. The Portuguese permitted the refugees to form camps in Angola as leverage against Mobutu's support for FNLA insurgents. Some exiles had been used by the Portuguese as military auxiliaries but when colonial rule crumbled in Angola, the refugees sided with the MPLA and continued to enjoy sanctuary. In March 1977 a small, lightly armed group of 1,500–2,000 men crossed the border into Shaba and advanced on the crucial copper centre of Kolwezi. The Zairian army offered almost no resistance and the invaders were only stopped by the intervention of Moroccan troops flown in French aircraft using American logistical support. The insurgents retreated into Angola without seeking engagement with the Moroccan forces. In May the following year the rebels struck again, this time capturing Kolwezi. The incompetence of the Zairian armed forces was again laid bare and it was French and Belgian paratroops, with overt American logistical backing, that drove the invaders back to Angola.[65] Also revealing was the popular reaction. No one rallied to the side of the Zairian army in resisting the invaders but neither did the incursion trigger

---

64 Economist Intelligence Unit, 'Zaire 1995–96'.
65 The best treatment of these episodes is Jean-Claude Willame, 'Contribution à l'étude des mouvements d'opposition au Zaire: le F.L.N.C.', *Cahiers du CEDAF* 6 (1980).

a public uprising as happened later in the successful 1996 Rwanda-supported rebellion led by Laurent Kabila in Kivu.[66]

The Mobutu regime had always relied in part on fear and intimidation to sustain its ascendancy, even in its expansive phase. With its authority and legitimacy in visible decline, the role of repression in securing the submission of subjects became more important. In the words of a former helicopter pilot, who served in the Zairian air force from 1975 to 1986, 'many of our soldiers are ashamed to belong to a corps capable only of terrorising our fellow citizens'.[67] The repressive arm of the state operated not simply with calculated coercive acts directed at specific opposition figures, but also through the generalised insecurity created by its undisciplined troops. Only a handful of élite units charged with protecting the inner corps of the regime were regularly, and in the case of the *Division Spéciale Présidentielle* handsomely, remunerated. The units deployed in the countryside received supplies and pay irregularly and they survived only by preying on the citizenry.[68] These oppressive aspects of the regime were long overlooked abroad but drew more attention when Amnesty International published damaging reports in 1983 and 1986.

With the decay of the Mobutu order opposition began to coalesce openly.[69] In the wake of the humiliating necessity to summon Moroccan troops to turn back the FLNC invaders in 1977, Mobutu gave a remarkably candid speech denouncing the flaws in the regime, though not of its president, and labelling the situation as the 'mal zairois'. His external patrons, particularly in the United States, pressed for a depersonalisation of power, the creation of a prime minister, and some empowerment of the single-party legislature. In 1978 newly emboldened parliamentarians interrogated ministers on a wide variety of issues involving corruption. The following year, after an incident in which army units slaughtered over two hundred clandestine diamond diggers in Kasai Oriental, deputies from the region boldly demanded a commission of inquiry, and defiantly circulated information about the atrocities overseas. In 1980, when Mobutu sought to close down political debate, thirteen parliamentarians published a fiery fifty-one-page open letter to Mobutu, claiming that the incarnation of the 'mal zairois' was Mobutu himself:

> We know how allergic you are to candour and truth. . . . For fifteen years now we have obeyed you. What have we done, during this time, to be useful and agreeable to you? We have sung, danced, animated, in short, we

66 Weiss, 'Zaire', p.167, underlines the significance of the inert popular reaction. Especially in 1977, for the brief moment when the insurgents seemed to advance without resistance, Zairians of high and low station confided secret hopes for their success. But no one made an overt move.
67 See the compelling memoir of a former Zairian army helicopter pilot, Pierre Yambuya, *Zaire: L'Abbatoir*, Editions EPO, Brussels, 1991, p.5. Yambuya, now in exile, working with Amnesty International, describes in chilling detail a number of sordid operations he observed in which officers or others suspected of infidelity to Mobutu were liquidated.
68 This pattern of oppression through generalised insecurity finds incisive analysis in Michael G. Schatzberg, *The Dialectics of Oppression in Zaire*, Indiana University Press, Bloomington, IN, 1988.
69 A Belgian journalist, Colette Braekman, provides an excellent description of the decline years; *Le Dinosaure: le Zaire de Mobutu*, Fayard, Paris, 1992.

have been subjected to all sorts of humiliations, all forms of subjugation which even foreign colonisation never made us suffer. . . .

After fifteen years of the power you have exercised alone, we find our-selves divided into two absolutely distinct camps. On one side, a few scan-dalously rich persons. On the other, the mass of the people suffering the darkest misery.[70]

Only complete political liberalisation could remedy the situation, they concluded.

At the end of 1980, the first imprisonment of the new opposition leaders occurred and throughout the decade, the leadership was in and out of prison. In his now well-honed style of coping with dissidents, Mobutu mingled threats with blandishments. Of the original thirteen parliamentary opponents some rejoined the regime but a hard core formalised their group as the *Union pour la Démocratie et le Progrès Social* (UDPS) in 1982. The movement shrewdly made its claims in terms of legitimacy, eschewed an armed uprising, and carefully avoided ideological terminology which might permit Mobutu to stigmatise it as externally orchestrated. 'Socialism', for example, was never mentioned and the discourse remained rigorously liberal and democratic.[71] In confronting Mobutu, the UDPS had one weakness. Although its leaders came from all regions and there was no trace of regionalism in its doctrine, prom-inence was given disproportionally to Luba-Kasai antecedents and, in particu-lar, to the group's leading voice, Etienne Tshisekedi wa Mulumba. Mobutu's most effective tactic of retaliation was probably to play the ethnic card and spread the word that the Union reflected Luba ambitions.

THE SHADOW GAME OF DEMOCRACY 1990–95

At the end of 1989 the shock waves from the fall of the Berlin Wall, and the simultaneous crumbling of autocracies across Africa, washed over Zaire and inaugurated the fourth phase of post-independence politics. Beginning in Benin at the opening of 1990, the concept of the 'sovereign national conference' swept across francophone Africa. In this moment of enthusiasm, the United States, France and Belgium formed a united front to insist that Mobutu par-ticipate in the 'wave' of democratisation. In the early weeks of 1990 Mobutu travelled the country, to engage in a 'dialogue with the people'. This technique, employed with useful effect in the past, no longer served as a therapeutic exercise. Expressing their bitterness with astonishing boldness, citizens told him in scathing terms about their quarter-century of accumulating discontent.

Mobutu's regal response was to announce on 24 April 1990 the demise of the Second Republic and the birth of a Third. The MPR monopoly of power was abandoned and a limited multi-party system was initiated. The symbolic

70 Jean-Claude Willame, *L'Automne d'un Despotisme: Pouvoir, Argent et Obéissance dans le Zaire des Années Quatre-Vingt*, Karthala, Paris, 1992, pp.132–3.
71 An excellent and detailed account may be found in Jean-Claude Willame, 'Chronique d'une opposition politique: l'UDPS (1978–1987)', *Cahiers du CEDAF* 7–8 (1987).

accoutrements of the party-state were jettisoned: citizens could reclaim their birth-names if they chose, and 'abacos' disappeared as obligatory attire. Mobutu, of course, would remain 'the arbiter, the ultimate recourse, and last rampart of the Nation', the 'pacifier', and the 'unifier' of the country.[72] The unleashed energies of popular discontent could not, however, be so easily controlled. The regained presidential initiative was lost again the next month when commandos were dispatched by Kinshasa to punish University of Lubumbashi students who had shown hostility towards colleagues from the president's home region. In a nocturnal raid on the campus dozens of people were murdered. The crisis was followed by an acceptance of an unlimited multi-party system and an immediate proliferation of political parties occurred. The UDPS of Tshisekedi drew upon the credit earned by its courageous role throughout the 1980s. Leading figures of the First and Second Republics created their own parties: the *Parti Démocratique Social-Chrétien* (PDSC) of Ileo, the *Union des Démocrates Indépendants* (UDI) of Kengo wa Dondo, the *Union des Fédéralistes et Républicains Indépendants* (UFERI) of Nguza, and others. With the multiplication of parties now the dominant pattern, Mobutu himself financed a number of small groups, and renamed his own party the *Mouvement Populaire de la Renouveau*. By 1991 the opposition sought to coalesce into a *Union Sacrée de l'Opposition Radicale* while the panoply of Mobutist parties was loosely coordinated as the *mouvance présidentielle*. In August 1991, a gargantuan National Conference was convened, composed of no less than 2,750 delegates.[73] For three years the national conference sought to render effective its claim of sovereignty, to force Mobutu from office, following the script successfully followed in neighbouring Congo, and also in Benin and Niger. At moments the delegates appeared on the verge of success but Mobutu was equally determined to cling to power. Throughout, he was able to retain control of the inner core of his security forces and also of the Bank of Zaire with its supply of foreign exchange.

Three threads ran through this tangled skein of events. One was the shifting flow of factional and personal rivalries. Both the *Union Sacrée* and the *mouvance présidentielle* were beset by frequent defections. On the left two parties claimed to be the legitimate heirs to Lumumba, one of them led by Antoine Gizenga, his former deputy prime minister. In the disillusioned observation of a former Lumumba associate, Thomas Kanza, power and money were indissolubly linked. 'It seems to me', he wrote, 'that it is money that directs the political dance in Zaire. Ideological differences are almost nonexistent, political opposition is only theoretical. Everything, or almost everything, is a function of money'.[74]

---

72 Jean-Claude Willame, 'Gouvernance et pouvoir: essai sur trois trajectoires africaines, Madagascar, Somalie, Zaire', *Cahiers Africains* 7–8 (1994), p.127.
73 1,095 representing 'civil society', 855 from the over 300 political parties, 14 from the presidency, 88 from the civil service, 222 from parliament, 340 from territorial entities, and 100 specially invited dignitaries; *ibid.*, p.131.
74 *Elima* (Kinshasa), 12 September 1991, quoted in Willame, 'Gouvernance et pouvoir', p.133.

A second thread was ethno-regional tension. A blacklist of the ethnic identities of national conference delegates was published in 1992 and purported to show that a majority were from Kasai.[75] A large-scale 'ethnic cleansing' of Kasai Luba had been officially instigated in the Copperbelt cities of Shaba in 1991, evoking unhappy memories of similar expulsions in the secessionist days of 1961. It was estimated that 100,000 people were driven out of Shaba. In North Kivu repeated attacks occurred, also incited by officials, against groups of 'doubtful nationality', particularly Tutsi and Hutu from Rwanda, most of whom had settled in the area many decades previously. The tactic, which left 6,000 dead and 150,000 displaced, bore bitter fruit in 1996 when an uprising of those who had been victimised plunged Zaire into its deepest crisis.

A third thread in the experience of the 1990s was the continuation of violence. In Kinshasa, especially, repeated mass demonstrations and strikes often met with army repression, resulting in numerous casualties. In September 1991 and again in January 1993, army units went on destructive rampages in the capital and elsewhere, protesting at their miserable conditions. On the latter occasion, the French ambassador was killed. Widespread looting occurred and army camps became 'thieves' markets' where stolen goods were openly for sale.

In 1992 Mobutu escalated his pressure on the opposition. The National Conference nevertheless appointed Tshisekedi as prime minister and he received the endorsement of 70 per cent of the delegates. A new transitional constitution was adopted by the National Conference in November 1992 and a Council of the Republic was appointed to supervise the transition to democracy. Meanwhile, Mobutu retaliated by reviving his own former parliament, whose electoral mandate had expired, and in December 1992 he announced the 'dismissal' of the Tshisekedi government. The Council insisted that Tshisekedi should remain in office although Mobutu had named his own alternative prime minister. Thus, by early 1993, Zaire had two governments, two parliaments, two constitutions – and virtually no state.

In October 1993, despite the vehement objections of the radical opposition, an accord was reached and a joint transitional parliament appointed Kengo to be prime minister in June 1994. A constitution was agreed and a referendum and national elections were planned for 1995. This timetable proved impractical and a new date was set for 1997.[76]

In 1995 Mobutu thus still appeared to be able to ride out the storm. Increasingly remote from the country, spending most of his time isolated in his palatial establishment in Gbadolite, Mobutu had long ceased dreaming of the 'terrestrial paradise' he would construct in Zaire. One of his former security agents, Emmanuel Dungia, argued persuasively that 'by 1979, [Mobutu] no longer had any illusions about his capacity to build a modern country and to restore a badly compromised situation. His ambition thereafter became limited

---

75 *Le Soft de Finance* (Kinshasa), 11 January 1992, cited in Willame, 'Gouvernance et Pouvoir', p.134.
76 For the most recent period, this account is based primarily on *Africa South of the Sahara 1996*, and the Economist Intelligence Unit Zaire reports, Europa Publications, London, 1996.

to the accumulation of personal wealth to prepare for his retirement'.[77] Retirement, however, became problematic when Mobutu underwent surgery in August 1996 for prostate cancer, a condition widely expected to be fatal.

Two decades of national decline had profound consequences for the survival of ordinary people. The decay of the public realm forced much of the population into a parallel economy which expanded in tandem with the progressive deterioration of the state. Janet MacGaffey, the most careful student of this phenomenon, wrote:

> Officially the economy of Zaire is in a state of disaster; exports cannot keep up with imports, production lags, industry barely functions, scarcities are rife, the infrastructure has deteriorated drastically, wages are at starvation level and nothing works as it should. But the reality on the ground is that, despite the severe economic crisis, a population of 35 million people, which is also the third largest in terms of urban population in sub-Saharan Africa, finds the means to survive, with some people thriving and becoming wealthy.[78]

The scale of the second economy is impossible to know or measure. It is not entirely disconnected from the state, whose agents prey upon it for their own survival. A large part of this parallel economy relies on foreign trade and access to currencies with real value. State employees purportedly engaged in policing and regulating foreign transactions have a privileged access to the benefits. Presidential wealth also derives from smuggling. The critical items of the hidden sector are easily transportable goods of high value relative to their volume. Thus, gold, diamonds and ivory are major second economy commodities. In 1993 an estimated 300 million dollars' worth of diamonds were smuggled. Coffee produced near the eastern frontier was also readily smuggled, as were stolen vehicles.

One measure of the magnitude of the 'real economy' was the array of consumer goods that continued to be available, even in small towns. Although prices far exceeded affordability for those who had formal employment, the market continued to find buyers as well as sellers. In reply to questions about survival Zairians claimed that 'we live mysteriously'.[79] There is considerable variation from one region to another as to the vitality of the parallel economy. Lower Zaire, Eastern Kasai, and the Butembo zone in Kivu have notably vibrant informal economies. Proximity to a border, the existence of a talented mercantile class,[80] and access to valuable resources such as gold or

77 Emmanuel Dungia, *Mobutu et l'Argent du Zaire*, L'Harmattan, Paris, 1992, p.15.
78 Janet MacGaffey, *The Real Economy of Zaire: The Contribution of Smuggling & Other Unofficial Activities to National Wealth*, University of Pennsylvania Press, Philadelphia, 1991, p.7.
79 *Ibid.*, p.8.
80 Vwakyanakazi Mukohya, 'Traders in Butembo', Ph.D. dissertation, University of Wisconsin-Madison, 1982, provides copious documentation on the emergence and role of a Nande trading network based on Butembo.

diamonds, all play a differentiating role. The parallel economy, through its regionalisation, maintains links from the countryside to major Zairian cities which possess distinctive external trade routes.

Thanks to local initiative, and to resources generated by the second economy, some local institutions operated surprisingly effectively despite their abandonment by the state. Private universities sprang up in several areas and operated with precarious resources. Schools functioned with parent and local community contributions. Non-governmental organisations became one of the few growth areas and largely replaced the state in service provision. External assistance, which totalled $169 million in 1993, was channelled through this sector.

An increasingly complex political economy arose as the burgeoning parallel markets intersected with pockets of state authority and with powerful local authorities which themselves often participated in the underground economy. With a domestic currency that was virtually worthless, accumulation often depended upon illicit trade both to gain foreign currency and to import foreign goods. International trade involved travel documents, visas, and evading or bribing customs agents. Protection from state depredation needed to be purchased and mafia-like organisations, often involving high officials, dealt in stolen property, ivory, smuggled vehicles of doubtful origin, and narcotics. These diverse networks extended into Europe, North America, neighbouring African states, and South Africa through a diaspora of established Zairian communities. Residual state institutions, representing an amalgam of the 'shadow state' described by Reno[81] and the 'rhizome state' of Bayart,[82] no longer bore any resemblance to 'Bula Matari'.

Far-reaching changes in Zairian society are hard to plumb. On the one hand the ravages of a decaying and largely predatory state have visited innumerable hardships on the subjects. Yet, from another perspective the period is marked by remarkable cultural creativity and transformation. Jewsiewicki has argued that Christianity and the colonial past have been absorbed as acknowledged elements in the collective heritage.[83] A particularly striking example of the reinvention of the past was the appearance of women's cloths bearing the effigy of Father G. Hulstaert, a colonial missionary ethnographer of the Mongo people. This was emblematic of a larger appropriation of missionary ethnography into a popular consciousness now permeated by a Zairianised reading of Christianity. A rich and distinctive popular culture also germinated in the paintings of urban folk artists such as Tshibumba,[84] and in ubiquitous Lingala songs. The media of cultural transmission were quintessentially modern – radios, cassettes, videotapes – but the content drew upon a syncretised Zairian heritage. Though much of popular culture was oral, literacy was surprisingly

81 William Reno, *Corruption and State Politics in Sierra Leone*, Cambridge University Press, Cambridge, 1995.
82 Jean-François Bayart, *The State in Africa: The Politics of the Belly*, Longman, New York, 1993.
83 I am particularly grateful to Bogumil Jewsiewicki for his astute and penetrating comments on cultural transformations in commentary intended for incorporation into this chapter.
84 B. Jewsiewicki (ed.), *Art Pictoral Zaïrois*, Editions du Septentrion, Sillery, Quebec, 1992.

high in spite of the disintegration of the state educational system. Schools supported by private initiative sprang up at all levels and a large proportion of the youthful urban population were pupils or students. According to Jewsiewicki, surveys in Kinshasa in the 1990s yielded the astonishing figure that less than 1 per cent of the men, and 2.2 per cent of the women, had received no education whatsoever; 38 per cent of the men and 21 per cent of the women had received some post-primary instruction. An emerging cultural and historical consciousness has a distinctively 'Zairian' cachet. It is perhaps these vital energies in the cultural realm, gravitating around a shared history and a common contemporary experience of struggle for survival, that explain the absence in the early 1990s of any serious efforts to dismantle Zaire, even though the degeneration of the state meant that a determined separatist movement would have met no effective resistance.

CONCLUDING REMARKS

The existence of Zaire is most visible as an imagined member of the world community of nation-states. One major trump card in Mobutu's hand, often adroitly played, has been the recognition which the regime continues to enjoy at least as a 'quasi-state'.[85] Emissaries from the opposition *Union Sacrée* appealed at OAU summit conferences in the early 1990s for a withdrawal of recognition for Mobutu, but their pleas fell on deaf ears. Belgium, especially after 1991, gave little support. By 1995 little remained of the once massive colonial presence, nor was there much inclination to restore it, even in changed circumstances.[86] France, after a momentary condemnation of autocrats at the La Baule francophone summit in 1990, restored Mobutu to respectable standing. The United States, though refusing entry to Mobutu after 1991, nonetheless continued to insist that he was a necessary element in Zaire's transition to a Third Republic. Through it all, Mobutu found ways to make himself indispensable to third parties. During the 1980s the CIA provisioning of the UNITA opposition in Angola had to pass through Zaire. In the 1994 Rwanda tragedy, when over a million Hutu refugees fled to Zaire, Mobutu discovered a new source of diplomatic leverage.

Two decades ago an article appraising the Zairian situation was entitled 'the unending crisis'.[87] The characterisation still applies. In the eyes of the citizenry, the state has lost whatever competence, credibility, and probity it once enjoyed. Skeletal remains may still be found in a handful of reliable military

85 Robert H. Jackson, *Quasi-States: Sovereignty, International Relations, and the Third World*, Cambridge University Press, Cambridge, 1990.
86 See the fascinating proceedings of a 1994 Brussels colloquium on the future of Belgo–Zairian relations. Belgium itself has profoundly altered in the postcolonial decades, into a loose-knit federation with an eroding national attachment. The question thus arises, as stated in the introduction to the volume, 'Who is still Belgian in Belgium? Is it not incongruous to ask what a Belgium which has ceased to exist can do for Zaire?' Gauthier de Villers, 'Belgique–Zaïre: une histoire en quête d'avenir', *Cahiers Africains* 9–10–11 (1994), p.13.
87 Crawford Young, 'Zaire: the unending crisis', *Foreign Affairs* 57, 1 (October 1978), pp.169–85.

units, a still proficient security service,[88] an often unpaid diplomatic cadre,[89] the presidential staff and palace, and the Bank of Zaire. The remaining official exports, especially diamonds, suffice to maintain this superstructure. Government offices around the country still have staff who deploy their energies in an unceasing struggle to ensure their own survival. But little remains of 'Bula Matari', or of the integrated state of which Mobutu dreamed in his regime's expansionist years. By 1993 Zaire even ceased to exist statistically when the World Bank stopped including Zaire data in the main tables of its annual *World Development Reports*. The IMF suspended Zaire's voting rights and placed its membership of the international financial community in limbo.

Nor can 'Bula Matari' be restored. Power has silently shifted downward, to several major regional nodes of the second economy, and to many more localised sites. This effective autonomy will not be readily surrendered to a successor regime aimed at restoring the unitary centralised state. Nor will such a regime have the coercive, institutional or material resources to compel compliance. Because of our disposition to imagine futures which are projections of the past, the future Zaire is beyond our ken. The only certainty is that it will bear little resemblance either to 'Bula Matari', or to the Mobutist state.

88 See the masterful portrait of 'the state as ear', in Schatzberg, *The Dialectics of Oppression*, pp.30–51.
89 In November 1994, the Zairian ambassador to Warsaw was found penniless and homeless in the railway station, evicted from the embassy quarters for non-payment of rent after having sold off all embassy property in a desperate effort to survive.

Map 6.1 Angola

CHAPTER 6

Angola: the challenge of statehood

CHRISTINE MESSIANT

Independence, which came to Angola in 1975 after fourteen years of armed struggle, brought dramatic change. Liberation was proclaimed amidst massive civil and international war; Portuguese settlers, who had dominated the life of the country, departed; and the winning *Movimento Popular de Libertação de Angola* (Popular Movement for the Liberation of Angola, MPLA) created a one-party system based on a 'Marxist-Leninist' model. Despite these tremendous ruptures, continuities over the years from 1960 remained apparent in 1996. The actors in the postcolonial conflict had already opposed one another during the anti-colonial war, and factors of social status and identity informed their political strategies. From 1961 the history of Angola's people developed under conditions of armed struggle, repressive regimes, and intrusive foreign influences. Although change was anchored in social processes, it was not inscribed in social, or ethnic, or cultural 'realities', but was determined by the armed confrontation of political forces. The colonial war had created divisions between Angolans, but the independence war and the subsequent armed conflict between UNITA *(União Nacional para a Independência Total de Angola)* and MPLA brought much deeper political antagonisms and social deaggregation. International factors and foreign military interventions bore a heavy responsibility for the dire situation which prevailed after two decades of independence.

When confronted with so convulsive a history, so many internal events and so many foreign actors, it seems well-nigh impossible to offer a 'simple' historical narrative, let alone an in-depth analysis of socio-political change.[1] Only the main structural factors and historical events will be underscored to give an image of how social struggles and political strategies were caught in the cogs of the Cold War. Ordinary Angolans may seem absent but they

1 This chapter is based mainly on fieldwork and research carried out in Angola since 1981. Syntheses of Angolan history can draw on only a limited number of original case studies and they are often heavily coloured by the ideological position of the writer. Although this chapter tries to take account of all 'hard facts', it is a personal analysis of Angolan history and exists alongside others that will be referred to both in the notes and in the bibliographic essay.

Christine Messiant

certainly were not. Forced into an historical process which was controlled by the confrontation of national and foreign military might, they adopted ingenious strategies but could barely master their circumstances.

'ULTRA-COLONIALISM' AND THE SOCIAL GROUND OF ANTI-COLONIAL REVOLT

The fifteen years after 1945 were for many African colonies a time of relative economic and social betterment, growing social differentiation, political liberalisation, and hopes for independence. For a great majority of Angolans, however, these years meant global economic regression, checked social promotion and a radical suppression of political activity. There was no hope that independence would arrive since Angola, like the other Portuguese territories, was trapped by the Salazar regime's refusal to decolonise. The empire was indispensable in creating a cohesive Portuguese nationalism. Moreover, the postwar economic profitability of Angola led Lisbon to hope that the 'jewel of the empire' could become a white man's colony. The armed struggle, which began in 1961 and was followed by important reforms of the Portuguese colonial regime, was grounded in this unreformed colonial society.

After the Second World War an increase in the international price of Angolan products, especially coffee, attracted hundreds of Portuguese to Angola. The majority were poor, with very little or no schooling or qualifications. The Portuguese state encouraged the process, but it was based on a backward economy and wanted the main benefits to go to Lisbon. In this period of 'ultra-colonialism'[2], racial discrimination and coercion were the primary means of achieving an expansion of the white economy and the protection of a vulnerable white population. Since the turn of the century, the colonial legal system had been based on the relegation of the 'non-civilised' population, the *indígenas* ('natives') to a status depriving them of civic and social rights and making them liable to wide-ranging coercion. Instead of being relaxed, the native code (*indigenato*) was put to full use after 1945, while the colonial state also 'managed' the corollary system of '*assimilação*' by which a minute part of the non-white population was recognised as 'assimilated' and, as such, was allowed entry alongside the whites to 'civilised' status although still subject to some forms of racial discrimination.

In Angola forced labour, commercial extortion and dictatorship were the structural elements of postwar colonialism, accompanied by an unprecedented extension of land alienation and the intensification of forced cultivation. For rural Angolans compulsory wage work represented a loss of labour for

2 The term was coined by Perry Anderson in his *Le Portugal et la Fin de l'Ultra-Colonialisme*, Maspero, Paris, 1963. On this period, see René Pélissier, *La Colonie du Minotaure: Nationalisme et Révoltes en Angola, 1926–1961*, Ed. Pélissier, Orgeval, 1978; Christine Messiant, '1961. L'Angola colonial, histoire et société. Les prémisses du mouvement nationaliste', Ph.D. thesis, EHESS, Paris, 1983; Gerald Bender, *Angola under the Portuguese: the Myth and the Reality*, Heinemann, London, 1978; Gervase Clarence-Smith, 'Capital Accumulation in Angola', in David Birmingham and Phyllis M. Martin (eds), *History of Central Africa*, Longman, Harlow, 1983, Vol.2, pp.163–99.

agriculture, which was their source of subsistence and their economic link to colonial society, while providing very low levels of income from the minimal commodity prices offered by Portuguese bush traders. In the cities, where Portuguese and African urbanisation and some industrial activity developed, only a tiny minority of the '*indígenas*' in suburbs and slums lived in conditions less miserable than in the countryside. The economic integration of 'natives' into colonial society was very weak since private enterprise was closed to them, and incoming whites filled all economic niches down to the most menial jobs. Portugal's proclaimed 'civilising' mission, especially in health and education, was left to the religious missions, and only the Catholic Church received state assistance. Even in the towns schools did not provide the 'natives' with more than a rudimentary knowledge of the Portuguese language. Under such conditions, churches and religion represented for most the only access to European 'civilisation'.

Despite profound colonial oppression, revolt was not rife throughout the country. After the Second World War, only two large-scale peasant explosions erupted, both in 1961, when severe economic crises affected living conditions of communities which had preserved a strong cohesion.[3] The one revolt which did develop into an anti-colonial war, that of the north-west, did so under the leadership of modern élites, mostly urban and 'non-native'. Indigenous Angolans did not have traditional leaders in a position to oppose colonialism or even to present local claims.[4] Economic, social and cultural marginalisation, coupled with coercion, left the majority with no alternative but to escape from colonial constraints, hiding in the towns or the countryside beyond government's reach, moving across the colonial borders or trying to find a place within colonial society, as a domestic servant with a 'good' patron or as an urban worker, or by joining Christian communities which gave education to a tiny minority. Angolan *indígenas* were thus particularly dependent on Western institutions and on the élites formed by them.

The harshness of colonisation was only alleviated for the very small minority which was recognized as 'assimilated' on conditions of literacy, values and customs. White immigration of the 1950s closed almost all other forms of promotion. In 1960, 'assimilated' families numbered 38,000 black and about 45,000 *mestiço* people (of mixed parentage). Although only about one per cent of Angola's six million inhabitants, *assimilados* formed a crucial group in the formation of the nationalist movement.

ANGOLAN ELITES: CREOLES, *ASSIMILADOS* AND BAKONGO EXILES

The distinctiveness and interrelations of Angola's modern élites were central to the divisions in the nationalist movement. Historical trajectories and actual

3 Pélissier, *La Colonie du Minotaure*, chapter 11.
4 Portuguese colonisation in Angola followed a systematic direct-rule policy. The paramount African chiefs were not recognised except the King of Kongo, and the chiefs (*sobas*) were reduced to village-level executors of colonial policy.

social experience differentiated three socio-cultural types of élite in the 1950s. Two were 'assimilated' élites, owing their status, whether they liked it or not, to their cultural separation from 'natives' and the third was the Bakongo African élite. The language, way of life and culture could no longer be African or 'ethnic' but 'Portuguese'. Their status protected them from the obligations imposed on the 'natives' and gave them access to distinct education and work. They were nonetheless discriminated against by whites and their right to independent economic activity was reduced by Portuguese immigration. Angola's assimilated élites were a wage-earning petite bourgeoisie, predominantly employed by the state in subordinate positions. But however distinctive, *assimilados* did not constitute a homogeneous social group.

The élite of the élite consisted of 'old *assimilados*' of mixed-race and black 'great families'. They were descended from the old multiracial colonial nucleus which had survived until the end of the nineteenth century. They were then downgraded, although their access to *civilizado* schooling enabled them to retain an élite position among non-whites. These families, mostly Catholic, no longer intermarried with whites, though Portuguese remained their maternal language. They retained the memory of their specific history and culture, and their multiracial composition and experience gave them a distinct awareness of themselves as Angolans rather than as 'Africans'. These 'old *assimilados*' of whatever colour were 'cultural *mestiços*' and can be called creoles. *Mestiços*, although visible as a group, were in reality neither socially nor culturally cohesive.[5] Creoles born to *mestiço* or half-*mestiço* parents had suffered with their black peers from the creole downgrading, while *mestiços* born of stable, albeit increasingly rare, unions between white men and non-white women enjoyed (if recognised and taken care of by their fathers) privileged white status and suffered little from racial stigmatisation. Many other children were abandoned by their white fathers and raised in their often 'native' family. Subjected to the obligations of the 'natives', they had little in common with *mestiços* or black creoles. 'Colour' could bring comparative privilege in this racially dominated society, but only within social class.

'New *assimilados*' were descended from commoners or chiefs who had never been part of the colonial nucleus. In the twentieth century, especially after 1945, they 'escaped' from the *indigenato* thanks to mission education, Catholic or Protestant, and to new needs for a more instructed labour force. Their maternal language was African, and their social relations were mostly conducted among their 'native' kith and kin. They had no place to socialise with

5 For further explanation of the meaning of terms such as 'creole' *assimilado*, *mestiço*, and *mulato* in Angolan history and at present, see Messiant, '1961. L'Angola colonial', pp.448–97, and 'Luanda 1945–1961: colonisés, société coloniale et engagement nationaliste', in M. Cahen (ed.), *Bourgs et Villes en Afrique Lusophone*, L'Harmattan, Paris, 1989, pp.153–76. Other analyses are found in Pélissier, *La Colonie du Minotaure*, pp.52–8, 63–75, 348–57; Basil Davidson, *In the Eye of the Storm: Angola's People*, Longman, Harlow, 1972, *passim*; John Marcum, *The Angolan Revolution, Volume I*, MIT Press, Boston, 1969, pp.9–120; Bender, *Angola under the Portuguese*, pp.219–24; F.-W. Heimer, *Der Entkolonisierungskonflikt in Angola*, Weltforum Verlag, Munich, 1979, pp.42–81.

whites, except for the rare few who reached secondary school, or had had social contact with creoles. The church had been their means of promotion, as qualified workers, catechists, teachers, nurses, and it remained important in their social life. Being black and more subject to growing white competition and racism than the creoles, they saw colonial society as racially stratified, with the *mestiços* in a privileged position. They mostly identified themselves as 'Africans', and often did not feel readily accepted by 'old *assimilados*' who lived and married among themselves and often claimed to be *the* élite. For the registered 'new *assimilados*', and for the more numerous *de facto* ones who had reached similar levels of schooling and employment without being legally acknowledged as *assimilados*, the struggle to achieve recognition had brought little gain.

The established church in Angola was the Catholic Church, and hostility towards Protestant missions, mostly staffed by foreigners, meant harrassment of and discrimination towards their congregations. This gave Protestantism a political importance. Protestant missions were also less hostile to African languages and customs than Catholic ones and facilitated the Africanisation of their churches which, by their dynamism, were an important focus of social life. Furthermore, Protestant evangelisation had been the work of three distinct denominations, with an 'ethno-linguistic' division of the territory between Baptists, Methodists and Congregationalists. Protestant 'new *assimilados*' became less 'Portugalised' than the Catholics, and were leaders of religious communities whose limits were ethnic. This 'ethnicity' emphasised the sociocultural differences between the 'new *assimilados*' and the creoles.

The composition of the rival segments of old and new *assimilados* was differentiated. Historically, colonial society had developed along three axes corresponding to the territories of three over-arching 'ethnic' groups.[6] They contained three-quarters of the Angolan population and produced most of the modern élite: the Ovimbundu in the centre-south, the Mbundu in the centre-north, and the Bakongo in the north-west. Before the twentieth century, colonial society only existed in Luanda, in the chain of small towns in its hinterland, and in Benguela. Auxiliaries and the non-white sons of colonisers – now creoles – were then mostly Mbundu with a few Ovimbundu settled on the coast. Only in the twentieth century did access to mission education lead to a more balanced opportunity for both Ovimbundu and Mbundu, though not Bakongo, to become 'new *assimilados*'. The relative weight of Protestant and Catholic élites also fluctuated by region, as did the attitudes of local white society to non-whites[7]. All these differences made for complex identities among non-white élites, and there was indeed a social and cultural gulf between a

6 In the 1950s, language was what characterised and mainly unified these groups, which can better be called 'ethno-linguistic groups'. See, notably, M. da Conceiçao Neto, 'Contribuições a um debate sobre "as divisões étnicas" em Angola', *Cadernos do CODESRIA* (Luanda) 2, (1991), pp.16–34, bibl.
7 The racist immigrants to the Bakongo towns during the coffee boom contrasted with the more mixed, albeit racialising, atmosphere of Luanda or of the 'white towns' of the Ovimbundu plateau.

black Protestant catechist in a little mission and the *mestiço* son of a Luanda white official with a very light-skinned wife.

The historical development of Angolan colonisation also produced a third, Bakongo, élite which was formed outside Angola. The Bakongo country was long marginalised inside Angola after the region was brutally repressed at the beginning of the twentieth century when a revolt had led to a first massive movement into exile.[8] Modern Bakongo élites were henceforth mainly exiled ones, socialised in the very different society of the Belgian Congo. They were marked by racial segregation, by strong ethnic affirmation, and were not initially recognised as being of élite, or '*évolué*', status. This non-Portuguese-speaking, non-assimilated élite identified itself as Bakongo and African. Although ethnic, it was no longer strongly 'traditional'. Positions linked to the hierarchy of the old Kongo kingdom were important, but those derived from mission affiliation, and particularly from Baptist education, were more significant in the urban modern economy. In the 1950s Léopoldville, and not Luanda, was their capital where, as foreigners, they worked not in the state but in the private sector. This atypical external ethnic élite had great importance for the way in which the nationalist struggle developed in Angola.

ELITE RIVALRY AND THE DIVISION OF THE NATIONALIST MOVEMENT

The Angolan nationalist contest was principally organised by modern élites. The *assimilados* who had been marginalised and humiliated led the anti-colonial action. Yet they were held back, both by the conditions under which the contest had to be waged, and by their singular alienation from Africanness, an alienation which was reinforced by their privileged position. The risks were obvious in the absence of democratic freedoms for black or white and as police surveillance was strengthened. Many *assimilados*, furthermore, demonstrated a strong élitism, which internalised the authoritarian and reactionary precepts of Salazarism. The prospect of an alliance with uncultured *gentio*, the *matumbo*[9], had little appeal. Creoles had, in earlier generations, engaged in cultural confrontations, proclaiming their specific Angolanity and emphasising African dignity. But not all were willing to emulate the initiators of the 1948 'Let us discover Angola' movement, and confront Portugal politically[10]. Only a small minority of the creoles, mainly among the young, engaged in political activity, embracing a radicalised nationalism in which they were joined by some *mestiço* sons of Portuguese and by a few rare whites. The

8 R. Pélissier, *Les Guerres Grises: Résistance et Révoltes en Angola (1845–1941)*, Ed. Pélissier, Orgeval, 1977, chapter 9, and *La Colonie du Minotaure*, pp.260–78, and Messiant, '1961. L'Angola colonial', pp.518–34, on this marginality. The 'memory' of the kingdom of Kongo strongly survived as a symbol of ethnic grandeur also due to this modern marginality.

9 *Gentio*, 'pagans'; *matumbo*, 'uncivilised, ignorant native'; *gentio* disappeared from everyday talk after independence, but *matumbo* did not.

10 Notable among the founders of this movement was Viriato da Cruz, the future first secretary-general of the MPLA.

anti-colonial movement among the 'new *assimilados*' was larger, notably among Protestants, in keeping with their distance from colonial society, yet also limited to a minority of mostly young people. Only the exiled Bakongo élite, beyond the reach of Portuguese repression and with no stake at risk in the colonial system, responded more widely to the nationalist awakening.

Repression increased when the Portuguese felt decolonisation on their doorstep. In the absence of freedom to make political debate possible, social fragmentation translated itself into a scattering of small nationalist groups.[11] They necessarily emerged clandestinely on the basis of trust among safe family, friends, and fellow church members. They rarely brought creoles and 'new *assimilados*' together, and distrust existed between socialists and anti-communists, believers and atheists, 'new *assimilados*' and *mestiços*. Even in Luanda where exceptional social intercourse occurred between all *assimilados*, attempts to unify nationalist groups, notably led by creoles who had adopted a progressive nationalism, failed.[12] Waves of arrests prevented any unification before 1960, by which time an MPLA leadership had been formed in exile and tried to regroup nationalist forces inside Angola. Even then, however, dispersion continued. The first armed, organised action against colonial power was an attack on the Luanda prisons by dozens of nationalists on 4 February 1961. Although the MPLA claimed to have organised the assault – and the date is still a national holiday celebrated as the launching of the armed struggle by MPLA – the assault was in fact coordinated by another nationalist network without links to the MPLA leadership or to any local supporters still at large.[13] The big March 1961 revolt in the rural north-west was instigated by yet another political group, based in Léopoldville. Outside Luanda fragmentation was even stronger and weak nationalist groups had even less success in achieving unification.

The repression of the 1950s meant that only the nationalists outside the country could organise themselves and be heard. In Portugal, Angolan creoles had arrived as students since the end of the 1940s. Many participated in anti-fascist activities while joining with other students from the empire to campaign against Portuguese colonialism. Maintaining links with their peers inside Angola, they mobilised for independence, emphasised African culture, and embraced European ideologies such as Christian humanism and especially Marxism. Their anti-imperialist stance involved a condemnation of 'lusotropicalism', the colonial claim that the Portuguese in the tropics were

11 See Pélissier, *La Colonie du Minotaure*, pp.240–56; Marcum, *The Angolan Revolution*, Vol.1, pp.23–46; Davidson, *In the Eye of the Storm*, chapters 5,6,7; Messiant, 'Luanda 1945', pp.176–81 which gives a first overview of the nationalist ferment as it emerged from interviews with nationalist militants carried out in the 1980s, in sharp contrast to 'official history'.
12 This view was notably expressed in a *manifesto* written in 1956 by Viriato da Cruz but which did not circulate. This became one of the founding texts of the MPLA in 1960.
13 The organiser, according to a great number of reliable testimonies, was the Catholic dignitary, Manuel das Neves. The recently opened archives of the Portuguese secret police also raise extreme doubts on 'official' history, according to the Angolan historian Carlos Pacheco (*Publico*, 4 Feb. 1996).

not racially prejudiced. Whatever their élite position, both their adoption of a European political ideology, and a firm anti-tribal and anti-racist nationalism reflected their creole culture. Only in 1960 did they finally form the MPLA as a separate Angolan movement, distinct from joint organisations with students from the other Portuguese colonies.

In a very different exile in the Belgian Congo, the Bakongo élites organised an anti-colonial movement which emerged from messianic movements, ethnic and clan networks and self-help associations, within a Congo political climate marked by racial affirmation and a strong Bakongo sub-nationalism. Many groups were formed, divided by regional origins and political stances, but all mono-ethnic in composition and outlook. Some initially joined Bakongo movements of Zairian *évolués*. When they turned politically to Angola, in 1957,[14] it was to form a *União das Populacões do Norte de Angola* (UPNA). Bakongo nationalism was thus very different from that evolving inside Angola, or in Europe. It reflected the dual nature of a modern ethnic élite which expressed a nationalism that was politically moderate but radical in its Africanness and in its opposition to whites. The UPNA had an enormous advantage over the student movements in Europe. It was close to Angola, was not cut off from its 'native' communities, and had ready access to followers among both the old Angolan emigré population and the newly arrived peasants driven off their land. In 1958 the UPNA widened its appeal to include all of Angola, changed its name to UPA, and made a firm bid for radical independence. The intolerable pressure of brutal Portuguese land alienation in the coffee regions and the stimulus of independence in Belgian Congo, combined with dense networks of families and Baptist communities which linked exiled nationalists and their home country, enabled the UPA to launch an insurrection in March 1961. The revolt inflamed all the north-west and caused violent attacks against whites and their associates, before being bloodily suppressed and contained by 1962.

The nationalist encounter between MPLA and UPA which took place in Léopoldville after the revolt was very unequal. The newly arrived leadership of the MPLA was almost without soldiers, whereas the UPA could claim to have launched an insurrection and had strong local support. The two leaderships were opposed on many grounds and did not recognise each other's legitimacy. To the MPLA's quasi-Marxist creoles the UPA leaders were not Angolans but tribalists and racist reactionaries. The UPA, on the other hand, considered MPLA not an African organisation but culturally alienated and dominated by *mestiços*. Opposing ideological stances crystallised socio-cultural distinctions, with UPA adopting a capitalist and pro-Western stand and MPLA defined by its socialist-oriented nationalism. International interference had also intensified the division and United States advisers supported the UPA president's refusal to accept unification with a weak MPLA.

---

14 July 1957 is the date given by Marcum. However, vying for the benefits of being the earliest organisation, the UPNA claimed 1954, and the MPLA 1956.

This extreme initial conflict had major consequences for the nationalist movement, exacerbating differences among Angola's élites, and creating lasting divisions. For both movements, 'new *assimilados*' were seen as a vital link to the 'natives' inside Angola. Those who quit Angola for Léopoldville after 1961 in order to join the armed struggle had to make choices in this polarised setting. Historico-social links with the Luanda creoles brought a majority of those from Luanda and the Mbundu towns to MPLA, whereas many others, among them 'provincial' and Protestant 'new *assimilados*', chose to join UPA. *Assimilados*, however, did not feel much affinity with the UPA ethnic leadership, and some who had studied in Europe, including the Ovimbundu student Jonas Savimbi, espoused Marxism. In the virulent identity and legitimacy struggles which mingled with the political ones, these *assimilados* favoured their 'Africanity' as a sign that, in contrast to creoles and particularly *mestiços*, they were a part of 'the people'. Their integration into UPA, and in 1962 FNLA[15], soon failed, however, as they faced the dictatorial and ethnic-oriented leadership of Holden Roberto. Most non-Bakongo cadres eventually quit FNLA, some to join the MPLA, and others, led by Savimbi, founded their own organisation, UNITA, in 1966.

The division of nationalist organisations can best be described by the hegemonic forces in each leadership. The FNLA was an 'ethno-nationalist' Bakongo group, dominated by exiled neo-traditional '*évolué*' élites. The MPLA brought together creoles and a part of the 'new *assimilados*' (mainly Mbundu but with significant Bakongo and some other additions), and maintained the Marxism, multi-racialism and anti-tribalism of the initial creole nucleus. UNITA was formed by provincial 'new *assimilados*', led by Ovimbundu but incorporating others, including Cabindans; its ideology was marked both by Marxism and by 'Africanism' and reflected hostility towards creoles and *mestiços*. The divisions are thus not principally ethnic. Nor can one say that UNITA, or even FNLA, principally represented peripheral societies[16]. The Angolan conflict appears mainly as a struggle between various élites for hegemony, in which each maximised its potential and constructed its identity to gain legitimacy in leading the Angolan people. The idealistic desire for justice and liberation which had led men and women into the nationalist struggle had to cope in Angola with this reality.

LATE COLONIALISM: WHITE EXPANSION AND SOCIAL CHANGE

The revolt of 1961 marked the beginning of a long armed struggle which from the start was deeply embedded in an international and an African context. Portugal was able to find Western support through NATO with a notable reversal of the United States policy. As one of the 'white regimes' of

---

15 *Frente Nacional de Libertação de Angola* was formed in March 1962 by UPA and another Bakongo party. A government-in-exile, the GRAE, was proclaimed in April.
16 This is the line of analysis of F.-W. Heimer which is more complex than the fundamentally ethnic ones of Marcum and Pélissier.

southern Africa, it tightened its economic and strategic ties with South Africa. On the nationalist side, each party of the divided anti-colonial movement, in seeking the necessary rear bases, as well as financial, political and military support, had to take into account the rising Cold War split and the schism inside the 'socialist bloc'. They also had to cope with divisions between 'moderate' and 'progressive' Africa, and with the crucial problem of Zaire, as the 'Congo crisis' developed. No strategically vital regions of Angola were affected by the war, nor were regions with dense populations. In such circumstances the late economic growth of colonial Angola was spectacular. Yet the political threat to Portugal's sovereignty resulted in the transformation of colonial society.

When faced with rebellion Portugal made it clear, in Salazar's words, that it would 'not bend to the winds of history'. It embarked instead on strengthening its hold on its colony, while modifying the more discriminatory aspects of its rule. Changes were now a political necessity to buffer Angolan opposition and calm growing international condemnation of Portuguese colonialism. The first and most symbolic reform was the 1963 abolition of the *indigenato*, thereby ending forced labour and cultivation, restoring some African rights to land, unifying the educational system, enabling all Angolans to become Portuguese citizens, and theoretically abolishing segregation and discrimination. The consequences of such a radical legal reform and of later changes were very uneven, limited by the same contradiction as before, since Portugal's sovereignty was still thought to depend on white immigration. Thus, new waves of migrants continued to arrive to make rapid money and they had to be protected from competition by Angolans. Late colonial society was greatly transformed in its last fourteen years, with spectacular developments in infrastructure, roads, towns, modern agriculture, and a surge of industries.[17] Benefits, however, went principally to white Angola and reached non-whites only if they did not jeopardise settler interests or if they facilitated colonial expansion. It was, moreover, out of the question for fascist Portugal to give Angolans democratic rights. To 'win hearts and minds' collided with the pursuit of an unwavering anti-subversion policy. Repression included a new prestige given to the chiefs so that they might discipline the peasants and a policy of removing whole villages to 'strategic settlements'. To lend credibility to the now loudly proclaimed 'Portuguese multiracialism', and give Angolan élites a stake in the system, would have required a check on continued racism and white domination of society.

In rural Angola, except for areas affected by guerrilla warfare, late colonialism brought a stronger incorporation into the colonial economy and

17 Gervase Clarence-Smith, *The Third Portuguese Empire, 1825–1975: a Study in Economic Imperialism*, Manchester University Press, Manchester, chapter 7; Carlos Rocha Dilolwa, *Contribuição à História Económica de Angola* (1978), pp.107–355; M. de Andrade et M. Olivier, *La Guerre en Angola: Étude Socio-Économique*, Maspero, Paris, 1973, pp.73–135; H. Guerra, *Angola: Estrutura Económica e Classes Sociais. Os Últimos Anos do Colonialismo Português em Angola*, Edições 70, Lisbon, 4th ed., 1979.

administration, which now reached communities hitherto unaffected by white expansion. Situations varied according to the form and intensity of white pressure, strategic considerations, and new policies initiated in the late 1960s to stem the degradation of African agriculture and form a class of modern farmers. The overall trend, however, was towards an impoverishment of African agriculture, a growing scarcity of good land, increased tax burdens and indebtedness to white traders. This resulted in a growing necessity for peasants to obtain waged work, sometimes by massive migration, in order to supplement family incomes. Some peasants did stabilise their condition on land now guaranteed to them, and a small minority bettered their lot, both chiefs and new beneficiaries of rural development programmes.[18] Coffee-growers across the country profited most, and some prospered. They were, nevertheless, a very small minority of the rural Africans who constituted 84 per cent of Angola's population.

By contrast, 'strategic resettlement' on the model used by the United States in Vietnam was implemented in areas thought to be militarily, politically or economically sensitive. A million people from displaced communities were settled on poor land under police control,[19] and suffered massive impoverishment and isolation from economic and social change. Relations with colonial society remained unfavourable, with low wages on farms, inadequate prices for produce, pervasive tax-collectors, and always the police. Churches still provided rural Angolans with the main opportunities for social integration. In spite of some development of state health facilities and a tenfold extension of schooling, the missions continued to offer primary classes for former *indígenas*. The mass of the pupils in rural schools, however, still failed to progress far enough to acquire literacy or skills for their adult lives. The Portuguese language was neither known nor used by the great majority. The search for education and better work, the dominant aspiration of rural Angolans, led gifted youths to migrate to the cities.[20]

The last years of colonisation were ones of rapid urbanisation. The whites, rich or poor, came to the towns, from abroad and from the Angolan countryside. Africans, needed by the new urban developments and attracted by possibilities well beyond those of their villages, flowed in, too. For the majority, however, city life meant crowding together with the poorest of the resident urban population in slums distant from the city centre with no basic amenities, often with insufficient work, and surviving on the solidarity of Luanda families from the same village.[21] The big opportunity in town was the availability of primary education provided by state and church, and in Luanda three-quarters of children spoke Portuguese, though few former *indígenas*

18 See H. Guerra, *Angola*, pp.95–112, on differentiations among peasants.
19 Bender, *Angola under the Portuguese*, chapter 6; and IDOC, *Angola. Secret Government Documents on Counter-Subversion*, IDOC-International, Rome, 1974.
20 On the limits of social and cultural integration, see F.-W. Heimer, *Educação e Sociedade nas Áreas Rurais de Angola. Resultado de um Inquérito*, Vol.2, *Análise do Universo Agrícola* (nd.), pp.21–34.
21 See Ramiro Monteiro, *A Família nos Musseques de Luanda. Subsídios para o seu Estudo*, FASTA, Luanda, 1973, pp.133–246.

completed primary schooling. The growing need for a more literate and qualified workforce for booming development projects benefited white children first, but Africans also gained more opportunities. Education provided their main route to promotion although much economic progress was still barred by competing white immigrants.

Removing racial barriers and extending schooling at primary and secondary levels did not eliminate discrimination, for example the salaries of non-whites remained inferior except in the state sector. Nor did education lead to a fundamental change in the social origins of the non-white élites. The legal and *de facto assimilados* of 1961, plus a new though tiny minority of farmers' children, gained most from late colonial development. Schooling led to some lessening of differences and, while senior positions continued to be the preserve of whites, many former 'new *assimilados*' now joined the creoles in secondary, technical and professional education and entered middle-salaried positions. In Luanda they also joined creoles in the new residential suburbs built to stabilise the urban élite and give them a stake in colonial society. As for the upper levels of the *indígenas* of 1961, they now constituted a better-qualified, more stable, and more numerous working class, living with difficulty in *musseques* (neighbourhoods) built closer to the town than the newer shanty towns housing the poor sub-proletariat who were mostly recent migrants. This three-tier social stratification, perceptible in Luanda's topography, was reproduced in most Angolan towns.

The processes of transformation did not turn Angola into a fully unified social formation, and some peripheral societies preserved strong ethnic reproduction mechanisms.[22] Yet the central regions became more deeply incorporated into the modern structures. The three 'historical' regional models of colonisation and ethnic homogeneity were now broken up, with increased diversification taking place inside 'ethno-linguistic groups', between peasants cultivating poor crops far from city markets, those linked to moderately profitable government-initiated development projects, and well-off modern commercial agriculturalists. Among the rural Bakongo[23] some chiefs and modern coffee-growers became large-scale African planters. The coffee boom of the 1950s and the colonial reconquest of northern Angola in 1961 had, however, allowed whites to expand their interests. The government subsequently created a number of 'strategic villages' into which many former coffee-growers were driven and where they lived in poor conditions alongside 100,000 returnees from Zaire. Catholic schools and the church did not provide development opportunities, while Protestant activity was notably curbed. Bakongo rural peoples remained closed in on themselves in a state of passive resistance.[24] Ethnic identification remained strong, both in the villages and in the exiled

22 Heimer, *Der Entkolonisierungskonflikt*, pp.81–5.
23 Cabindans and urban coastal Bakongos have, furthermore, always been in rather different situations from those living in the rural Bakongo heartland. The finding of oil in the mid-1960s transformed the conditions for some of the Cabinda enclave population.
24 Bender, *Angola under Portuguese Rule*, pp.165–77.

urban community, where those with skills or the best mission schooling now survived in commerce and in service industries. Only a few Bakongo lived in Luanda, however, forming inward-looking communities in some *musseques*.[25] Social differentiation also deepened among the Mbundu at the regional and local level.[26] The old rural élites which had succeeded in keeping their land holdings through historic links with local Portuguese were again able to prosper, making use of salaried and migrant labour. Elsewhere, outward migration continued from rural areas where the population experienced difficulties. Links between town and country remained close among the strong Catholic majority, and also in the active Methodist minority with its centres of Quessua and Luanda. On the Ovimbundu plateau a growing scarcity and exhaustion of land and low prices for produce led to massive labour migration without the need for compulsion. The rural Ovimbundu were, with the exception of a few coffee growers and some *sobas* and modern farmers, poorer and more socially fragmented in 1974 than they had been in 1961. Their acceptance of migrancy and low-paid employment by the Portuguese – enforced by military isolation, social atomisation and widespread confinement in 'strategic settlements' – led to a colonial stereotype of the 'faithful' or 'submissive' Bailundu. By 1974, however, the Ovimbundu had produced several modern élites, mainly through the missions. Rural entrepreneurs had legalised their holdings and developed commercial agriculture and artisan activity. Many had settled on the coast south of the Kwanza and supplied a labour force for the port of Lobito, the Benguela railway, and the administrations of railway towns. Increased opportunities for secondary schooling created an educated élite proportionate in size to their demographic importance. Their long aspiration to modernity was preserved as was the weakness of their identification with 'ethnic' groups or old highland polities. Marked differences in social experience also separated the Ovimbundu plateau from the coastal cities.[27]

In the Angolan towns homogenisation of upper social levels occurred through schooling and social experience. Increased social contact in secondary schools between young blacks, *mestiços* and some whites meant that creoles and 'new *assimilados*' of the younger generation enjoyed greater social intercourse, while the difference between Catholic and Protestant 'cultures' was lessened and new links were forged between 'ethnically' distinct pupils.[28] Luanda, however, remained the only town with a significant multiethnic composition, and the Mbundu predominated. They constituted three-quarters of the city's

25 Interviews; also, Monteiro, *Musseques*, pp.95–125.

26 For an example of this strong local differentiation for agriculture in the region of Malange, see Fernando Pacheco, *Agricultura e Sociedade Rural na Angola dos Anos 60. O Caso de Malanje*, Luanda, 1991.

27 Hermann Pössinger, 'Interrelations between economic and social change in rural Africa: the case of the Ovimbundu of Angola', in F.-W. Heimer (ed.), *Social Change in Angola*, Weltforum Verlag, Munich, 1973, pp.31–52. Also, Messiant, '1961, L'Angola colonial', pp.534 50; M. da Conceição Neto, *Entre a Tradição e a Modernidade: os Ovimbundu do Planalto Central á Luz da História*, Luanda, 1994.

28 Notably among the Protestants. See Lawrence Henderson, *A Igreja em Angola*, Editorial Além-Mar, Lisbon, 1990, chapters 10 and 11.

African population, the Ovimbundu only 18 per cent and the Bakongo 6 per cent.[29] Each community was organised by its own mission. The Luanda Ovimbundu worked in white agriculture outside the city or in low-paid urban work and were dispersed rather than consolidated but, like the city's Bakongo, they were little integrated into Luanda society at large.

Except for the Bakongo, where a historically strong ethnic identification had been reinforced by the trauma and exile of 1961, there did not exist in Angola in 1974 any strong ethnic tradition. One could not speak of the Mbundu or the Ovimbundu as 'corporate groups' and late colonialism had led to 'the structural regression of tributary societies'.[30] No traditional élites provided social models or leaders of opinion. Assimilated élites had a strong Angolan identity alongside their social, cultural and religious ones, which remained important among the stabilised urban population. Ethnicity could be polit-ically mobilised in rural areas, where socio-cultural integration was minimal, or in the cities due to social fragmentation and inequalities, but it was not a paramount identification.

Beyond ethnicity, the 'racial question' was obviously central to a white-dominated settler society where social identities were always in part racially defined. Despite a loud official multiracialism, and some social mixing at the bottom level of white society,[31] no historical rapprochement between whites and creoles occurred during the late colonial period. But while ever more *mestiço* children were abandoned by their settler and soldier fathers, the few *mestiço* sons still acknowledged by their white fathers continued to be accepted into white society where they benefited from its privileges. The social origins of the non-white élites did not change, and the children of creoles were still at the top, above the now more numerous children of former 'new *assimilados*'. While the younger generation of the 'new *assimilados*' became less colour-conscious in relation to *mestiços*, and more similar to creoles in their social perceptions, the older generation still tended to see *mestiços* as a racially privi-leged group. *Mestiços* could thus be a focus of both élite rivalry and of the popular vision of colonial domination and social inequality.

By 1974, however, Angolan city dwellers defined themselves more by their attitude to white domination and the issue of independence. The absence of civic rights, enduring discrimination, the social remoteness or outright racism of white society, all meant that, except for a tiny minority, the élites aspired to independence. Even the small proportion of creoles and former 'new *assimilados*' that had bettered their social condition and accommodated them-selves to the late-colonial situation, found white privilege and domination intolerable. Their hopes and fears were mixed as they aspired to an independ-ence that would strengthen their élite position. The wish for an orderly inde-

29 Monteiro, *A Família nos Musseques*, p.97.
30 Heimer, *Der Entkolonisierungskonflikt*, p.95 and *O Processo*, pp.21–5. Also, see Bender, *Angola under the Portuguese*, chapter 6, and IDOC, *Angola*.
31 Although rarely implying racial mixing in social life, a small number of Portuguese traders in the *musseques* still had stable unions with black women as did some settlers in the countryside.

pendence was strong even among nationalist militants and it was only among the urban nationalist youth that the appeal of a socialist independence found a wider echo. The stabilised urban working class also hoped for independence and the departure of whites, as a condition for improving its position. As for the floating slum population, for whom religion and church were still a strong focus of identification, they strongly aspired to independence, whatever the attitude of their church.[32] Their expectation was a vague and vehement hope to 'live a better life', a cause supported by their kin in the countryside. The general wish for independence manifested itself when nationalist organisations came to towns and were welcomed by large crowds. However, only small minorities had already strongly identified themselves with one or other of the movements. The complex of social identities and political expectations among Angolans in 1974 could have led to other political developments, had not the acute power struggle between the three nationalist organisations occurred in a context where one-party systems were the norm rather than the exception, and where high foreign interest in Angola resulted in all-out war.

ARMED STRUGGLE

When the Armed Forces Movement (MFA) put an end to the dictatorship in Portugal in 1974, the nationalist movement in Angola was still divided. The competition between nationalists of different élites had given way to a struggle for hegemony between three organisations. Their conflict was exacerbated and ideologised by Cold War division, by foreign support and by military necessity. Thirteen years of consolidating organisational cultures, identities, legitimacies, modes of leadership and visions of the enemy fostered growing antagonism between the organisations and subsumed their internal contradictions. As well as a massive Portuguese war effort, and the quasi-monopoly which the FNLA enjoyed on the crucial Zaire frontier, this division severely weakened guerrilla advance in Angola. The FNLA was reduced to frontier action in the north, while MPLA and UNITA guerrilla activity was confined to the remote east, where Zambia provided bases after its own independence in 1964. No organisation was able to reach the central regions of the country[33] or to organise significant links with the clandestine networks in the cities. Under these circumstances the political organisation of 'liberated zones' was weak, and little social and political change occurred in the leadership or among the cadres of the movements. Through their exclusive access to foreign support and their very centralised control over their organisation – which war justified – all three leaders maintained themselves at the head of their

32 The hierarchy of the Catholic Church remained unsympathetic to independence, but after the individual participation of a number of Catholics and some eminent church personalities in the nationalist movements in the 1950s, a growing distancing from the colonial government occurred in various sectors of the Church. See Emílio de Carvalho, *A Igreja Africana no Centro da sua História*, Ed. do autor, Luanda, 1995, pp.81–3.
33 The exception being the survival from 1961 of an isolated guerrilla force of the MPLA known as its 'First Region' in the Dembos north of Luanda.

movement until 1974. Colonial Angola never experienced democratic rights, or open political expression, but neither did nationalist movements practise democracy at a time when discipline in war and for the struggle against each other was essential. Such conditions of rivalry also helped perpetuate the FNLA and UNITA leaderships' rivalry with the MPLA creole and *mestiço* leaders, while inside MPLA more complex political and social processes occurred.

Despite initially receiving exclusive support from the Organization of African Unity (OAU) for its government in exile, the FNLA soon declined as a national political organisation and as an active guerrilla force. The autocratic and narrowly parochial leadership of Holden Roberto, his personal links with Mobutu, and his integration into emigré business life much weakened the front. Many guerrillas and cadres, including some Bakongo, progressively abandoned an exiled army waiting for independence. The dwindling movement soon lost the exclusive support of the OAU, became more dependent on Zaire, and was alienated from the needs of its initial supporters inside Angola and among the refugees. Having lost the all-Angolan membership it had gained in 1960–63, the FNLA's external character grew. At the same time the movement maintained its ethnic outlook, its racial vision of society and its strong opposition to the 'creole communist MPLA' and to the 'assimilated Maoist UNITA'[34].

The evolution of UNITA was marked by its isolation. In the Cold War alliances, its Maoism brought some Chinese training for its leaders but minimal material help and no recognition by the OAU. Even support from Zambia soon stopped. Whereas the MPLA and FNLA had bases outside the country, UNITA was forced to operate inside Angola's borders under very difficult conditions, with few guerrilla forces which were located among marginal populations. Since the Portuguese put much effort into protecting the central highlands, UNITA guerrillas were unable to organise Ovimbundu communities before 1974. Under these circumstances UNITA established links between leaders, guerrillas and people according to a Stalinist 'red army' discipline. A brothers-in-arms cohesion was forged among its leaders, reinforced by a strong Maoist ideology and a self-proclaimed legitimacy as the true national movement representing the black, rural, peoples of 'deep Angola'. In the hardship of its isolated struggle UNITA also developed a strong pragmatism in order to survive, and in 1972 Savimbi did not hesitate to make a pact with the Portuguese army of eastern Angola to overcome the rival MPLA guerrillas active in the region.[35]

After suffering a major crisis in 1961–63 and being expelled from Zaire, the MPLA moved to Brazzaville in Congo, and obtained better political conditions and the assistance of socialist countries, though without any access to mainland Angola. Military action began in the Cabinda enclave, won some

34 Marcum, *The Angolan Revolution*, Vols.1 and 2, remains the main source for the nationalist movement and the guerrilla war.
35 On UNITA, see Marcum, *The Angolan Revolution*, Vol.2; and Fred Bridgland, *Jonas Savimbi: a Key to Africa*, Ashanti Publishing, Gibraltar, 1986.

OAU support and served to train guerrilla cadres and fighters, but the drive met with very little popular support. Decisive new momentum came with Zambia's independence, and from 1966 MPLA guerrillas based on the eastern frontier could receive help through Tanzania. For some years they penetrated the interior, organising populations fleeing Portuguese rule or repression, and gained OAU recognition. The forces failed, however, to break out from the '*terras do fim du mundo*', the lands at the end of the earth. Instead heavy Portuguese offensives at the beginning of the 1970s drove them back and brought a grave new crisis to the movement.

On the eve of the Portuguese regime's collapse, the MPLA was in a very precarious military and political position.[36] The crisis was aggravated by the harsh conditions of exile, by endemic problems underlying the evolution of the armed struggle and by the uneasy coexistence between the initial creole leadership and the 'new *assimilado*' rural and urban cadres, Mbundu and Bakongo, which had joined the movement in Léopoldville. Agostinho Neto embodied[37] and promoted this alliance at a time marked by violent FNLA attacks on *mestiços* and *assimilados*, which exacerbated the MPLA's own colour rivalries and cultural mistrusts. The crisis crystallised around the place of *mestiços* at the head of the leadership. The defection in 1963 of the first leader of the movement, Viriato da Cruz, who briefly joined the FNLA then went into exile, caused much demoralisation. In the ensuing struggle for the survival of the MPLA, and now under Neto's uncontested leadership, opposition continued to manifest itself in struggles over leadership and privilege. Neto arbitrated in these struggles, defending the ideological orientation of the MPLA and protecting the creoles while also building a personal power base among 'new *assimilados*' loyal to him by virtue of colour, religion or origin in the region of Catete.

In the absence of democratic practices linking the leadership and the dispersed guerrilla fronts, a silent power struggle continued, despite the consolidation of control by Neto. Segments of 'new *assimilados*' opposed creole 'hegemony' and 'privilege', using racial and ethnic arguments to promote their position as the more genuine representatives of 'the people', while simultaneously competing among themselves on ethnic and micro-regional lines.[38] During the years of armed struggle, 'new *assimilados*' won promotion in the MPLA more readily than did *indígenas*. Several dozen also achieved social advancement through scholarships offered to the movement and absented themselves for long periods of study during the guerrilla years.

---

36 This analysis results from MPLA internal documentation and personal interviews; also, Marcum, *The Angolan Revolution*; Davidson, *In the Eye of the Storm*; and Jean-Michel Mabeko Tali, 'Dissidences et pouvoir d'État: le MPLA face à lui-même (1962–1977)', PhD thesis, EHESS, Paris, 1996.
37 Neto was black and came from the region of Catete near Luanda. He was one of the few Protestant creoles. He was of communist conviction and had participated in the anti-fascist movement in Portugal and had been jailed for his activities.
38 See the novel written in 1971 by a MPLA cadre, Artur Pestana 'Pepetela', *Mayombe*, Heinemann, London, 1996.

Until 1974 the MPLA continued to consolidate its basic alliance and maintain its initial ideology, but it lost sections of two groups. In 1972 an attempt at democratisation and politicisation was initiated by cadres in the east. The initiative could not, however, strengthen the movement but instead caused the emergence of two dissident tendencies. An important part of the eastern guerrilla forces which resented the abuse of power by some of its commanders, rallied to the so-called 'Eastern Revolt', a regional movement led by an Ovimbundu, Daniel Chipenda,[39] who had challenged Neto's leadership. Later, in 1974, a small group of creoles joined together in an 'Active Revolt' which called for an end to undemocratic leadership and a united nationalist front. Entrenched leadership habits, the necessity to present a cohesive front against the hostile UNITA and FNLA, the imminent prospect of independence, and the denunciation both of tribalism and of intellectuals disengaged from the struggle, enabled Neto to find support among a large majority of MPLA cadres and avoid compromise with dissident factions, despite heavy pressure on him from friendly African states. After an aborted 'unification congress' the 'Eastern Revolt' quit the movement and later made an alliance with the FNLA. The members of the 'Active Revolt' were internally discredited as being 'petit-bourgeois intellectuals' and several leaders were later arrested. Meanwhile the Neto leadership reasserted its authority in a 'purified' congress, the 'Inter-Regional Conference', held in September 1974, at which guerrilla leaders and the 'underground' wing of the movement met in joint support of Neto against both dissident factions. The MPLA emerged from remote guerrilla camps and foreign exile to enter open politics and global society with an uncompromising claim to revolutionary legitimacy.

INDEPENDENCE AND THE WAR FOR POWER[40]

Angola was one of the key pawns in the manoeuvring which followed the 'revolution of the carnations' in Portugal on 25 April 1974. Rival Cold War factions inside and outside Africa tried to consolidate or create alliances in Angola[41]. Meanwhile, the three armed movements, all claiming to be 'the sole legitimate representative' of the people, looked for both new and 'historic' allies to reinforce their bargaining power. Neither the FNLA nor the MPLA was prepared to share state power. The FNLA, strongly backed by Mobutu,

39 On the Active Revolt and Eastern Revolt, see J.-M. Mabeko Tali, '"Tribalisme", "régionalisme" et lutte de libération nationale: la question "tribale" et "ethnico-régionale" dans la dissidence au sein du MPLA dans l'est angolais en 1969–1974', *Année Africaine, 1992–1993*, CEAN, Bordeaux, 1993, pp.463–79.
40 On this crucial period, see Heimer, *Enkolonisierungskonflikt*; Claude Gabriel, *Angola: le Tournant Africain*, Editions La Bréche, Paris, 1978, pp.145–268; Mabeko Tali, *Dissidences*, chapters 10 and 12; Marcum, *Angolan Revolution*, Vol.2, pp.240–8; Cahen, *Bourgs et Villes*, pp.218–53; and Valdir Carlos Sarapu, '"Pouvoir populaire" et coopératives en Angola (1974–1977)', 'Diplôme', EHESS, Paris, 1980.
41 The CIA resumed its support to the FNLA and began to think of larger options; the Soviet Union, which had suspended its support to the MPLA, started it again; Western, Portuguese and African pressures led to a last-minute recognition of UNITA as a liberation group by the OAU.

opted from the start for a military takeover, counting on Zairian participation and western support. The MPLA had a revolutionary appeal but needed time and help to consolidate itself. Only UNITA, which had neither military nor diplomatic strength, saw any virtue in an election or in compromise.

For some time the political prospects were unclear. As the nationalist movements signed ceasefires with Portugal and entered Angola, a power struggle occurred in Lisbon between factions with divergent views on the future of the empire. At the same time parts of the white community in Angola laid claim to an autonomy of their own or tried to preserve privileged positions for whites in an independent Angola. Once independence was on the agenda, however, 'revolutionary legitimacy' prevailed and the armed organisations gained exclusive favour,[42] forming a coalition government in January 1975, with elections to precede independence proposed for November 11.

The coalition government broke down between March and July 1975 after the FNLA had tried and failed, with Zairian support, to take military control of the capital. The MPLA secured its hegemony in Luanda and expelled UNITA from its city positions. The logic of military confrontation thereupon drew in Cold War allies. The CIA coordinated a Zaire-supported FNLA and chose to intervene directly.[43] Cuban 'advisers', with increased Soviet help, supported the MPLA, and UNITA, after some hesitation, turned to the west and to South Africa. Three foreign armies entered Angola, the South African one from the south, a Zaire–mercenary one from the north, and the Cuban troops supporting MPLA forces by air. The latter were decisive in stopping the overland advances and protecting Luanda, allowing the MPLA to proclaim independence on November 11 and to gain prompt African recognition since its FNLA–UNITA opponents had sought help from the unacceptable forces of apartheid South Africa. As the United States was unwilling, so soon after its defeat in Vietnam, to risk even covert intervention, South Africa's exposed forces were finally foiled and had to pull back. The MPLA thus gained power through a military victory – a victory won against the hated enemies of imperialism and apartheid, against Mobutu's tyranny, and against their Angolan 'agents', all of them, UNITA and the FNLA, now branded 'traitors to the Angolan people'.

The Cold War confrontation which dominated the power struggle gave the Angolan state a particularly strong ideological charge and coloured foreign opinion of Angola's politics. The choices for the people of Angola after April 1974 depended, however, on much more complex factors. Only a minority of people had joined a movement or even had a definite sympathy with one or the other, through family, religion, 'old boy' networks, or political inclination. The majority simply welcomed 'liberators-at-large'. Even party sympathisers had no idea that division would lead to war and that they would be caught on opposing sides of a bloody barrier. As the three little-known

42 Heimer, *Processo*, chapter 5.
43 John Stockwell, *In Search of Enemies: a CIA Story*, Norton, New York, 1978.

movements claimed military monopolies of sections of the countryside, and moved into towns, perceptions changed according to the appeals made for their support and the dangers feared in a rapidly changing situation.

Some factors carried particular influence. One was the arrival of the FNLA, whose soldiers had been brought up in French-speaking Zaire, often did not speak Portuguese, and who were thus widely seen as 'non-Angolan'. Another issue resulted from an attack on the African population in the summer of 1974, led by radical settlers. In Luanda this led to a spontaneous political mobilisation, organised by radical militants, former political prisoners and members of the MPLA's underground cells. After the settlers had been expelled from the *musseques*, local 'popular commissions' were formed to tackle the problems left by stampeding whites. While the FNLA violently opposed this grass-roots movement, the MPLA leadership supported it, gaining among the urban poor and the radicalised youth a significant popular advantage. The fact that some right-wing racist settlers favoured either the FNLA or UNITA also played a part in position taking, while Protestant participation in nationalist politics was an important factor in rallying Mbundu Methodists to the MPLA, Ovimbundu Congregationalists to UNITA and Kongo Baptists to the FNLA. In the hope of winning power, however, all three movements tried not to alienate any part of the population by proclaiming a precise political orientation, but chose to stimulate ethnic sentiment.[44] A massive ethnic polarisation of support between the MPLA and UNITA (no longer only the FNLA) emerged in rural areas, heightened by the threat of civil war. Soon war against 'the enemy camp' took a more brutal ethnic reality.

Arising from this convulsive accession of Angola to its independence, domestic and foreign factors intertwined and led to rapid resumption of war from 1978–80, and from then to ever-escalating violence. UNITA found determined foreign allies to help mount heavily-armed guerrilla attacks, while the MPLA government could count on socialist support and oil revenue to resist. The strength of both parties in terms of wealth and allies reinforced the dynamics of war and obliged people to seek shelter in one camp or the other. The violence of the other side seemed to legitimise each party or make its protection necessary. Through their war and a parallel building of instruments of coercion, both sides consolidated their grip on the lives of Angolans. Through the powerful instruments of propaganda of their international allies, they were also able to disseminate the 'useful' part of any truth about the war and the country, and any 'useful' lies that might help their cause and that of their foreign supporters.

THE CHAOTIC CONSTITUTION OF A POWER BLOC

The victorious MPLA had to cope with the ruin and disruption caused by war and by the sudden departure of nine-tenths of the 330,000 Portuguese who

44 Heimer, *Processo*, pp.71–4.

had dominated the colony and had left behind a completely disorganised administration and economy.[45] Fired by a conviction of the legitimacy of its 'revolutionary power' the MPLA disregarded the fact that it was not the sole representative of the people. Its political constituency consisted of some of Angola's rural peoples, an important section of the urban sub-proletariat and city workers, and a significant proportion of the wage-earning petty bourgeoisie. But large parts of the population, and important segments of the élites, did not accept the legitimacy of MPLA power and felt themselves to be under Cuban 'occupation'.

Despite the weakness of its base, the MPLA did not seek any reconciliation with those it considered to be reactionaries or representatives of foreign interests. Political exclusion prevailed and a policy of severe repression was directed against those suspected of sympathy for defeated movements. Political loyalty became the prime qualification for a post in the 'movement-state': guerrillas and underground militants formed the backbone of the new power, while counsellors, advisers and foreign-aid workers from socialist countries staffed the various ministries. To establish its authority the MPLA also decided to get rid of radical political groups and place under central control the activities of popular commissions. This was carried out by popular young leaders, among them Nito Alves, under the radical banner of 'People's Power'. They adopted strong revolutionary, anti-bourgeois and sometimes racist rhetoric against those excluded from the loyal core of the party.

While radicalism was growing on the street, the MPLA also faced the difficult task of running a state. Strategic and pragmatic considerations dominated policy. Political allegiance was pledged by cadres from the colonial civil service and private sector, belonging to the creole and 'new *assimilado*' middle class. Social position being now dependent on the single-party state, both groups preserved their social position by joining the new power. Whatever their personal ideological inclination – notably a lack of sympathy for 'communism' and for the 'people's power' that was spreading through the slums – social and family links to the MPLA leaders facilitated their integration. The affiliation of creoles to the MPLA was strengthened by the anti-creole and anti-*mestiço* stance of both the FNLA and UNITA, while many 'new *assimilados*', notably in the older generation, resented what they perceived as a despising of their African identity under creole and *mestiço* hegemony. Furthermore, in contrast to the creoles, only a part of 'new *assimilados*' had joined the MPLA, since most Bakongo and almost all Ovimbundu élites were excluded for political if not for 'ethnic' reasons.

While social élites joined the political MPLA as the new 'state-class' and benefited from the Portuguese departure, the ordinary people in the cities, who had been deeply radicalised, experienced economic degradation and few positive results from independence or their participation in war. A political

---

45 For a vivid account of the stampede of the Portuguese to leave, see R. Kapuscinsky, *Another Day of Life*, Viking Penguin, New York, 1987.

faction around Nito Alves and other young MPLA leaders who had taken control of 'people's power' now defended an orthodox communist orientation.[46] Using a radical and populist rhetoric, they began to challenge the 'rightist' orientation of the party leadership and the 'new bourgeoisie' inside the MPLA, using strong anti-*mestiço* language. Their appeals gained a popular audience in Luanda and other towns as well as support from militants, cadres of the movement, state, army, and mass party organisations.

After being politically criticised for factional activity the 'Nitistas', counting on Soviet neutrality, attempted a coup in Luanda on 27 May 1977. Although poorly organised, and rapidly checked with Cuban help, the plotters killed several well-known leaders. The MPLA leadership reacted with hundreds of executions, killing not only coup activists and leaders, but also sympathisers and suspects as the political police eradicated 'factionalism'.

The MPLA transformed itself into a purged Marxist-Leninist party some months later, that is after a serious rift in the regime's already narrow base and the loss of much cadre and popular support. It was seen as implacably repressive even inside its own ranks. Exorbitant repression traumatised the whole of Angolan society for years, decimated a political generation and reduced the country to silence. Only a muted 'passive resistance' was now offered by formerly enthusiastic supporters. In the crisis creoles and *mestiços* who had been attacked closed ranks in support of the party. So, too, did many 'new *assimilados*' either through opposition to 'Nitist' communism or through loyalty to Agostinho Neto. The crisis had, however, revived *assimilado* resentment of creole and *mestiço* hegemony while entrenching a popular opinion of the MPLA as a repressive *mestiço* power.

The claim to a 'triumphal march of the revolution' was belied by the weakness of the party and by guerrilla attacks from defeated FNLA and UNITA forces. After two abortive invasions of Shaba launched from Angola by Zairian exiles, Neto tried to settle Angola's conflict with Mobutu in an accord signed in 1978, one year before his death. Zaire agreed to expel opposition groups, including the FNLA and the separatist FLEC which was active in Cabinda.[47] The FNLA, deprived of its base, soon abandoned armed action, and some of its cadres accepted the clemency offered by Neto and were integrated into the MPLA party-state. The accord launched a tide of returning Bakongo exiles and refugees who, after years in Zaire, now sought a place in Angola. These *regressados* (returnees) bore, however, the double stigma of a real or imagined sympathy for the FNLA, and an alien language and way of life.

A unified power bloc had thus constituted itself around the winner, which

46 David Birmingham, 'The twenty-seventh of May: an historical note on Angola's 1977 coup', *African Affairs* 77, 309 (1978), pp.554–64; Gabriel, *Angola*, pp.311–37; More recently, see Mabeko Tali, *Dissidences*, chapter 14.

47 *Frente de Libertação do Enclave de Cabinda* was formed in 1963 by various separatist groups, but suffered from internal divisions and interferences from Congo, Zaire and western oil companies. See Phyllis M. Martin, 'The Cabinda connection', *African Affairs* 76 (1977), pp.47–59, and João Baptista Lukombo, 'Cabinda: uma problemática de sociologia política à luz de traçados fronteiriços em Africa', *Africana*, no.15, University of Porto, Porto, 1995, pp.73–85.

controlled the enormous resources of the state as well as the future political and social development of the nation. Power was now strongly urban-based. Few of those with the means to determine the destiny of the country adhered to the officially proclaimed socialist aims, but in the repressive atmosphere no one challenged them, nor their 'multiracial' and 'anti-tribal' ideology, nor their professed atheism, even though influential sectors of the party did not recognise some or indeed any of these orientations. Political orthodoxy reigned and conviction was hidden. Conflicts over policy direction and fights over group interests took the form of silent struggles for posts and privileges. To preserve state authority, and the precarious cohesion of a heterogeneous party, the MPLA leadership gave the priviliged élite of the *nomenklatura* great legal advantages not enjoyed by the people. Before South Africa launched its destabilisation policy, the MPLA had thus defined a mode of exercising power and dealing with opposition. Although narrowly tied to the socialist camp, the regime had also initiated the joint exploitation of Angolan oil by western – notably American – firms, despite the strategic antagonism of the United States towards an Angolan government which it did not recognise.

THE SOUTH AFRICAN WAR AND THE RISE OF UNITA

The war of the 1980s was not triggered simply by Angola being South Africa's neighbour but also by its oil, its strategic position adjoining Zaire, and its importance to Soviet foreign policy. The presence of a Cuban military contingent also made the country an issue for the United States in the Cold War. Under a Republican administration, the United States chose to support South Africa against 'international communism' through a policy of 'constructive engagement' which sought to force a Cuban departure from Angola before allowing Namibia to become independent, as demanded by the United Nations. Powerful enemies created a siege mentality and strengthened a conviction of legitimacy in the MPLA camp while also bringing military help from the Soviet Union and Cuba. The dynamics of an internationalised war continued until the emergence of Gorbachev's perestroika.

Angola's commitment to the independence of southern Africa, and its hosting of liberation movements, made guerrilla and refugee camps the first objective of South African attack. This remained the justification for later interventions and prolonged military occupation of parts of Angola. After 1980 and Zimbabwean independence, South Africa in reality developed a 'total strategy' against its neighbours, allegedly to resist a 'total onslaught' by communism. The United States gave political acquiescence and then military support to the policy in Angola. And in that country UNITA's armed opposition to the regime could be used to bring about Angola's political destabilisation.[48]

48 William Minter, *Apartheid's Contras: an Inquiry into the Roots of War in Angola and Mozambique*, Zed Press, London, 1994; Robert Davies and Dan O'Meara, 'Total strategy in southern Africa: an analysis of South African regional policy since 1978', *Journal of Southern African Studies* 11, 2 (1985), pp.118–211.

The commitment of its ally was crucial to UNITA's military progress. Armed interventions destroyed economic targets, saved UNITA troops from Cuban and Angolan offensives, tied down government forces, and permitted UNITA guerrillas to spread deep into Angolan territory. South Africa helped Jonas Savimbi's movement to establish a conventional military force. It also provided UNITA with a sanctuary which could be supplied overland in the *terras livres* ('free lands') around Jamba in remotest south-east Angola, and a shield from air attacks to protect people from the growing war. With increasing American support during Reagan's second presidential term, and with supplies received through Zaire, UNITA guerrillas spread north, their foreign supplies minimising the need to plunder villages and conscript fighters and labourers by terror. Terror was, however, used against towns and villages, and land mines were planted to deny civilians access to roads and to deprive peasants of their livelihood in the fields. Counter-terror by government forces forcibly removed villagers in order to empty prospective zones of guerrilla advance. Government bombs and land mines served to bring to UNITA not only conscripted but also voluntary recruits.[49] The wealth of UNITA's allies allowed it to give the people under its control better physical security, health, and schooling, than was enjoyed by most guerrilla armies. The western alliance also gave many UNITA cadres scholarships and access to university studies abroad.

Savimbi and his officials were granted access through right-wing lobbies to the Reagan government, and given the prestigious status of 'freedom fighters', yet the movement held a disciplined grip on its population, fighters, élites and cadres, building in Jamba a truly totalitarian 'society' in which the militarised political party dominated all aspects of life. Over the years the organisation itself became more centralised and its leader came to manipulate all traditional, religious, military and Stalinist sources of power. Savimbi promoted ever more of 'his men' from his own province and family to direct and police the movement, and brutally suppressed any critic or potential rival, executing several leaders and sometimes even their families. Public humiliation, arrest, or marginalisation became Savimbi's way of exercising power over the cadres.[50]

UNITA changed a great deal after independence. The war of 1975–76 had brought in a large Ovimbundu contingent and an urban component. The Ovimbundu, together with populations of the war-torn south and east, now formed the bulk of UNITA's people. Their experience, however, changed as UNITA society became ruralised and militarised in its closed environment.

49 Africa Watch, *Violations of the Laws of War on both Sides*, London, 1989, and *Angola: Civilians Devastated by 15-Year War*, London, 1991.
50 Accusations coming from former members of UNITA began to surface in 1988. On UNITA and Savimbi's power, see Fred Bridgland, 'Savimbi et l'exercice de pouvoir: un témoignage', and Guilherme de Loanda, 'La longue marche de UNITA vers Luanda', both in *Politique Africaine* 57 (1995), pp.94–102, 63–70.

Strong political indoctrination, a blend of Maoist Stalinism and African populism, which carried the anti-*mestiço* and anti-creole message of the UNITA founders, was now directed against the 'Luanda creole dictatorship of the oppressed genuine Africans', thereby ensuring that cohesion was based not only on coercion but also on a strong belief in UNITA legitimacy. Military discipline and totalitarian control gave UNITA some aspects of a sect, a reality far removed from the image of a 'free state' portrayed to guided visitors and United States lobbies and publicists. But neither coercion nor external alliances could account alone for UNITA's military or political successes. As the war eliminated alternative choices, the evolution of opposition to the MPLA regime gave UNITA much of its political strength.

WAR, OIL AND THE *NOMENKLATURA*

Despite the growing destruction of war, the MPLA could count on oil wealth which affected the course of the conflict and greatly influenced social and political affairs. Oil in Angola constituted an economic enclave, exploited jointly by the Angolan state and by western firms. It was not governed by 'socialist' norms and was easily protected since it was located on the coast or off-shore. Oil revenue, moreover, was totally centralised by the managers of the state. As war progressed, and the economy dramatically deteriorated, with sharp falls in agricultural and industrial production, oil output increased and oil revenue came to represent almost all of Angola's currency earning and the bulk of state income. Oil enabled the government to wage an ever more expensive war. It also allowed the consolidation of a privileged *nomenklatura* which was often more committed to its own advancement than to the politics of the 'worker–peasant alliance'. In effect, thanks to oil the Angolan regime had no need of the production of most of its population. The joint influence of an urban-based ruling class and a Soviet-conceived development strategy made agriculture the poor relation of the budget, with state farms preferred to peasant farming. Inadequate agricultural policies and their inefficient implementation soon led to failure. Oil permitted the government simply to abandon efforts to build an economic and social link with the countryside and imports were used to feed the cities. When peasants ceased to sell produce, since they received less in exchange than they could have expected at the end of the colonial period, the regime abandoned them to care for themselves or drafted them into the army.

Oil also influenced the general evolution of MPLA policy and brought a deep and rapid transformation of the social system. As the war spread peasants were neglected and sometimes welcomed UNITA guerrillas. The MPLA used its oil revenue for defence and to ensure growing privileges for the *nomenklatura*. In a first phase town people were provided with basic food and goods, health and education services, according to a classic 'socialist' model, although at low levels due to the war. Immense wastage was caused by bad management, uncoordinated bureaucratic planning of the economy, prevailing political criteria for promotions and incoherent policy decisions based on personalities or factions and the growing corruption among cadres.

As the cost of war grew, and the mental gap between the *nomenklatura* and the people widened, oil revenue was increasingly oriented to waging the war and supporting the *nomenklatura*, until the state appeared to have abandoned its socialist-style contract with its people. The situation further deteriorated when oil prices fell, bringing more austerity to the people. Public revenue was ever more oriented to the *nomenklatura* to provide privatised access to goods, transport, water and electricity, and to pay for education and health facilities abroad. At the same time, public services collapsed. As a result of growing scarcity, imports were diverted and, with contraband goods arrived on a black market. Efforts at repression of this market were soon reversed and it flourished as part of a non-productive economy where the dollar dominated all transactions and enormous differences between exchange rates allowed profitable speculation. During the 'transition to socialism' the only way to survive at the bottom of society, when salaries were derisory, was through theft, embezzlement and reselling in the informal economy. Such practices enabled the urban population to survive, though the impoverished masses had been inflated by hundreds of thousands of rural people who fled from war and famine. Technicians who were given access to goods at official prices speculated on the market and lived somewhat better. Some individuals even grew rich and built fortunes.

This wild parallel market of Angola was, however, in no way a free economy. The state controlled oil revenue and foreign exchange, import licences and the allocation of goods. The major benefits from the only partially visible informal economy went to the *nomenklatura*. Its senior members appropriated oil revenue which did not feature in the state budget. They negotiated commissions on military imports and were protected from prosecution when organising high-level embezzlement networks. Among lower echelons the allocation of dollars or goods at official rates allowed lucrative reselling on the black market. Freelance producers and traders at the bottom of the informal sector coped with people's most basic needs,[51] but state control ensured that the biggest profits passed through the hands of members of the *nomenklatura*.[52] Status in the party-state and proximity to power-holders determined social position, access to legal privilege, and one's opportunities for illegal private speculation. Goods and services no longer reached the people directly but through embezzlement and redistribution among family, friends, 'ethnic' net-works and micro-regional clientship.

51 R. Duarte de Carvalho, *Ana Manda: Os Filhos da Rede*, IICT, Lisbon, 1989, pp.101–10, 170–6; David Sogge (ed.), *Sustainable Peace: Angola's Recovery*, SARDC, Harare, 1992, chapters 3,6,8.
52 Diamonds were the most lucrative product and smuggling, private dealing and embezzlement by officials brought enormous loss to the Angolan state.

This evolution of the political economy was accompanied by one within the power bloc[53] with a transfer of decision-making from the party to the president and a change from the ideological Marxism of the old guard to pragmatic single-party rule. Power relations between creoles and 'new *assimilados*' also shifted as part of the latter continued to struggle against creole and *mestiço* hegemony, now with the support of the *regressados*, claiming cultural forms of 'genuine African' identity as against a distinctive 'Angolan' identity claimed by creoles. No change in official cultural ideology occured though, and the creoles and *mestiços* remained in the power bloc. Antagonisms also continued along ethnic, political, cultural, colour and regional lines, now growing as networks of corruption and clientship. Despite increased rivalries, factors of cohesion also developed. A common membership of the *nomenklatura* closed some divisions between 'old' and 'new' *assimilados*. All the power factions grew more distant from the common people, and their common commitment to winning the war and staying in power increased with their growing privilege. The arrogance of dominance fed on an élitism grounded in disdain for the *matumbo*, 'the ignorant native', common among *assimilados* under Portuguese colonialism and also present in Marxist-Leninist avant-gardes. Salazarism and Stalinism provided common 'heritages' of dictatorial authority and order.[54] No significant modification in the general composition of the *nomenklatura* occurred. Domination of the party-state reinforced the positions of the original power élites, and social promotion ensured that their children reached the highest levels. Former 'natives' with a good record in guerrilla or political activity had gained *nomenklatura* status, and the original popular orientation of the MPLA also permitted some promotion of non-élite middle cadres among youths from all over the country. But former *assimilados* – creoles and Mbundu 'new *assimilados*' – continued to dominate the nucleus of the *nomenklatura*, with a Bakongo segment in a profitable but politically subordinate position.

Deep social change occurred in the country as the population rose to some 11 million inhabitants. The massive exodus from the ever-spreading rural war to the protection of the towns caused Luanda and the provincial capitals to crumble under the weight of refugees. A huge reintegration of *regressados* also took place. Many settled in Luanda and used the skills acquired in exile to invest in the informal economy and in cross-border trade. The Bakongo returnees were the first petty traders and continued to be the most successful ones even when traders of other ethnic origins were active in Luanda's markets.[55]

53 C. Messiant, 'Angola, les voies de l'ethnisation et de la décomposition. I. De la guerre à la paix (1975–1991): conflit armée, les interventions internationales et le peuple angolais', *Lusotopie* 1–2 (1994), pp.187–206, and D. Sogge, *Sustainable Peace*, chapter 7.
54 For literary visions of the evolution of the political and social situation and of the relations of power-holders, see Pepetela, *O Cão e os Calús*, Publicações Dom Quixote, Lisbon, 1985, and *A Geração da Utopia*, Publicações Dom Quixote, Lisbon, 1992; J. Mendes de Carvalho, *O Ministro*, União dos escritores angolanos, Luanda, 1990; Jose Eduardo Agualusa, *A Estação das Chuvas*, Publicaões Dom Quixote, Lisbon, 1996.
55 J. M. Mabeko Tali, 'La "chasse aux Zairois" à Luanda', *Politique Africaine* 57 (March 1995), pp.71–84.

The disruption of land transport to the regions made Luanda an enclave which received but did not distribute imported goods. The growing prevalence of clientship impeded proletarianisation in the country. With token salaries and little production, a worker's status became a formality, and work a sham; no social justice was conceivable when the possession of a dollar note meant that one's purchasing power was raised thirty or even more times by comparison with the local currency.

The development of clientship meant that political exclusion resulted in economic marginalisation. Membership of the *nomenklatura* took on a new importance and perceptions of political power and social inequalities changed. In the provinces marginalised groups tended to blame their misery not on the nature of the regime but on what people saw as privileged groups. The 'Luanda regime' was seen to favour Luanda's people, as well as the *mestiços*, the Mbundu, and also, in the eyes of some, the Bakongo, for selling goods at inaccessible prices. Some regional groups felt cheated of their wealth, especially so where armed opposition parties claimed they would restore provincial well-being. In oil-rich Cabinda armed separatist groups mobilised the population with a claim for independence. Many Ovimbundu hoped that misery could be alleviated and pride restored by UNITA. In the diamond-producing Lunda and Chokwe provinces regional resentment was fuelled by the brutal and wholesale pillaging conducted by outsiders.

Among the supposedly privileged groups perceptions of power evolved in a more complex manner. The absence of rights, the threat of repression, the disappearance of 'legal' career options, the need for state-party support to live, all entrenched a strong allegiance to powerful patrons. Yet Luandans, urban cadres, Bakongo, Mbundu city-dwellers or peasants also knew that a common identity with those in power did not enable them to live decently if they were not included in political or personal networks of clientship. Growing hardship and the sentiment of social injustice and oppression led many into disaffection or even opposition.

The war-time polarisation into two camps caused some disaffected sectors to see in Savimbi's party the only means to an end of MPLA power. A much wider reaction to the misery, however, was the ardent popular and middle class desire for peace and a withdrawal from politics into the private spheres of life, be they commercial, cultural or religious. The years of official atheism saw a considerable growth of all the churches in Angola as places of hope and refuge. The Catholic Church profited most by virtue of its social assistance activities and its public criticisms of the war and of MPLA policy. When the church denounced the power of the 'lords of war' and demanded peace and democracy, it voiced the aspiration of large popular and élite circles. In the towns and in Luanda, significant minorities also distanced themselves politically both from the MPLA and from UNITA to claim social and democratic rights for Angolans. Despite the wartime logic which drove those who rejected one party to support the other, despite the strength of clientship and the repression of protest, political discontent and a movement in favour of citizen autonomy and democratisation grew. A proliferation of social, civic and political initiatives ensued, when they were given free reign in 1991.[56]

But the regime, although aware of growing disaffection, feared reform. It was ever more reluctant to reverse its social policies and to meet people's economic needs, resisting attempts at economic reform which checked *nomenklatura* privilege. Relaxing its undemocratic grip over society might mean losing political control. Least of all was the regime ready to compromise with UNITA. Savimbi remained the arch enemy, and power-sharing would put considerable economic interests at risk in an electoral contest.

On the UNITA side, power through war remained the agenda. Democracy, though an explicitly proclaimed objective of UNITA, was out of the question. The whole history of Savimbi's organisation was one of military power fundamentally impervious to democracy.

A FLAWED PEACE PROCESS

While the population longed in silence for peace and freedom, the first steps to end the war came from the outside. The Soviet Union wanted to extricate itself from its external military engagements. South Africa had learnt, after its retreat in the enormous battle for Cuito Cuanavale, that enabling UNITA to win the war would involve a much greater effort than hitherto imagined and would have grave political repercussions at home.[57] Under American mediation, and with Soviet agreement, two accords were signed in December 1988 in New York, on the eve of the end of the Cold War. Angola, Cuba and South Africa agreed that Cuba should leave Angola in exchange for Namibia's independence and an end to South Africa's military help for UNITA.[58] The accords, however, were not followed by a lessening of the war effort, but by its intensification. The MPLA saw the end of South African help to UNITA as an opportunity to neutralise its enemy rather than to compromise politically. At Gbadolite, in 1989, it merely offered UNITA positions in an unchanged MPLA one-party system. The United States therefore increased its military support to UNITA to pressurise the government into accepting a multi-party solution with a political place for UNITA. Only after a year of this ever-growing military pressure did the government negotiate, then accept

56 C. Messiant, 'Social and political background to the "democratization" and the peace process in Angola', in *Democratization in Angola*, African Studies Centre, Leiden, 1993, pp.32–4; Sogge, *Sustainable Peace*, chapter 7.
57 On Cuito Cuanavale, see Fred Bridgland, *The War for Africa: 12 Months that Transformed a Continent*, Ashanti Publications, Gibraltar, 1990; Horace Campbell, *The Siege of Cuito Cuanavale*, SIAS, Uppsala, 1990; also Karl Maier, *Angola: Promises and Lies*, SERIF, London, 1996.
58 C. Messiant, 'Le retour à la guerre ou l'inavouable faillite d'une intervention internationale', *L'Afrique Politique, 1994*, Karthala, Paris, 1994, pp.199–229; Minter, *Apartheid's Contras*, chapter 6; and Chester Crocker, *High Noon in Southern Africa: Making Peace in a Rough Neighbourhood*, Norton, New York, 1992.

multi-party politics as the basis of a new agreement with UNITA, and finally signed the peace accords in Portugal in May 1991.

The Bicesse accords were supposed to lead to peace through demilitarisation, democratisation and a general election. They were hailed as an example of the 'new international order'. They were, however, marked by the very unequal relations of power between the Angolan parties and their allies rather than by any consideration of Angola's need for peace and democracy.[59] The widespread expectation among international negotiators, shared by the MPLA itself, was that UNITA would win an electoral contest. Indeed the foreign peace-brokers conceived the accord to 'accompany' this outcome rather than to tackle the difficult problem of creating conditions for a lasting peace after so acute a confrontation. The international intervention was, furthermore, given no adequate mandate and derisory means of control.

The transition instituted a 'dual monopoly' of power by UNITA and the MPLA.[60] Responsibility for pacification and democratisation was given to two armed forces very far from reconciled in spirit, or ready to answer people's needs. In contrast to the South African road to democracy, no provision was made for a multi-party transitional executive before the elections or for a government of national unity after the vote. A 'winner takes all' option prevailed, and the election thus became the last battle of the war, exacerbating the power struggle. The transition also gave Angolans too little time to settle down and come to believe in peace. Worse still, the signatories were authorised to retain their respective hegemonic practices.[61] UNITA showed itself to be less a political movement and more an army waiting impatiently for power and believing in force. It failed to comply with demobilisation agreements, and showed no sign that it could be a benevolent or democratic winner. Those associated in any way with 'the ruling cast' feared that they would be in danger if UNITA won the election. On the other side, the government abused for political ends its control of the instruments and resources of the state, such as oil revenue, government services, the police, and the media. It accelerated the plundering of public assets in case it should lose the election, while simultaneously giving material and symbolic signs that it wanted peace and would now care for its people. It also warned the country of the barbarous dictatorship it could expect should UNITA win.

A turning point in the transition came at the beginning of 1992 when two senior leaders of UNITA defected and accused Savimbi of having executed two of his lieutenants. Many sympathetic Angolans began to distance themselves from UNITA and the government saw the first signs that the political tide could be reversed. Henceforth, no further compromises were sought by

59 Messiant, 'Social and political background', and 'Le retour à la guerre'.

60 Messiant, 'Le retour à la guerre'; Moises Venâncio, *The United Nations, Peace and Transition: Lessons from Angola*, Instituto de estudos estratégicos e internacionais, Lisbon, 1994.

61 On the policies of the two sides and their consequences during the transition to elections, see C. Messiant, 'Angola: les voies de l'ethnisation et de la décomposition. II. Transition à la démocratie ou marche à la guerre?', *Lusotopie* (1995), pp.181–212.

MPLA with small parties and no democratic niceties were tolerated. The many parties that had been founded after the signing of the Bicesse accords were relegated to the margins of the political arena, while UNITA and MPLA propaganda and disinformation competed, unhindered by the international community. The international monitors did not even accomplish the most necessary task of ensuring that disarmament and demobilisation were accomplished. UNITA was permitted to keep the core of its army ready for remobilisation. The MPLA, having indeed demobilised its demoralised army, was rapidly able to build an alternative paramilitary police force. Instead of appeasing the political antagonisms, the transition fostered a growing logic of war which was aggravated by the failure of both sides to disarm and by the discrediting of the international community.

THE FACE OF THE ENEMY AND THE STAKES IN THE VOTING

By the end of the transition, the balance of power between the two contenders had been reversed. Fear of brutal retribution had lost Savimbi's party the sympathy of many who would have voted for it. But this was not the only change, and hope of better relations between winner and people had dwindled with the experience of the transition. Angolans no longer sought the best government but only the most generous protector and the least bad master. Fear of a return to war was at the heart of the election. Voters wanted to be protected by a strong force, a sentiment which strengthened both parties.[62] The electoral terrain was thus a military, political and social mine-field. Although it had become obvious that there could be no effective demobilisation or army unification before the date set for the election, the international community nevertheless determined to hold the ballot on 29 and 30 September 1992. The most basic political and military conditions needed to ensure acceptance of the outcome were, however, missing. Angolans voted massively and enthusiastically in a desperate longing for peace and in the hope that the international community would recognise their sovereign act and prevent a return to war.

The parliamentary election result gave a majority of 53.7 per cent to the MPLA while UNITA only reached 34 per cent. The small parties, among them the FNLA, received less than 2.5 per cent each. In the election for the presidency, José Eduardo dos Santos, the president of Angola and of the MPLA, only received 49.5 per cent of the 50 per cent vote necessary to win. Savimbi received 40 per cent. A second round of voting became necessary. UNITA protested that massive fraud had occurred and did not accept the result, even after the United Nations had made some checks and declared the elections 'generally free and fair'. UNITA threatened that, if the result was not cancelled, a destructive war could bring about Somali-style destruction in Angola, and moved its army to strategic points in the country. The international

62 Messiant, 'Angola: les voies, II', pp.208–10.

community now tried anxiously to avoid a return to war by sponsoring power-sharing before the second round of voting, but the government was not ready to see its new legitimacy dented, and UNITA was not willing to see power slip from its grasp. The second vote never occured and war began again, despite all appeals from a now impotent international community.

After a month of growing tension, disinformation, armed incidents, and UNITA military movements in the provinces, the first central strike came from the government. During the last weekend of October 1992, the special police, commandos, militias and armed militants launched a 'cleansing' operation to eliminate UNITA from Luanda and from several provincial capitals. The attacks targeted military bases, civilian installations, political cadres and party militants, causing at least 1,200 deaths in Luanda, and killing several senior UNITA leaders and hundreds of their soldiers. The survivors fled from Luanda or were imprisoned. Civilians were also attacked, in the city, in the suburbs, and in the slums of Luanda. Some were murdered simply for having voted for UNITA, for being Ovimbundu, or as returnees.[63] One perverse effect of the election had been to reveal an ethnicisation of political choice. The murderous ethnic turn taken by the 'battle for the towns' (according to the MPLA) or the 'All-Saints Day massacre' (according to UNITA) did not, however, give way to longer-term ethnic reprisals or massacres. The roots of political confrontation in Angola had not been, and still were not, ethnic. But an ethnic dimension had indeed grown from a flawed process of democratisation and a failed peace, which expressed itself in the government offensive and was entrenched by it.

The two years of war from 1992 to 1994 were to be the most destructive and disruptive that Angola had known in its agonised history. In the cruelty of that war new fears played a part, as civilians were remobilised to wage pitiless war against civilians who were now considered enemies. The driving force behind this cruelty was, however, the confrontation of two hegemonic leaderships with irreconcilable ambitions and each resolved to annihilate the other. Both sides prevented humanitarian aid from reaching starving populations. During long months of deadly siege UNITA surrounded provincial towns, even ones which had voted for it, while government forces indiscriminately bombed the towns and villages which UNITA held.[64]

After the first shock of its expulsion from the cities, the superior, non-demobilised, UNITA army was able to seize a majority of the provinces. Deprived of help from the American and South African governments, it revived its networks of support among South African security forces. In Zaire

63 Human Rights Watch, *Angola: Arms Trade and Violations of the Laws of War since the 1992 Elections*, HRW, New York, Nov. 1994, pp.61–70; and on the resumption of the war, Messiant, 'Le retour à la guerre', pp.223–7; also, Cicero Queiros, *Angola: Outubro de 1992. Um Passo para o Abismo*, Edições Pesquisa, Lisbon, 1995.
64 On the war of 1992–94, see Alex Vines, 'La troisième guerre angolaise', *Politique Africaine* 57 (1995), pp.27–39; Human Rights Watch, *Angola: Arms Trade*; Maier, *Angola: Promises and Lies*.

it could sell the diamonds captured from the Lunda provinces. While military success lasted, UNITA eschewed all negotiations. Only after the United States had recognised the MPLA government and the Angolan army had rearmed and re-equipped itself by mortgaging the country's oil, did UNITA seriously agree to negotiate. Despite the sanctions imposed by the United Nations, it took a year and another major military offensive by the government before UNITA signed the Lusaka Protocol, in November 1994, in a vain last attempt to avoid the loss of its stronghold of Huambo. Only international pressure persuaded the reluctant government army chiefs of staff to desist from a more radical neutralisation of UNITA in defiance of the accord.

SOCIAL DISLOCATION AND THE NEW PEACE PROCESS

The war of 1992–4 brought levels of destruction hitherto unknown, with cities in ruins and exceptional social dislocation. Hundreds of thousands of people were enclosed for months in towns, villages and war zones on the verge of starvation. Survival meant fighting, violence, a disintegration of solidarity and a generalised culture of pillage. Those under the rule of UNITA suffered the most severe economic hardship and arbitrary, unchecked and ruthless militarised power. Three million Angolans fled from war and famine to places where they could find food or shelter. In this war only Luanda, the coastal cities and the protected zone around Lubango were safe. The misery of refugee life, dependent on international food aid, in camps, in slums, or on the streets caused utter distress.[65] Violence pervaded the lives of Angolans not only due to war but also from the threat of plunder and assault by armed criminals, soldiers or policemen. Two years of war saw an unparalleled increase in armed urban criminality by ever more organised gangs. The war was also a time of extreme ostentation and enrichment by many at the top of the party, the state and the army. An unprecedented surge in corruption linked to war profits occured in private business, whether, national or international. The government blamed the war, the enemy, and the structural adjustment measures imposed by international institutions for the people's misery, but permitted no social or political challenges. Under a façade of parliamentary life the MPLA controlled the media, neutralised critics and maintained a monopoly of power. More dangerously, it deflected mass discontent, pointing at scapegoats against whom popular frustration could be directed. In January 1993 rumours of a Zairian infiltration designed to kill the Angolan president were spread as a pretext to 'hunt down' so-called 'Zairians', and Angolan *regressados* were chased out of the markets of Luanda by civilians and police. Murder, the violation of women, and plunder went unpunished.[66] In the following December, as social misery bred further discontent, it was against the Lebanese,

65 On displaced persons, see Fernando Pacheco, 'Les déplacés et la question du retour', *Lusotopie* (1995), pp.213–20.
66 Mabeko Tali, 'La "chasse aux Zairois"', pp.71–94.

some of them business associates of sectors of the *nomenklatura*, that the so-called 'popular rage' was directed.

The 1994 Lusaka Protocol, founded on the government's electoral legitimacy, demanded, unlike the Bicesse accord of 1991, the unilateral demobilisation and disarming of UNITA forces. The treaty did furthermore represent notable political progress since Bicesse, proposing a transitional period with power-sharing, a coalition government, and an international intervention force ten times stronger than had been offered in 1991. The war, however, had opened a new chasm of deep hatred between the signatories. No good faith or good will could be expected from either side. The new peace process had to deal with extreme mistrust and a fierce desire by both sides to preserve military forces, and by UNITA not to disarm unilaterally. The second, political, step in the Lusaka peace process also suffered from ambiguities. The government of national unity and reconciliation designed at Lusaka excluded all political and civil entities other than UNITA and the MPLA from a political role. In the eyes of the MPLA, the sharing of power was an imposition by the international community since electoral victory had given it a right to full power. The prospective entry of UNITA into government did not imply any agreement over policy, which remained the MPLA programme. The planned return of UNITA deputies to parliament would create a forum for debate, but the MPLA majority ensured that decisions would not be contrary to the party policy. In any case, real political and economic power was held neither by government nor by parliament but was in the hands of the president and of unofficial power groups.

Under such conditions UNITA delayed implementation of the first military phase of the settlement, though it solemnly, if very improbably, proclaimed at the end of 1996 that it had completed its demobilisation and disarmament. The MPLA managed, despite the integration of some UNITA men, to keep control of its police and barely disarmed the militias and civilians it had armed in 1992. At the end of 1996, the coalition government was scheduled to meet before the United Nations forces departed in February 1997, but the situation remained one of political warfare rather than unity and reconciliation.

The Lusaka Protocol brought no real peace. Under its umbrella the two parties saw a renewed licence to dominate their own sections of the country as partitioned in November 1974. The free movement of persons and goods was hampered by checkpoints on either side, by murderous armed attacks along the roads, and by the laying of millions of land mines. In UNITA zones people continued to be subjected to the rule of the party and no expression of opposition could breach the necessity for silence and submission. In government zones the vicious circle of misery and corruption continued unabated alongside nominal parliamentary democracy. The arbitrary rule of the *nomenklatura* carried on providing personal profit, with political impunity. Inside the party critics of corruption remained timid, still fearing to weaken the party in the face of UNITA but now also at risk of reprisals from their own ranks. Fear spread everywhere as ordinary Angolans were subjected to criminality, the abuse of power, and intimidation[67]. Despite difficult conditions, a few independent organisations gained strength, particularly in education and in hospitals. They formed the embryo of civil society, but fear and despair remained heavy. In contrast to 1991, the majority of displaced persons did not go back to their homes. A new surge of charismatic churches and a multitude of sects developed among people hoping for miracles of fortune and health, and among disoriented youths wanting to escape from a world they saw as decidedly bad.

With social discontent brewing in many quarters, the MPLA could opt for real democratisation and the redistribution of the considerable national wealth to marginalised populations. But it could also try to reform its domination without changing its basic way of exercising power. The Lusaka Protocol left intact the socio-political system and power continued to lie with whoever controlled the oil reserves and essential distribution. In early 1997, after two years of a 'peace process', UNITA and the MPLA were about to coexist politically in a planned government of national unity designed to be in place for an indefinite period. No election was on the agenda for the near future. The rule of law, the guaranteeing of civic and social rights, and an end to arbitrariness and economic marginalisation, were essential in order that this coexistence should not deteriorate into further national dramas. Having intervened so decisively in war and then so ambiguously in peacemaking, the international community had done little to help Angola on its uncertain way.

---

67 The murder of a leading journalist of the small independent press was a serious warning to opponents and critics.

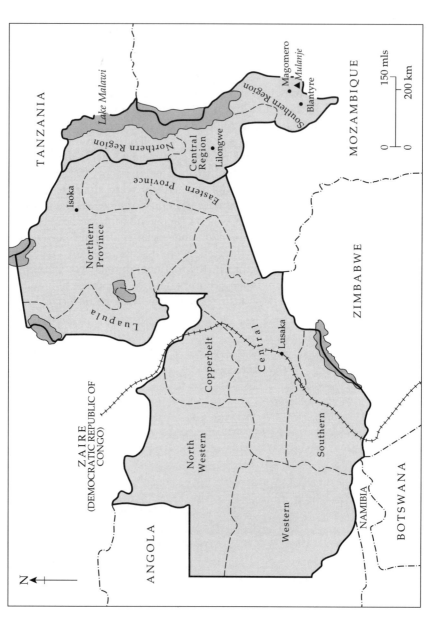

Map 7.1 Zambia and Malawi

CHAPTER 7

Exploitation and neglect: rural producers and the state in Malawi and Zambia

MEGAN VAUGHAN

In the Isoka district of Zambia, which borders Tanzania, *amapulani* was widely held to be essential to survival in the late 1980s. People with *amapulani* were admired but not trusted, for they were succeeding where others failed. The meaning of the word *amapulani* in the Ichinamwanga language had shifted since the 1960s, according to the anthropologist Owen Sichone.[1] In those heady days of state-directed development crusades, the word had been used to describe those who were 'getting ahead' in the context of 'development'. Twenty years later it carried an unmistakable resonance of cunning. With the failure of 'rural development' here and elsewhere in this part of Africa, survival in an uncertain cash economy depended more than ever on individual initiative and the ability to out-manoeuvre others. The people with *amapulani* were risk-takers, but they were not rich and their livelihoods remained vulnerable. Examples of behaviour labelled *amapulani* included the hoarding of maize and beans which would be used to pay casual labour from poor households short of food; buying second-hand clothes, soap and salt that were scarce in the 1980s and using them to pay casual labour; changing a registered birth-date to qualify for retirement benefits; befriending a headmaster to obtain access to the labour of schoolchildren; and using magic charms to undermine the work of neighbours and enhance one's own harvest. Access to the institutions of the state was useful in 'getting on' but access to labour was more important, though hiring labour might not be a straightforward transaction. Commodity shortages in Zambia in the 1980s meant that the value of cash to a rural dweller, and even to some town dwellers, was uncertain. To be certain of securing labour then, one might have to pay in kind. All over

1 O. Sichone, 'Development dynamics: views from a village in Isoka district' in K. Crehan and A. von Oppen (eds), *Planners and History: Negotiating 'Development' in Rural Zambia*, Multimedia, Lusaka, 1994, pp.63–91.

the region, men and especially women were 'working for salt', or 'working for soap', or working for maize, millet or cassava.

Women with *amapulani* were frequently beer-brewers. Elsewhere in northern Zambia beer was also central to the economic survival of many households, particularly those headed by women. In Mpika and Kasama districts women performed 'food for work', or *ukupula* in chiBemba. The food they earned might be consumed directly or might enter a longer cycle of exchange. A woman might work for another household in order to obtain millet, an essential component of some favoured types of beer, and then sell her beer to men in exchange for cash, or use it directly to recruit male labour through a work party.[2] This *ukupula* was not new and had been noted in the 1930s and the 1950s, and a newly-arrived development worker in northern Zambia in the 1980s might have thought that little had changed over fifty years. Barter exchange remained central to the local economy, households were still vulnerable to seasonal fluctuations and cycles of subsistence, and the collection of 'traditional' wild foods such as caterpillars seemed to completely dominate the lives of many people. Labour was obtained through complex sets of social negotiations, and accusations of witchcraft were rife. Few seemed to be engaged with the process of 'development', and some farmers relied more on 'ancient' practices of shifting cultivation than on 'improved' methods of farming. Yet, the development worker would have been wrong in one crucial respect: the strategies of rural people in northern Zambia in the 1980s were not simple vestiges of a pre-capitalist past, but rather the product of a long and volatile engagement with the market and the state, an engagement in which, in the words of Sara Berry, 'no condition is permanent'.[3] Except, one might want to add, that of poverty.

The Mulanje district of southern Malawi also lies on an international border, in this case along the Mozambique frontier. Here, too, the condition of poverty had the appearance of permanence, but the configuration of that poverty was different from that of northern Zambia. Whereas land in northern Zambia is not in absolute short supply, this is far from the case in southern Malawi. In 1987, Mulanje district had a population density of 185 persons per square kilometre.[4] Many households appeared to be locked into a vicious

---

2 Accounts of *ukupula* and its variants can be found in Johan Pottier's account of Mambwe villages in the 1980s: J. Pottier, *Migrants No More: Settlement and Survival in Mambwe Villages, Zambia*, Manchester University Press, Manchester, 1988, in Moore and Vaughan's re-study of the work of Audrey Richards: H. L. Moore and M. Vaughan, *Cutting Down Trees: Gender, Nutrition and Agricultural Change in the Northern Province of Zambia, 1890–1990*, James Currey, London, 1994, and in Evans and Young's account of agricultural change in Mpika District: A. Evans and K. Young, *Gender Issues in Household Labour Allocation: the Transformation of a Farming System in Northern Province, Zambia*, Report to the Overseas Development Administration's Economic and Social Research Committee, London, 1988.
3 S. Berry, *No Condition is Permanent: the Social Dynamics of Agrarian Change in Sub-Saharan Africa*, University of Wisconsin Press, Madison WI, 1993: Sara Berry uses the Northern Province of Zambia as one of her examples in her comparative study of agrarian change in Africa.
4 This figure includes around 10,000 hectares taken up by tea estates – therefore the true density for smallholders is much higher.

cycle involving both a land and labour shortage. The overall shortage of land, signalled by population pressure and by an ever-increasing number of land disputes, combined with a shortage of local employment possibilities, led many men to leave their households and seek work elsewhere. In the past they had gone to the mines of South Africa, but when that labour market closed many migrated north to low-paid work on the tobacco estates of the central and northern regions. Many women left in Mulanje, old and young, headed households in which the provision of subsistence was a daily struggle. Most had tiny plots or small fragmented parcels of ground, some of which were 'borrowed' from a neighbour in return for a share in the crop. In addition to being short of land, they frequently suffered from a lack of labour, especially if they were sick or disabled. Some households had to give up the struggle to stay in the business of cultivation and relied instead on hiring out their labour to others. *Ganyu*, in southern Malawi, once had much the same meaning as *ukupula* in northern Zambia, but in this area of deepening impoverishment and differentiation it had begun to lose the element of reciprocity between cultivators which it retained elsewhere. Though 'permanent' *ganyu* labour is a contradiction in terms, this was in fact an accurate description of the survival strategy of many poorer women in Mulanje in the 1980s. Even when they retained a foothold on a piece of land, they had ceased to be cultivators and had become agricultural labourers, with all the vulnerability which that condition implied.

In 1988 research workers for the non-governmental organisation, OXFAM, attempted to piece together a pattern of poverty prevailing in Mulanje from the perceptions of the poor themselves.[5] Most saw the source of their poverty as being land shortage, and many households grew only enough food to last two to three months. Most also complained of the deterioration in the quality of the soil, which was tired, depleted and impossible to plant without fertilisers, which few could afford. They felt a desperate need for employment and for cash. Some found work on tea estates in the wetter regions of the Mount Mulanje foothills, but there was never enough work for all and the wages for casual labour were low. Here, as in Isoka, the agents of 'development' were mostly regarded with cynicism. 'Farmers' Clubs' were thought to be only for the rich, and agricultural extension workers never visited the woman farmer with her tiny plot of land. Poverty had become, for some, a matter of shame. When asked why they did not visit government-run health clinics in the area, many women replied that they lacked appropriate clothing to do so. In Malawi, the public rhetoric of the Banda government continued to insist that poverty was a thing of the past, of the colonial past, which had long since been eradicated along with 'ignorance and disease'. The reality was very different.

In both Isoka and Mulanje poverty was a daily reality in the late 1980s. Yet not everyone in Isoka or in Mulanje was grindingly poor, and those who were had often reached that state by different routes. In Mulanje, the structural

5 R. Trivedy, *Action Research in Southern Malawi*, Oxfam Research Paper no.1, Oxford.

poverty of the land-short poor was deepening. In Isoka, it was not so much land as labour which remained the scarce resource. In both places the lack of local employment and the decline of male labour migration to the mines of the Copperbelt or to the south had radically altered the structure of livelihoods. In both places access to scarce resources, whether cash, labour, land, fertiliser, employment or, crucially, credit, depended on who you were and whom you knew. Relations with the institutions of the state and political party, with the cooperative society machinery, with the local headmaster and the agricultural extension officer were perhaps the most valuable resources of all. Negotiability was a fact of economic life, and economic life was indissolubly linked to political life and to social institutions.[6] In both Zambia and Malawi state-led 'rural development', which had been around since the late colonial period, appeared by the 1980s to have failed to benefit the majority of the rural population. Rather, the policy had added to the web of institutions and relationships which stood between the farmer and 'the market', creaming off a surplus and distorting incentives. Structural adjustment programmes and market liberalisation, largely imposed from the outside, attempted to break these links, these 'distortions' of the market system, and to put the rural producer in a more direct relationship with 'the market'. By the mid-1990s the effects of these new policies began to be assessed.

THE LATE COLONIAL PERIOD: CREATING 'DEVELOPMENT' AND CONTROLLING THE MARKET

Institutionalised 'rural development' in Zambia and Malawi did not begin with independence in 1964, but rather in the period after the Second World War which some historians have labelled the 'second colonial occupation'.[7] African colonial economies were drawn into a closer relationship with the metropole in an attempt to make the empire pay and to relieve pressure on the pound sterling. Rural East and Central Africa were seen as having the potential

6 This is essentially the argument put forward by Sara Berry in her account of the politics and social relations of agararian change in Africa: Berry, *No Condition*.
7 Studies of this period include J. Lonsdale and B. Berman, *Unhappy Valley*, Book 2, James Currey, London, 1992; S. Feierman, *Peasant Intellectuals: Anthropology and History in Tanzania*, University of Wisconsin Press, Madison WI, 1990; P. Maack, '"We Don't Want Terraces"' in G. Maddox, J. Gilbin and I. Kimambo (eds), *Custodians of the Land: Ecology and Culture in the History of Tanzania*, James Currey, London, 1996, pp.152–71; J. Iliffe, *A Modern History of Tanganyika*, Cambridge University Press, Cambridge, 1979; S. N. Chipungu, *The State, Technology and Peasant Differentiation in Zambia: a Case Study of Southern Province, 1930–1986*, National Education Company of Zambia, Lusaka, 1988; N. Long, *Social Change and the Individual: a Study of Social and Religious Responses to Innovation in a Zambian Rural Community*, Manchester University Press, Manchester, 1968; J. Gould, *Luapula: Dependence or Development?*, Zambia Geographical Association and Finnish Society for Development Studies, Vammala, 1989; E. C. Mandala, *Work and Control in a Peasant Economy: a History of the Lower Tchiri Valley in Malawi, 1859–1960*, University of Wisconsin Press, Madison WI, 1990; W. Beinart, 'Agricultural planning and the late colonial technical imagination: the Lower Shire valley in Malawi, 1940–1960', in *Malawi: an Alternative Pattern of Development*, Centre of African Studies, University of Edinburgh, Seminar Proceedings No.25, 1984, pp.93–149; O. Kalinga, 'The Master Farmers' Scheme in Nyasaland, 1950–1962', *African Affairs* 92 (1993), pp.367–89.

to produce more dollar-earning cash crops, and money from the Colonial Development and Welfare Fund was directed towards raising the incomes and the income-producing capacity of rural dwellers. Nyasaland, an entirely agricultural country, devoid of mineral resources, was much the poorer of the two territories. Nyasaland had a tripartite economy: a small white settler population, concentrated in the south, but increasingly present in the central region, produced tea and tobacco and employed both wage labourers and 'visiting tenants'; peasant producers in the southern and central regions grew cotton, dark-fired tobacco, maize and other crops; migrant labourers left every year in large numbers for South Africa, and Northern and Southern Rhodesia. Some migrants came from the more prosperous peasant-producer areas, but more were drawn from remoter regions of the north and the centre, where the major constraint on local incomes was not land shortage but the absence of infrastructure and markets. Some 'Nyasas' found their way to neighbouring Northern Rhodesia – Nyanja and Tumbuka were widely spoken on the Copperbelt in the 1940s and 1950s. Many educated 'Nyasas' from the north of the country also moved to form part of a distinct labour aristocracy in the mining regions.

The migrants found an economy very different from the one which they left behind and, despite some close ethnic links, a very different society. Northern Rhodesia had wealth derived from copper which had formed the heart of its economy since the 1920s.[8] Even the remote parts of this large country were firmly linked to the copper economy through the migration of men and, increasingly, women. By the 1940s the rural economy of Northern Rhodesia could be characterised as falling into two halves. Those areas which lay along the 'line of rail' turned mainly to cash crop production for the urban market and experienced low rates of out-migration, whilst those further away from this crucial line of communication became migrant labour reserves. Hence the Southern Province produced maize for sale to the Copperbelt towns and to Lusaka,[9] while Barotseland provided labour. There were some exceptions to this pattern. Both Luapula and the Northern Provinces lay far from the 'line of rail', but whilst the Northern Province as a whole was a labour-exporting area with little potential for cash-cropping, the economy of Luapula rested less on migrancy and more on fish, for which there was a buoyant market, not only on the Copperbelt, but also across the border in the Belgian Congo.[10] Many Northern Rhodesians from even remote parts of the country thus gained an experience of urban living and many men and some women spent their whole working lives in urban areas, with infrequent visits home.[11]

8 See R. H. Bates, *Rural Responses to Industrialization: a Study of Village Zambia*, Yale University Press, New Haven, CN, 1976; A. Roberts, *A History of Zambia*, Heinemann, London, 1976.
9 Chipungu, *The State*.
10 Bates, *Rural Responses*; I. Cunnison, *The Luapula Peoples of Northern Rhodesia*, Manchester University Press, Manchester, 1959.
11 J. Ferguson, 'Mobile workers, modernist narratives: a critique of the historiography of transition on the Zambian Copperbelt', Parts 1 and 2, *Journal of Southern African Studies* 16 3 (1990), pp.385–412; 16 4 (1990), pp.603–21.

Despite the efforts of the colonial administration to avoid creating an African urban class, this had very clearly emerged on the Copperbelt by the 1940s. Yet, most urban workers did eventually return 'home', and this was a rural home.

Colonial administrators and commentators on Northern Rhodesia had long recognised the danger of over-dependence on the copper industry, and the experience of the Depression of the 1930s had deepened these fears. The Depression on the Copperbelt, however, was shortlived and the new war industries in Europe soon stimulated production until copper accounted for 90 per cent of the territory's exports, a situation which prevailed into the 1980s. Postwar development policies aimed, in part, to redress the imbalance between mining and farming by stimulating agricultural production and generating employment and services in rural areas. 'Development', however, had no sooner been invented in Northern Rhodesia and in Nyasaland than it became embroiled in the politics of African nationalism and debates over the Central African Federation.

In parts of Northern Rhodesia, the 'problem' of African agriculture had long been perceived as one associated with mobility. In less populous areas villagers continued to practise shifting cultivation which involved the periodic movement of villages. Not only was this system regarded as 'wasteful' and unsustainable in agricultural and ecological terms, it also implied in colonial eyes an absence of social control.[12] The movement of people was an administrative nightmare which made tax collection and census enumeration difficult. The dispersal of settlement also appeared to undermine the authority of local agents of government, the Native Authorities, and was a source of anxiety which persisted into the post independence period. The postwar planners felt that agricultural development had an inescapable social dimension and that the key to increased agricultural productivity and to better use of the soil lay in forging an attachment between the male farmer and a piece of land, encouraging investment in permanent housing, and providing services to rural areas. Economic development and social development were inextricably linked. Men would be attracted back to the countryside from urban centres and bring their families to live on peasant farming 'blocks', where, with the help of agricultural officers and community development experts, a new kind of social settlement would come into being. Farming, instead of being left to women, would become a male affair.

By the late 1940s, colonial agricultural officials in both territories were pessimistic about 'reforming' the agricultural practices of most African producers. They began to concentrate, instead, on producing a peasant élite whose profitable agricultural practices would, hopefully, act as an example for others. Late-colonial experts enjoyed a bold technically-driven optimism and, taking a long-term view, thought on a large scale. For the first time in the colonial history of this region, they had significant sums of money with which

12 Moore and Vaughan, *Cutting Down Trees*, chapters 1 and 2.

to plan. Certainly, some of their proposed technical solutions were expensive and highly interventionist. In the Lower Shire valley of Nyasaland, for example, an ambitious plan involved not only the resettlement of communities but a reconfiguration of the whole landscape.[13] By 1957, however, the project had been abandoned, largely owing to the unwillingness of peasants to be forcibly removed. Meanwhile, in the Northern Province of Northern Rhodesia funds from the mining companies were channelled through the colonial government for the purposes of 'resettlement'.[14] The 'rural town' of Mungwi was built, at great expense, with the intention of attracting African men back from the mining districts to become 'progressive' farmers. Here, as elsewhere, an ambitious scheme failed as a result of the unwillingness of Africans to be 'resettled'. Unwillingness to move was soon whipped up into overt hostility by nationalist leaders. Institutionalised development proposals came to be seen as representing the inequities of the Federal system, and 'development' projects were sitting targets. But Mungwi and other large projects would in any case have faltered through economic miscalculation as well as from a failure to understand the social relations which underpinned African production. An ambitious African producer, even with the aid of a plough and colonial sub-sidies, could not afford to cut himself off from his wider kin group as was expected in Mungwi and elsewhere, for it was mostly on his kin that he relied for additional labour to grow tobacco or cotton. Colonial experts looked on in dismay as their neat lines of nuclear family housing took on the more familiar appearance of an African village settlement with new huts erected next to brick houses and the 'colonial village' fragmented into what was essentially a set of lineage settlements. The most successful farmers frequently moved out altogether and explained to each successive colonial anthropologist that big settlements meant more adultery and more witchcraft.

Linked to the question of labour was that of profitability, as was shown by the outcome of the Master Farmers' Scheme of the 1950s in Nyasaland.[15] That the scheme failed to benefit its participants financially was in part due to the heavy burden of debt involved in becoming technically 'improved'. The 'profits' made by some Master Farmers were more apparent than real and in many cases losses were only covered by a government subsidy in the form of a 'bonus'. The relationship between the participants in these colonial schemes and the nationalist movement needs to be inserted into a larger story of economic and social differentiation.[16] While some African commercial

13 Mandala, *Work and Control*, chapters 6 and 7; Beinart, 'Agricultural planning'.
14 Moore and Vaughan, *Cutting Down Trees*, chapter 5.
15 Kalinga, 'Master Farmers'.
16 Kalinga, 'Master Farmers'; J. Momba, 'The state, rural class formation and peasant participa-tion in Zambia: the case of Southern Province', *African Affairs* 88 (1989), pp.331–59; M. Dixon-Fyle, 'Agricultural improvement and political protest on the Tonga Plateau, Northern Rhodesia', *Journal of African History* 18 (1977), pp.579–96; Chipungu, *The State*; M. Bratton, *The Local Politics of Rural Development: Peasant and Party-State in Zambia*, University of New England Press, Hanover, NH, 1980; Bates, *Rural Responses*.

farmers owed part of their success to colonial loans and subsidies, others made profits despite a state-led 'development' policy. 'Master Farmers' in Nyasaland, like the occupants of Mungwi in Northern Rhodesia, were probably not the colonial 'stooges' they have been made out to be, but they became easy targets for nationalists who represented them as 'slaves' of the colonial government.

Colonial governments of the late 1940s and 1950s made much of the need to 'advance' African agriculture, but when it came to the macroeconomic framework of pricing policies and marketing, it was the influence of European settler interests that continued to be felt. African nationalists were right to see that rural development for Africans was a sham, when marketing structures in both territories were geared explicitly to benefit white farming interests and the Federation threatened to enhance the political power of the white community. Although nationalist leaders were themselves 'modernisers' who shared much of the agenda of the postwar colonial development 'experts',[17] they concluded that Africans were unlikely to gain significantly from these efforts while they remained politically disenfranchised. Furthermore, postwar 'development', and its sometimes coercive conservation regulations touched rural communities more directly than almost any other colonial intervention and so presented a perfect opportunity for nationalist leaders to tap into rural grievances. The fact that conservation rules directly affected women and entailed a further burden on their labour, gave these measures a powerful if unintended symbolic meaning. Conservation was seen as coercive and transgressive, touching the basis of African life through demands on female labour and direct intervention in household production. In southern Nyasaland the story spread that the powerful and enduring spirit of 'Mbona' was displeased with the ridges agricultural officers had insisted farmers should construct since, in in his embodiment as a snake, Mbona's movement in the fields was impeded.[18] The colonial director of agriculture, Dick Kettlewell, became a target of nationalist attack wherever he went. He was, in fact, an unusually energetic and far-sighted agriculturalist, but for many his name had come to represent the coerciveness of 'conservation'. The Nyasaland African Congress was quick to seize on the opportunity offered by dissatisfaction with conservation measures. 'After all', as Kettlewell was later to observe, 'almost everyone in the country was concerned with agriculture, and so if you could develop their hostility to agricultural activities you had a very solid body of support'.[19] At Magomero, in the middle of Nyasaland's 'white highlands', women's songs by 1953 astutely linked 'contour ridging' with the birth, and anticipated death, of the Federation:

17 Kenneth Kaunda, for example, was an early enthusiast for 'progressive farming', as were many other members of the mission-educated élite. Moore and Vaughan, *Cutting Down Trees*, chapter 4.
18 Mandala, *Work and Control*, p.229.
19 Mss Afr.s.1742: R. W. Kettlewell Papers: Nyasaland, ORDP: Rhodes House Library, Oxford.

Federation capitões
e – e – e
Sooner or later you will die
e – e – e
Contour ridging capitões
e – e – e
Sooner or later you will die
e – e – e
e – e
You will die but you don't know it
a – i – a
You will die but you don't know it[20]

In both Nyasaland and Northern Rhodesia the imposition of Federation crystallised and intensified fear of further land alienation by whites. Conservation measures were seen by some peasants as a cynical attempt by the colonial governments to exploit African labour to 'improve' the land prior to its inevitable transfer to white farmers. These fears were further heightened by the vociferous European demand, in both territories, that 'non-African agriculture' should be the responsibility, not of the territorial governments, but of the Federal government. For many Africans, especially in the southern parts of both territories, this demand by Europeans was seen as a direct threat to African land security. In Nyasaland, the question of European possession of land was also linked to labour. On the Shire Highlands the practice of *thangata*, the extraction of a labour rent from African tenants on private estates, lived on in the collective memory, even on estates where the practice had been abandoned.[21] In 1953 a disturbance on an estate in Thyolo district linked local grievances to the politics of the Federation, while in the Central Region, the 'visiting tenant' system which operated on European-owned tobacco estates was likened to *thangata* by the nationalists of the Nyasaland African Congress. Agitation against conservation measures was a factor in mass nationalism in Northern Rhodesia, linking the concerns of remote rural communities with the politics of colonial chieftaincy, and hence with the nationalism of urban workers. The role of marketing boards was also important. In Northern Rhodesia the economic interests of a relatively weak white settler population had, since the Depression, been explicitly subsidised by the colonial state through the operations of the Maize Control Board. Faced with competition from African peasants in the south and from neighbours in Southern Rhodesia, white farmers owed their survival to a deliberate distortion of the market.[22]

20 L. White, *Magomero: Portrait of an African Village*, Cambridge University Press, Cambridge, 1987, p.217.
21 White, *Magomero*.
22 K. P. Vickery, 'Saving settlers: maize control in Northern Rhodesia', *Journal of Southern African Studies* 11 (1985), pp.212–35.

In Nyasaland, meanwhile, colonial control over marketing focused not only on maize but, perhaps more importantly, on tobacco. The Native Tobacco Board was, despite its title, designed to limit the production of tobacco by African smallholders.[23] There was also a paternalistic element to this policy. The serious famine of 1949 appeared to demonstrate the vulnerability of food production as communities became enmeshed in the market economy.[24] African producers were, therefore, thought to need 'protection' from aspects of the operation of the market 'for their own good'. Both the overtly manipulative and the paternalistic dimensions of this control survived into the postindependence period. One colonial officer recognised the major functions of marketing boards when he was placed in charge of the Maize Marketing Ordinance in Nyasaland in the 1950s:

> Having become responsible for the marketing department I was able at last to put my finger on what before that I had felt was functionally wrong. So the penny dropped. The Maize Marketing Ordinance, the Board and the Organisation it created was not a marketing organisation. The so-called Marketing Board was gloriously mis-named. In reality, it was a body acting on behalf of the consumers of maize, not the producers; it was simply an organisation created to buy the maize needed by the large employers of labour to issue as rations. Their demand in effect determined the price and set a maximum to the quantity bought each year.[25]

In the 1950s, then, while agricultural officers pursued their sincere, if sometimes misguided, strategies to 'improve' African farming, a structural economic and political bias in favour of European interests was all too evident, and made more explicit through the operations of the Federation after 1953.[26] The impressive growth rates of the early Federal economy were achieved primarily through high world copper prices. Fiscal laws ensured that a large proportion of these profits were drained away from their source in Northern Rhodesia. An economic bias towards Southern Rhodesia in particular, and towards white populations in general, was more pronounced than ever. Between 1955 and 1963 the Federal government spent £37 million on 'non-African' agriculture in the Rhodesias, while the three territorial governments combined spent only £27 million on African agriculture. Yet the clear political bias of the economics of the Federation was not the whole story. Although discriminated against in the market, African producers in parts of Northern

23 J. McCracken, 'Planters, peasants and the colonial state: the impact of the Native Tobacco Board in the Central Province of Malawi', *Journal of Southern African Studies* 9 (1983), pp.172–92.
24 M. A. Vaughan, *The Story of an African Famine: Gender and Famine in Twentieth Century Malawi*, Cambridge University Press, Cambridge, 1986.
25 Mss Afr.s.1742(5): Stuart T. Bell papers: Nyasaland, ORDP, Rhodes House Library, Oxford. Bell was development secretary in Nyasaland from 1949 to 1953.
26 For accounts of the Federal economy see: R. Baldwin, *Economic Development and Export Growth: a Study of Northern Rhodesia, 1920–1960*, University of California Press, Berkeley, 1966; Roberts, *History of Zambia*; A. Hazlewood, 'The economics of Federation and dissolution in Central Africa', in A. Hazlewood (ed.), *African Integration and Disintegration: Case Studies in Economic and Political Union*, Oxford University Press, Oxford, 1967, pp.129–85.

Rhodesia and Nyasaland did manage to take advantage of the growth of markets for their produce. It would appear that during the Federal period differentiation between Africans increased and regional imbalances were aggravated. The failures and biases of state-directed 'development' initiatives did not prevent some Africans from 'getting on'. In the Southern Province of Northern Rhodesia, for example, Tonga farmers who had long produced maize for the Copperbelt food market, continued to expand their production in the 1950s and a distinct group of 'rich peasants' with distinct political views and alignments emerged.[27] Some richer producers launched transport businesses to satisfy increased demands for African passenger and freight haulage which European companies could not meet. In Luapula Province, where postwar prosperity rested on the huge regional market for fish, prosperous Africans became fish buyers and transporters. Luka Mumba, for example, earned his initial capital through migrant labour, travelled as far afield as Uganda, Tanganyika and Southern Rhodesia. He later returned to Luapula and purchased an old lorry to transport fish from Lake Bangweulu to the Copperbelt. He progressed to owning a fleet of trucks, buses, a number of stores and an hotel.[28]

With the exception of Luapula and its fishing industry, the economic growth of the 1950s in Northern Rhodesia was largely confined to those areas along the 'line of rail' which enjoyed relatively easy access to urban markets. Rural prosperity remained linked to the urban economy and, hence, to copper prices. The need for further rural development was recognised but it was argued that investment would be more likely to reap rewards if targeted on areas which had already exhibited high potential. The 1961 Report of the Rural Economic Development Working Party argued that such concentration would produce a 'snowball effect' which would ultimately benefit the whole territory.[29]

In Nyasaland regional imbalance was perhaps less acute than in Northern Rhodesia but prosperity for some in the 1950s highlighted the increasing differentiation within communities. On the Shire Highlands the gradual demise of *thangata* on European estates freed more men to take the route south as labour migrants. Some returned home to grow maize and tobacco for the market on their wives' land. Most ignored official government resettlement schemes in favour of more 'informal' resettlement through matrilocal marriage. For women with land, marriage was a 'buyers' market'. Opportunities for making a reasonable cash income from the sale of one's own produce meant that 'for the first time there was money in the villages'.[30] Money in the villages also meant more opportunities for small businesses such as bicycle menders, bricklayers, carpenters and blacksmiths, who found a market for

27 Momba, 'The state'.
28 Y. N. Seleti, 'Entrepreneurship in Colonial Zambia' in S. N. Chipungu (ed.), *Guardians in Their Time: Experiences of Zambians Under Colonial Rule, 1890–1964*, Macmillan, London, 1992, pp.147–80.
29 Northern Rhodesia, *Report of the Rural Economic Development Working Party*, Government Printer, Lusaka, 1961.
30 White, *Magomero*, p.227.

their skills among those who were themselves finding a market for their produce. In 1958, the year in which Dr Hastings Banda returned to Nyasaland to lead the nationalist campaign against the 'hated Federation', a group of musicologists recorded songs in the Central Province. In Lilongwe they arrived just as smallholders were being paid for their fire-cured tobacco. The farmers' songs were not about nationalist politics but about sexual politics. Known locally as the 'snatching season', this was the time when men with money in their pockets were 'snatching' women and girls from their husbands and boyfriends, thereby giving rise to, according to the district assistant, Mr Phiri, 'many, many court cases'.[31] As elsewhere, the gains made from economic growth fell largely to men. Women, especially in matrilineal societies, had long preserved a degree of economic and social independence, but 'development' was a male affair, both in its conception and its practice. This, amongst other features of life in the late colonial period, was not to change with political independence.

In 1964, both Malawi and Zambia attained independence after a struggle against the Federation and against colonial domination which had united ethnically, economically and socially diverse societies against a common enemy. Central to this struggle had been the moral campaign against the economic discrimination and white domination which the Federation represented. For both Kenneth Kaunda in Zambia and Hastings Banda in Malawi, the most pressing task was to raise the living standards of ordinary people and to lift them out of the poverty and 'underdevelopment' which were the most immediately obvious legacies of colonialism. Both leaders had inherited situations in which the state had been heavily involved in the management of the economy, often with the explicit aim of furthering the interests of whites. That both leaders, in different ways, continued to employ the structures of the state to control the market, should therefore have come as no surprise. During the period of interim government from 1961 to 1964, Hastings Banda, as Minister of Natural Resources, had had time to learn the ropes from colonial officials. Banda, according to a number of these officials, was quick to recognise that in the colonial Marketing Board he had inherited an invaluable instrument of economic control and political patronage. He lost no time in extending its operations to cover all crops grown on Trust Lands.[32] In Zambia, meanwhile, the racial and regional bias of the colonial economy became the target for transformation through state intervention in marketing and subsidies. A uniform territorial pricing of crops would, it was hoped,

31 'Report of the ILAM Nyasaland Recording Tour, 1958', *African Music* 2 (1958), pp.65–8.
32 Charles Johnson, who was director of agriculture in Nyasaland from 1960 to 1964 recalled that 'Banda quickly saw the opportunities offered by the Board for extending his authority in the agricultural sector, and conferred additional responsibilities on it by making it the sole buyer of all produce from the Trust Lands': Mss Afr.s.1742(19): Nyasaland, ORDP: Rhodes House Library, Oxford. Dick Kettlewell also recalled that 'I think it fair to say that in the end he [Banda] recognised that there was much wisdom in the work that had gone before . . . and particularly that the Marketing Board gave him an instrument for development and the efficient handling of African grown crops'. Mss Afr.s.1742(3): Kettlewell papers.

deliver benefits to less economically developed parts of the country away from the 'line of rail'. As in the colonial period, 'development' in both states was as much a political and social project as it was an economic one but, despite cultural and historical similarities, Zambia and Malawi were in very different situations at independence.

RURAL DEVELOPMENT IN THE AGE OF COPPER: ZAMBIA, 1964–75

Zambia attained its political independence at the height of a boom in copper prices, a mixed blessing as it turned out, since the problem of over-dependence on this single commodity soon resurfaced. In the short term, however, revenues from copper (71 per cent of total government revenue in 1965) enabled the government to embark on an ambitious programme of nationalisation and social investment. Kaunda's philosophy of 'Humanism', which he articulated in 1967, was a mixture of Fabian socialism, nineteenth-century liberalism, Christian morality and idealisation of the communal values of Zambia's pre-capitalist past.[33] Though Humanism was a philosophy which placed 'man' above ideology and institutions, in practice what the people of Zambia experienced in the first decade of independence was the increasing role of the state and the domination of its proliferating institutions by a new ruling class. In a country never short of satirical commentators, the policy of 'Zambianisation' and nationalisation of many business and manufacturing enterprises was frequently the target of amused and cynical comment. In his column in the *Times of Zambia* in 1968, Kapelwa Musonda proposed the nationalisation of criminal activity under the heading 'If Crime Pays it's Time we Took it Over'.

'Humanism', many commentators suggested, was no more than an ideological gloss. The structural features which in fact characterised the politics of the First Republic (1964–72), and the 'one-party participatory democracy' of the Second Republic, had nothing to do with 'Humanism' or socialism, except when represented rhetorically by the leadership. Political struggles during the First Republic often took on a regional or an ethnic dimension and this continued to be a lasting feature of Zambian politics. Kenneth Kaunda attempted to address 'tribalism' through a kind of ethnic balancing, with each group holding important positions in turn, but the policy could be interpreted more straightforwardly as a grabbing for spoils by an emerging ruling class.[34] The First Republic saw the demise of the multi-party system, and a marked concentration of power in the hands of the executive and of the president. The apparent aim of national politicians was to gain control over the state and restructure the political and economic system to suit their own interests. Despite notable improvements in the welfare of Zambians in the first decade after independence, their long-term interests were sacrificed to an increasingly

33 K. D. Kaunda, *Humanism* (Part I), Government Printer, Lusaka, 1967; K. D. Kaunda, *Humanism* (Part II), Government Printer, Lusaka, 1974; M. M. Burdette, *Zambia: Between Two Worlds*, Westview Press, Boulder CO, 1988, chapter 4.
34 Burdette, *Zambia*, p.73.

powerful and corrupt élite which used the state to expand its role in the economy and penetrate sectors previously dominated by foreign capital. Nationalisation in the name of anti-imperialism and the creation of massive parastatal organisations such as the Zambia Industrial Mining Corporation (ZIMCO), enabled the élite to control the most lucrative areas of the economy and accumulate capital for their own ends. Expanding state control thus 'put vast public resources at the disposal of the elite'.[35] While the money kept flowing there was little incentive to address the structural problems of a copper mono-economy and early signs of the economic decline, which was to hit Zambia from the mid-1970s, were ignored. The urban bias of political and economic policy remained marked, and measures to address agricultural and rural development were largely subordinated to this agenda.

Securing the urban food supply was the ultimate goal of rural development policy. The Zambian government initially concentrated on expanding the network of crop collection depots inherited from the colonial period to enable more farmers to produce for the market. In the rural sector, as in the mining sector of the economy, parastatals were the central instruments of economic policy. A state marketing organisation, Namboard, was established in 1969 as a successor to the old Maize Control Board, and it became one of the largest employers in the country. Through this board, the government moved towards uniform crop pricing to encourage production for the market in less developed regions and banned private trading of the main food crops. In a large country like Zambia, a uniform pricing policy inevitably involved heavy subsidies to producers in remote areas. Furthermore, the political significance of maize as the food of urban workers led to a concentration on this crop, sometimes at the expense of diversity of production and food security for rural producers. Cooperatives were encouraged, state farms were established, credit extended and extension services were supplied, though mostly to wealthier, more 'progressive', male 'farmers', as distinct from mere 'villagers'. The meaning and practice of 'development' had changed little since the late-colonial period. Yet even those who were accorded the title of 'farmer' in the late 1960s and 1970s hardly had an easy time. Overall, prices for their products did not keep up with the cost of manufactured goods, thanks to the superior political muscle of urban workers, especially the mining unions. Farming was not an attractive way to earn a cash income, and migration from countryside to town continued, thereby intensifying labour supply problems for rural producers.[36]

Problems were compounded by the inefficiencies and corruption of Namboard which, far from providing the reliable market thought essential for the

35 J. O. Ihonvbere, *Economic Crisis, Civil Society, and Democratization: The Case of Zambia*, Africa World Press, Trenton NJ, 1996, p.50.
36 Urban wages rose rapidly in the first few years after independence: between 1964 and 1969 the average earnings for African workers rose by 97 per cent, whilst the consumer price index rose by only 37 per cent: Burdette, *Zambia*, p.91. For migration in the postindependence period see also Bates, *Rural Responses*, 1976, chapter 8.

encouragement of a regular agricultural surplus, in fact produced ever greater uncertainties for farmers. Crop pricing was often erratic and the prices were sometimes announced very late. When production costs continued to rise they were not matched by increases in the prices paid to producers. Fertiliser was delivered late and crop collections were unreliable so that bags of maize rotted by the roadside when rains turned the roads to mud. Successful farming came to depend, not only on commanding a supply of labour through the adept manipulation of 'customary' notions of seniority and obligation, but also on close and continually reconstituted connections with the organs of the state and the party. Success in farming thus depended crucially on who you were and whom you knew.[37] Gaining access to some part of state resources in a parastatal like Namboard was a far surer way of making money than farming for the market.

Despite the aim of achieving regional equity and uniformity, the effects of these agricultural policies differed greatly from place to place. In general the 'line of rail' bias was reinforced rather than eradicated, those who were already wealthy gained access to credit, extension advice and subsidies; women were neglected or their economic strategies seriously undermined. The lack of any official market for many traditional household food crops, such as millet, sorghum and cassava, which were grown by women, as well as institutional biases in favour of men increased the marginalisation of women.[38] In some cases, this neglect of women was to contribute to the increasing vulnerability of many rural households.

When the copper price collapsed in 1974, independent Zambia had had ten years of prosperity. Most commentators agreed that much of this advantage had been wasted. Agricultural policy had done little to increase productivity and even less to raise the living standards of the poorest rural dwellers. According to some analysts, a 'confusion between rural development and agri-cultural production' had led to a stress on consumption and on the redistribution of resources, rather than on production.[39] This analysis implied that if market conditions had been more favourable, or agricultural advice more useful, or the state less interventionist, then the story of Zambia's agricultural sector would have been very different. And yet it is hard to see how this 'confusion' between rural development and agricultural production could have been entirely avoided. In a country built on an 'urban bias', rural constituencies expected an independent government to replicate for them some of the advant-ages of urban living. In fact, social investment was impressive in this period, with a rapid expansion in education and health facilities for rural as well as

37 Berry, *No Condition*, pp.88–100.
38 For a case study of the effects of this concentration on maize, see K. Crehan and A. von Oppen, 'Understandings of "development": an arena of struggle: the making of a develop-ment project in North-Western Province' in Crehan and von Oppen (eds), *Planners and History*, pp.257–307.
39 A. P. Wood, 'Agricultural Policy since Independence' in A. P. Wood et al. (eds), *The Dynam-ics of Agricultural Policy and Reform in Zambia*, Iowa State University Press, Ames, 1990, p.292.

Megan Vaughan

urban populations.[40] By the mid-1970s, however, it became clear that the economic foundations were inadequate to pay for much-needed social improvements. Furthermore, an entrenched élite had little interest in reforming a system which, for the time being, served them well.

FEUDALISM IN THE GUISE OF CAPITALISM: MALAWI, 1964–80

Urban bias was not a problem which the new government of Malawi had to face. From the perspective of many Malawians, urban bias would probably have been viewed less as a problem and more as a luxury. There was both jealousy and smugness in the Malawian stereotype of a 'typical' Zambian as one with money (probably obtained illegally), but no food. Zambians, meanwhile, satirised their Malawian neighbours as 'country bumpkins', peasants whose eyes were easily dazzled by the bright lights of the town. Blantyre, the largest urban concentration in Malawi, was a slow-moving place in comparison with the towns of the Copperbelt, or with the city of Lusaka. While Zambia faced the need to increase imports of maize in the late 1970s, President Banda of Malawi was boasting of his country's continued self-sufficiency in foodstuffs. This was only a partial truth, however.

At independence the people of Malawi were some of the poorest in this part of Africa.[41] Not only was the country without mineral wealth, but throughout the colonial period the territory had been saddled with an enormous debt arising from the building of the railway to Beira.[42] When President Banda assumed power in 1964 the three central tenets of economic policy had to be: maintaining food production, earning foreign exchange from cash crops, and balancing the budget. Banda's economic philosophy was firmly neo-classical, pleasing his western donors and allies who came to see Malawi as a buffer against socialism in south-central Africa.[43] In the so-called 'cabinet crisis' of 1964 Banda eliminated the younger, leftist members of the Malawi Congress Party and concentrated power in his own authoritarian hands. Rid of the necessity for internal debate, Banda proclaimed his unequivocal commitment to the west and to the capitalist system. He suppressed consumption and reinvested surpluses in order to guarantee a high growth rate. The people of

40 Between 1964 and 1974 there was a doubling of enrolments in primary school, while enrolments in secondary schools almost quintupled. Government achievements in the health sector were also impressive. Between 1964 and 1972 the number of hospitals had increased by more than 50 per cent and there was a great expansion of primary health care: Burdette, *Zambia*, pp.67–8.
41 Pike estimated that in 1966, Malawi's GDP was 25 per cent of that of Zambia and 22 per cent of that of Tanzania: 'If Malawi's GDP is expressed in terms of "per capita", the resulting figure of £13 is the lowest in Africa': J. G. Pike, *Malawi: a Political and Economic History*, Pall Mall Press, London, 1968, p.218.
42 L. Vail, 'The political economy of East-central Africa' in D. Birmingham and P. M. Martin, *History of Central Africa*, vol. 2, Longman, London, 1983, pp.200–50.
43 On Malawi's foreign relations and its role in regional politics see G. C. Z. Mhone (ed.), *Malawi at the Crossroads: the Postcolonial Political Economy*, SAPES Books, Harare, 1992; J. L. Lwanda, *Kamuzu Banda of Malawi: a Study of Promise, Power and Paralysis*, Dudu Nsomba Publications, Glasgow, 1993; P. Short, *Banda*, Routledge Kegan Paul, London, 1974.

Malawi did not experience the spending spree on social infrastructure or production subsidies which their Zambian neighbours enjoyed. Their duty, as Banda made clear, was not to consume but to work hard. With an annual growth rate of 5.8 per cent per annum between 1965 and 1980,[44] and with self-sufficiency in food, the Malawian story came to be viewed by some observers, including the World Bank, as an 'economic miracle'[45] and a model of peasant-based capitalism compared to the disastrous centralising and social-istic policies of neighbouring Tanzania and Zambia.

A closer analysis produces a rather different picture. The Malawi Congress Party had come to power voicing its concern for the ordinary farmer, the peasant producer. Nationalist rhetoric dwelt not only on grievances against the Department of Agriculture's conservation rules, but also on the colonial practice of *thangata*. The 'visiting tenants' system of the Central Province tobacco estates was seen by many as a mere variation on this theme of 'slavery'. Yet even before independence Hastings Banda was beginning to take a rather more favourable view of estate production.[46] In the first years of independence policy still aimed to bolster smallholder production and the Ministry of Agriculture's local resources were directed towards smallholder projects.[47] In 1967 the growing of sun/air-cured and fire-cured varieties of tobacco was still reserved entirely for peasants. In 1968, however, the estates were given a monopoly on the production of tea, sugar, burley and flue-cured tobacco. The following year marked the beginning of a period of rapid growth in estate pro-duction, labelled by one commentator the 'years of the Presidential fiefdom'.[48]

The declaration of unilateral independence in Rhodesia in 1965 improved the prospects of Malawi's tobacco industry. Some estates were transferred from Europeans to Africans, but the major expansion occurred on new estates located on 'customary' land. The 1965 Land Bill had confirmed the colonial division between 'private', 'public' and 'customary' land and allowed for the granting of leases of 'customary' land to prospective estate owners. Initially, these new owners were mostly members of the President's entourage, politi-cians, security officers and public officials, who obtained large areas of land at virtually no cost. They also benefited from subsidised loans. The govern-ment, unable to interest donors in the financing of estates, directed Malawi's commercial banks to do so. Owning an estate came to mean a great deal more than a commercial investment and the borrowers regarded their loans as gifts from the President, who exercised his patronage on a national scale. His

44 V. Scarborough, *Agricultural Policy Reforms under Structural Adjustment in Malawi*, Agricultural Development Unit, Wye College, Occasional Paper No.12, 1990.
45 World Bank, *Accelerated Development in Sub-Saharan Africa*, Washington D.C., 1981.
46 McCracken, 'Planters', pp.56–7; see also the recollections of Charles Johnson, director of agriculture 1960–64 in Mss Afr.s.1742(19) and Robert Dewar, permanent secretary in the Min-istry of Natural Resources and then in the Ministry of Economic Affairs, Mss.Afr.s.1742(8). Both in ODRP (Nyasaland) records, Rhodes House Library, Oxford.
47 J. Kydd, 'Malawi in the 1970s: development policies and economic change', in *Malawi: an Alternative Pattern of Development*, Centre of African Studies, University of Edinburgh, Seminar Proceedings, No.25, 1984, pp.293–381.
48 Kydd, 'Malawi in the 1970s'.

supporters, in turn, regarded their bank loans as a means to exercise local patronage.[49] Many of these estates were disastrously inefficient, but by the mid-1970s, estate owners were a political force at least as powerful as European planters had been during the colonial period. In his speeches President Banda had begun to refer to 'development' or *chitikuko* as what happened on estates rather than smallholdings. At the same time, the government marketing board, ADMARC, extended its operations. Although estate owners conducted business directly with their markets, smallholders had to sell their produce directly to ADMARC. In the 1970s ADMARC profits averaged MK14 million a year, representing a hidden tax on smallholders of over 50 per cent. The massive growth in the estate sector was, thus, financed by a tax on smallholders with declining real incomes. Agricultural wage-employment meanwhile increased. Following an air crash in which many Malawian labour migrants died, President Banda, in 1975, curtailed the export of migrant labour to South Africa, thereby cutting off a major source of wealth for many rural families and forcing them onto the local labour market instead. For some this meant working as casual labour for wealthier peasant farmers, but for others it meant employment on the new estates, either as direct labour, or as tenants. The 'visiting tenant' system against which the nationalists had protested, was far from dead.

Though the World Bank might think that high growth rates in Malawi were the result of liberal, capitalist, market-oriented policies, in fact the economy of Malawi was anything but an open one. Through a set of interlocking connections between ADMARC, the commercial banks and the so-called private sector, Banda had sewn up the whole economy for the benefit of himself and a small élite, largely from the Central Region, to whom he extended his patronage. Much direct government expenditure was wasted on high profile, self-aggrandising projects, such as the building of the new capital of Lilongwe and the construction of lavish presidential residences, but more went into parastatal investment.

What made Malawi different from Zambia, however, was not the role of the parastatals, but the nature of the 'private sector'. A large proportion of the indigenous private sector was actually controlled either by the Malawi Government through the Malawi Development Corporation, or by the President himself through a holding company, Press (Holdings) Ltd. This huge company was 99 per cent owned by the President and grew rapidly in the 1970s by investing in estate agriculture and absorbing, in takeovers of varying degrees of legality, many existing industrial and commercial enterprises. Press Holdings was a major producer, purchaser and exporter of tobacco, owned the biggest retailing company in Malawi, was a large distributor of agricultural produce, owned the largest national bakery and controlled a company manufacturing clothing. Press Holdings had foreign partners in the estate production of sugar and rubber, and held a major stake in a large civil

49 Kydd, 'Malawi in the 1970s', p.326.

engineering business and in a firm of stuctural engineers. Furthermore, Press Holdings also had major interests in the financial sector and by 1977 was the largest shareholder in the country's two commercial banks. The 'private sector' was, in fact, Press Holdings, and Press Holdings was the President. Perhaps the most important aspect of the dominance of Press Holdings was its relationship to the government marketing board, ADMARC, for it was through this relationship that Malawian peasants were effectively taxed for the benefit of the estate-owning political élite. The large profits shown by ADMARC in the 1970s were largely made through not handing on to the peasant farmers the improved export prices which the board received for their crops. ADMARC profits were then invested in Press Holdings and its subsidiaries as low-interest, unsecured loans. Press Holdings, in turn, invested in projects such as the building of the Kamuzu Academy (Malawi's 'Eton') and the purchase of aircraft used to transport Banda's faithful supporters to rallies of the Malawi Congress Party.

When the economic crisis of the late 1970s hit Malawi, it was perhaps less dramatic than that experienced in Zambia, but it exposed a terrifying level of vulnerability and impoverishment amongst Malawian people. In the early 1980s, as President Banda toured the country on his 'crop inspections', exhorting the populace to work harder, and reminding them of the dark days of hunger under colonialism, many Malawians were, in fact, on the verge of starvation.

ADJUSTING TO THE CRISIS: ZAMBIA AND MALAWI IN THE 1980S

Conditions for the rural producers of Zambia in the late 1970s were hardly favourable. Not only were they disadvantaged by low producer prices and by the inefficiencies of Namboard, but even those who were successful in the rural economy could find little or nothing to spend their money on. This was the period of 'shortages'. Price controls and inflation in the cost of imported materials led to such low profit levels for some manufacturers that they curtailed the production of less profitable items.[50] Rural traders, especially in the remoter rural areas, found that even if they could procure the goods they required, they could hardly make a profit on them after meeting transport costs. Shortages affected urban dwellers too. Bottled beer, an essential commodity of Zambian urban life, was frequently unavailable, for lack of beer or bottles or bottle-tops. Queues formed for cooking oil, soap and salt, and a lively black market developed. Zambia's politicians, always alert to the political volatility of the urban working class, continued to attempt to satisfy their needs before those of the rural dwellers.

Although Zambia's economy had always been 'a house of cards balanced narrowly on the prosperity of the copper mines',[51] it was still a shock when

50 Wood, 'Agricultural policy', p.28.
51 Burdette, *Zambia*, p.95.

the house of cards tumbled down, beginning with the collapse of the copper prices in 1975. In 1973 copper and cobalt had represented 95 per cent of export earnings and revenue from the mining industry constituted over half of all government revenue. When the slump came, government revenue was reduced overnight. While the economic crisis deepened, Zambia's leaders were still preoccupied with extending their control over what was now a one-party state. Zambians were now ruled by a party which saw itself as supreme,[52] though few bothered to become party members. In the 1980s, terms of trade continued to be unfavourable, and the economic situation worsened. People saw their living standards fall dramatically and the government, hampered by patronage and corruption in its highest ranks, failed to carry through economic reforms. Increasingly obliged to follow the dictates of the International Monetary Fund and World Bank, to whom the country was now heavily indebted, Kaunda's government was unable and unwilling to take political responsibility for the ills affecting the country. The poor, both rural and urban, bore the brunt of the imposed 'adjustment' policies which the government now followed, while the élite continued to flaunt their wealth. Economic dependence on copper had always entailed political dependence on the urban working class which now increasingly felt the effects of unemployment, inflation and the withdrawal of food subsidies. They expressed their anger in strikes and food riots. 'Adjustment' was supposed to benefit the rural dwellers and rid them of inefficient bureaucracy, thus turning the terms of trade in their favour. 'Adjustment', however, rarely worked straightforwardly and Zambia was no exception.

By 1980, in the midst of economic crisis, the government of Zambia was spending 19 per cent of its shrinking revenue on agricultural subsidies and 10 per cent of its precious foreign exchange on food imports. The decline in local maize and the political necessity of maintaining low urban food prices accounted for this situation.[53] Under pressure from aid donors the government raised producer prices and, in 1980, launched 'Operation Food Production', revived the cooperatives and extended state farms. The emphasis remained on the production of hybrid maize for the urban market, though new prices were also announced for sorghum and millet, and an official market for cassava was established. The long period of 'adjustment' continued into the 1990s, sometimes under the supervision of the IMF and at other times under the government's own 'home recovery programme'.[54]

Raising producer prices led to a phenomenal extension of hybrid maize production in the 1980s. It seemed that producers beyond the 'line of rail'

52 Burdette, *Zambia*, p.104.
53 Wood and Shula, 'The state and agriculture in Zambia', in T. Mkandawire and N. Bourenane (eds), *The State and Agriculture in Africa*, Codesria, London, 1987, p.299.
54 For accounts of the 'reform' of the agricultural sector in Zambia in the 1980s see Wood, 'Agricultural policy'; R. Gulhati, *Impasse in Zambia: the Economics and Politics of Reform*, EDI Development Policy Case Series, Study No.2, World Bank, Washington D.C., 1989; J. Kydd, 'Changes in Zambian agricultural policy since 1983: problems of liberalisation and organisation', *Development Policy Review* 4 (1986), pp.243–69.

were finally entering the market in large numbers, and by 1986–87 the country had almost returned to self-sufficiency in maize. Aid donors, eager to participate in the country's agricultural revival, carved up the country into 'Intensive Development Zones' or 'Integrated Rural Development Projects', extending credit, giving advice and improving infrastructure.[55] In many ways these efforts at 'rural development' were very similar to those of the late colonial period. They benefited returned migrants, those who were able to take risks, who could command large amounts of labour, and who were well-connected politically. Though the increase in marketed maize was welcomed by the government, there were indications that this was not a sustainable increase. In the Northern Province, for example, the massive increase in hybrid maize production would not have come about without huge government subsidies and was not sustainable without them. Large parts of the province were ecologically unsuited to hybrid maize and required large inputs of fertiliser which had to be transported over long distances.[56] Producing for the market was a risky business requiring precise timing for planting and fertiliser application. Neither Namboard nor the Provincial Cooperative Societies proved able to maintain an efficient service to remote producers.[57] For many facing rising unemployment and declining remittances, hybrid maize offered the only real possibility for earning cash.

President Kaunda urged the urban unemployed to return 'home' to rural areas, to invest in agriculture and to contribute towards the drive towards self-sufficiency. At the same time, a debate was emerging on the social and nutritional effects of extending maize cash-cropping in Zambia. Central to this debate was question of gender. In most cases it appeared that maize cash-cropping was a male-dominated affair, and that women's economic independence was the main casualty of this development.[58] Indeed, a major problem facing many Zambian communities was how to absorb, or reabsorb, the young men who would, in the past, have become labour migrants. In some areas, such as the Northern Province, the absence of cash-earning possibilities for men had become an acute problem by the 1980s, giving rise to increasing levels of poverty and of frustration. In the Mambwe area, as

55 For more detailed accounts of these development projects see P. Gatter, ' Deaf to reason?: agricultural extension agents and their construction of rural Luapula' in Crehan and von Oppen (eds), *Planners and History*, 1994, pp.91–131; Crehan and von Oppen, 'Understandings of "development"'; J. Pottier, *Migrants No More: Settlement and Survival in Mambwe Villages, Zambia*, Manchester University Press, Manchester, 1988; J. Gould, 'Local strategies and directed development: cooperatives between state and community in Luapula' in Crehan and von Oppen (eds), *Planners and History*, pp.213–257.
56 Moore and Vaughan, *Cutting Down Trees*, chapters 7 and 8.
57 Namboard was, in fact, under increasing pressure in the 1980s, for whilst government maintained pan-territorial pricing, the extension of maize cash-crop production beyond the 'line of rail' meant that transport costs rose enormously.
58 For the effects of maize cash-cropping on gender relations see Moore and Vaughan, *Cutting Down Trees*, chapters 7 and 8; G. Geisler et al., *The Needs of Rural Women in the Northern Province*, Report to NCDP/NORAD, Lusaka, 1985; A. Evans and K. Young, *Gender Issues in Household Labour Allocation: the Transformation of a Farming System in Northern Province, Zambia*, Report to ODA's Economic and Social Research Committee, London, 1988.

elsewhere, some men turned to maize production.[59] Mambwe women, like many Zambian women, had previously held well-defined rights over the distribution of food crops. Women were always reluctant to sell food crops for cash, since it was their responsibility to ensure that the household was adequately fed. Selling food at the beginning of the season often meant buying it back at an inflated price later in the year. As men became more involved in food production, however, household negotiations over the rights to dispose of any surplus food intensified. Maize had the ambiguous status of being both a food and a cash crop. While men claimed their rights to dispose of it as a cash crop, women held on to it as a food crop. In parts of the Northern Province and in Eastern Province this conflict undermined women's economic independence.[60]

Some members of maize cash-cropping households experienced a deterioration in food security and nutritional status. Evidence remains inconclusive, but it would appear that struggling in the cash-cropping stakes could sometimes decrease household food security. This was partly due to the enormous pressure on family labour which maize production imposed. For some households, there was simply not enough time to produce food on traditional millet plots, as well as to produce hybrid maize. Other households sold too much. Women were losing control both over their own labour and over their allocation of surplus. Cash from maize sales went, in the first instance, almost entirely to men, depriving women of direct access. This was, perhaps, not such a radical change since married women had always found it difficult to gain access to cash earnings of their labour migrant husbands. What had changed was that women's labour was now being increasingly subordinated to the production of a crop over which they had little ultimate control. Other women, especially those who headed their own households, also had no direct access to this new source of cash. Short of labour, they were also ignored by the credit-giving institutions of 'development'. As rural differentiation increased, so these poorer households relied on working for others, sometimes for cash, but often for food or other goods. In the middle of this 'cash-crop revolution' there were many women who hardly set eyes on cash at all, rather they supported their households through complex exchanges of goods and labour.[61] While the drive to increase national food production had succeeded, it also had its casualties.

In the late 1980s the maize boom came to an end in many places. Pressure from donors led to the gradual withdrawal of subsidies on fertiliser, the ending of uniform pricing and the introduction of private trading. Private traders

59 Pottier, *Migrants No More*, p.114.
60 We should be careful, however, not to overgeneralise this point. Han Seur found a number of successful women maize cash-croppers in Serenje district: H. Seur, 'Sowing the Good Seed: The Interweaving of Agricultural Change, Gender Relations and Religion in Serenje District, Zambia', Doctoral thesis, University of Wageningen, 1992, pp.223–67.
61 Evans and Young, *Gender Issues*; P. Vedeld and R. Oygard, *Peasant Household Resource Allocation: a Study of Labour Allocation of Peasant Households in Zambia's Northern Province and Market Constraints on their Increased Agricultural Production*, SPRP Occasional Paper, No. 3, Kasama, 1982; Moore and Vaughan, *Cutting Down Trees*, chapters 7 and 8.

showed little interest in collecting maize from remoter areas, particularly given the declining state of many roads. Some maize growers calculated that, without the fertiliser subsidy and with the continued uncertainty around marketing, producing hybrid maize was no longer a viable option.[62] In some cases it seemed that a retreat from the market was taking place just as the government had 'opened up' the market. Many exchanges took place without the medium of money, and 'traditional' food crops and 'traditional methods' of cultivation experienced a revival. Isolation came to rural areas which had been connected through labour migration to the urban economy for nearly one hundred years. With typical self-deprecating humour, people of one small rural town in northern Zambia told the following story in the late 1980s. One morning a bus was spotted moving slowly down the main street. It was so long since anyone had seen a bus, that people stopped whatever they were doing to come out and stare at it 'as if it were an elephant'. Many jumped on, regarding the destination as irrelevant. As the bus reached the edge of town the chassis collapsed under the weight of the crowd. The last bus had broken down.

As this story indicates, most Zambians did not choose to live in rural isolation. Furthermore, even the remotest Zambian villager had an increasing need for cash in the late 1980s in order to purchase, not only clothing and soap, but also health care and education, which were no longer free.[63] A retreat into subsistence was never a real possibility, and so people continued to seek ways of making cash, through petty trading and casual labour. In the early 1990s poverty continued to deepen in Zambia[64] and, though the decline in living standards was most immediately apparent in urban areas, the rural poor also continued to get poorer. The rural poor were more likely than urban dwellers to be malnourished and their children were less likely to see their fifth birthday.[65]

---

62 G. Geisler, 'Who is losing out? Structural Adjustment, gender and the agricultural sector in Zambia', *Journal of Modern African Studies* 30,1 (1992), pp.113–39; G. Geisler and K. T. Hansen, 'Structural Adjustment, the rural–urban interface and gender relations in Zambia' in N. Aslanbeigui, S. Pressman and G. Summerfield (eds), *Women in the Age of Economic Transformation*, Routledge, London, 1994, pp.95–113; L. Ndalamei, 'Liberalisation of agricultural marketing in Zambia in the 1980s: implementation problems and future prospects', in J. Benyon (ed.), *Market Liberalisation and Private Sector Response in Eastern and Southern Africa*, Food Studies Group Working Paper No. 6, Oxford, 1992, pp.28–9.

63 Geisler, 'Who is losing out?'. The decline in Zambia's government health service is described in detail in P. Freund, 'Health care in a declining economy: the case of Zambia', *Social Science and Medicine* 23,9 (1986), pp.875–88. User fees have been introduced since Freund's piece was written. For effects of structural adjustment policies in Zambia more generally see R. Gulhati, *Impasse in Zambia; the Economics and Politics of Reform*, EDI Development Policy Case series, Study No.2, World Bank, Washington D.C., 1989; S. Jones, 'Structural Adjustment in Zambia' in W. van der Geest (ed.), *Negotiating Structural Adjustment in Africa*, James Currey, London, 1994, pp.25–47; R. Young and J. Loxley, *Zambia: an Assessment of Zambia's Structural Adjustment Experience*, North–South Institute, Ottawa, 1990; C. Fundanga, 'The Role of the IMF and World Bank in Zambia' in B. Onimode (ed.), *The IMF, the World Bank and the African Debt*, Zed Press, London, 1989, pp.142–49.

64 E. Kashambuzi, 'Poverty still deepening in Zambia', *Southern African Economic and Political Weekly* (June 1995), p.13.

65 Siandawazi concluded that malnutrition in Zambia is worst in regions furthest away from the 'line of rail': Siandawazi, *Household Food Security*, p.15.

In theory 'structural adjustment' was a process by which the rural producer was put into direct contact with 'the market'. Without the distortions produced by subsidies, by government political objectives, by cumbersome and inefficient institutions, rural people would be able to make rational production decisions and their incomes would increase. In practice, however, 'structural adjustment' and 'the market' do not come unmediated by social and political relations or by institutions. Neither, of course, is 'the market' always reliable. For many rural people in Zambia, life in the 1980s and 1990s was harder than it had ever been, and also more confusing than ever before. Some blamed the Kaunda government. In September 1991, for example, 27,000 bags of maize were set on fire at Mumbwa where they had stayed uncollected for three years. Although the official reason for the delay was transport difficulties, this explanation was hard for local producers to swallow since the Mumbwa depot was on a main road and only 100 kilometres from Lusaka.

Other disaffected Zambians looked for more immediate targets to blame. In the Ngoni villages of the Eastern Province there were frequent rumours that politicians were diverting stocks of fertiliser and food and selling them to neighbouring Malawi. Local preachers and witchfinders continually warned that the 'bus' of prosperity was passing villagers by, as 'witches stole the neighbours' hybrid maize and flew off to the Copperbelt on nocturnal celestial highways'.[66] The tarmac road, that great symbol of modernity connecting villagers to the urban centres of power, was viewed with great suspicion, not least by farmers whose seed and fertiliser failed to arrive along it each year. Mysteriously, however, some lucky individuals *did* get their seed and fertiliser each year, managed to avoid the misfortunes of illness, death, crop disease or drought, and made a healthy profit. Down the same road in 1988 arrived Doctor Moses, a witchfinder of some repute who had been making his way through the province. He turned the gaze of the villagers inward to their own community and to their own relationships of generation and gender. Old people, it seemed, were responsible for the misfortune, the poverty, and the frustration experienced by everyone. Young men were quick to agree. They wanted to 'get on' and make money, but the elders always seemed to be holding them back with one kinship obligation or another and with their insistence on the maintenance of a proper sense of social hierarchy. Women were also central to Doctor Moses' diagnosis. Moving around on the road, engaging in petty trade, they were suspected by their husbands, not only of keeping large profits to themselves, but also of selling their bodies, 'altering' their wombs, and bringing AIDS to the villages. When Doctor Moses moved on after a few days, some members of the community, at least, felt that they had been provided with an explanation for their continued lack of economic

---

66 The following account is taken directly from Mark Auslander's work: M. Auslander, '"Open the wombs!": the symbolic politics of modern Ngoni witchfinding' in J. and J. Comaroff (eds), *Modernity and its Malcontents: Ritual and Power in Postcolonial Africa*, Chicago University Press, Chicago, 1993, pp.167–93.

success. The blame had been laid at the door, not of the politicians in Lusaka, or of the IMF in Washington, but of their immediate neighbours.

Not everyone in Zambia was listening exclusively to the likes of Doctor Moses, however. Among the urban population in the late 1980s, dissatisfaction with increasing food prices spilled over into rioting. The UNIP government was losing the support of its central source of popular power among trade unions. Opposition to the ruling UNIP party had been mounting since the mid-1980s and culminated in the formation of the Movement for Multi-Party Democracy (MMD) in 1990. This was a coalition of dissatisfied UNIP politicians, some professionals and intellectuals, and the trade union movement. In 1991 the MMD, headed by the trade unionist, Frederick Chiluba, swept to power in the country's first multi-party elections, and Kenneth Kaunda retired gracefully to the wings.[67] Chiluba committed the MMD to a political and economic programme which would appeal to foreign donors. The new government was in favour of 'free enterprise' and committed to the eradication of the corruption of the Kaunda regime. It planned to release the Zambian people from the burdens of excessive bureaucracy and liberate their economic intitiative and potential. Most importantly, it would address the continuing economic crisis by following 'adjustment' through to its conclusion.

Though the government had changed, and the rhetoric had changed, the basic configuration of Zambian politics was the same.[68] The MMD, like UNIP before it, came to power by appealing to the dissatisfied and increasingly impoverished urban population.[69] Urban consumers and workers, feeling themselves to be the main victims of 'structural adjustment', had brought the old government down,[70] but the MMD faced the same intractable economic problems as its predecessor. Unable to implement campaign promises of greater prosperity and more open government, President Chiluba faced mounting

67 For 'multi-party' politics and the fall of the UNIP government see C. Baylies and M. Szeftel, 'The fall and rise of multi-party politics in Zambia', *Review of African Political Economy* 54 (1992), pp.75–91; S. Wina, 'An open letter to the Fifth Zambia National Convention', *Southern African Economic and Political Monthly* (May 1990), pp.31–4; A. Mwanza, 'UNIP routed in Zambia's elections', *Southern African Political and Economic Monthly* (November 1991), pp.28–30; O. Sichone, 'Zambian elections: an example for Africa to emulate?', *Southern African Political and Economic Monthly* (December/January, 1991/2), pp.3–4; E. Bjornlund et al., 'Observing Multi-Party Elections in Africa: Lessons from Zambia', *African Affairs* 91 (1992), pp.405–31; Ihonvbere, *Economic Crisis*.
68 For full and critical assessments of the Chiluba government see Ihonvbere, *Economic Crisis* and van Donge, 'Zambia, Kaunda and Chiluba: enduring patterns of political culture' in J. A. Wiseman (ed.), *Democracy and Political Change in Sub-Saharan Africa*, Routledge, London, 1995, pp.193–220.
69 Van Donge, 'Zambia: the pains of continuity', *Southern African Political and Economic Monthly* (September 1994), p.3; G. Mudenda, 'MMD: Two Years Later', *Southern African Political and Economic Monthly* (August 1992), p.4; C. Cheushi, 'Zambia: Warming Up for the 1996 elections', *Southern African Political and Economic Monthly* (November 1994), pp.20–1.
70 There is evidence, however, that rural voters also turned to the MMD during the 1991 election. Rural people were affected, through declining remittances, by the urban economic collapse: M. Bratton. 'Economic crisis and political realignment in Zambia' in J. Widner (ed.), *Economic Change and Political Liberalization in Sub-Saharan Africa*, Johns Hopkins University Press, Baltimore, 1994, p.119.

criticism of authoritarianism and corruption. Many Zambians were disillusioned with 'multi-party' democracy, indeed, with government altogether. As one woman put it, 'I am yet to see any serious differences between Chiluba and Kaunda and we are tired of excuses upon excuses which do not affect the rich'.[71] The 1996 election was unlikely to have much impact on this woman's cynicism. Kenneth Kaunda (known as 'Super-Ken') and UNIP had been engineering a comeback since 1992, but the government, alleging a plot to produce instability and stage a military coup, arrested senior UNIP members and then declared a state of emergency which it later revoked. With an election looming, Chiluba accused Kaunda of being 'really' a Malawian, and therefore not eligible to stand for the office of president. Kaunda responded by alleging that Chiluba was 'really' a Zairian. After much postponement and a threatened constitutional crisis, the election went ahead in November 1996, but Kaunda was banned from standing. UNIP urged its supporters to boycott the poll. The official result showed Chiluba to have taken 82 per cent of the vote. It was far from convincing and many donors cut off aid.

In the late 1980s many farmers in the Eastern Province of Zambia sold maize across the border to Malawi. Malawi, too, had been going through a process of 'structural adjustment' and agricultural reform since the late 1970s. At one level there were similarities between rural producers in Zambia and in Malawi, but there were also marked differences. In the 1970s and 1980s any Zambian, and particularly one in the Eastern Province with relatives over the border, could have enumerated these differences. It was true that you could buy soap in Malawi without queuing, and it was sometimes true that you could get a better price for your maize over the border, but life on the other side was not easy. Malawians were not only poorer than their Zambian neighbours, they were also oppressed and frequently frightened. Both Malawians and Zambians lived in one-party states, but the stranglehold which Dr Banda had on his subjects had become legendary. It is impossible to understand the political economy of Malawi since independence without some sense of the effects of this stranglehold, not only on society, but also on the psyche of the people.[72] His Excellency, the Life President, Dr H. Kamuzu Banda had elaborated a web of political and social control which, at many times, looked unassailable. Not only had he reduced parliament to a sham, he and his close political allies closely controlled the media, whipped up regional rivalries, imprisoned large numbers of 'subversives', and, through the impressive grass-roots organisation of the Malawi Congress Party with its youth and women's wings, kept close control over the affairs of the remotest village. Carefully constructed rivalry between the police, the Special Branch and the army, helped keep potential opposition at bay. Local resentments and jealousies were played upon to great effect, and everyone, especially those in middle-class occupations, walked a tightrope where one false step might lose you a job or

71 Quoted in Ihonvbere, *Economic Crisis*, p.176.
72 For a recent analysis, see Lwanda, *Kamuzu Banda*. On human rights violations see also Africa Watch, *Where Silence Rules: the Suppression of Dissent in Malawi*, Africa Watch, New York, 1990.

land you in jail. There was a strong ethno-regional dimension to Banda's politics but his expanded notion of 'Chewa' ethnicity and his persecution of 'northerners' was not a straightforward case of ethnic absolutism driving the political agenda.[73]

Serious analysis of independent Malawi politics was delayed during the Banda years by heavy censorship of social science publications. Furthermore, 'western' observers were often so mesmerised by Banda's eccentric character and bizarre political style that they rarely delved deep into an analysis of the nation. Banda's very authoritarian and idiosyncratic style was one, but only one, important part of the whole picture, since it created paralysing fear and uncertainty among many of his subjects. State violence was more often implicit than explicit, but the fear of violence worked powerfully to create the impression of a regime with all-pervasive power. Control never was complete, but the belief in its completeness was sufficient to keep most incipient opposition at bay.

Malawi's economy, like Zambia's, was run for the benefit of a small élite – very small in the case of Malawi. In each country, a small number of politicians and civil servants was able to take control of the most productive sectors of the economy through the ever-growing parastatals and through relationships with foreign investors. In Zambia, with its mining economy, the parasitic spoils were great while the copper prices remained high, and some social investment was not incompatible with increasing wealth differentiation. Malawi, though it shared some of these features, was different in a number of ways. Firstly, the welfare of the Malawian people was scandalously neglected, as was clearly demonstrated by their health statistics, their nutritional standards and their educational levels. Secondly, the Malawian 'rent-seeking' élite exercised its control over the economy, not only through the mechanism of the state and its parastatals, but also through the 'private sector'. This was little more than a cover for the economic ambitions of the President and his entourage, who convinced donors that they were dealing with a liberal, capitalist regime, a bulwark against socialism in the region.[74] Thirdly, the Malawian élite, unlike most of their Zambian counterparts, did invest, albeit inefficiently, in productive activity within the country.[75] Despite the stranglehold of Press Holdings, during the 1970s and 1980s a group of entrepreneurs emerged in Malawi who combined investment in estate agriculture with

73 For a revisionist account of the Banda regime which argues that the ethnic dimension has been much exaggerated, see H. Englund, 'Between God and Kamuzu: the transition to multi-party politics in central Malawi' in Richard Werbner and Terence Ranger (eds), *Postcolonial Identities in Africa*, Zed Press, London, 1996, pp.107–36. Though Englund's discussion is interesting and illuminating, it is also rather far removed from the realities of life under Banda's oppressive rule at its height and overstates its case in criticising, for example, the work of John Lwanda: Lwanda, *Kamuzu Banda.*
74 Malawi's relationship with South Africa, its position on Mozambique and its pro-western stance during the Cold War, were of course very important factors keeping the donors on Banda's side, and keeping criticism of human rights violations at bay.
75 See M. Chipeta, 'Political process, civil society and the state' in G. C. Z. Mhone (ed.), *Malawi at the Crossroads: the Post-Colonial Political Economy*, Sapes Books, Harare, 1992, pp.35–49.

investment in small-scale industry and urban property. At the lower end of this group, small businessmen and entrepreneurs were less dependent on the state for capital accumulation than were the political élite. Like their predecessors of the 1940s and 1950s, these African businessmen eventually played an important part in bringing about political change. It took an economic crisis, however, to begin the process.

The high economic growth rates of the 1970s, which so impressed economists in Washington and Banda's political allies in the United Kingdom and South Africa, would almost certainly not have been possible if the ordinary people of Malawi had had any political voice. Ultimately, however, the economic system which Banda had elaborated could not survive. With the faltering of the economy came greater donor intervention and this, amongst other factors, helped to trigger the eventual collapse of the Banda regime. The external shock of the oil crisis of 1979 revealed the vulnerability of Malawi's export economy and its heavy dependence on tea and tobacco. In 1980, the economy registered a negative growth rate of −5.2 per cent, and a 'crisis' was acknowledged.

Initially, the conditions attached to loans from the World Bank were relatively mild. Malawi was still thought of as a model 'market economy' whose government already followed many of the policies recommended by the IMF. The international financial institutions appeared little interested in the evidence which was emerging of huge and increasing wealth disparities and of worsening conditions among the poor. Their emphasis was on 'efficiency', and this Banda appeared to be able to deliver through dictatorship. In the course of the 1980s, it became apparent that Banda's political system was less than 'efficient' in economic terms. Many of the tobacco estates, created in the 1970s as part of the system of political patronage, were found to be appallingly inefficient and a significant drain on the country's financial resources.

The terms of the 1981 second structural adjustment loan called for a rise in the smallholders' price for export crops. A growing conflict emerged between the World Bank, whose objective was to promote export crop production among smallholders, and the government, which aimed to preserve estate monopolies on the most lucrative crops while maintaining national self-sufficiency in food.[76] In 1981 an increase of 66 per cent in the price paid for maize led to oversupply and the need to export at a loss. From 1982 there was some realignment of prices and real producer prices for maize declined. The worsening financial position of ADMARC in the 1980s resulted in 'market liberalisation' which the World Bank had called for. Liberalisation of the lucrative tobacco market, however, met with greater political resistance. Only in 1990 was the production of burley tobacco by smallholders legalised.

---

76 Kydd, 'Malawi in the 1970s', argues for the existence of this conflict between the World Bank and the Malawi government. Mhone, 'Agriculture and Food Policy' thinks that this conflict has been exaggerated and that 'The World Bank has a good record in supporting and promoting large-scale private farming' (p.83).

Underlying this process of 'liberalisation' was a more complex story. Throughout the 1980s the tobacco estates continued to expand. By 1989 they occupied about 9 per cent of the land area of the country, and an estimated one million of Malawi's ten million people lived on them. These newest estates had again been obtained by converting customary land, mostly in the less-populated parts of the central and northern regions, into leasehold properties. But whereas in the 1970s most of the land newly brought under leasehold was formed into large estates held by corporations, or prominent politicians and civil servants, most of the new estates in the 1980s were a great deal smaller. Some 71 per cent of the estates registered in the 1980s measured less, sometimes much less, than 30 hectares. These small estates were being established by groups of growers confusingly referred to as 'progressive smallholders'. These individuals and families acquired new land or registered their own land in order to gain the right, denied to ordinary smallholders, to grow burley tobacco.

As the 'land grab' progressed in some areas, traditional smallholders began to feel that their customary land tenure was no longer secure. To prevent further alienation, they, too, began to register their land as estates. In some cases an 'estate' essentially represented one extended family group, whose members had pooled their customary holdings and registered the land in the name of one or two household heads, while maintaining a claim to 'customary' land. The 'dualistic' Malawian rural economy, in which 'smallholders' and 'estates' were distinct, separate groups, had become more complicated as large smallholders circumvented the tobacco licensing system by registering their land as estates. In the mid-1990s, the long-term effects of this process were yet to be worked out, but the liberalisation of the tobacco market removed one of the most powerful incentives for the land registration. Many small estate owners, however, especially those in areas of land shortages, might prefer to retain their leases as a form of security. As men from the better-off smallholder families found ways to increase their land security, women suffered a loss of their security. All but a handful of the approximately 15,000 estates registered by the end of the 1980s were held by men. Even in areas where wives rather than husbands were traditionally the holders of the land, women found themselves in a potentially very different situation. They were particularly vulnerable in the event of their husband's death.

By the late 1980s, then, the 'estate sector' had become highly differentiated. At one end were the huge estates, owned by international companies, by white residents, and by Dr Banda and his immediate entourage. At the other end were the small estates of the 'progressive smallholders', and in the middle were many estates created through patronage in the 1970s and often belonging to absentee Malawian landlords such as civil servants, politicians and businessmen. While the efficiency and profitability of estates varied enormously, most of them had in common a heavy reliance on tenant families to grow their tobacco. The 'visiting tenant' system, once attacked by Dr Banda as a vestige of colonial 'slavery', was alive and well on his own estates. In order to understand this survival we need to turn again to the 'smallholder' sector and examine growing levels of differentiation and population growth.

In the 1970s and 1980s, while the estate sector grew, Malawi's smallholders became more differentiated. Some were able to produce a surplus and others were not even able to meet their subsistence needs. Not only did many small-holders in the 1970s and 1980s face serious constraints in access to fertiliser and credit, many had insufficient land on which to make a living. Malawi, always a relatively densely populated part of Africa, experienced an annual population growth rate of 3.3 per cent between 1977 and 1987, with a fertility rate in 1987 of 7.6 per cent. In 1977 the population was just over five and a half million; in 1987 it was nearly eight million, and by the year 2000 the estimated population will reach twelve million.[77] Population density was low-est in the north and highest in the south. In 1977, the Southern Region had a population density of 87 per square kilometre and by 2000 it will likely rise to around 186. Districts such as Chiradzulu, Mulanje and Thyolo were pro-jected to have densities of between 275 and 400 by the year 2000. This meant that many people in the south, and in other parts of the country too, were completely unable to satisfy their subsistence needs due to lack of land. In 1990, 26 per cent of households had access to less than half a hectare of land each, and a further 26.9 per cent had access to less than one hectare. One commentator has estimated that households with less than half a hectare could only produce 38 per cent of their requirements, while those with less than one hectare were able to produce about 75 per cent. Smallholder 'development' projects in Malawi, as in Zambia, did not touch this growing group of house-holds. Agricultural extension advice was rarely offered to those with small plots, and credit was available only in small packages and too risky to take on. Even with extension advice and credit it would have been hard for households to manage to feed themselves, let alone produce a surplus. While a 'green revolution' was hailed by some as a possible solution for Malawi, others were much less optimistic.[78]

In effect, a growing proportion of Malawian rural households could not be self-sufficient in foodstuffs or gain directly from the liberalisation of the tobacco market.[79] They had to buy a significant proportion of their food, and, as consumers, they were affected by changes in food and fertiliser prices, unlike their more self-sufficient neighbours. In order to feed their house-holds, adults in these land-short families had to find employment. In areas such as Mulanje district people 'managed' in different ways.[80] About 35 per cent of

77 W. J. House and G. Zimalirana, *Rapid Population Growth and Poverty Generation in Malawi*, Labour and Population Series for sub-Saharan Africa, Document No.15, ILO, Geneva 1991, p.7.
78 For the optimistic view see M. Smale, 'Maize is life: Malawi's delayed Green Revolution', *World Development* 23 (1995), pp.819–31. For a more pessimistic evaluation of the possibilities of a 'green revolution' see S. Carr, 'The unique challenge of Malawi's smallholder agricultural sector', n.d., circulated paper.
79 This fact seems lost on many policy-makers, who, despite the wealth of data on the rural population of Malawi, often treat 'smallholders' as if they were a homogeneous group.
80 Trivedy, *Action Research in Southern Malawi*, Oxfam, Oxford, 1990.

households were female-headed, adult men often having gone to work on the tobacco estates of the Central and Northern Regions. Labour migration was far from a new concept, but wages for agricultural labourers on the estates were extremely low, and remittances therefore small or non-existent. Between 1982/ 83 and 1989/90, for example, the rural minimum wage in Malawi halved relative to the consumer price for maize, and many estates and richer small-holders paid well below the minimum wage. Despite an average annual decline in estate wages of 2.8 per cent between 1981 and 1986,[81] there was an increase in estate wage employment of 8 per cent per annum, indicating lack of alternative opportunity and political voice among rural workers. Female heads of households in Mulanje and elsewhere could not realistically expect to see much in the way of cash remittances from absent husbands and had to try to satisfy their household needs in other ways. But performing casual labour, *ganyu*, on other people's land, in exchange for food or cash, often meant neglecting their own small plots. The primary aim of these women was to feed their families and, in female-headed households in both Malawi and Zambia, where women had greater control over resources, a higher proportion of total food calories was allocated to children.[82]

Some households in places like Mulanje opted for more radical alternatives. As the tobacco estates expanded in the 1980s, so estate owners and managers competed for labour. Many relied heavily on tenants, and areas of land shortage proved a frequent source of potential tenants. Not all tenant families on the tobacco estates lacked land in their own homes, however. As they had in the late colonial period, some opted to be tenants in order to gain access to credit and to earn a higher income than they could do on their own plots.[83] These tenant families were not wholly dependent on the estate for their livelihood for they might well pay someone to cultivate their own land at home, and they might return there in the slack season. Tenant families from places like Mulanje were often in a very different position, however. They were usually recruited at home by a roaming estate manager in a pick-up truck, transported with their few belongings to a remote estate in the Central Region, and attached to their employer through debt for at least the coming year. The tenancy system worked by relying on a male household head to control and exploit his family's labour. No estate manager would recruit a tenant who did not have a wife, or preferably two, and several 'strong' children.[84] Tenants were usually illiterate and were rarely presented with a written contract. They were given everything on credit – the seeds, the fertiliser, and

81 Harrigan, 'Malawi'.
82 E. Kennedy and P. Peters, *Household Food Security and Child Nutrition: The Interaction of Income and Gender of the Household Head*, Development Discussion Paper, No.417. Harvard Institute for International Development, Cambridge MA, 1992.
83 For the wide variations in tenant incomes see S. Jaffee, R. Mkandawire and S. Bertoli, *The 'Migrant Smallholders': Tenant and Laborer Participation, Remuneration and Social Welfare within Malawi's Expanding Estate Sector*, IOA, Binghamton, NY, 1991.
84 M.Vaughan and R. Mkandawire, *Report on Recent Developments in the Estate Sub-Sector of Malawi*, Government of Malawi and UDA, Lilongwe, 1991.

often their food – and at the end of the season received a proportion of the price which the owner obtained for their tobacco. The high interest rate and the profit extracted by the owner were rarely apparent to the tenant. The well-managed estates made more money, paid their tenants more, and took greater care of them. For the vulnerable, with few alternative sources of live-lihood, however, taking on a tenancy could be a risky business and at the end of a bad year those making a loss might have to abscond with their family to avoid further indebtedness. Some tenants, then, were among the poorest people in Malawi, and their numbers were expanding in the 1980s.

Tenant families and estate workers were an almost invisible section of Malawi's rural population in the 1970s and 1980s, due to the political sensit-ivity of the estates and the power of the government to control access to information. The many donor-funded surveys of rural land-holdings, incomes, labour profiles, health and nutrition explicitly excluded those living on estates. Only in the late 1980s, as donor pressure to reform the estate sector grew, did studies begin to emerge. The nutritional status of these estate house-holds, which would allow comparison with that of smallholders, remained unknown, however. Though a relative wealth of data existed for small-holders, real obstacles were placed in the way of any public discussion or analysis of this data until the late 1980s. Poverty, as Dr Banda repeatedly reminded his people, was a thing of the past. In public discussions someone was always present to remind participants of this fact. Meetings on 'devel-opment' therefore frequently took on a bizarre and unreal character, as the pretence was maintained that every Malawian was well-fed, well-dressed and happy. Only a few courageous individuals insisted on mentioning the word 'poverty' in relation to the present rather than the past,[85] and UNICEF and other international organisations published data which spoke for itself.[86] Other factors also helped break the silence.

In 1992 the rains failed in Malawi, as they did over large parts of southern Africa. Malawi was already playing host to refugees from the war in Mozam-bique, who constituted around 12 per cent of the country's population. The government's response to the refugee crisis had been much admired by inter-national organisations working in Malawi. In fact, the impact of refugees on the local economy had been complex. Though in many areas refugees had placed a further strain on limited land resources and had contributed to a further deterioration in an already vulnerable environment, they had also, in some cases, brought a revival of local economies through the influx of aid agencies and money. The focus on refugees also revealed something of the poverty of the host population. Traffic across the Mozambique border had always been two-way, and identities were fluid. While many Mozambicans

---

85 The late Louis Msukwa, Director of the Centre for Social Research, University of Malawi, was one such person.
86 For example, Government of Malawi and UNICEF, *The Situation of Women and Children in Malawi*, Lilongwe, 1987.

passed themselves off as Malawians in order to gain access to land and employment, many Malawians masqueraded as Mozambicans to obtain donor food.

In part due to the refugee crisis, and in part as a result of the economic crisis and 'adjustment', Banda's Malawi was opened up to greater scrutiny by the outside world. At the same time, an underground opposition was beginning to coalesce, helped by exiled opposition movements which were growing in coherence. In October 1991, Malawians watched Zambia's 'multi-party' elections with interest. Increasingly, the Malawian government's control over information and opinion was faltering. Imported fax machines and photocopiers allowed the circulation of opposition pamphlets so critical of the government that previous methods of coercion and control ceased to be viable. In March 1992 the Catholic bishops of Malawi published a Lenten Letter which amounted to a full-scale criticism of the Banda government. Not only did it address questions of poverty, and lack of educational and health facilities, it also argued, in terms familiar in the world of aid donors, that 'accountability is a quality of good government'. This made it impossible, according to the bishops, to ignore 'our peoples' experience of unfairness and injustice, for example those who, losing their land without fair compensation, are deprived of their livelihood, or those of our brothers and sisters who are imprisoned without knowing when their cases will be heard'.[87] Though Malawi Congress Party activists responded initially to this criticism by plotting the murder of the bishops, and though President Banda attacked them as seditious, the tide was already turning and the edifice of Banda's extraordinary system of political control was beginning to reveal serious cracks.

When drought struck in 1992, there was little possibility of 'covering it up'. Not only was Banda's government under scrutiny from the donors, but internal opposition was beginning to find its muscle. Furthermore, aid agencies and non-governmental organisations already in the country to handle the refugee crisis could not turn a blind eye to the threat of mass starvation in the host nation.[88] Perhaps one of the most important effects of the 1992 drought was not the need which it created for imported food and the greater dependence on donors which this implied, but the fact that it revealed the underlying reality of Malawian rural life – serious long-term malnutrition, and a marginal existence for many of the rural poor. Chronic malnutrition, evidenced by the stunted growth of children, was revealed to be extremely high, even in non-drought years. Over 56 per cent of children were stunted, according to the National Sample Survey of Agriculture of 1981/2,[89] and a 1989 survey in Ntchisi District revealed that 70 per cent of children there were

87 Quoted in Lwanda, *Kamuzu Banda*, appendix 1.
88 Accounts of the drought can be found in United Nations, *Malawi: Monthly Drought Reports, 1992*; SADCC, *Food Security*: Monthly Bulletin of the SADCC Regional Early Warning Unit, Harare, 1992; J. MacAskill, *Food Security in Malawi*, Save the Children Fund, UK, 1993.
89 Government of Malawi, *Report of the National Sample Survey of Agriculture,1980/1981*, Volumes 1–3, National Statistical Office, Zomba, 1984. For a full review of the nutritional data for Malawi over time see V. Quinn, 'Nutrition and National Development: an Evaluation of Nutrition Planning in Malawi from 1936 to 1990', Doctoral thesis, University of Wageningen, 1994.

stunted. A 1992 national survey showed that nearly one half of children under five were stunted, and about a quarter severely stunted.[90] Stunting was the result, not of one season's drought and food shortage, but of continuous undernourishment, probably exacerbated by frequent bouts of illness. There was plenty of evidence to show that, despite Dr Banda's continuous proclamations of prosperity, many rural people were living on the margin of existence. Data on infant and child mortality rates confirmed this picture. In 1988–1992, the under-five child mortality rate amounted to 234 deaths per 1000. One in four Malawian children did not see their fifth birthday, a figure which compared very unfavourably with neighbouring countries.[91]

In 1992 it looked as if Malawi, like Zambia, would have a trade unionist as its next leader. Chafukwa Chihana, secretary-general of the Southern Africa Trade Union Coordinating Council, arrived back in Malawi from exile and declared himself ready to lead Malawians into democracy. He became a founder of the first opposition party to declare itself, the northern-based Alliance for Democracy (AFORD). Chihana's personal leadership style displayed some worrying similarities to that of Banda, however, and he never became a leader with national appeal. The Malawian opposition took on a marked regional dimension with the foundation of the southern-based United Democratic Front, (UDF) led by the businessman Bakili Muluzi. In 1993 the people of Malawi voted in a referendum to end one-party rule. Multi-party politics were legalised and preparations for an election began. In the elections of 1994, Bakili Muluzi was elected president with 47 per cent of the votes, while Chafukwa Chihana won 19.5 per cent, and Kamuzu Banda, a substantial 33 per cent. Malawians had voted very largely on a regional basis,[92] with Banda's Malawi Congress Party (MCP) still dominating the Central Region, the UDF winning in the south, and AFORD in the north.

Muluzi's UDF did not have a majority in the national assembly, however, and the reformed MCP was far from dead. Indeed, under a 'memorandum of understanding' the MCP and AFORD cooperated in opposition from June 1994 until January 1995, when AFORD ended this arrangement. In July 1995, AFORD and UDF formed a coalition, but it was never stable, and was finally dissolved by AFORD in June 1996. Many old members of Banda's Malawi Congress Party had meanwhile turned up in new guises within Muluzi's UDF. Ordinary people in Malawi, as in Zambia, were far from idealistic about their politicians. The trial of ex-president Banda and his close associates, John Tembo and Cecilia Kadzamira, for conspiracy to murder four senior politicians in 1983, ended in their acquittal.

90 Government of Malawi, *Demographic and Health Survey*, National Statistical Office and Macro International Inc., Zomba, 1992, p.104.
91 Government of Malawi, *Demographic and Health Survey*, p.71. Quinn argues that nutrition is a key factor affecting morbidity and mortality rates in Malawi: Quinn, *Nutrition*.
92 N. Kamwambe, *Post-Mortem of the 1994 Elections in Malawi*, Montfort Press, Limbe, Malawi, 1994; T. Dumbutshena, 'Malawi: the end of a dictatorship', *Southern African Political and Economic Monthly* (September 1994), p.3; J. K. van Donge, 'Kamuzu's legacy: the democratisation of Malawi', *African Affairs* 94 (1995), pp.227–57.

Meanwhile, poverty in Malawi continued to deepen. The Muluzi government was accused of corruption, though it was probably not on the scale experienced in Zambia. Neither government had many real options in economic policy, and both were driven to push through privatisation and structural adjustment programmes. The fact that both Chiluba's MMD and Muluzi's UDF represented local business interests made such policies look as though they were designed to benefit the ruling élites. In Zambia, Chiluba avoided the privatisation of the mining industry, and the depletion of copper resources was a serious long-term threat to the economy. The Malawi economy, meanwhile, remained dangerously dependent on tobacco, which accounted for 75 per cent of the country's exports. Not only was the world market for tobacco uncertain, the extension of its cultivation in Malawi already showed signs of being ecologically unsustainable. A liberalisation of the tobacco market could break the dominance of the estate sector and produce greater prosperity for Malawian smallholders, but in the long run other sources of income needed to be found. For the land-hungry Malawian poor, the future depended on the creation of more jobs and better-paid employment.

In the Mulanje District of Malawi during the elections of 1994, a long queue of men formed outside the small building which had served as the office for the South African mine labour recruiting organisation, WENELA. Opposition parties had promised a resumption of labour migration to South Africa. The men waited patiently. A new government was elected. Unfortunately for them, their labour would not be required.

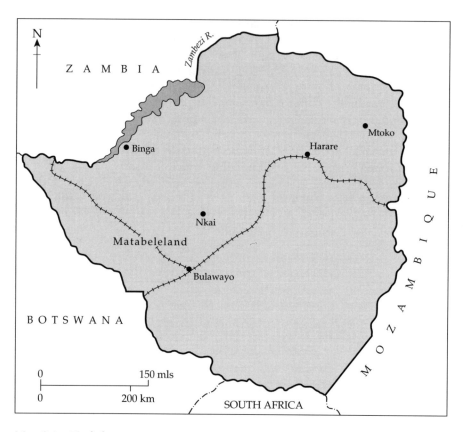

Map 8.1   Zimbabwe

CHAPTER 8

Zimbabwe and the long search for independence

TERENCE RANGER

Zimbabwe may seem the odd one out in this book. Most of the other countries of Central Africa obtained their independence in the early 1960s. Zimbabwe achieved majority rule only in 1980. But there is another way of looking at Zimbabwe's history over the last thirty-five years. One could say, without complete absurdity, that Zimbabwe has had as many as three attempted 'independences' during that time, two abortive and one enduring. These were Ian Smith's 'independence' of November 1965; Abel Muzorewa's 'independence' of April 1979; and finally Robert Mugabe's independence of April 1980.

Of course, these three regimes were very different from each other and possessed very different degrees of legitimacy. Still, they had certain things in common. Each had two main problems to resolve – how to settle the rural areas, and how to revive the urban and industrial economy. Each had to confront both internal and external enemies. None of them was completely successful, though the Mugabe regime has certainly been more successful than either of its predecessors.

The contested succession from Smith to Muzorewa to Mugabe, the bitter violence of the liberation war of the 1960s and 1970s, and the terror and counter-terror of the 'dissident' war of the 1980s, has meant that Zimbabwe has experienced constant debate and mobilisation. Questions of race, ethnicity, religion, gender and generation have been central. Erosion of state services due to violence or to economic stringency, in combination with a rapid increase in population, has brought about crises of environment and crises of disease. A history of Zimbabwe since 1960 has to be much more than a political narrative. Nevertheless, political history has continued to be centrally important. There has been no 'collapse of the state' in Zimbabwe, which remains a recognisable modern nation, with a functioning bureaucracy, police force and army. Its modern history has been as much a matter of the excessive ambition of states as of their incapacity to carry out their plans.

The year 1960 makes a good beginning date for a modern history of Zimbabwe. 'Everyone is agreed' ran the blurb for Philip Mason's book on the fate of the Federation of Rhodesia and Nyasaland, 'that 1960 is a year of decision in Africa'.[1] It was a year of decision not only for the Federation but for Southern Rhodesia as well. During 1960 everything accelerated. The arrests of black nationalist leaders, protest marches, urban riots, the deaths of Africans in the repression of urban discontent – all this changed everything. Garfield Todd, who a bare two years before had been a paternalist prime minister, joined with African nationalist leaders in late July to demand that Britain suspend the Southern Rhodesian constitution and send in troops. He was right to see that politics had polarised. There was no longer room for 'moderate' blacks or for 'liberal' whites. The black nationalists moved reluctantly from non-violence and constitutional negotiations to sabotage campaigns and ultimately to guerrilla war. The split in 1963 between Joshua Nkomo's Zimbabwe African People's Union (ZAPU) and Ndabaningi Sithole's Zimbabwe African National Union (ZANU) stimulated competition between them to be the first to discover how to use violence effectively. Whites, many of them increasingly proclaiming their own brand of Rhodesian nationalism, moved from 'reform' to repression.[2]

The Rhodesia Front's victory in the elections of December 1962 made this polarisation starkly apparent. In December 1963 the Federation broke up, most of its war-planes and military equipment going to Southern Rhodesia. In 1964 Malawi and Zambia achieved independence, thereby stimulating both black and white nationalism in Rhodesia. Each struck out at the other. In April 1964 Joshua Nkomo, the leader of ZAPU, was restricted in remote and arid Gonakudzingwa. On 4 July the 'Crocodile Gang,' a group sent in from Zambia to stimulate the ZANU campaign of confrontation and sabotage, killed the first white man to die in the black nationalist confrontation with the Rhodesian state. On 26 August 1964 both ZAPU and ZANU were banned and every leading nationalist detained. Everything was set for Ian Smith's 'unilateral' declaration of independence.

SMITH'S 'INDEPENDENCE' IN THE AFRICAN RURAL AREAS

On 11 November 1965 the Rhodesia Front government issued a proclamation of independence. As one analyst of the Unilateral Declaration of Independence (UDI) wrote, it 'was couched in archaic and convoluted syntax reminiscent of the eighteenth-century American Declaration of Independence'.[3] These

1 Philip Mason, *Year of Decision. Rhodesia and Nyasaland 1960*, Oxford University Press, London, 1960.
2 The most recent treatment of the events of 1960 in Southern Rhodesia and their significance is Terence Ranger, *Are We Not Also Men? The Samkange Family and African Politics in Zimbabwe, 1920–1964*, James Currey, London, 1995.
3 Kenneth Young, *Rhodesia and Independence*, Eyre and Spottiswoode, London, 1967, p.286. Other treatments of UDI are James Barber, *Rhodesia. The Road to Rebellion*, Oxford University Press, London, 1967, and Robert Good, *UDI. The International Politics of the Rhodesia Rebellion*,

echoes were deliberate. The Rhodesia Front was appealing to a long tradition of settler revolts against imperial power in north and south America. Like the American Declaration, the Rhodesia Front's proclamation appealed to 'Almighty God, who controls the destinies of nations', and Smith himself told his supporters that 'history has cast us in a heroic role', no less than 'the preservation of justice, civilization and Christianity' in a world of 'appeasement and surrender' to godless communism.

Even at the time many whites in Rhodesia believed that the time for such settler declarations of independence had long since passed. The British prime minister, Harold Wilson, announced that UDI would 'be over in weeks.' In retrospect, UDI looks an even more improbable and doomed enterprise. Nevertheless, it endured for over a decade. Most of what has been published about 'independent' Rhodesia has focused on international sanctions and on the guerrilla war. But for more than ten years Smith's government also made internal social and economic policy. The legacies of these policies were inherited first by Abel Muzorewa and then by Robert Mugabe. They need to be better understood.

One of the major problems for the UDI regime was posed by the Tribal Trust Lands (TTLs), the areas in which hundreds of thousands of African peasant families lived. By 1965 most of the TTLs had become bases for black nationalist opposition. The roots of such opposition lay deep in a past in which white political power had been used to give white farming unequal advantage over black.[4] Peasant resentment had intensified after the Second World War. A sustained boom in maize, tobacco and beef brought prosperity to white commercial agriculture. It also led to the evictions of whole peasant populations from land designated as 'white' under the Land Apportionment Act. Very large numbers of African families were forcibly moved from the plateau, where they had lived close to schools, clinics and markets, into the remote and unhealthy areas of the Zambezi escarpment and valley, into the southern low veld and into the frontier areas of east and north-east Rhodesia. These evicted people were pioneers of radical nationalism in the undeveloped areas which surrounded the central core of white commercial agriculture. Such areas later provided ideal territory for guerrillas. In the early 1960s they were strongholds of mass nationalism.

Eviction was followed up by intensified state interference in African crop production and cattle raising. Large-scale destocking was enforced; conservation measures were imposed; the TTLs were surveyed and mapped in preparation for a revolution in residence patterns and land tenure rights. By means of the Native Land Husbandry Act of 1951, the Rhodesian government had sought to create a 'contented peasantry' and a 'stable working class'. In practice

---

Faber and Faber, London, 1963. A fascinating unpublished study is Michael Evans, 'The role of ideology in Rhodesian Front rule, 1962–1980', PhD. dissertation, University of Western Australia, 1993.

4 For an account of the history of African rural society see Terence Ranger, *Peasant Consciousness and Guerrilla War*, James Currey, London, 1985.

what developed was a discontented peasantry, deeply opposed to destocking and 'expert' interference, and a large landless class. The Land Husbandry Act aroused protest in many places and was impossible to implement in some. By 1960 and 1961 there was a widespread passive resistance and sabotage in the rural areas.

Well before the election of the Rhodesia Front in 1962, let alone UDI in 1965, Sir Edgar Whitehead's government had begun to change its policies. It abandoned any attempt to implement the Land Husbandry Act. It tried to find new land for African occupation by amending or even repealing the Land Apportionment Act. At the same time it adopted 'community development'. What this involved is described by Jocelyn Alexander:

> A new orthodoxy . . . rejected the possibility of 'modernizing' the reserves . . . [and] brought together the traditionalist beliefs of administrators in search of order, the 'expert' advice of community development advisers seeking 'natural' communities, and white politicians' needs for allies other than the nationalist leadership. The weight of these combined forces led to policy measures which effectively blocked land desegregation and set the stage for the exclusion of Africans other than chiefs from political channels.[5]

The Rhodesia Front regime espoused these new policies with enthusiasm, though showing 'a more dogmatic interpretation of tradition and a more authoritarian understanding of community development'. It rejected any further distribution of land to Africans and entrenched 'possessory segregation'. Instead of making more land available it embarked on tsetse fly clearance, road building, water development and irrigation within the 'wild' areas to which so many African families had been removed. 'Our policy is to place as many people on as little land as possible', announced an Internal Affairs official in 1971.[6]

These measures were combined with effective political repression in the rural areas. After the ban on ZAPU and ZANU in August 1964 many rural nationalist activists were arrested. The first tentative guerrilla incursions were broken up. In the late 1960s Noel Hunt was district commissioner of Nkai in northern Matabeleland. He later remembered these initial guerrilla thrusts. 'Oh, they came into Nkai a couple of times, and we killed them . . . There was a lot of unrest over land ownership in Nkai at the time, and this fell in with the classic guerrilla thing, you know . . . exploit a local grievance . . . and there they were exploiting it. And I kept on stamping on them every time they did it – never had so much fun in my life'.[7]

Hunt was a firm believer in an alliance with the chiefs – 'the hereditary aristocracy, who'd been ruling these people ever since they emerged from the

---

5 Jocelyn Alexander, 'The state, agrarian policy and rural politics in Zimbabwe,' D. Phil, Oxford University (August 1993), p.87.
6 *Rhodesia Herald*, 14 July 1971, cited in Alexander, p.90.
7 Interview with Noel Hunt, 27 November 1983, ORAL/240, National Archives, Harare, pp.61/62.

Congolese forests . . . They know how to rule blacks'. He thought that UDI in combination with chiefly power was enough in itself to break the nationalist hold on the rural areas. He heard Smith's UDI broadcast in a 'dirty little store . . . at the bottom end of Nkai District':

And when I went out and got into my truck and drove off, the word had spread all over the tribal area that something terrible had happened, that the white man had taken over the country and was going to rule it and that he'd kicked the British out. And wherever you went the Africans were taking their hats off and clapping their hands . . . The Chiefs were one hundred per cent behind us on that. They thought that we were going to get busy and kill every damn Afro-Nat in Rhodesia.

According to Hunt, one of the Nkai chiefs had 'hauled out every Afro-Nat', lined them up and flogged them. 'Ha, my friend, Ian Smith has taken the country over. Now, *now* I remind you, *you* were the one who said you were going to cut my legs off . . . Wack . . . Wack . . . Wack'.[8]

Rhodesia Front policy in the African rural areas did not amount only to repression, however. What Hunt called 'the bleeding hearts' in the Internal Affairs Department of UDI Rhodesia tried to take community development seriously as a policy which could appeal to Africans as well as cut costs for the white state. Some administrative intellectuals genuinely believed that community development could stimulate a 'vigorous system of local government [which] offers the only hope of protecting local values, sustaining local identities and resisting the claims of centralization over decentralization, nationalism over localism and uniformity over diversity'. The policy was 'a far-reaching assertion of the rights of minorities as against the tyranny of majorities'.[9]

The Department began an extensive research programme in order to discover the 'democratic' potential of chiefs and headmen. It announced the result in 1966 – 'an aggregate of communities is the basis of the state . . . [and] those communities have a right to representation in Parliament'.[10] Rural local communities were defined as chieftancies; chiefs were to represent their communities in a hierarchy of district, regional and national councils; a few selected chiefs would sit in senate as part of parliament. Between 1963 and 1967 an elaborate 'delineation' exercise was undertaken throughout the Tribal Trust Lands. Tribal histories were recorded; the boundaries of wards and chieftancies were mapped; communities were invented. Their 'felt' and 'unfelt' needs were painstakingly recorded.[11] Tribal Land Authorities were set up, chaired by chiefs. District commissioners went to great, sometimes absurd, lengths

8 Interview with Hunt, p.60.
9 Secretary for Internal Affairs, *NADA*, 1963, pp.108–12.
10 Roger Howman, 'Chieftanship'; Internal Affairs Memorandum on 'Tribal Psychology and Tribal Structure,' *NADA*, 1966.
11 The delineation reports are held in the National Archives, Harare, as series S 2929. By 1966 970 communities had been identified; 60 councils and 77 community boards had been established.

to identify 'legitimate' chiefs, consulting the senior spirit mediums and great aunts of the lineage.[12]

These policies won some African support. In many areas chiefs, themselves owners of large herds, were able to stop destocking. The takeover of mission primary schools by local councils between 1967 and 1972 was popular with the many critics of missionary authoritarianism. Some of the Rhodesia Front's irrigation schemes provided fertile land for peasant entrepreneurs. But the designers of community development were not satisfied themselves with their creation. Chiefs were unable – or unwilling – to implement land conservation measures; peasant settlers on irrigation schemes resented expert direction; nationalist emotions kept on bubbling to the surface. Obviously, people did not have their hearts in local 'communities'.

So the Rhodesia Front intellectuals went on searching for the 'real' community unit. In 1973 secretary for internal affairs A. B. Yardley circulated a memorandum to all district commissioners. 'In the past we have had some unfortunate experiences in using the tribal system, notably with our conservation drive, but these disappointments resulted not from the tribal structure or organization as such, but from using incorrect levels of the organization. One must always work with groups of tribesmen.' But it was 'the sub-community we are after': the extended family village, 'small enough for the problems to become real, to affect the individual sufficiently to make him willing to do something about it'. DCs were told that 'it is now urgently necessary to recognize and identify the various constituent communities and their leaders'; another great delineation exercise was commanded, which would establish 'a clearly defined boundary' between each village and its neighbours. Throughout 1973 district officers began to delineate 'villages'.[13]

The guerrilla war swallowed up these desperate attempts to find and map the key unit of rural collaboration. But in any case by the 1970s the contradictions of community development had become plain. Local 'tribal' councils found that maintaining primary schools was beyond their resources; Rhodesia Front irrigation schemes became in effect state farms, as peasant settlers deserted them; instead of working 'with groups of tribesmen', district commissioners became increasingly authoritarian as they sought to enforce conservation rules and to combat guerrilla infiltration.[14] Above all, government refusal to make any further land available undercut the capacity of the chiefs to play

12 Terence Ranger, 'Tradition and travesty: chiefs and the administration in Makoni District, 1960–1980,' in J. D. Y. Peel and Terence Ranger (eds), *Past and Present in Zimbabwe*, Manchester University Press, Manchester, 1983, pp.20–41.
13 Memorandum by provincial commissioner, Mashonaland South, 15 January 1971; Secretary of Internal Affairs Circular, February 1973, Nkai file LAN 23. Rural Planning, Dev. 82/84. In Matabeleland district commissioners were ordered to restore 'traditional' chiefs' councils, or *in-Khundla*, which would come together at a central gathering, presided over 'by a senior member of this Ministry, to take the place of Lobengula'. A. B. N. Beale, 'Tribal Organisation, Matabele', February 1973, *ibid.*
14 Alexander writes that 'the Natural Resources Board remained decidedly authoritarian in its approach, producing, for example, pamphlets entitled "Obey or Die" for chiefs' consumption'. See her 'The state, agrarian policy and rural politics', p.100.

the role of significant patrons. In any case, Ian Smith himself did not take the community development ideology, or the chiefs, nearly as seriously as the Internal Affairs intellectuals.

Noel Hunt has a vivid passage in which he describes Smith speaking at the Chiefs' Hall in Seke:

> making a fighting speech to them. Telling them '*You* are the leaders of the African people' . . . they all clapped their bloody heads off! Then he'd say, 'Well, that's it chaps, I'll leave it to you now, I've got to go and do something else'. And off he'd go and next morning you'd see in the paper that night he'd met with Joshua Nkomo.[15]

Smith was always the supreme political pragmatist.

THE CAPITALIST ECONOMY UNDER THE RHODESIA FRONT

The break-up of the Federation in 1963 was the first blow to the Southern Rhodesian economy, which had prospered so greatly in the previous ten years. The Rhodesia Treasury took over most of the Federal debt; meanwhile the great mining companies abandoned Salisbury and set themselves up in Zambia. 'Sheer survival was the first consideration' for Southern Rhodesia in 1963.[16] UDI and the subsequent imposition of sanctions by Britain and the United Nations seemed a much greater threat. Many industrialists and businessmen strongly opposed UDI. But in fact the short-term success of the capitalist economy under UDI, at least in the ten years between 1965 and 1975, was one of the Rhodesia Front's most striking achievements.

As in other periods of Rhodesian economic growth, industry thrived on protection from competition. Colin Stoneman and Rob Davies noted in 1981 that:

> The imposition of economic sanctions caused a small drop in national income initially, but much less than most Western trained economists expected. After two or three years of near stagnation, the economy then moved ahead rapidly until 1974, led by the expansion of manufacturing needed to substitute for goods that could no longer be imported. GDP per capita in constant 1965 prices rose from $157.5 in 1965 to a peak of $223.2 in 1974 but then fell to $166.5 in 1979 . . . Up to 1975 it could be maintained in broad terms that UDI had in a sense worked, allowing an economic growth rate higher than in some (though by no means all) poor countries, and higher than in some (but not all) earlier periods of Rhodesia's history.[17]

In the early 1990s, reacting to drought and price inflation, many Zimbabweans told each other that 'it was better under Smith'. But the economic 'successes' of UDI were partly an illusion. By the mid-1970s growth ended,

15 Interview with Hunt, p.51.
16 Kenneth Young, *Rhodesia and Independence*, p.95.
17 Colin Stoneman and Rob Davies, 'The economy: an overview', in Colin Stoneman (ed.), *Zimbabwe's Inheritance*, Macmillan, London, 1981, p.96.

as import substitution opportunities declined. The continuing poverty of African peasants and the low wages of African workers restricted the size of the internal market. Towards the end of UDI inflation began to increase. By 1980 the average income of the population was only one-fifteenth of the average income in Britain, compared to one-twelfth in 1965. By the late 1970s the peasant share of marketed maize had dropped to almost nothing. The inequalities between the white and the black economies became yet greater under UDI.[18] Nor were the achievements of industry under UDI a triumph for free enterprise. State investment amounted to nearly 50 per cent of the total in the mid-1970s; there was close state supervision of 'sanctions-busting' and state inducements for foreign investment. Rhodesia Front economic management was a continuation under war conditions of long-established state discrimination in favour of white enterprise. The rhetoric of community development could not long conceal this.

DEALING WITH EXTERNAL AND INTERNAL THREATS

During its proclaimed 'independence' the Rhodesia Front regime faced both external and internal threats. Smith's external enemies were not prepared to use force against him. Britain depended upon economic sanctions and a series of futile and often absurd negotiations. At the same time successive British governments maintained that Rhodesia was exclusively a British rather than a United Nations responsibility.[19] The communists, against whom UDI Rhodesia rhetorically stood, did not employ force directly either but contented themselves with training, arming and advising the guerrilla armies of Joshua Nkomo's ZAPU and Ndabaningi Sithole's ZANU. During the 1960s neither the British nor the Soviet Union and China had much success in their strategies of opposition to UDI.

After 1970, however, things changed. Sanctions began to have an effect on the Rhodesian economy and guerrilla incursions began to be much more effective. Even British negotiations began to have some important consequences as they helped to bring about a revival of nationalist activity inside Rhodesia. On 24 November 1971 Ian Smith signed an agreement in Salisbury with the British foreign secretary, Sir Alec Douglas Home. The details of that agreement need no longer concern us. The important thing was that it was subject to an expression of opinion by the people of Rhodesia. A Commission was established to test public opinion, chaired by a British judge, Lord Pearce, and largely staffed by ex-colonial officials. While the Commission was operating, it was agreed, 'normal political activity' must be allowed.

The effect of this was to reveal the hollowness of the structures which the Rhodesia Front had erected to displace African nationalism. On 16 December 1971 an African National Council was formed on the initiative of ex-detainees

18 *Ibid.*, pp.96,103.
19 Elaine Windrich, *Britain and the Politics of Rhodesian Independence*, Croom Helm, London, 1978, is the best account.

210

from both ZAPU and ZANU, to oppose the Smith/Home proposals. It was fronted by the prominent churchmen Abel Muzorewa and Canaan Banana.[20] At once 'ANC branches sprang up like mushrooms . . . Sometimes an old branch of either ZANU or ZAPU formed a nucleus'.[21] The Pearce Commission found, much to its surprise, that 'the African population of Rhodesia was alive with political activity . . . not only in the urban areas where one might have expected it but also in the Tribal Trust Lands'.[22]

In particular, the Commission found that chiefs were neither unanimous in supporting the proposals nor accepted as the political spokesmen of rural people. Indeed, 'the majority of the Chiefs lined up with their people in the TTLs in the rejection of the Proposals or chose to remain silent'.[23] When the commissioners met Chief Mutassa on 12 January 1972, for instance:

> Several people spoke against the Proposals. Then came the moment for Chief Mutassa to state publicly his position. The chief said: 'My people do not want these Proposals. I am chief of the people. I do what my people want. I therefore say *Kwete* – No'! At that word 4,000 people rose up and started jumping, shouting, throwing their hats in the air and cutting the earth with their axes. Women shrilled a joyful noise.[24]

Community development seemed to dissolve before the eyes of the dumb-founded district commissioners. The African National Council rapidly brought together the essential elements in the old nationalist coalition – trade unionists, students, resentful rural evictees. Churchmen, however, now played a more prominent role. In the early 1960s mass nationalism had competed with the churches, deliberately holding huge rallies on Sunday mornings and increasingly appealing to 'traditional' religion. Ten years later the ANC was powered by a radical Christianity which denounced the Rhodesia Front's claim to defend Christian civilisation. Muzorewa himself preached on the coming together of the dry bones. 'I'm a free agent of the Holy Spirit,' announced Reverend Thompson Tirivavi, 'and I'm opposed to Christian Imperialism'.[25]

In the aftermath of the Pearce Commission's report in May 1972, when Africans had rejected the proposals, the African National Council reconstituted itself as a political party. On its side, the Rhodesia Front regime could think of no other recourse save to make community development yet more authoritarian. The Pearce Report:

> marked an important point in the turn from a notional adherence to participatory, voluntary community development to an over reliance on chiefs and direct state control. The 1973 African Councils Act strengthened chiefs'

---

20 The most detailed examination of the formation of the ANC is A. H. Rich, 'Social, ethnic and regional factors in the development of Zimbabwean Nationalist Movements, 1963–80', Ph.D. dissertation, Manchester University, 1983.
21 Abel Muzorewa, *Rise Up and Walk*, Evans, London, 1978, p.97.
22 *Rhodesia. Report of the Commission on Rhodesian Opinion*, Cmnd. 4964, May 1972, p.37.
23 *Ibid.*, p.51.
24 Muzorewa, *Rise Up and Walk*, p.99.
25 Rich, 'Social, ethnic and regional factors', p.166.

administrative and executive powers . . . After 1972 district and provincial commissioners assumed paramilitary powers under the much amended Law and Order (Maintenance Act) and Emergency Powers Act. PCs could impose collective fines, DCs could marshall forced labour for security reasons, control the movement of food and stock, administer corporal punishment, control entry and exit to TTLs, and prohibit any meeting whatsoever.[26]

After 1972 British control of negotiations with Smith could no longer be maintained. The United States and South Africa now tried to broker a solution and South Africa put sufficient pressure on Smith to compel him to go along with the attempt. In the end the so-called détente exercise of 1974 broke down. But it had one significant effect. On 3 December 1974 it was announced in Salisbury that Nkomo, Mugabe, Sithole and other nationalist leaders had been released from detention in order to participate in talks. Under heavy pressure from the presidents of the Front Line States of Tanzania, Zambia and Mozambique, ZAPU and ZANU agreed to join under the umbrella of the ANC, led by Muzorewa.[27] From these developments flowed the political events of the later 1970s.

GUERRILLA WAR

In the early 1980s the bookstalls at South African airports were loaded with triumphalist volumes explaining how the Rhodesians had won the guerrilla war. They also explained that the unbroken victories of the gallant Rhodesian forces had been betrayed by the politicians and particularly by the British. The South African and exiled white Rhodesian public had a particular appetite for books about 'dirty tricks', such as Peter Stiff's two best sellers on the Selous Scouts and the Central Intelligence Organisation.[28] These presented a tale of 'blacking up', infiltration, assassination, poisoning. They sought to make two things clear – that black guerrillas were no match for Rhodesian soldiers, and that it was legitimate to use any measures against them.

Stiff's book on the Central Intelligence Organisation, for instance, narrates the adventures of 'Taffy,' leader of its 'most secret external operating team,' who is credited with the successful killing of Herbert Chitepo and with unsuccessful attempts on both Nkomo and Mugabe. Its tone comes out clearly from a scene where 'Taffy' needs poison for his attempt on Mugabe. He is directed to Sam Roberts, 'an elderly man with grey hair and bushy eyebrows . . . everybody's idea of what a grandfather should be, kindly, concerned and always prepared to listen to people's problems'. Sam had a little hobby, however, 'researching for and distilling rare poisons'. In his private laboratory in Borrowdale he distilled thalium for poisoning mealie-meal and parathian for

26 Alexander, 'The state, agrarian policy and rural politics', pp.101–3.
27 The most vivid account of these developments is given by Maurice Nyagumbo, *With the People*, Allison and Busby, London, 1980.
28 Reid Daly, 'as told to Peter Stiff', *Selous Scouts. Top Secret War*, Galago, Alberton, 1982; Peter Stiff, *See You in November. Rhodesia's No Holds Barred Intelligence War*, Galago, Alberton, 1985.

doctoring clothes. 'It was said that there were some months when Sam Roberts had killed more terrorists than the Rhodesian Light Infantry'. Sam claimed credit – 'beaming' the while – for the deaths of large numbers of ZANLA guerrillas in the eastern districts, who ate meal doctored with thalium; he also claimed credit for soaking 'several hundred pairs of under-pants and T-shirts' with parathian – these were then distributed to stores for supply to guerrillas. 'Parathian is a poison that works its way into the human body through hair follicles. The score achieved was considerable'.[29]

These books could easily be dismissed as macabre macho adventure stories. But they are in fact very revealing. Rhodesian forces *did* win most formal encounters with guerrillas; Selous Scouts' counterinsurgency and dirty tricks operations *were* very effective; poison *was* used on a large scale – even though Ian Smith insists to this day on the 'clean' way in which his Christian war was fought.

But they overlook two things. One is that guerrilla wars are fought to win political victories rather than military ones. Rhodesian politicians did not betray their army by eventually negotiating; their great error was that for far too long they took no sort of political initiative at all.[30] The other is that, while some Rhodesian civilians believed any means was justified in the defence of 'civilisation', many white soldiers were sickened and demoralised by the sort of war they had to fight.[31] White Rhodesians had come to believe that as great trackers and hunters they were masters of the environment. It was a shock to them to discover that the guerrillas were even more at home in the bush. The costs of the war bore more and more heavily. It was by no means only politicians who undermined Rhodesian capacity to go on fighting. 'By 1980', write their chroniclers 'the large majority of White Rhodesians would settle for peace at any price'.[32]

By the late 1970s the large majority of Africans were also longing for peace, even if not at any price. As Joshua Nkomo reflected when the war was over:

> Our war of independence was longer and more cruel than any yet fought in Africa . . . Hardly a family in our country was unaffected by the bloody war that was forced upon us. Tens of thousands of young people grew up knowing nothing but chaos and disruption – living in danger, in the bush, in exile, in makeshift camps, outside the steadying framework of

29 Stiff, *See You in November*, pp.308–10. The poisonings were confirmed by a book published both in Britain and in Zimbabwe, Ken Flower, *Serving Secretly*, John Murray, London, 1987. Flower continued to act as Robert Mugabe's intelligence chief. ZANLA was the acronym for the army of ZANU.
30 This is the conclusion reached by a South African military study of the Rhodesian war, J. K. Cilliers, *Counter-Insurgency in Rhodesia*, Croom Helm, London, 1985. Cilliers warns that military victories are useless without a political programme that can win African support.
31 The most explicit, but by no means the only, statement of this is Bruce Moore-King, *White Man Black War*, Baobab, Harare, 1988. Peter Godwin and Ian Hancock's *Rhodesians Never Die*, Oxford University Press, London, 1993, documents the traumatic postwar fates of many white soldiers, p.283.
32 Godwin and Hancock, *Rhodesians Never Die*, p.3.

established communities. The focus of their lives was the false glamour of the gun.[33]

Their elders suffered equal disruptions. Many of them were forced out of 'the steadying framework of established communities' into so-called Protected Villages, designed to cut the guerrillas off from their source of food and intelligence. Others found themselves caught in the middle or in the crossfire of competing groups with guns: ZIPRA guerrillas, ZANLA guerrillas, 'rogue' guerrillas, Selous Scouts' pseudo-guerrillas, Security Force units. A woman from an area contested between both guerrilla armies and the security forces remembers:

> The Zipras had come into our area. They always came at night and asked for food. We cooked and gave it to them. We never told anyone because, had the soldiers known, we would have been beaten and our homes burned down. The Zanlas came a little while after the Zipras. They were very troublesome. They always wanted food and they made us sing their songs. We dreaded sunset because we knew that once the sun had set the Zanlas would arrive and make us sing . . . The soldiers would say how surprised they were that we said we loved our children, the comrades, for after all they troubled us so much . . . On the other hand, when the Zanlas came they accused us of hating them and loving the soldiers . . . We were caught between these two groups . . . both groups blamed us and both groups were armed, but we were not.[34]

Both sides employed calculated terror. The security forces displayed the butchered bodies of guerrillas and their young civilian helpers at schools and on the steps of churches; the guerrillas forbade the burial of the bodies of 'sell-outs', which were left for the dogs to eat. Communal rituals of mourning and settling of spirits were disrupted. Diseases spread, some of them, such as anthrax, almost certainly being used by the regime as a weapon against Africans and their cattle. In areas where guerrillas were poisoned by impregnated clothing and did not understand what was happening to them, very many people were identified and killed as witches. The war left deep scars in the African communal areas.[35]

A large literature has already grown up on the war.[36] Some of it describes how, despite all the suffering, most Africans in the rural areas supported the aims of the guerrillas.[37] This was achieved because guerrillas appealed to local

33 Joshua Nkomo, *The Story of My Life*, Methuen, London, 1984, pp.xiii and xiv.
34 Josephine Ndiweni's story is reproduced in Irene Staunton (ed.), *Mothers of the Revolution*, Baobab Books, Harare, 1990, pp.208–9. ZIPRA was the acronym for the army of ZAPU.
35 A graphic account of the war from within is Patricia Chater, *Caught in the Crossfire*, Zimbabwe Publishing House, Harare, 1985. For the actualities and memories of wartime terror I draw upon the research of Jocelyn Alexander, JoAnn McGregor, David Maxwell and Heike Schmidt.
36 Useful collections of such recent research are Ngwabi Bhebe and Terence Ranger (eds), *Zimbabwe's Liberation War: Soldiers and Society*, University of Zimbabwe, Harare, 1995.
37 For example David Lan, *Guns and Rain*, James Currey, London, 1985 and Terence Ranger, *Peasant Consciousness and Guerrilla War*.

traditions and consulted local religious shrines and mediums. It was also achieved because they promised to restore peasant land. In the border areas to which so many people had been forcibly evicted guerrillas were able to appeal to long-harboured resentment. But other work shows that there were many divisions within peasant societies and that these profoundly affected how people responded to the war. It has been argued that the dominated groups in rural society, especially women, commoners, youths, tried to use the guerrillas to break the power of elders and chiefly lineages. But these groups were more 'revolutionary' than the guerrillas themselves, who had no desire to offend the power-holders in the communal areas.[38]

Much research has been directed to the experience of women in the war, whether in the camps in Zambia and Mozambique, in guerrilla groups or as civilian women in the rural areas. There is no doubt that African women played many quite new roles during the war: as cooks and comforters to guerrillas; as carriers of weapons to the front; as young trainees in the camps; in a small minority of cases as gun-bearing combatants. During and soon after the war some people claimed that these new experiences amounted to a gender revolution, and that women would emerge from the war as equals of men. Such claims depended on a very exaggerated estimate of the numbers of female guerrillas and too great a readiness to believe the progressive propaganda of the African parties. In reality, a gender division of labour continued to operate in the camps and in the bush. ZIPRA did not deploy women combatants at all and ZANLA only deployed them in 'semi-liberated' zones.[39] Recently, work has begun on masculine dilemmas during the war and it has been argued that the basic paradigm of rural masculine power – the patriarchal elder, controlling the young and the women – was radically undermined by the arbitrary authority of young men with guns. When those young men withdrew or were disarmed at the end of the war, male elders hastened to reinstate the old system. Returning women combatants had no choice but to fit into it.[40]

A periodisation of the war has begun to emerge. In the mid-1960s the parties sought to use armed and trained men to stimulate and supplement civilian sabotage. When that failed, there were a series of purely military intrusions, which tried to avoid interaction with the civilian population. These also achieved no lasting gains. The key changes came in the early 1970s. The Mozambique front opened up with the victory of FRELIMO, the Front for the Liberation of Mozambique, which offered facilities to the guerrilla armies. These opportunities were first offered to ZIPRA but divisions within ZAPU prevented them from being taken up. Instead ZANLA began to infiltrate north-eastern Rhodesia and to adopt the new strategy of swimming among the people like fishes. They had many difficulties at first in districts which had

38 Norma Kriger, *Zimbabwe's Guerrilla War. Peasant Voices*, Cambridge University Press, Cambridge, 1992.
39 I draw here on the doctoral research of Josephine Nhongo.
40 I draw here on the doctoral work of Michael Kesby.

supported ZAPU in the past, but by 1974, they had rooted themselves firmly and begun to present a real threat to the Smith regime's hold on the communal areas. Thus began a dichotomy between the two major nationalist parties, with ZANLA working out of Mozambique into Shona-speaking areas, and ZIPRA working out of Zambia into Ndebele-speaking districts.

The détente exercise of 1974–75 confused the situation both politically and militarily. Politically, the losers were Muzorewa and Sithole, who both lost any authority over the guerrillas. The winner was eventually to be Robert Mugabe, though his command of ZANU and its guerrilla army was not secure until 1977. For a time in 1975 and 1976, with the formation of the Zimbabwe People's Army (ZIPA), the war was resumed by the young soldiers themselves, without political direction. ZIPA brought together soldiers from both ZIPRA and ZANLA. It aimed at a radicalised and politicised army and disliked the dependence upon spirit mediums and local traditions which had grown up among the guerrillas.[41] But there were bloody clashes within ZIPA between ZIPRA and ZANLA soldiers. The ZANU politicians managed to gain the ear of FRELIMO and ZIPA was broken up and its leaders imprisoned. By 1977 the war was again being waged by two party-based armies, ZANLA under the direction of Robert Mugabe and ZIPRA under the direction of Joshua Nkomo.

There was a contrast between the two armies. ZANLA certainly had many more recruits, so many in fact, that it began not to take them to Mozambique for training but to make use of them immediately on the ground. This situation led to many cases of indiscipline and to bitter complaints by civilians, but it also led to the swamping by guerrillas of many areas of eastern Zimbabwe. The Smith regime virtually withdrew from these 'semi-liberated' zones; women guerrillas were moved into them, and male detachments went on into 'contested' zones further inside the country. ZIPRA meanwhile deployed fewer guerrillas in the forests of northern Matabeleland – and no female combatants at all – but also achieved its own 'semi-liberated' areas. At the same time, ZIPRA began to prepare and train for conventional warfare on the assumption that this was the only way to smash the iron ring which the Rhodesians had thrown around the key farming and mineral areas and eventually to capture the towns.[42] The two parties viewed each other's efforts with suspicion. ZAPU regarded Mugabe's guerrillas as ill-trained political lobbyists, concerned mainly to persuade or to compel peasants to support Mugabe as leader. ZANU regarded Nkomo's preparations for conventional war as a strategy to leave ZANLA to fight the whites to a standstill and then to march in and seize the spoils.

Despite these tensions between the parties and their guerrilla armies – which led to clashes whenever they met each other on the ground – the Rhodesian

---

41 For ZIPA see David Moore, 'The Zimbabwe People's Army: strategic innovation or more of the same?' in Bhebe and Ranger (eds), *Soldiers in Zimbabwe's Liberation War*, pp.73–86.
42 For the conventional strategy of ZIPRA see Jeremy Brickhill, 'Daring to Storm the Heavens,' in Bhebe and Ranger, *Zimbabwe's Liberation War*, pp.48–72.

position had become untenable by 1977. The policy of community development was in ruins. Chiefs were either killed by guerrillas, lived under armed
police guard, or made secret alliances with the 'boys'. District commissioners
abandoned any pretence of local democracy and ruled their districts with an
iron hand and often with martial law. The economic successes of the early
1970s had ended and the cost of the war was increasingly felt. Ian Smith
decided that he must now ally himself with Muzorewa and Sithole against the
parties which controlled the guerrilla armies. This internal settlement ushered
in the brief attempt at a second independence – this time the majority rule
government of Abel Muzorewa.

MUZOREWA'S 'INDEPENDENCE' AND THE FAILED NATIONALIST SOLUTION

Little more than a year before entering into negotiations with Ian Smith,
Muzorewa had been in intransigent mood. 'The ANC is not here in a spirit
of give and take', he told the Geneva conference in October 1976. 'We have
come only to take'.[43] He boasted of his command of 'dedicated Zimbabweans
fighting barefoot in rugged valleys and mountains' and asserted that 'we shall
lay down our arms only when there is majority rule'. He demanded that
independence day for a majority-rule Zimbabwe be 12 September 1977, the
twentieth anniversary of the refounding of the Congress movement and 'the
87th anniversary of the Pioneers taking possession of Rhodesia.'[44] A year later
the situation was very different. Muzorewa was back inside the country. He
had no control over any of the fighting men. The only way he could participate in a movement towards 'independence' in 1977 was to negotiate with
Ian Smith.

Meanwhile Smith had decided to abandon community development and
the representation of communities by chiefs. He planned to negotiate with the
representatives of Zimbabwean nationalism so as to frustrate the spokesmen
of Zimbabwean socialism. He invited the bishop to talks. Muzorewa's auto-
biography gives an engaging account of their encounter. Smith spoke of the
intolerable cost of the war: 'business people tell me that the economy will not
survive much longer'. Muzorewa challenged him: 'If you are now prepared
to accept universal adult suffrage, not in principle but in practice then we are
in business'. Smith's answer was 'as completely unexpected as it was revolutionary': 'Well, Bishop, I would accept such a commitment provided, of
course that I received, in return, guarantees for whites under majority rule . . .
White confidence is absolutely essential'.[45]

On 24 November Smith announced to his shocked supporters that he was
ready to negotiate 'a Rhodesian solution' on the basis of majority rule. Two
days later Muzorewa 'issued the UANC's Final Demand for Freedom at a
National Youth Rally'; he was given a standing ovation and authorised to

43 Draft Preamble to the ANC Position paper, Geneva, October 1976, Samkange Papers, Harare.
44 Notes of Discussion of 14 November 1976, *ibid*.
45 Muzorewa, *Rise Up and Walk*, pp.227–8.

enter negotiations. Muzorewa was 'enthralled when the youth of Zimbabwe endorsed my decision'.[46]

Negotiations between Smith, Muzorewa and Sithole began on 9 December 1977. There was heavy bargaining over the guarantees to be given to whites. But on 3 March 1978 Smith signed the agreement which marked the transition from white rule. Government officials brought along a water-colour of Cecil John Rhodes; Muzorewa wore his Liberian costume. The mixture nicely symbolised the hybridity of the new state of Zimbabwe Rhodesia. A Transitional Government was formed with an Executive Council consisting of Smith, Muzorewa and Chief Chirau. December 31 1978 was set as the target date for a full transition to majority rule and for a declaration of independence.

Muzorewa proclaimed 1978 as 'a year of sacred events, a golden year in our history'; December 31 was to be a 'holy day' when 'we shall turn the graves of national heroes into national monuments, see tears turned into smiles and atrocities into history'.[47] But things went slowly. The white referendum on the new constitution was not held until January 1979, when 84.4 per cent voted in favour. The universal adult suffrage elections did not take place until April 1979. Muzorewa won 51 of the 72 African seats. The 'independence' which he had craved came at midnight on May 31 1979.

Muzorewa's 'independence' was thus very short-lived. The Zimbabwe Rhodesia flag was not unfurled at Rufaro Stadium in Salisbury until 5 September 1979, five days before the beginning of the Lancaster House Conference, which was to bring about the transition to Robert Mugabe's regime.

MUZOREWA AND THE NATIONALIST SOLUTION

Muzorewa's United African National Council was by design a throwback to the mass nationalism of the late 1950s and early 1960s. A youth league and a women's league were set up. An Organising Department prepared a 'master plan' to penetrate every part of the country and to take over every sort of association. Aware that 'the strength of the Party lies in the urban areas', the Department urged that every effort be made to penetrate rural society. Muzorewa should write a personal letter to each chief 'thanking him for his relationship with the people' and chiefs as a whole were to be assured 'of their existence in the future Government as true, traditional and hereditary leaders of the people'. The party should make use of 'women with hawkers' licences who trade within Protected Villages' to establish branches there. It should seek to take over burial societies, clubs, teachers' associations, football clubs, etc, etc, 'implanting the aims of the party within the members'. Schoolchildren should be encouraged 'to sing nationalist songs promoting the party'. And 'since the church is a common meeting ground for many people the

46 *Ibid.*, p.231. UANC was the United African National Council.
47 Muzorewa's New Year Message, 31 December 1977, Samkange Papers.

organisation should be well represented within the government body of that church, so that that body will influence the congregation'.[48]

Veteran nationalists, like George Nyandoro who had founded the 1957 Congress, were brought back from Zambia to 'add fire to those enthusiastic crowds'.[49] In short, while Muzorewa still claimed that most of the guerrillas had been sent out by the UANC, the main emphasis was upon the prewar nationalist tradition and on prewar nationalist policies. There would be a truly 'internal' settlement of the sort that Rhodesian whites might have had in the early 1960s, before the radicalisation of the war and the influence of Russia and China. When the UANC described itself as 'revolutionary' and set aside a special budget for 'revolutionary activities', it was to be a nationalist revolution.[50]

This determined the party's answers to the three great questions which confronted every attempt at independence. Economic problems were to be addressed by deracialising the capitalist economy. The problems of the rural areas were to be resolved by closing the Protected Villages, restoring the legitimacy of the chiefs, and planning a programme of land redistribution. The hated white presence of the Internal Affairs Department was to be replaced by African 'auxiliaries' of the UANC and Sithole's ZANU. The internal and external enemies of the new regime were to be won over or neutralised by the rapid implementation and perceived success of these programmes. Emissaries were sent out to negotiate with guerrilla groups and to establish local cease-fires. When all this was done, or under way, it was believed that Britain would endorse the new regime.

The question was how all this was to be done. The radicals in the UANC wanted simply to *do it*. In mid-1978 a committee set up to consider how the rural areas might be reclaimed, recommended merely that: 'all PVs be dismantled and the ceasefire made effective, e.g. Government forces should stop hunting guerrillas'.[51]

THE FAILURE OF THE NATIONALIST SOLUTION

The Muzorewa regime was quite good at the negative aspect of the nationalist revolution. The Rhodesia Front's land segregation legislation was repealed, all racial discrimination was abolished, and many Protected Villages were closed down. It was not so good at the positive action needed to follow up these changes. The economic stress of the continuing war meant that there were no

48 Organising Department, UANC, 18 December 1977, Samkange Papers.
49 Enoch Dumbutshena to Stanlake Samkange, 23 October 1977, Samkange Papers.
50 Even this degree of radicalism soon lapsed, however. On 7 June 1978 the Central Committee of the UANC voted to stop paying for 'revolutionary activities' and agreed to divert the funds to increase the allowances of committee members! Minutes of the meeting of 7 June 1978, Samkange Papers.
51 Ad Hoc committee report, 6 June 1978, Samkange Papers. The Committee urged that 'this time of year is the best for people to move back into their former homes'; Protected Villages should at once be abolished; guards and soldiers withdrawn; and village vigilante groups be set up.

funds to launch a land resettlement programme or to make loans to black entrepreneurs or even to offer assistance to the inhabitants of the Protected Villages. A report by the Catholic Justice and Peace Commission issued on Muzorewa's 'holy' date of 31 December 1978, remarked that when Protected Villages were closed:

> it soon became apparent that this did not benefit the former inhabitants who were left almost entirely to their own resources in relation to the problem of the reconstruction of the homes and the replacement of livestock and planting of crops. The opening of these villages was stopped after only some seventy in number had been re-opened.[52]

The first budget of 'independent' Zimbabwe Rhodesia revealed its poverty both of resources and ideas. With the war costing some 45 per cent of government expenditure, sales tax was not lowered nor were wages increased. In the first few weeks of the Muzorewa 'independence' meat prices rose by 11 per cent and milk by 8 per cent.[53]

The crucial problem was, of course, that the regime could not end the war. Command of the security forces remained firmly with white officers, and they had no intention whatsoever of stopping hunting guerrillas. From their point of view the auxiliaries were not an African *replacement* for a white army but a valuable supplement. The auxiliaries, many of whom were ex-guerrillas who knew the civilian networks of support and supply, established themselves in forts inside the communal areas. For most peasants 1978 and 1979 were the worst years of the war, as they were caught between auxiliary brutality, increasing guerrilla indiscipline and security force bombing. Muzorewa could do nothing to prevent devastating raids on the guerrilla camps in Mozambique and Zambia. Time and time again the UANC radicals demanded that something be done to gain control of the army or to withdraw from collaboration with the whites. Time and time again they were defeated by the UANC pragmatists.

The truth was that Zimbabwe Rhodesia was too strange a hybrid. Many white supporters of the old Rhodesia Front policy felt betrayed. The authoritarian Hunt, who in 1975 had formed the Rhodesian Conservative Alliance 'for white rule only', emigrated in 1979. He left with a curse on the white electorate: '85 per cent of them voted for black rule. So I don't really care what happens to them now, as long as it is very, very unpleasant . . . The sooner whites with a genetic inheritance like that are wiped off the face of the earth the better'.[54]

On the other side most guerrillas were deeply suspicious of the internal settlement leaders. When UANC mediators took clothes as gifts to guerrilla groups they suspected an attempt at poison and the emissaries were killed. An

52 Chairman's report, CCJP, 31 December 1978, Church of Sweden Archives, A 6241 1979:55.
53 Tony Rich, 'Social, ethnic and regional factors', pp.464–5. Rich's thesis is in general a rich source for the Muzorewa period.
54 Interview with Noel Hunt, 27 November 1983, ORAL 240, National Archives, Harare.

ex-combatant, Emmanuel Musara, describes how he explained the situation to 'a group of girls and *mujibas*' in 1979. Now that the auxiliaries were leaving 'no stone unturned to [kill] if they could all us guerrillas':

> no-one could say our war was a white versus black thing. To us guerrilla combatants the war was a class war – a war against the capitalists and all exploiters ... I explained that people were to be very wary about the machinations of nationalists in our midst who ... wanted only to remove the white man from power so that they could take over the vacated seats and then carry on exploiting the people.[55]

In Zambia Nkomo's ZIPRA continued to prepare for a conventional war on Zimbabwe Rhodesia. From Mozambique Robert Mugabe declared 1979 *Gore re Gukurahundi*, the Year of the People's Storm: 'Every Zimbabwean must be cleansed by the storm, for as much as it washes away the dross it also purifies the gold.[56]

MUGABE'S INDEPENDENCE

The Mugabe government responded to the problems of the communal areas, of the economy and of internal and external opposition in ways that were significantly different to those of the Smith and Muzorewa regimes. Yet there were nevertheless significant continuities. One of these was the continuity of a strong state. In contrast to many other Central African countries, the Zimbabwean state did not wither away in the years after 1980.

Omens did not look good at the beginning of Zimbabwe's independence. The Muzorewa regime had lost control of much of the countryside; the white-controlled army was riven with internal feuds and had been fighting a series of regional wars against the guerrillas rather than a single coordinated campaign; many of Mugabe's own guerrillas resented and suspected the Lancaster House Constitution which had been drawn up by the British government and the Zimbabwean political parties. Many guerrillas did not go into the Assembly Points; others soon deserted; yet others used the Assembly Points as bases from which to attack the infant institutions of the new state. In 1980 in Mtoko, for example, ex-ZANLA guerrillas consistently attacked the police station; at this stage 'dissidence' in Matabeleland, though it did exist, was dwarfed by the scale of disorder in central and eastern Zimbabwe. The Mugabe regime, in short, was faced with the classic dilemma of how to restore 'governability' out of a long-fostered 'ungovernability'.

Morever, the new regime faced a crisis of reconstruction in the rural areas. Merely to rebuild schools and clinics and cattle dip tanks would be vastly expensive. It was unclear which local government institutions would share in this task. The new regime was determined not to continue with chief-led

---

55 Emmanuel Musara, 'Zimbabwe – The Great War of Liberation,' unpublished ms.
56 *ZANU. 1979 The Year of the People's Storm*, Maputo, January 1979.

'communities' but nothing had yet taken their place. Local party committees and 'people's courts' had seemed admirable from the ground-level perspective of the guerrilla war, but they did not look like reliable instruments of the state when seen from the centre. At the centre itself, the new ministers faced a suspicious and resistant white civil service. 'I feel like a fly in a glass of milk' one of them said after his first visit to his ministry. There were fears of deliberate sabotage by white leaders of industry and commerce.

Yet in fact Robert Mugabe inherited effective mechanisms for state control of the economy and functioning professional associations. He also inherited a still formidable army, which in the end was made yet more formidable by the integration of guerrillas with elements of the Rhodesian forces. The Matabeleland dissidents found the Zimbabwean army in the 1980s much more effective than the Rhodesian army in the 1970s. Return to 'normalcy' in the rural areas which had voted for ZANU/PF in 1980 was astonishingly rapid. Rural patriarchs were anxious to restore their prewar dominance and every-one else in the communal areas wanted peace more than anything else. Pamela Reynolds has argued that diviners engaged in healing the traumas of the war were responding to a quite new sense of the immanence of evil; nevertheless, their ministrations returned youth to their submission to elders and young women to their submission to men.[57]

Foreign donors proved ready to finance rebuilding and welfare, though not land acquisition and redistribution. Survivors of the Internal Affairs Depart-ment continued to act as administrators of the rural areas until a new system was put in place.

In short, the Mugabe regime had at its disposal the effective persuasive and coercive powers of a modern state. It had every intention of making use of these. The Zimbabwean government was one of the last unequivocal modern-ising regimes in Africa. It felt its legitimacy to lie not only in the two-thirds vote it received in the 1980 elections, but also in its commitment to 'develop-ment.' Loyal ZANU/PF members and voters were to be rewarded, but even those areas which had supported Nkomo were to be 'developed,' as were the minority ethnicities on the edges of the state:

> The battle for Binga is on! War is being waged upon the ugly enemies of poverty and starvation which have stalked the stricken Ba-Tonka in the most remote and underdeveloped region of Zimbabwe . . . The Ba-Tonka had never managed to raise themselves much above subsistence level . . . Deep-rooted superstition and beliefs in witchcraft and primitive Gods ren-dered the Ba-Tonka slow in adapting to a new way of life . . . [But] the Ba-Tonka are no longer a forgotten people. There are devoted health workers, educationalists and even businessmen fighting to haul the district and its people into the light of modern day.[58]

57 Pamela Reynolds, *Traditional Healers and Childhood in Zimbabwe*, Ohio University Press, Athens, 1966. ZANU appropriated the name Patriotic Front (PF).
58 *Chronicle*, 10 March 1981.

On May 10 1992 the *Chronicle* headline ran 'New Hope for the People of Binga'. This new hope, it said, came from a government which for the first time really cared for the Tonga and which had 'responded with unprecedented speed to an SOS to save the whole population from starvation'.

As these reports suggest, the modernising government inherited a great deal of colonial paternalism and condescension. It also inherited the development plans which the Rhodesian government had drawn up in the late 1950s and early 1960s before community development had replaced the development thrust. The Mugabe regime was going back more than twenty years but the 'experts' were still available. 'Development' once again meant conservation, villagisation, surveys and increasingly individual tenure. Planning became more and more top down. In the terms of Mahmood Mamdani's recent analysis[59] the radical modernisers of the Mugabe regime moved in the rural areas from party dominance to the party state and finally to the state as such. In Matabeleland, where neither ZANLA nor ZANU/PF had enjoyed support, the move to the directive state was yet more rapid.

THE DISSIDENT WAR

Before exploring the regime's attempts to resolve the problems of the rural areas and of the national economy, it is necessary to deal with internal and external opposition. It was incapacity to end the war which doomed the Muzorewa regime. In 1980 peasants had voted for ZANU/PF as the only party able to achieve peace, yet this was difficult as in 1980 there were 'dissidents' all over the country. Gradually, however, the term came to be applied only to Matabeleland.

The regime's relationship with Matabeleland was tense for several reasons. The government was determined to 'develop' the region almost despite its elected ZAPU representatives.[60] For their part, the Sindebele-speakers of northern Matabeleland, with their memories of eviction and forced resettlement in the 1950s and 60s and of poisoning and repression in the 1970s, continued to distrust the state. They passively resisted state development plans. The government felt that its moral authority was being wantonly disregarded. It took a simple majoritarian view of democracy. 'We worship the majority as much as Christians worship God', Edson Zvogbo told a Matabeleland audience.[61] It sought to 'convert' Matabeleland to ZANU/PF as a party, and then to a party state in the interests of the unhindered power of the state as such. For this reason great government displeasure was visited upon

59 M. Mamdani, *Citizen and Subject*, James Currey, London, 1996.
60 For an account of ZAPU's role in the aftermath of independence see Jocelyn Alexander and JoAnn McGregor, 'Democracy, development and political conflict: rural institutions in Matabeleland North after Independence,' University of Zimbabwe, Harare, 1996. Alexander and McGregor – with whom I have been carrying out research on northern Matabeleland – do not share my emphasis upon the 'development' commitment of the Mugabe regime.
61 *Chronicle*, 12 September 1983.

Matabeleland when the 1985 elections revealed its stubborn persistence in voting for ZAPU.

There were other reasons for tension. A new nation had to have a usable history. But the usable history of Zimbabwe was exclusively one of 'Shona' empires, just as the authorised version of the liberation war was exclusively an account of ZANLA's victory. Matabeleland and ex-ZIPRA fighters, although by no means exclusively Ndebele, felt excluded.

There were also more immediate and practical tensions. ZANU/PF feared that ZAPU had not accepted the election result and was plotting a coup. In an atmosphere poisoned by sabotage and assassination attempts by South African agents, it was not difficult for surviving white members of the Central Intelligence Organisation to persuade Mugabe that treason was being plotted in Matabeleland.

Ex-ZIPRA men also had tangible reasons for alarm. Plans to integrate the ex-guerrillas into the new army broke down into savage fighting between ZIPRA and ZANLA. ZIPRA guerrillas fled from their 'integrated' units. Many tried to return to civilian life or migrated to South Africa. Some took to the bush with guns. There they were joined by disaffected returning refugees and unemployed youth and by some chancers and thugs. South Africa naturally tried to exploit this situation. It set up a Sindebele broadcasting station, Radio Truth, and offered arms and support to ZAPU refugees in Botswana, creating an armed force which came to be called Super-ZAPU.

Everything seemed set for a classic destabilisation scenario. This did not happen and for reasons which again distinguish Zimbabwe from many other Central African territories. The *state* in Zimbabwe survived. So too did the idea of the *nation*. However one-sidedly the new regime imagined the history of Zimbabwe as nation; however ruthlessly it used its specially established Korean-trained and Shona-speaking Fifth Brigade, *Gukurahundi*, as the purging storm intended to wash away the dross of Matabeleland and to purify the gold of ZANU/PF support; however urgently the dissidents called on ZAPU to back them; the idea of the nation was in the end too strong. Joshua Nkomo at one point fled from the country but he never abandoned his image as 'Father Zimbabwe', founder of nationalism and representative of the nationalist aspirations of the whole country. When young hotheads in Dukwe refugee camp in Botswana opted to ally themselves with South Africa, claiming to have been 'born ZAPU', Nkomo's representative in the camp replied that no one was born ZAPU. Membership was a matter of ideology and political education. The ZAPU tradition held as a national tradition; ZAPU did not back the dissidents and Super-ZAPU was destroyed by the dissidents themselves.[62]

The idea of the nation-state as the objective mediator of interests persisted. In Matabeleland both Shona-speaking policemen and Sindebele-speaking district administrators sought to maintain this ideal and themselves became

---

62 A fascinating discussion of the dissident experience is Jocelyn Alexander, 'Dissident perspectives in Zimbabwe's post–independence war', Oxford, 1996.

objects of Fifth Brigade attack, along with councillors and churchmen. For a while all the institutions of local government and rural society in Matabeleland were under threat. But in the end, after five years of terrible violence, the idea of Zimbabwe as a plural nation emerged. The Fifth Brigade was withdrawn, retrained, and in effect disowned by the national army. After long-drawn out negotiations Nkomo and Mugabe signed a Unity Agreement in December 1987 which provided for the integration of the two parties. In April 1988 an amnesty was declared for the dissidents and for everyone else involved in the Matabeleland war. A peace, partly of exhaustion and partly of rejoicing, fell on Matabeleland.[63]

In this way the Mugabe regime fared better than either of its predecessors. Internal war *did* end; a political solution *was* found. By the 1990s external threats had also ended. South Africa no longer sought to destabilise; Zimbabwe was able to withdraw its troops from Mozambique; and RENAMO raids into the country came to an end. Yet this outcome was far from a total victory for the Mugabe regime. Even though Nkomo and ZAPU had long supported the idea of an executive president and a one-party state, and even though the Unity Agreement had guaranteed the unchallenged political dominance of ZANU/PF from 1987, the change was nevertheless profound.

It became clear that the new Zimbabwe had to be imagined in plural ways. 'Killing has become a political language', wrote a Matabeleland intellectual, Edwin Mkwananzi, five months before the Unity Agreement.

The people of Matabeleland in particular have lost that sense of human touch . . . they no longer know that a stranger can be helped with a glass of water when thirsty . . . Children no longer play in the moonlight . . . This is a time when we must halt once and for all the ZANUeering and ZAPUeering. It is a time when we must put an end to sloganeering and return to civilised life. The individual must cease to be seen only as a political instrument but should be elevated to full status as a human being . . . This violent society must go. ZANU (PF) and ZAPU cannot afford to be rigid in a plural world like today.[64]

The experience of the 1980s had persuaded Nkomo and many others of the dangers of unrestrained state power. Ex-ZAPU men within the new united party were among those who opposed the formal legislation of a one-party state. Events in Eastern Europe, especially in Zimbabwe's close ally, Romania, were taken as a warning. Zimbabwe drew back from a majority/minority conflict which was becoming dangerously close to an ethnic war. The rhetoric of 'civil society' and of 'transparency' replaced that of the majoritarian state.

63 A vivid and profound accont of the impact of Fifth Brigade violence in Matabeleland is given in Richard Werbner, *Tears of the Dead*, Edinburgh University Press, Edinburgh, 1991; 'In memory: a heritage of war in southwestern Zimbabwe', in N. Bhebe and T. O. Ranger (eds), *Society in Zimbabwe's Liberation War*, James Currey, London, 1996.
64 *Sunday News*, 26 July 1987.

Terence Ranger

APPROACHING THE PROBLEMS OF THE RURAL AREAS

The Mugabe regime differed sharply from both Smith and Muzorewa in its approach to the African rural areas. There was to be no courting of the chiefs and no return to Rhodesia Front 'communities.' Chiefs were allocated merely 'cultural' and 'traditional' duties and stripped of their power to distribute land or to hear cases. Spirit mediums, who had been so courted during the liberation war, were now closely controlled and defined as healers rather than as prophets. During the war, Mugabe and many others had appealed to the heroic memory of the female spirit medium, Nehanda, who was believed to have issued commands to begin the 1896 *chimurenga* uprising against the whites. After 1980, however, ministers were anxious to cut the heroic tradition of Nehanda down to size, stressing that the spirit's reputation was due to their own invocation of it and that no Nehanda medium had any longer independent power to determine war and peace. A powerful Nehanda medium, based at Great Zimbabwe, around whom ZANLA guerrillas from the local Assembly Point gathered, was summarily dealt with. Her kraal was stormed by the police and she herself was tried and convicted for incitement to murder. As Simon Muzenda said, once Prime Minister Mugabe had declared that the war had ended it was treason for a spirit medium to seek to launch her own *chimurenga*.

Rural local government was to become resolutely modern. Land allocation was entrusted to elected district councils. Below them a network of village and ward development committees was constructed. Cases were to be heard by newly constituted local courts. These arrangements were hailed by ZANU/PF activists as a revolutionary democratisation of the countryside. In theory development plans were to originate at the local level and to succeed because of popular participation and involvement.

There were several contradictions built into these provisions. One was that the most important government policy to redress rural grievances, i.e. the acquisition and redistribution of land, was not under the control of the new district councils at all. The resettlement areas answered to no local authority but directly to the responsible ministry. That ministry was determined that the resettlement areas should not be extensions of the social, or tenurial, or farming system of the African communal zones. Local people watched with increasing scepticism as successive models of producer cooperatives, of state farms, of resident male farmers, of paddocked grazing schemes, failed in their objectives. In Matabeleland especially, where people had been moved so many times, the call was that cattle rather than human beings should be resettled, using the newly acquired land as supplementary communal grazing. The government constantly resisted these demands, arguing that they would merely increase rural inequality. The resettlement areas were to be a 'modern' zone in the countryside.

Another contradiction was that for many years the elected district councils only represented the impoverished communal areas and could not levy rates

226

on the still surviving rural councils which represented commercial farmers. District councils thus had no capacity to fund schools, clinics or development projects.

Finally, so far as the communal areas themselves were concerned, official thinking began by believing that the solution to their over-crowded poverty was land redistribution. But officials soon came to believe that what was needed was internal 'land reform'. Government therefore turned to all the old blueprints for consolidated settlement, demarcation of grazing and arable zones, cattle permits and cultivation rights which had marked government policy in the 1950s. These schemes were no more popular in the 1980s than they had been thirty years before. Nor were official calls for conservation. When Joshua Nkomo himself called upon the people of the Matopos communal area to evacuate their stony home so as to safeguard the rivers of southern Matabeleland, they told him: 'You forget that we fought for you – *and* for these rocks'.

A sort of stalemate arose. Government alone had the power to initiate development schemes; peasants had only the capacity, which they widely deployed, to frustrate these plans. Chiefs began to be thought of by their people as representative of local communal interests; mediums and shrine priests, freed from political alliance with the state, came to articulate peasant demands for land and 'custom'.[65]

In all this Zimbabwe was following the pattern of other radical modernising states like Tanzania and Mozambique. It was also following the pattern of previous modernising Rhodesian regimes. As we have seen, when the modernising, transforming impulse which inspired the Land Husbandry Act of 1951 exhausted itself in political and fiscal crises, Rhodesian regimes turned to chiefs and community development. After 1990 one could see the same trajectory in independent Zimbabwe. This reached its height in the 1995 Land Tenure Commission's recommendations which were accepted by the government. The village and ward development committees were to be abolished and replaced by village assemblies under headmen and chiefs. In a striking innovation the village assemblies were to own freehold title to their own land. But there were echoes here of the Rhodesia Front's attempts to find the true organic units of development in the 'real' village of the extended family kraal. Just as in the 1970s so in the 1990s the 'traditional' villages were to be identified, mapped, and fenced. Whether the main impulse behind these policy changes was a belated desire for rural democratisation or withdrawal of the exhausted modernising state was not clear.

---

65 An illuminating account of the local dynamics of 'development' is Steven Robins, 'Contesting the social geometry of bureaucratic state power: a case study of land-use planning in Matabeleland, Zimbabwe', *Social Dynamics* 20, 2, summer 1994; an account of the prophetic critique of the state is Abraham Mawere and Ken Wilson, 'Socio-religious movements, the state and community change: some reflections on the Ambuya Juliana cult of Southern Zimbabwe', *Journal of Religion in Africa* 25, Fasc. 3, August 1995.

INDEPENDENT ZIMBABWE AND THE ECONOMY

The 1980s were a paradoxical decade. They saw unsuccessful interventions in rural society, a brutal war in Matabeleland, and a thrust towards a majoritarian, 'general will', one-party state. At the same time, however, there were real successes. There was significant economic growth. Above all there was effective welfare provision. All the indices of life expectancy, child survival, literacy, health and educational provision improved steadily between 1980 and 1990. 'Real' socialists mocked what they called 'mere Scandinavian welfarism,' but outside Matabeleland the 1980s seemed a golden age.

The early 1990s saw the opposite paradox. As the state began to lose its heroic legitimation and hence its monopoly over national life, there was a flowering of 'civil society', a debate about human rights and an acceptance of a more plural national identity. But at the same time all the welfare indices were reversed. Structural adjustment resulted in the abolition of subsidies; in the demand that state agencies like the Grain Marketing Board, so essential to peasant participation in the sale of crops, must make a profit; in severe inflation in commodity prices; and in the decline of health and educational standards. Structural adjustment had been justified by the argument that Zimbabwe's economy had developed as much as it could under conditions of protection. It needed to make itself more efficient through competition and to develop an internal market. If all this were to come about it would indeed be a dramatic change from Rhodesia Front economic policy.

But there were few signs of the policy succeeding. Many local industries, unable to compete with imports, closed down. Inflation put the price of goods out of the reach of the urban poor and the peasantry, so that the internal market did not develop. Workers with doubts, like civil servants, nurses and doctors, increasingly challenged the government through strike action. The civil service strike of August 1996 was the most widespread labour protest since the 1948 General Strike. In the rural areas even old nationalist activists condemned the new economic policy and asserted that 'things were better under Smith.' Droughts intensified the popular belief that the governing regime of independent Zimbabwe had never made peace with the land nor submitted itself for cleansing to the spiritual authorities of the nation.[66]

CONCLUSION

There have been substantial continuities of dilemma and even of solution between the three Zimbabwean 'independences' since 1960. At the same time there was no sense in which Zimbabwe was a mere hostage to its history. The uses made of this history have been so varied and selective that it is obvious

66 Two papers delivered to the International Conference on Democracy and Human Rights, University of Zimbabwe, September 1996, reviewed the current economic situation. These were Hevina Dashwood, 'Economic justice and Structural Adjustment in Zimbabwe'; Manuel Nunes and Colin Stoneman, 'Economic justice'. They will appear as chapters in a volume to be edited by N. Bhebe and T. O. Ranger and published by the University of Zimbabwe.

that the past does not in itself possess the power to determine the future. What now came under discussion in Zimbabwe was the possibility of a real trans-formation. Mamdani's analysis of postcolonial Africa as a whole suggested that there were two tasks for nationalist regimes. One was to capture and deracialise urban civil society. The other was to democratise the rural areas, which in his terminology had been under 'decentralised despotism'. The inhabitants of urban civil society were 'citizens', those of the rural areas were 'subjects.' In his view no postcolonial regime had succeeded in doing both. Uganda under Museveni had democratised rural society but did not know how to cope with the towns while South Africa under Mandela had captured urban civil society and would deracialise it but had abandoned the rural areas to traditional authority.

An optimistic view of developments in contemporary Zimbabwe might be that there are elements of transformation both in the rural communal areas and in urban civil society. Perhaps the recommendations of the Land Tenure Commission contain the possibility of rural democracy; perhaps the flowering of civil society contains the possibility of democratic politics in the towns. It must, however, be stressed that these dual developments have to break the moulds not only of the majoritarian one-party state but also of all previous Rhodesian regimes. In 1997 the opposition parties were all urban-based and all supported structural adjustment more enthusiastically than did the Mugabe regime. They left the countryside to the unenthusiastic ruling party.

The leaders of the main opposition parties, Sithole, Muzorewa, and others, came from the same nationalist generation as Mugabe himself. They could not break out of the assumptions derived from mass nationalism, the libera-tion war, the Muzorewa regime and from Lancaster House. Zimbabweans will have to wait for a new generation of political leaders to see whether innovative combinations of rural and urban democracy can be achieved. Nevertheless, such prospects are within the realm of possibility and so distin-guish Zimbabwe from most other countries in Central Africa.

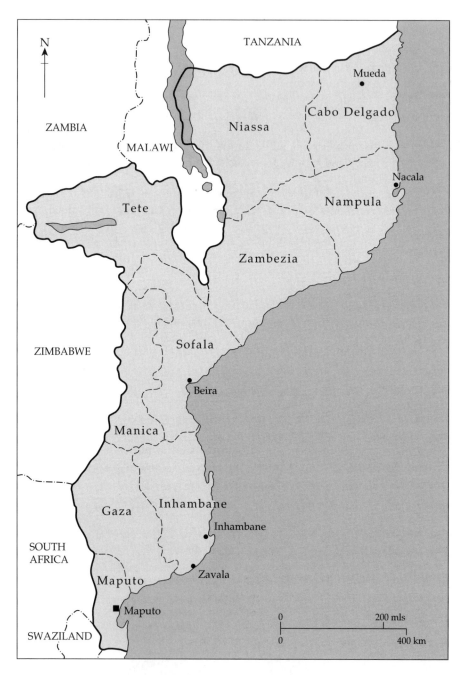

Map 9.1   Mozambique

CHAPTER 9

Mozambique: a tapestry of conflict[1]

JEANNE MARIE PENVENNE

In July 1992 Leia Paunde Zandamela celebrated her hundred and tenth birthday.[2] She was born in the Zavala area of Gaza province in southern Mozambique at the time of the *watsimbakulalela* ('it is forbidden to have dinner') famine. She was a girl of thirteen when the Portuguese capture of Gungunhana, chief of the Gaza state, marked the defeat of African political and military authority in her region. Her life under Portuguese colonial rule revolved around farming, family, neighbours, village elders, and religious life. Social conflicts and disruption due to plagues and drought were mediated through the family. Very serious matters were addressed by village chiefs and elders who gathered at the *kokolwene da gumane*, the ceremonial place, to evoke the intercession of ancestral spirits.

Like most Mozambicans, Leia never had an easy life. She savoured the good times, and persevered through locust plagues, famine, arbitrary beatings, forced labour, abandonment by one husband and widowhood by another. Unlike most Mozambicans, however, her lifetime spanned Portuguese conquest, the implantation and dissolution of Portuguese colonialism, and the emergence of an independent Mozambican state in 1975 headed by the Front for the Liberation of Mozambique, Frelimo.[3] For most of her life Leia farmed Zavala's sandy soils, but in 1989 she and thousands of others fled the increasing danger of armed attacks in Gaza to take refuge in the capital city of Maputo. When she celebrated her hundred and tenth birthday in Maputo, her birthday wish was to go home to Zavala. Leia had a clear perspective on her life during the colonial era but was uncertain about the benefits and exigencies of the first two decades of independence:

1 This essay does not seek to engage the contentious academic debates around recent Mozambican history except to note them in the bibliographic essay.
2 The following paragraphs are based on 'Um Século e Picos de Vida', interview by Beimiro Adamugy with Leia Paunde Zandamela in *Domingo*, Maputo, 12 July 1992, XI, 508.
3 The *Frente de Libertação de Moçambique* originally used the acronym FRELIMO. Upon independence, FRELIMO became a political party and adopted the spelling Frelimo. The latter spelling is used throughout the text. The *Resistência Nacional de Moçambique* Mozambican National Resistance, RENAMO, or MNR, is spelled Renamo in the text. John Saul, *Recolonization and Resistance in Southern Africa in the 1990s*, Africa World Press, Trenton, NJ, 1993, p.xiii, n.1.

In our time, life was difficult because of *xibalo* [forced labour], since from one minute to the next you could be seized, taken from your family, without any explanation . . . You would be beaten for no reason. We also had many famines caused by droughts and [locust] plagues. . . . Fine, now we no longer have *xibalo*, but we have this war . . . If the war ends, I want to go home . . . I do not know why we have this war.[4]

Leia knew that war, state officials and soldiers, whether related to the politics of Gaza, the Portuguese or Frelimo, were all to be avoided. Hardship and conflict were common enough in her life, but nothing had prepared her for 'this war', the 'complicated war' that in 1989 forced her to leave behind all she had ever known to seek refuge in Maputo.[5] By 1992–93, Leia was only one of an estimated 5.7 million Mozambicans uprooted by the war.[6]

The events of Mozambique's past thirty years certainly cannot be framed simply within a local or regional context, but ordinary Mozambicans like Leia experienced them in very personal local terms. The subtleties and complexities that were so important and clear at the local level were often lost on the emerging regional and national leadership. Similarly, Mozambique's leadership often wrestled with issues or adopted strategies that seemed distant or wrong-headed to local people. The impact of national government decisions on local situations could be grossly distorted by international Cold War conditions or regional drought. Similarly, local resistance could totally thwart national policies and international initiatives.[7]

Despite miscommunication, arrogance, and mutual disdain, people had to engage one another. Sheer coercion had its limits. No government, military or non-government group could develop or sustain strategies without some level of local cooperation, and as drought and agricultural disruption worsened, civilians became dependent upon outside food supplies. Tragically, people were often trapped between contending groups or between the uncoordinated directives of different levels of government or international agencies. Within their range of possibilities, ordinary Mozambicans spared themselves and maintained an acceptable balance between the demands of local and more distant powers.[8] This chapter explores thirty-five years of Mozambican history with the experience of ordinary Mozambicans like Leia Paunde Zandamela in mind.

4 Zandamela interview in *Domingo*.
5 William Finnegan, *A Complicated War: The Harrowing of Mozambique*, University of California Press, Berkeley, CA, 1992; Kenneth B. Wilson, 'Cults of violence and counter-violence in Mozambique', *Journal of Southern African Studies [JSAS]* 13, 3 (Sept. 1992), pp.527–82.
6 U.S. Committee for Refugees (USCR), *No Place Like Home; Mozambican Refugees Begin Africa's Largest Repatriation*, Committee for Refugees, Washington, DC, 1993, p.9.
7 These themes are strongly evident in the contentious debates around contemporary Mozambique. For further readings, see bibliographic essay.
8 Alice Dinerman, 'In search of Mozambique; the imaginings of Christian Geffray in "La cause des armes au Mozambique. Anthropologie d'une guerre civile"', *JSAS* 20, 4 (Dec. 1994), pp.575–7; Judith Marshall and Otto Roesch, 'The "Green Zones" agricultural cooperatives of Nampula city: a new phase in the Mozambican cooperative movement?' *JSAS* 19, 2 (June 1993), pp.246–7.

A TAPESTRY OF CONFLICT, PLAYERS AND ARENAS

Mozambique's people, like the rivers and mountain ranges, spill outside the national frontiers and feed the centrifugal forces which challenge the bounded political entity called Mozambique. Makonde, Shona, Chewa, Yao and Shangaan people link Mozambique to Tanzania, Zimbabwe, Malawi and South Africa, just as the Zambezi, Chire, and Limpopo rivers link headwater villages of the hinterland watersheds to the country's river ports and Indian Ocean harbours. Railways link its Indian Ocean export enclaves in Nacala, Beira and Maputo to production centres in Malawi, Zambia, Zimbabwe and South Africa. The railways were typically joint projects, built, maintained and run in conjunction with the political, business and financial interests of Mozambique's hinterland neighbours and their colonial metropoles.[9] Workers found employment at Mozambique's ports and on the railways as well as in the mines, farms and cities in the hinterland. Families shared social claims to resources, spaces, markets, and jobs on both sides of the borders with all six of Mozambique's neighbours.

This socio-economic and cultural mesh presented governments, businesses and the governed with opportunities and constraints that promoted untidy linkages. Throughout the twentieth century Mozambicans have worked, visited, traded and sought refuge in neighbouring countries to such an extent that the posture of these countries toward Mozambicans has had important implications for experience and policy on both sides of all borders. Legal and illegal trade, labour migration and revenue, political support for or opposition to insurgency, and internationally supplied refugee camps form fundamental links within the region. Although the people and economic infrastructure of many areas connect more coherently to the neighbouring interior than to the rest of Mozambique, the national whole is nevertheless much more than simply a collection of arenas or trade 'corridors'.[10]

Central Africa's colonial heritage extended these regional networks beyond the African continent to Great Britain, India and Portugal. The nationalist and guerrilla struggles which contested colonialism in the 1960s and early 1970s introduced another layer of players who supplied their military and technical support: Algeria, the former Soviet Union and Eastern Bloc allies, China, South Africa, Southern Rhodesia and the United States. After independence in 1975 bilateral and multilateral technical and cooperative agreements introduced still more players: Scandinavians, Italians and others. Finally, the extent of Mozambique's international links increased greatly in the late 1980s and early 1990s when the deeply indebted and enfeebled state began to lose its ability to direct and pace the intervention of foreign capital, international

9 Leroy Vail, 'The political economy of East-Central Africa', in David Birmingham and Phyllis M. Martin (eds), *History of Central Africa* 2 vols, Longman, Harlow, 1983, Vol.2, pp.200–50.
10 Joseph Hanlon, *Mozambique: Who Calls the Shots?*, James Currey, London, 1992, p.29.

private voluntary organisations and non-governmental organisations engaged in relief and aid projects.[11] In sum, over thirty-five years, a great array of players in interlocking arenas, from local to global, public to private, and communist to capitalist became engaged in Mozambique's history.

How does one begin to understand this tapestry of conflict, displacement, cooperation, accommodation, and endurance? How did the changing mix of players and arenas shape key events? How do most Mozambicans understand, explain and assign meaning to experiences both within and beyond their influence or control? When did the conflict begin and what events defined the time frame? The armed conflict of the 1960s and 1970s grew out of changes that took place in the 1950s. By the 1960s some Mozambicans organised themselves into political and military groups to wrest power from the Portuguese colonial regime and the foreign companies and settler population it sheltered and promoted. Others rode the tide of Portuguese reform to a better life within the colonial model, and still others continued their daily struggles, scarcely aware that profound changes were afoot.

Although similar patterns of contention, opportunism, accommodation and isolation obtained after Mozambique's independence from Portugal in 1975, those struggles reached far deeper into local communities than had their colonial predecessors. The political and economic markers that structured the first two decades of Mozambican independence will be considered in turn below. In 1995, however, Mozambique entered its twentieth year of independence under the same political party that came to power at independence. Although the ruling party was the same, the country had new political and economic systems in place. For all the change some fundamental issues like the ownership of land remained unresolved.[12] If Leia managed to return to Gaza she would have found peace, but she would probably have had to renegotiate her access to land.

THE ROOTS OF INSURGENCY: 'THIS IS PORTUGAL'

The beginning of the end of Portuguese colonialism in Africa is generally identified with events that took place in Angola between January and March 1961.[13] Six months prior to the Angolan uprisings, however, the Mueda Massacre, as it became known, occurred in the Cabo Delgado district of northern Mozambique. Unarmed Makonde demonstrators seeking a fairer regime for the sale of their agricultural products, clashed with the Portuguese district governor and a platoon of colonial troops in Mueda on 16 June

11 Hanlon, *Who Calls the Shots?*; Barry Schultz, 'The heritage of revolution and the struggle for governmental legitimacy in Mozambique', in William Zartman (ed.), *Collapsed States: The Disintegration and Restoration of Legitimate Authority*, Lynne Rienner, Boulder, CO, 1995, pp.109–24.
12 Joseph Hanlon, 'Land law sets precendents for debate', *Mozambique Peace Process Bulletin*, Issue 17 (November 1996), Part 2.
13 Christine Messiant on Angola in this volume.

1960. Estimates of the resulting deaths range from thirty-six to five hundred.[14]

At the time, the incident at Mueda was little known beyond Mozambique. Some men and women throughout the north, however, responded by joining political movements and taking their families to exile camps across the borders, while others, no doubt, hoped that the events would simply pass into history, leaving them to get on with their lives. Portuguese soldiers, intelligence and administrative officers also heard what happened and most responded by closing ranks. To date, wildly different versions of the 1960 events at Mueda persist, but there is little doubt that the Mueda clash fuelled tensions throughout the region. By the time the Angolan events of 1961 became public knowledge, the smouldering situation in Mozambique was ready to burst into flames.

Faced with the rise of African nationalist politics throughout the continent and the increased pace of urbanisation, industrialisation and manufacturing in neighbouring areas, Portugal could not sustain its African colonies without broader investment and a stronger political strategy. From the 1940s to the 1960s the regime suppressed all serious political opposition to its policies in the metropole or the colonies. In an era when colonial powers were renegotiating the political rights of colonial peoples, the Portuguese regime clung to an ideology that linked domestic legitimacy to maintaining authoritarian rule in the colonial empire.[15]

In the early 1950s Portugal invested in the fuller incorporation of Mozambique into the white-dominated regional economy by expanding service and transport links between Mozambique's Indian Ocean harbours and the production centres of South Africa and Southern Rhodesia, thus enhancing the colony's service capacity rather than its productive capacity. Throughout the twentieth century Mozambique's foreign exchange revenues from services (transport, repatriated wages, migrant labour conventions, and South African and Rhodesian tourism) strongly complemented production earnings from the country's key agricultural exports. The great majority of workers, however, laboured in agriculture rather than in service industries. Sugar, tea, and citrus fruits were produced largely by local workers on Portuguese or foreign-owned plantations, whereas cotton and cashews were produced principally on family farms and cooperatives. Until the early 1960s, production of cotton and rice continued under a coercive regime.[16]

Since the 1930s, the Portuguese regime had discouraged both state-supported white settlement and large-scale urban industry or manufacturing.

14 Thomas Henriksen, *Revolution and Counterrevolution; Mozambique's War of Independence, 1964–1974*, Greenwood Press, Westport, CT, 1983, p.19; Alberto Chipande, 'The massacre of Mueda', *Mozambique Revolution* (Dar es Salaam) 43 (April–June 1970), p.7.
15 Kenneth Maxwell, 'The legacy of decolonization', in Richard J. Bloomfield (ed.), *Regional Conflict and U.S. Policy: Angola and Mozambique*, Reference Publications Inc., Algonac, MI, 1988, pp.7–39.
16 Allen Isaacman, *Cotton is the Mother of Poverty: Peasants, Work and Rural Struggle in Colonial Mozambique, 1938–1961*, Heinemann, Portsmouth, NH, 1996.

Jeanne Marie Penvenne

From the 1950s, however, the regime urged nationals to invest in colonial manufacturing and industry.[17] Portugal also committed itself to extensive state-sponsored white settlement in Africa.[18] Investors purchased some of Mozambique's extensive foreign farms and ambitious agricultural settlement schemes were planned along some of the most fertile river valleys. Most settlers, though, had neither the will nor the experience to work the large-scale agricultural projects designed for their occupation. Contrary to policy aims, they avoided the farms and flowed steadily into civil service jobs. Those with sufficient skills swelled the ranks of insurance and bank employees in the capital city, where they typically enjoyed job security with low cash wages but generous benefit packages such as group transport to and from work, child care, health, life and retirement insurance, group-owned recreational centres and discount-rate holiday outings. Unskilled settlers clung to urban petty trade or service opportunities in direct competition with Mozambicans.[19]

State-sponsored Portuguese immigration sharply increased white domination of public culture, especially in the cities and towns of central and southern Mozambique. Portugal promoted a political and demographic fiction through festivals, gatherings and conferences under the banner '*Aquí é Portugal!*' or 'This is Portugal!' Newspaper photographs, municipal bulletins and media coverage of public social events from the late 1950s to the early 1970s corroborated the fiction. Except for a very few African notables, whose immaculately dressed presence was regularly recorded in photographs, most Africans pictured were either uniformed or carrying trays.[20]

Portugal's commitment to white settlement directly fuelled local anger and unrest. Peasants competed with Portuguese settlers for land, water, credit, market share and technical assistance. Townspeople competed with them for housing, municipal services, schools and jobs. Neither group was spared the bitterness and irony of blocked opportunity.[21] Mozambicans had long pressed for improved infrastructure and services for working families, farmers and ranchers, but when these finally materialised they were monopolised by recently arrived Portuguese.[22] African taxes and labour enhanced the value of lands

17 'Annual Economic Reports', US Department of State Consular Despatches, 1950 through 1973, Mozambican Documents, Freedom of Information Collection, Boston University; Jens Eric Torp, 'Industrial planning and development in Mozambique: preliminary considerations and their theoretical implications', in *Mozambique; Proceedings of a Seminar held in the Centre of African Studies*, University of Edinburgh, 1–2 December 1978, pp.122–41.
18 Keith Middlemas, 'Twentieth century white society in Mozambique', *Tarikh*, 6, 2 (1979), pp.30–45; Gervase Clarence-Smith, *The Third Portuguese Empire, 1825–1975: A Study in Economic Imperialism*, Manchester University Press, Manchester, 1985, chapters 6 and 7; *História de Moçambique*, Vol.3, Departamento de História, Universidade Eduardo Mondlane, Maputo, 1995.
19 Maria Clara Mendes, 'Maputo antes da independência; geografia de uma cidade colonial', *Memórias do Instituto de Investigação Científica Tropical*, 68, Segunda Série, Lisbon, 1985; Middlemas, 'White society in Mozambique'.
20 Social pages of *Notícias, Lourenço Marques Guardian, Notícias de Beira* and *Boletim Municipal.*
21 Jeanne Marie Penvenne, *African Workers and Colonial Racism; Mozambican Strategies and Struggles in Lourenço Marques, 1877–1962*, Heinemann, Portsmouth, 1995, p.5.
22 Merle Bowen, 'Peasant agriculture in Mozambique: the case of Chokwe Gaza province', *Canadian Journal of African Studies* [*CJAS*], 23 (1989), pp.355–79; Bowen, 'Beyond reform:

and markets from which Africans were displaced. Despite African exclusion from rural settlement schemes, they were frequently burdened by agricultural reforms linked to the schemes.[23] In tones that foreshadowed agricultural development schemes under Frelimo after independence, Portugal painted a portrait of 'modern' efficient and productive agrarian settlements populated by state-sponsored families. Instead, the colonial government fell short in building the promised infrastructure, supplying the necessary tools and agricultural inputs and embracing the culture, society and aspirations of settler families.

MIGRANTS, FARMERS AND INTELLECTUALS: THE FORMATION OF FRELIMO

The thousands of Mozambicans who worked as migrant labourers in South Africa, Rhodesia, Malawi, and Tanzania also faced disappointment. Throughout Central Africa, rapid population growth fuelled unemployment and frustration among young school-leavers seeking placement. In order to quell dissatisfaction among their nationals, several neighbouring states adopted legislation making it more difficult for Mozambican migrants to compete for positions. Skilled and semi-skilled Mozambicans found themselves squeezed by competition with nationals in neighbouring areas, and with the growing settler population in Mozambique.[24] By the early 1960s at least three groups of migrants had formed associations outside the country to consider their political future: the National Democratic Union of Mozambique (UDENAMO) in Southern Rhodesia, the Mozambican–Makonde Union (MANU) in Kenya and Tanzania and the National African Union of Independent Mozambique (UNAMI) in Nyasaland.[25]

The country's most highly skilled urban Africans not only experienced declining real wages and consumption-driven inflation, but also lost jobs directly to unemployed whites.[26] The whitening of public institutional life and the injection of Portuguese culture into the school curriculum finally rekindled activism among the urban intellectual élite. A postwar generation of urban Africans reasserted pride in their heritage, reviving literary publications, highlighting the absurdity of the idea that Mozambique was Portugal, and expressing the growing anger of Mozambicans.[27] Noemia de Sousa's poems

adjustment and political power in contemporary Mozambique', *Journal of Modern African Studies* [*JMAS*] 30, 2 (1992), pp.255–79; Otto Roesch, 'Renamo and the peasantry in southern Mozambique: a view from Gaza province', *CJAS* 26, 3 (1992), pp.462–84.
23 José Firmo de Sousa Monteiro, 'Resgate dos Machongos do Sul do Save', in Rodrigues Júnior, *Transportes de Moçambique*, Editorial Ultramar, Lisbon, 1956, pp.219–54.
24 Jeanne Marie Penvenne, '"Here everyone walked with fear!" The Mozambican labor system and the workers of Lourenço Marques, 1945–1962', in Frederick Cooper (ed.), *Struggle for the City: Migrant Labor, Capital and the State in Urban Africa*, Sage, Berkeley, 1983.
25 Allen Isaacman and Barbara Isaacman, *Mozambique: from Colonialism to Revolution,1900–1982*, Westview Press, Boulder, CO, 1983, p.79ff.
26 Penvenne, '"Here everyone walked with fear!"' esp. pp.153–61.
27 Gerald Moser and Manuel Ferreira, *Bibliografia das Literaturas Africanas de Expressão Portuguesa*, Imprensa Nacional, Lisbon, 1983; Fátima Mendonça, *Literatura Moçambicana; A História e as Escritas*, Universidade Eduardo Mondlane, Maputo, 1988.

Jeanne Marie Penvenne

invoked 'mother Africa' and echoed the dignity and restraint of Langston Hughes's images of redemption. José Cravarinha's famous poem, *Eu sou carvão!* ('I am coal!'), juxtaposed images of black exploitation and black energy. The poem ended with the assertion that the white boss, who forced black workers to dig out coal in dangerous and difficult conditions, would one day be consumed by the fiery anger and energy of that black coal and coal miner.[28]

The challenge in this literature circulated among the intelligentsia in the same way as news of the Mueda massacre spread among Makonde farmers in northern Mozambique and word of political meetings spread among migrants. Each person brought to the texts, the stories, and the meetings her or his own experience. In the end the poems written by Cravarinha and de Sousa, the stories that grew up around Mueda, and the nascent political formations in exile catalysed a growing sense of tension into direct challenge.

The point finally came home that Portugal had conceived and launched the blueprints of the country's economic and political future for the second half of the twentieth century without so much as consulting the Mozambicans whose lives and livelihoods bore its direct impact. Africans decided to do something about it and the Portuguese vowed to nip that action in the bud. Nationalist politics across the continent had exacerbated the already marked tendency of the Portuguese to be both watchful and suspicious of Africans. The 1960 incident at Mueda was simply the red sunrise warning of a storm. By the middle of the decade, guerrillas from political groups of Mozambican exiles who had been trained in Algeria launched their first armed attack into northern Mozambique, Noemia de Sousa was in exile in Paris, and José Cravarinha was incarcerated with hundreds of others in a Mozambican prison.

FRELIMO AND THE 'ARMED STRUGGLE'

In the early 1960s organised African groups and public figures of all descriptions became suspect as tensions rose: urban journalists, officers of the *Associação Africana*, and the *Centro Associativo dos Négros de Moçambique*, workers in colonial syndicates, traders and artisans in 'native' associations and members of rural agricultural cooperatives. Any legitimate or popular figure was suspect and many were jailed.[29] The Portuguese secret police had been active in Mozambique since the late 1940s. By the mid-1960s arrests and disappearances at their hands occurred regularly and white vigilante groups organised themselves openly.[30] Arrest without charge was commonplace, but experiences of incarceration varied greatly. Long-time civil servant Raul Bernardo Honwana was released after serving just five days in prison, his son Luis Bernardo Honwana remained in gaol much longer, but he survived. Presbyterian catechist Zédéquias

28 Gerald Moser, *Essays in Portuguese African Literature*, Pennsylvania State University, University Park, 1969.
29 Raúl Honwana, *The Life History of Raúl Honwana; An Insider View of Mozambique from Colonialism to Independence, 1905–1975*, edited with an introduction by Allen F. Isaacman, translated by Tamara L. Bender, Lynne Rienner, Boulder, CO, 1988.
30 Honwana, *Life*, chapter 5.

238

Manganhela did not. He allegedly committed suicide in December 1972 after six months in a Maputo gaol. The authorities would not allow the coffin to be opened.[31]

Political initiatives among African élites from throughout Portugal's colonies combined in important ways with dissident movements within Portugal. *Movimento Unida Democratica* (MUD) and later *Movimento Anti-Colonialista* (MAC) brought African intellectuals and politicians (Amilcar Cabral of Guiné, Agostinho Neto of Angola, Marcelino dos Santos and Eduardo Mondlane of Mozambique) together with a coalition of Portuguese, including Mário Soares who opposed Salazar's authoritarianism and Portugal's colonial policies. The Portuguese coalition included a substantial contingent of the clandestine but well organised Portuguese Communist Party and the Socialist Party.[32]

MAC was formed in 1957 in Paris by dissidents who had fled a crackdown by the secret police in Lisbon and Coimbra. In contrast with Mozambique's early exile political groups, MANU, UNAMI and UDENAMO, which were isolated and spent much of their energy contesting one another, MAC brought dissidents from Portugal and all its colonies together and focused on a common strategy to end Portuguese colonialism. By 1961 an allied group, the *Conferência de Organisações Nacionalistas das Colónias Portuguesas* (CONCP) was formed in Casablanca to provide an African base for insurgents to lobby the United Nations, the Organization for African Unity (OAU), and other potential national and international patrons for recognition, training, funding and supplies.

The alliances and trust built from experience in MAC and CONCP contributed a special stamp to Lusophone Africa. During the wars for independence such collaboration enhanced the impact of the challenge. Personal bonds between African and Portuguese anti-colonial allies were eventually instrumental in facilitating the transition to independence, and since independence those bonds have sustained links among five independent nations that have little in common except the experience of Portuguese colonial rule. Ironically, such links encouraged the retention of the Portuguese language, which, to some extent, enabled Portugal to continue to wield some measure of influence.[33]

Creating and sustaining insurgency against Portuguese colonial rule in Mozambique was no easy task. In 1962 the three Mozambican exile political groups (UNAMI, MANU and UDENAMO) met. They were pressed by the OAU, the United Nations and independent African leaders in the region to unite Mozambique's political opposition.[34] In June 1962 Frelimo was formed

31 Honwana, *Life*, chapter 5; Alf Helgesson, *Church, State and People in Mozambique; An Historical Study with Special Emphasis on Methodist Developments in the Inhambane Region*, Uppsala University, Uppsala, 1994, pp.368–74.
32 Maxwell, 'Legacy of decolonization'; Francisco Tenreiro and Mário Pinto de Andrade, *Poesia Negra de Expressão Portuguesa*, Editor Africa, Lisbon, 1982.
33 Michel Cahen, 'Le Portugal et l'Afrique; le cas des relations Luso-Mozambicaines (1965–1985): étude politique et bibliographique', *Afrique Contemporaine* 137 (1986), pp.3–55.
34 Ronald Chilcote, *Emerging Nationalism in Portuguese Africa: Documents*, Hoover Institute, Stanford, 1972.

under the leadership of Eduardo Mondlane. Mondlane was the eldest son of an important lineage leader from Gaza and one of a very few Africans from the Portuguese colonies to hold a doctoral degree. Before he returned to Africa to take up the struggle for Mozambican independence, he was a university professor in the United States and a United Nations official.[35] In short, Mondlane was a man of considerable stature, and he used it to bridge tensions within Mozambique's exile community and to sustain the front.

Mondlane and Frelimo's twenty-four other founding members immediately faced many pressing demands. The Mozambican exile community of women, men and children was growing, fuelled by the news that a united front had been established. Soldiers, intelligence gatherers, and military strategists had to be identified, recruited, trained, armed, supplied and eventually led in workable battle strategies. Women had to be assigned land to plant, children had to be schooled and cared for, and supply networks, trade and services had to be negotiated with the host country. Those tasks all required organisation, political work, money, unity and personal sacrifice.

Some members brought prior political experience to the challenges they faced in Tanganyika. Marcelino dos Santos, for example, had been a member of earlier movements and sustained his political role into the early 1990s. In 1950, when studying at a technical institute in Lisbon, dos Santos wrote home to the *Associação Africana's* membership:

> We must work together. We must instruct, cultivate and educate ourselves to improve our culture and raise our standard of living . . . parochial issues must be subordinated to general concerns and personal and group concerns must be subordinated to collective interests.[36]

The letter revealed both an ambivalent awareness of the culture and material conditions of the majority population and a commitment to the greater good and collective interests that characterised Frelimo's first-generation leadership. As an intellectual who was fluent in key global languages, dos Santos soon became Frelimo's spokesman at the United Nations and the OAU. Funding and training of Frelimo's military depended, in the first instance, upon dos Santos's success in arguing their case to potential sponsors.

A negotiated independence for Portuguese colonies was out of the question in 1962, so Frelimo's leadership committed itself to a sustained campaign of guerrilla warfare.[37] Initially, Frelimo enjoyed financial support from private foundations in the United States, and some covert support from the Kennedy administration. Under the growing shadow of the Cold War, however, Portugal's membership in the North Atlantic Treaty Organization and its con-

35 Eduardo Mondlane, *The Struggle for Mozambique*, Introduced by John Saul. Biographical sketch by Herbert Shore, Zed Press, London, 1983.
36 *Brado Africano*, 14 January 1950.
37 Mondlane, *The Struggle*; John Saul (ed.), *A Difficult Road: The Transition to Socialism in Mozambique*, Monthly Review Press, New York, 1985; Saul, *Recolonization*, chapter 3.

trol of the strategically important Azores military bases, combined with the Republican rise to power in Washington, moved the United States increasingly toward cooperation with Portugal.[38]

The Soviet block eventually became Frelimo's main financial and military supporter. Framed by the politics of the Cold War, Frelimo's movement toward the Eastern bloc generated increased hostility from the United States. Since political exiles from other areas of southern Africa also gathered in Tanzania, white minority governments in Southern Rhodesia and South Africa found it expedient to label them all as communist threats and increasingly the United States, Southern Rhodesia and South Africa all supported Portugal in the conflict.[39]

Frelimo was easily recognised in international circles as the most credible of the Mozambican insurgent groups, but its major challenge was always closer to home. In Tanzania, military, social and political strains within the exile community, personal rivalries and ambitions provided fertile ground for conflict and contest along predictable lines.[40] Scarcely a year after its formation, tension within Frelimo's own student body led to a series of small schisms. The military and administrative components of the armed struggle had to be of one mind, but contending political visions were complicated by the ethnic and regional implications of every decision. Makonde speakers of northern Mozambique, for example, were overrepresented in Frelimo's fighting force, as were Shangaan-speakers of the south in the leadership positions. Further fighting placed the Makonde of northern Mozambique in imminent danger, whereas Shangaan villagers, in the short-run, remained outside the fray.

On the political front, sharp disagreements about the goals and strategies of the struggle arose and transformed the movement between 1968 and 1970. Eduardo Mondlane, whose stature and energy had provided the necessary force behind the original union in 1962, was murdered by a parcel bomb in 1969.[41] His loss and the subsequent speculation and recriminations about responsibility for the bomb checked Frelimo's momentum and led to the group's most important crisis. One founding member, Uria Simango, and several others left with their followers. The groups that emerged from that schism never managed to raise a serious challenge to Frelimo or to Portuguese colonialism during the subsequent half decade of the independence war, but Simango, among others, re-emerged to contest Frelimo's claim to political hegemony later.[42] By May 1970, Samora Machel, whose political influence grew out of his role in the military, consolidated his leadership in the Central Committee. Machel, who had not been a founding member, replaced Mondlane and remained Frelimo's leader until his death a generation later.

38 Maxwell, 'The legacy of decolonization'.
39 *Ibid.*, esp. pp.16–18.
40 Leroy Vail and Landeg White, *Capitalism and Colonialism in Mozambique; A Study of Quelimane District*, University of Minnesota Press, Minneapolis, 1980, chapter 9.
41 Saul and Shore in Mondlane, *The Struggle*.
42 Isaacman and Isaacman, *Mozambique*; Barry Munslow, *Mozambique: The Revolution and its Origins*, Longman, Harlow, 1983.

Although the military struggle was obviously critical, political struggles had a direct impact upon the military campaign and on Frelimo's overall effectiveness. In September 1964 a small group of guerrillas, trained in Algeria, carried the challenge from Tanzanian bases across the Rovuma River to Mozambican soil.[43] Thus began what Frelimo calls the 'Luta Armada' or the 'Armed Struggle', as distinct from the armed conflict that arose after independence and dwarfed the earlier situation. From 1970 Machel firmly committed Frelimo to the military challenge against the Portuguese. Certainly, Frelimo's decade of armed struggle included costly mistakes born of inexperience and ineptitude, incidences of unnecessary brutality toward innocent farming families, and ruthless purges in the name of security or ideology.[44] Portuguese garrisons were sometimes attacked and corpses displayed to civilians to undermine the sense that whites were too powerful, too strong to challenge.[45] In comparison with Portugal's resort to scorched-earth techniques, terror and massacres, however, Frelimo's treatment of captured Portuguese recruits won it a reputation for 'humanitarianism' that enhanced its capacity to promote itself as a politically responsible organisation and 'the sole legitimate representative of the Mozambican people'.[46] The balance sheet of human rights abuses during Mozambique's war of independence (1964–74) reveals Portugal's marked brutality in comparison with Frelimo.[47]

Parallel to the military operation, Frelimo, which could not take the loyalty of local people for granted at that point, conveyed its goals to the people of northern Mozambique through public meetings, song, dance and performance.[48] The record suggests that mutual communication and accountability were important features of Frelimo's strategy in the war for independence, but Frelimo was unable to extend an auspicious beginning through its transformation from a liberation group to a ruling party.[49]

After independence, Frelimo framed its policy in terms of the experience it gained in the north during the war for independence. Although this 'founders' myth' may not hold up under close scrutiny, the trust and solidarity forged in the cauldron of the liberation struggle remained critical. The single factor that was most likely to influence a person's appointment to an important position of trust or authority in any branch of the Frelimo government was her or his participation in the liberation struggle.[50]

43 Henriksen, *Revolution and Counterrevolution*, p.41.
44 *Ibid.*
45 Wilson, 'Cults of violence', pp.549–50.
46 Adrian Hastings, *Wiriyamu*, Search Press, London, 1973.
47 Henriksen, *Revolution and Counterrevolution*.
48 Schultz, 'The heritage of revolution', pp.117–19.
49 Michel Cahen, 'Check on socialism in Mozambique – what check? what socialism?', *Review of African Political Economy* [*ROAPE*], 57 (1993), pp.46–59 esp.; Henriksen, *Revolution and Counterrevolution*, pp.92,148; Schultz, 'The heritage of revolution'.
50 Kathleen Sheldon, 'Women and revolution in Mozambique: *a luta continua*', in Mary Ann Tetreault (ed.), *Women and Revolution in Africa, Asia and the New World*, University of South Carolina Press, Columbia, 1994.

SOLDIERS, SETTLERS AND BUREAUCRATS: PORTUGAL AND THE COUNTER-INSURGENCY

In 1961 there were only about 3,000 Portuguese troops in Mozambique, but by 1964 that number had increased to 35,000.[51] By the late 1960s, Portugal began to Africanise its colonial forces and the incorporation of black Mozambicans into the military was judged one of Portugal's few successes in the twilight of the colonial era. About 40 per cent of the troops fighting on Portugal's side were Mozambicans. Unlike the limited number of women in Frelimo's detachments, who seem to have clustered in the lower ranks, Africans participated at all levels of the colonial army, from the poorly armed village militia to the *Flechas*, the best trained and best supplied élite units.[52]

The Portuguese population was no more homogeneous than the Mozambican population. Administrators, bureaucrats, military officers, intelligence gatherers, troops, settlers, business people, housewives and missionaries shared Portuguese nationality, but not necessarily a great deal more. The weight of social differentiation, authoritarianism, fiscal conservatism and political intrigue in Portugal exacerbated an already socially fragmented situation in Mozambique. During the 1960–75 war, the Portuguese wrestled with tensions common throughout colonial areas. Bureaucrats and policy-makers may have been exasperated by African resistance but they also chafed under settler demands and abuses. Although many leaders planned to make their political and military careers in Mozambique, few planned to settle their families there or spend their lives in Africa. Personal and professional ambitions contributed to the marked disunity among military, intelligence and political cadres. Portugal mounted a military strategy to defeat the armed insurgents and a socio-political and economic strategy to win the 'hearts and minds' of the masses. Its military, paramilitary and intelligence forces often worked at cross purposes, a costly failure in every sense. Portuguese and Mozambican conscripts shared a sense of cynicism. By the early 1970s, the frustrations of guerrilla war and a series of scandals, such as the gruesome revelations of the massacre at Wiriyamo, contributed to the Portuguese junior officers' sense that the African wars were more likely to blight than to distinguish their careers.

Portuguese and international business people who responded to Portugal's belated opening of export, import and production initiatives were attracted by profits, infrastructure, tax breaks and investment potential. Their interests did not always dovetail with the 'hearts and minds' claim that Mozambicans could look to a bright future with good jobs, fair wages and even-handed racial treatment. Ironically, if the companies had been free to hire whomever they pleased the future might indeed have been brighter for Mozambicans. Instead, most companies were pressured to hire unemployed Portuguese.[53] Settlers

51 Henriksen, *Revolution and Counterrevolution*, p.23.
52 *Ibid.*, pp.101,68.
53 Clarence-Smith, *The Third Portuguese Empire*.

recognised from the outset that concessions to ordinary Mozambicans in the 'hearts and minds' campaigns were made at their expense. They were concerned about security and sustaining their privileged position and were directly threatened by the proposed reconfiguration of race relations. Thus, they regularly undermined the 'hearts and minds' campaign by their presence and actions.

THE SEA OF CIVILIANS

The military struggle of 1964–74 took place in the fields, forests and towns occupied and worked by millions of civilians. Although revolutionaries may have described the people as the sea in which the guerrillas, like fish, had to swim, that metaphor privileged the fishes' dependence upon water, not the water's vulnerability to the fish. The experience of ordinary people in conflict zones is more accurately suggested by the African proverbs: 'Soldiers eat, peasants provide' and 'A woman is a cob of maize for any mouth that has its teeth'.[54] Food, fuel, shelter and anything of material value could be seized. Valued services like sex, cooking, carrying, and washing could be commandeered. Military discipline ideally set limits and conditions on force and expropriation but the likelihood of abuse was high. The civilian sea, ordinary Mozambicans, experienced a host of problems that actually increased after independence when Frelimo repeated many of Portugal's mistakes.

Portugal established so-called strategic hamlets as part of its military cum 'hearts and minds' campaign. The gathering of scattered farmsteads into a fortified enclosure was a familiar wartime strategy for centuries in many parts of Mozambique.[55] Mozambicans also experienced displacement due to forced labour raids, flood and drought, but such crises passed and people were then generally free to resettle as they liked. The Portuguese strategic hamlets were designed for two purposes: firstly, to make better use of scarce resources and to provide basic services, such as health care, education, piped or pumped water and military protection to rural people and, secondly, to make it more difficult for Frelimo to contact farmers of the area for supplies, intelligence and shelter. The emphasis was on denying Frelimo access to the farmers rather than providing the rural population with improved services. The farmers noticed.

Farmers also noticed a decade later when Frelimo promoted its policy of communal villages. Some locations were the same, the names and the ideology were different. Most importantly, the infrastructure and services were still grossly inadequate, and the farmers still preferred to live on their own scattered lands. Their intimate knowledge of the local environment – the

54 John Iliffe, *The African Poor; A History*, Cambridge University Press, New York, 1992, p.15; Ferdinand Oyono, *Houseboy*. Translated from the French by John Reed, Heinemann, London, 1966, p.71.
55 Newitt, *A History of Mozambique*, Hurst & Co., London, 1995; Isaacman and Isaacman, *Mozambique*.

configuration of local soils, rain shadows, and flood areas – convinced them that the scattered pockets they regularly planted and tended minimised their risk from the whole range of predictable and unpredictable problems the environment throws at farmers everywhere. The dispersal of homesteads seemed inefficient to bureaucrats and technocrats, whether they were sent out by the Portuguese or by Frelimo. Technocrats assumed that farmers would benefit from the agricultural inputs that the state was supposed to provide at appropriate junctures throughout the agricultural cycle. Mozambican farmers knew better.

Portugal's military strategy required substantial investment in the colonial infrastructure of the central and northern regions. The need to move and provision troops spurred the development of roads, air strips, markets and communications that potentially benefited people living in those areas. North–south communication routes were developed and much more extensive transport networks were forged throughout the northern provinces, altering the existing south-centred and east-west corridor emphasis. The northern and central provinces bore the brunt of the war, but they also experienced the greatest investments in transport and communications infrastructure.[56]

Portugal's most dramatic contribution to Mozambique's capital plant in this period was clearly the construction of the Cahora Bassa [Cabora Bassa] hydroelectric dam, power station and irrigation scheme which was undertaken between 1960 and 1974 when it began operation.[57] The Cahora Bassa Dam, which spans Africa's third largest river system, the Zambezi, produced the fifth largest reservoir in Africa. The dam has a 2,075 megawatt installed capacity, but it has never functioned at full capacity. It was built by an international consortium under Portuguese management and a Portuguese company administers it. Security and political concerns dogged it from the outset. South Africa was designed to be, and long remained, Cahora Bassa's principal consumer. Mozambique consumed less than 4 per cent of Cahora Bassa's power capacity in the mid-1990s.

Over 225,000 Mozambicans were relocated both upstream and downstream of the dam to accommodate the reservoir and to comply with strategic hamlet considerations. Although Mozambique gained control of Cahora Bassa, the Portuguese have continued to service the debt incurred by its construction. By 1995 Cahora Bassa had seriously altered the environment, agriculture and fisheries of the region. Incidences of schistosomiasis, malaria and trypanosomiasis had increased substantially because the reservoir surface and the slower stream flows below the dam provide breeding grounds for the vectors of these diseases. Diminished flooding and flow have influenced fish populations in some areas, and contributed to salt intrusion at the estuary which threatens the

56 Mendes, 'Maputo antes da independência'; Alfredo Pereira de Lima, *História dos Caminhos de Ferro de Moçambique*, Edição dos Portos, Caminhos de Ferro e Transportes de Moçambique, Lourenço Marques, 1971 Vols 1 to 3.
57 Keith Middlemas, *Cabora Bassa: Engineering and Politics in Southern Africa*, Weidenfeld and Nicolson, London, 1975.

important relationship between mangrove clusters and shrimp and prawn production.[58] This supposed monument to colonial investment and development provided little benefit to ordinary Mozambicans and may indeed have contributed to the further deterioration of the environment upon which their health and livelihoods depend.

COUP AND TRANSITION

Frelimo's guerrillas sustained the uneven conflict with Portugal's colonial forces for about a decade. The combination of guerrilla challenges throughout Portuguese colonial Africa and shifting coalitions of military, civilian and economic interests, both within Portugal and Mozambique and between Portugal and its African colonies, ultimately convinced officers of the Portuguese Armed Forces Movement to topple a regime that had wedded itself to Portugal's colonial era in Africa. The bloodless coup took place in Lisbon on 25 April 1974.[59]

When the 1974 military coup in Lisbon initiated the transition that led to the independence of Mozambique under a Frelimo government, Frelimo troop levels stood at between 9,000 and 11,000 combatants. Most were men, but there was also a small group of women.[60] Portugal had deployed 65,000 to 70,000 troops, around 60 per cent of whom were metropolitan Portuguese. Portugal reckoned it suffered about 4,000 casualties, of whom more than 70 per cent were caused by land mines. Frelimo's casualties were five times higher, about 20,000, but whereas the Portuguese tallied only uniformed soldiers, Frelimo's figure included civilian supporters and accident victims. It had been a difficult struggle. Toward the end, the brutality of Portugal's war record became an international scandal.[61]

The military coup in Portugal came as a surprise. Suffice it to say that it was not simply a response to Portugal's military situation in Africa.[62] Although Frelimo had made some stunning military advances in the Tete and Zambezi areas, the Portuguese still held cities and towns even in areas Frelimo claimed to control. A Frelimo military victory over the Portuguese was certainly not imminent in April 1974. Yet Frelimo did not come to power in Mozambique simply 'because they endured' in the military struggle.[63] It triumphed at least in part because the leadership seized the opportunity at the critical moment. Barely two months after the coup, in the OAU-sponsored preliminary talks

58 Dlemneh Djene and José Olivares, *Integrating Environmental Issues into a Strategy for Sustainable Agricultural Development: The Case of Mozambique*, World Bank, Washington, 1991.
59 Cahen, 'Le Portugal et l'Afrique'.
60 Henriksen, *Revolution and Counterrevolution*, pp.40–4.
61 João Paulo Guerra, *Memória das Guerras Coloniais*, Edições Afrontamento, Porto, 1994; Hastings, *Wiriyamu; Tortura na Colónia de Moçambique (1963–1974)*, Afrontamento, Porto, 1977.
62 Cahen, 'Le Portugal et l'Afrique'.
63 Quote from Thomas Henriksen. Henriksen argued that Frelimo's military triumphalism in 1975 did not square with history. Portugal was able to sustain the fight for as long as it did, not because Portugal's efforts were strong, but because Frelimo's military was weak. Henriksen, *Revolution and Counterrevolution*, p.68.

with the Portuguese in Mogadishu, Samora Machel confidently pressed his opportunity to consolidate Frelimo's position.[64]

In the wake of the Lisbon coup key figures with whom Frelimo members enjoyed secure and trusting relationships came to power in Portugal. This was the critical juncture when alliances forged decades earlier in the anti-colonial movements proved critical. Frelimo militants found themselves sitting across a negotiating table from men they had known on a first-name basis for years, and with whom they shared some fundamental political principles. Mário Soares, among others, negotiated the Lusaka Accord, signed in Zambia in September 1974, that outlined the process for political and military transition and recognised Frelimo as the 'sole legitimate representative of the Mozambican people'.[65] The agreement called for Mozambique's independence as a single political entity, from the Rovuma River in the north to the Maputo River in the south.[66]

Samora Machel had little to fear from the men across the table in Lusaka, but he was well aware of the hostile forces that remained in the surrounding region and within Mozambique. Portugal was a small country with a relatively small army, and its essential national interests were a continent away. South Africa, by contrast, was a big country with a powerful military, whose industrial, manufacturing and agricultural heartland was just across the border. The similarly impressive Southern Rhodesian military establishment knew that it would soon face incursions across its border from Mozambique, and was unlikely to sit still in anticipation. Finally, although Machel felt Frelimo had the support of the majority population in Mozambique, Portugal had taken pains to sow fear and misinformation. Popular support could not simply be assumed.

Before taking their seats at the negotiating table in Lusaka, Frelimo political and military forces faced a rash of crises. Between July and August nearly 4,000 workers went on strike on the Lourenço Marques (Maputo) waterfront. On 7 September an ill-planned coup was launched by a loose coalition of settlers and Mozambicans who had either left Frelimo in the schism of the late 1960s or simply opposed one-party rule under Frelimo.[67] The rebel group took control of the radio transmitting station in the centre of the city. They seemed to harbour a vain hope that their uprising would trigger intervention from Southern Rhodesia and South Africa. Portugal had forewarned Mozambique's neighbouring white governments not to intervene should any such incidents arise. In the event, both countries apparently had their own reasons for rejecting any military involvement in Mozambique at this point.[68] Portuguese and Frelimo troops arrested the plotters with little loss of life.

---

64 *Ibid.*, p.57.
65 Henriksen, *Revolution and Counterrevolution*, p.57; Isaacman and Isaacman, *Mozambique*, pp.105–7.
66 Henriksen, *Revolution and Counterrevolution*, p.57; Saul, *Recolonization*, p.79.
67 Henriksen, *Revolution and Counterrevolution*, pp.57–9.
68 *Ibid.*, p.181; Maxwell, 'Legacy of decolonization', pp.16–18.

A more violent situation occurred in the capital's suburbs in the wake of the Lusaka Accords. Dozens of people were killed or injured and a great deal of property was destroyed in rioting and confusion. Once again calm was restored by a joint force. No further serious disturbances occurred before independence ceremonies in June 1975.[69] The identified leaders of the suburban riots and the radio station débâcle were arrested. Some were deported or eventually released, but, perhaps because of their earlier relationship with Frelimo, two, Uria Simango and Joana Simião, were held to be traitors. They were sent to prison camps that Frelimo referred to as '[political] re-education' camps. Several years later they were shot, without benefit of trial. Mozambican dissidents who avoided or survived these confrontations during the transition period eventually emerged twenty years later under the shelter of an internationally imposed shift to 'multi-party democracy' to challenge Frelimo hegemony.[70]

Although the formal end to the war for independence was accomplished through legally binding accords signed by politicians and diplomats in national and international arenas, the scars of that era were borne locally and personally. When Mozambicans saw a new flag raised on 25 June 1975, signalling the country's transition from a Portuguese colony to the People's Republic of Mozambique, they understandably hoped their sacrifices would lead to a better life. The Frelimo leadership probably had higher hopes and fewer illusions than ordinary Mozambicans. The leadership retained the group's motto from the days of the liberation struggle, *A Luta Continua!*, ('The Struggle Continues!').

PEOPLE'S POWER IN THE ERA OF COLD WAR AND APARTHEID

On the morning after independence ceremonies Frelimo's leadership 'found itself in power', faced with transforming itself from a liberation group into a government.[71] Despite the successful quelling of disturbances in the capital, Frelimo could not afford to take military and security issues lightly at home or abroad. Furthermore, the settlers clearly did not share the Portuguese government's faith in Frelimo and they left Mozambique by the thousand. They took everything they could pack, and frequently maliciously destroyed whatever they had to leave. Frelimo could not allow the panic and discontent of fleeing settlers to shake the confidence of the larger population. The party had to implant political structures and initiate its programmes quickly if it hoped to direct the course of events. From the party's perspective, they faced a slippery slope. Major transformation was required, and yet change would

69 Ndabaningi Sithole, *Frelimo Militant: The Story of Ingwane from Mozambique, an Ordinary, yet Extraordinary, Man, Awakened* . . . Transafrica Press, Nairobi, 1977.
70 Pepe Diniz, 'Mozambique's 1994 General Elections', *Portuguese Studies Review* 4, 2 (Fall/Winter 1995–1996), pp.43–61; Brazão Mazula (ed.), *Moçambique: Eleições Democracia e Desenvolvimento*, Lisbon, 1995.
71 Quote from John Saul, *Recolonization*, p.59. See also David Birmingham, *Frontline Nationalism in Angola and Mozambique*, James Currey, London, 1992, chapters 4–6; Schultz, 'The heritage of revolution'.

have to be accomplished in an atmosphere that had no tradition of national legitimacy or trust, let alone good governance and democracy.

Not surprisingly, the leadership felt it could only trust itself. Frelimo drew troops and support from a broad ethnic, regional and national base, but in the cauldron of war, treachery, and ambition, Frelimo's leaders had closed ranks. Political murders, spies, and an awareness of the high cost of betrayal promoted a tendency to trust only those who had survived the test of battle.[72] The inexperienced leadership, faced with transforming itself from a military to a governing body with stronger, more sophisticated and hostile South African and Rhodesian forces along half of its western borders, tended to read political neutrality as opposition.[73] Despite Frelimo's stated commitment to 'People's Power', most of the people were barely known to Frelimo and Frelimo was barely known to them, given the fourteen months' notice they had to prepare to govern. Despite the euphoria of independence, it is hardly surprising that both 'the people' and the Frelimo leadership should have approached their relationship with caution and mutual distrust.

The reforming energy that forged unity among the Frelimo cadres eventually promoted an arrogance of the sort commonly associated with the missionaries and colonial administrators who were Frelimo's immediate predecessors. All had their projects and too many assumed that they knew better than 'the people' what was in their best interest. Whether the approach was described as 'arrogance of ostensibly progressive élites', 'benevolent authoritarianism', or 'development dictatorship' the sense that policy flowed from the top down was increasingly evident.[74] Frustrated cadres were determined to implement the desired changes, and were often unaware of the social costs until it was too late.

Before 1975, the bureaucratic machinery of the colonial state controlled and extracted value from the majority population. It served the interests of Portugal and its small client population in Mozambique, rather than the masses. The difficulties of transforming that ponderous, highly centralised, repressive machine into a tool to serve Frelimo's developing political goal of 'people's power' had scarcely been imagined. The old system could not be simply discarded before a workable new system was in place. Such a vacuum would have aggravated a climate of uncertainty that could easily have pushed the country over the line into chaos. Yet the day-to-day work required to sustain the old system robbed the new leaders of the energy necessary to develop responsive tools. From the outset, it was clear that if Frelimo cadres swam hard upstream, they might just keep pace with the current, but any lapse of effort would sweep the entire project swiftly downstream. The kind of upstream movement Frelimo envisaged required Olympic strength, and even Olympic champions could not sustain that pace month after month.

---

72 Saul, *Recolonization*, p.10.
73 The treatment of Jehovah's Witnesses is a case in point. *The Watchtower* (15 August 1992), pp.21–5; Sithole, *Frelimo Militant*, p.19.
74 Saul, *Recolonization*, pp.10, 70–1.

Frelimo's decision to implement sanctions against Southern Rhodesia was as politically necessary as it was economically costly to the already reeling economy. Climatic crises exacerbated the generalised distress: severe drought in 1975–76, record flooding in the populous Limpopo and Incomati river valleys in 1977, and a hail storm that smashed window panes and roof tiles throughout the capital city in the same year. In such circumstances, damage control heavily shaped what was articulated as policy. Efforts to curb the haemorrhaging of capital, the destruction of infrastructure and capital plant, and loss of capacity through sabotage and abandonment of property by white settlers made nationalisation and the formation of state enterprises obvious choices. Their mutual articulation was compelling in circumstances that held few options.

The painful transformation of government machinery proceeded piecemeal with some inspired innovations and successes, but in many more cases the weight of resistance, sabotage, naiveté, miscommunication, arrogance and miscalculation led to counterproductive conundrums or to a sullen acceptance of a default mode of government. In some cases the worst features of the old system were perpetuated without incorporating the anticipated innovations of the new.[75] Frelimo repeatedly sought to overcome these frustrations by promoting bold new political structures and sweeping economic transformations. The first of these was the Third Party Congress in 1977. At that congress, Frelimo declared itself a Marxist-Leninist Vanguard Party, wedded to collective agricultural production, state farms, mechanisation and industrialisation. Somehow, the larger-than-life Vanguard murals and confident rhetoric that accompanied the congress were expected to empower the same people with the same tools to accomplish goals that remained well beyond their capacity.

With or without the Marxist-Leninist label, development and implementation of 'people's power' proved as difficult and frustrating as transforming the machinery of government. From the outset Frelimo ruled in the name of 'the people', Mozambique's ordinary people. The party consistently mistook its own construction of a disembodied, generic peasantry, free from the complications of racial, class, religious and ethnic identities, for the great diversity and complexity of Mozambique's breathing citizenry.[76]

The party cleverly developed cartoon figures to convey its 'people's policies' to Mozambicans who spoke scores of different languages but read none.[77] The cartoons featured Frelimo's heroes and heroines: new men and new women who were young, uniformly tidy, humourless, correct and determined. They would have been equally at home on the pages of mission journals throughout the twentieth century. These heroes and heroines were regularly portrayed in juxtaposition to *Xiconhoca*, Chico the Snake, or Chico the Enemy, a pointedly untidy, corrupt, lazy, drunken swashbuckler who ironically emerged as more

75 Saul, *Recolonization*, p.10.
76 Jeanne Marie Penvenne, 'A Luta Continua', *International Journal of African Historical Studies* 18, 1 (1985), pp.109–38.
77 *Xiconhoca o Inimigo*, Edição do Departamento de Trabalho Ideológico, Frelimo, Maputo, 1979.

engaging than the bland and obedient state servants who consistently foiled his evil plans. *Xiconhoca* was familiarly human, whereas Frelimo's cartoon agents of change were dull, predictable and unconvincing.

Frelimo's real cadres inevitably included a range from courageous, dedicated people to scoundrels. In the rush to set up political machinery, some party agents proved to be less than sincere. Stories of agents who walked away with the party dues, funeral collections, or collaborative accounts were common.[78] To Frelimo's great credit, the party took an active hand in identifying and prosecuting abuses by its agents, at least in the early period of independence. From the outset the thousands of hard-working party members and agents were better able to take advantage of policy changes and avoid the constraints of the deteriorating economic situation than many of their neighbours, and may have earned some resentment on that count alone. As the security situation deteriorated in the 1980s, people willing to do the party's bidding or to serve as a state-paid teacher, health-worker or agricultural extension agent did so at risk to life and limb, since insurgents targeted anyone connected with the government for death or mutilation.

Frelimo developed political communications through its government-owned press and radio, and through public rallies, songs and dances. The choice of media reflected their recognition that ordinary Mozambicans 'mapped their experience', criticised their leaders, and conveyed and interpreted their history through song, story and performance.[79] Such mapping was variously accomplished by well-known artists, 'peasant intellectuals' and ordinary women and men who contributed songs or spirit voices at ceremonial rituals.[80] Fabião, a young Mozambican migrant worker and a locally recognised poet, performed for a large crowd in the streets of the capital just six months after Frelimo proclaimed itself a Marxist-Leninist Vanguard party in February 1977.[81] Fabião was undeterred by the presence of Vanguard elements in his audience.[82] His interpretation of recent Mozambican history provided a window into popular consciousness and a lively foil to Frelimo's official texts.

Fabião opened his performance by confirming a shared past that featured conquest and colonialism and then proceeded to warn of a hauntingly horrific future. Although the song was full of irony and sarcasm, it was an open challenge to Frelimo's leadership to recognise the important gap between many of its national directives and the will of 'the people' in whose name it claimed to govern. The challenge was forcefully confident, but respectful. Fabião

78 'O partido – a luta dos trabalhadores na "Caju Industrial"', *Tempo* 405 (9 July 1978), pp.15–20; Marshall and Roesch, 'The "Green Zones"'.
79 Leroy Vail and Landeg White, *Power and the Praise Poem: Southern African Voices in History*, Virginia University Press, Charlottesville, 1991, esp. chapter 2.
80 Steven Feierman, *Peasant Intellectuals: Anthropology and History in Tanzania*, University of Wisconsin Press, Madison, WI, 1990, pp.4–5, 11 and 31; Vail and White, *Power and the Praise Poem*, chapter 7.
81 'Fabião of Mavalane', Wenela [Witwatersrand Native Labour Association] Compound, Malanga, Maputo, 15 July 1977. Tape D.
82 The performance was attended by Gaspar Salamão Guevende, the 'grupo dinamizador', or Frelimo party organiser, of Maputo's City Hall government, 15 July 1977.

solemnly hailed Samora Machel as the embodiment of Frelimo, and confirmed the seriousness and fragility of the new nation's position in a hostile region of powerful white neighbours. He supported Frelimo's militarism and urged enhanced vigilance to ward off any attempts to wrest Mozambique's hard-won independence from its hands:

> Very Sorry, Machel
> We worked without pay for the Portuguese
> We worked like donkeys
> Very Sorry President Machel, President of Frelimo, President of the Shangaan
> (They even know about him in Lisbon)
> Be strong. Do not let the Portuguese make trouble here again.
> If you do, they will be worse than ever
> They will harness us [like cattle] and make us pull the ploughs
> There will be fighting in every village
> They will burn the houses, and even the field rats will flee.

Fabião irreverently mocked Frelimo's taboo on ethnic or tribal discourse and highlighted a growing cult of personality by clearly identifying Samora Machel as both the president of Frelimo and 'president' of the large Shangaan ethnic group in southern Mozambique – thus firmly conflating Frelimo and Shangaan interests. He then went on to attack Frelimo's unpopular stance against the bridewealth which a husband's family customarily conveyed to the bride's family to publicly confirm the legitimate consummation of the marriage in Mozambique's patrilineal social systems. Frelimo argued, following the missionaries of Mozambique's past, that such payment was tantamount to the groom's purchase of the bride, and should be abolished. Fabião argued that most people did not agree. He taunted Frelimo by advocating bridewealth, employing the same discourse Frelimo commonly used to condemn it. Frelimo warmed up political meetings and explained its political agenda through songs that culminated with a series of *Vivas* (Long Live!) for the relations and institutions it wished to promote and *Abaixos* (Down With!) for those it wished to suppress or condemn. These related to the virtues and vices portrayed through the cartoon campaign, and although most of the *Vivas* were uncontested, the *Abaixo* repertoire was a different matter. Fabião cleverly set up the contrast in his repeated chorus:

> President Machel says *abaixo* bridewealth
> but, the people say
> *viva* bridewealth

Frelimo's commitment to transform the popular institutions and social relationships that it deemed oppressive or a threat to its authority sat poorly with many ordinary Mozambicans from the outset. Its campaign against specific social institutions such as bridewealth, sexual initiation at puberty and polygyny, and its hostility toward ethnic, religious or spiritual leadership that might compete with its own secular authority always featured strongly in

Viva and *Abaixo* choruses. The party's attack on fundamental indigenous social and cultural institutions has been criticised under the rubric 'abaixism'![83]

Fabião's critique was heartily acclaimed by the audience, including the party's representative. Like most critiques of that era it was openly conveyed, but it seemingly failed to sway the central political leadership which was aware of popular dissent but was determined to root out what it deemed anti-modern and iniquitous relations.[84] If the leadership was unwilling to 'hear' urban residents in the southern capital city where its headquarters were based, its deafness to the farming populations in central and northern Mozambique was not surprising.

Specific policies enhanced Frelimo's international standing among liberation support groups, academics, professionals and international aid agencies, but, at the same time, proved controversial within Mozambique. Non-racialism, the promotion of women's rights and extension of medical and educational services immediately after independence were well received internationally. The extension of health, education and welfare services to ordinary citizens, although broadly popular throughout Mozambique, ironically threatened Frelimo's ability to retain the loyalty of key groups. The new Mozambican élites and the few thousand skilled and semiskilled Portuguese who remained in Mozambique experienced a decline in the quality of the medical and educational facilities they had come to expect as services were opened to the general population. Those facilities deteriorated rapidly once stretched beyond capacity. Indeed, within two years of independence, basic municipal and state services that had largely served the Portuguese communities in Maputo and Beira were already swamped by excess demand and inadequate maintenance.[85] Thousands of the best-educated and skilled citizens of all racial and ethnic backgrounds eventually left the country because they feared that their children would suffer from declining standards in basic health and educational facilities. The challenge of political and economic reform was soon overshadowed, however, by the changing security situation.

THE FAILURE OF PEOPLE'S POWER

Mozambicans enjoyed a brief respite from armed conflict immediately following independence in June 1975, but it was barely sustained. The continuing conflict in Rhodesia increasingly spilled into Mozambique, and after a short

83 Saul, *Recolonization*.
84 In the 1990s the Maputo-based theatre group 'Mutembela Gogo' staged plays that openly mocked the governing élite and exposed the contradictions that generated support for Renamo. *Amor Vem*, staged August 1992.
85 Jeremy Grest, 'Urban management, local government, reform and the democratisation process in Mozambique: Maputo City, 1975–1990', *JSAS* 21, 1 (March 1995), pp.147–64; James Sidaway, 'Urban and regional planning in post-independence Mozambique', *International Journal of Urban and Regional Research* 17, 2 (June 1993), pp.241–59; Maria Clara Mendes, 'Les répercussions de l'indépendance sur la ville de Maputo', in M. Cahen (ed.), *Bourgs et Villes en Afrique Lusophone*, Karthala, Paris, 1989.

period of seeming indecision, South Africa undertook a focused programme of regional destabilisation and sabotage. While Rhodesia and South Africa became more effective in identifying and supporting potential Mozambican collaborators to suit their national and regional projects, Frelimo's internal policies generated widespread resentment that channelled disaffected refugees into the Rhodesian and South African camps. Soon Mozambique was again 'at war.[86]

This time the war was between the Frelimo government's military forces and the forces of what came to be called the Mozambican National Resistance or Renamo.[87] The renewed armed conflict was politically and ideologically complex, but its most important implication for most ordinary Mozambicans was that it greatly narrowed the margin of error. Once road, rail and communication networks were destroyed in the conflict or rendered useless by mines, the safety nets for all kinds of emergencies disappeared. Risks were greatly increased, and the smallest error could yield the most chilling results. Such strained circumstances were particularly difficult for the still young and inexperienced Frelimo cadres.

Renamo was created by the Rhodesian Intelligence Service in the mid-1970s as part of its effort to undermine the guerrilla forces of Zimbabwean nationalists who had moved their bases from Tanzania to central Mozambique with Frelimo support. The Rhodesians recruited disaffected Mozambicans and mercenaries to penetrate central Mozambique, attack the Zimbabweans, and raise the cost to Mozambique of aiding the nationalists by destroying roads, bridges and railways. In 1979–80 Rhodesia and the guerrillas reached a political settlement and Zimbabwe became independent under the Patriotic Front led by Robert Mugabe. Renamo quickly moved from Rhodesian to South African military sponsorship. The South African military continued to arm, train and supply Renamo until the late 1980s. Even when South Africa's political leadership decided that it was in their interest to withdraw support, some parts of the military command continued to assist Renamo. With the transformation of South African politics in the early 1990s support for Renamo passed to private interests, and by that time the group had taken on a life of its own.

As a military surrogate for Rhodesia, Renamo abducted a larger percentage of its military and supply force than Frelimo conscripted into its army. It did not develop anything like a political platform for almost a generation into its existence. This suggests that Mozambicans who joined Renamo were more likely to have come to their decision through disaffection with the politics of Frelimo than through affinity to those of Renamo.

Several Frelimo policies contributed directly to the ranks of Mozambican dissidents. The first was its decision to nationalise certain kinds of property

86 Alex Vines, *RENAMO: Terrorism in Mozambique*, James Currey, London, 1991.
87 Frelimo, following in the footsteps of the Portuguese, refused to accord Renamo the legitimacy of a name, referring to them in the disaggregate as *banditos armados*, the armed bandits. Renamo is the title the group has used in documents since at least 1990. Vines, *RENAMO*.

and services, including housing, church holdings, education, medical, legal and funeral services. As we have seen, settler hostility and sabotage partly shaped Frelimo's decision on nationalisations, but people who lost their property and livelihood through these decisions became potential dissidents. The second factor was Frelimo's range of disastrous agricultural policies: its commitment to unwieldy state farms, its hostility to successful private farmers, and its forced relocations to communal villages.

Monitored, bureaucratic removals of Mozambican farmers were begun in earnest with Portugal's settler schemes and strategic hamlets in the late colonial era. Frelimo continued the trend with its communal villages and state farms. On balance, all were ill-conceived impositions on the farming population, but their implications changed over time. During the war for independence, Mozambicans who were forced to relocate to 'strategic hamlets' considered the enemy to be the colonial government, rather than the Frelimo insurgents from whom they were being strategically protected. A decade later, when Frelimo's communal villages were targeted by Renamo, Frelimo could not always protect villagers. Yet it nonetheless insisted that farmers return to those communal villages. In some cases when Frelimo burned farm homesteads to guarantee compliance, they left farmers defenceless to face future attacks. By the mid-to late 1980s, farmers in some communal villages did not receive supplies, services or protection from the government that had required them to live there. After a while Mozambicans, facing assault from the government in their own homesteads and assault from Renamo in communal villages, quite sensibly joined refugee flows to escape the reach of both Frelimo and Renamo[88].

Perhaps no Frelimo policy produced more recruits for Renamo than the infamous Operation Production. In 1983 a national directorate known as Operation Production ordered the removal of all unemployed and 'marginal' people from urban areas and their relocation to underdeveloped rural zones where they could contribute more fully to the greater good through collective agricultural production. Frelimo bears unambiguous responsibility for the disaster that ensued. Innocent people were removed to areas totally unsuited to receive them, families were broken up and lives ruined. To their credit, those responsible for implementing the disastrous policy soon recognised its counterproductive impact and halted the process, but not before irreparable damage had been done. People who felt their lives had been destroyed joined Renamo's effort to destroy Frelimo.

From the late 1970s to the early 1990s Renamo's depredations made the violence of the armed struggle of the colonial era seem haphazard. Under Renamo, violence was not incidental but focused and designed to immobilise through terror.[89] The high price of conflict-related disruption of communications and agricultural production was evident by the early 1980s. A drought

---

88 Bowen, 'Beyond reform'; Otto Roesch, 'Renamo and the peasantry', in Kenneth Hermele, Peter Gibbon, Kjell Havnevik, *A Blighted Harvest: The World Bank & African Agriculture in the 1980s*, Africa World Press, Trenton, NJ, 1993.
89 Wilson, 'Cults of violence'.

in southern Mozambique, that previously would have raised the already high incidences of hardship and morbidity but little else, became a crisis that consumed an estimated one hundred thousand lives.[90] That proved to be only the warning bell. By the end of the decade Renamo's destruction of infrastructure, crops and processing machinery virtually extinguished Mozambique's agricultural exports. Between 1981 and 1988 sugar and cotton exports dropped 80 per cent by value. Renamo set fire to tea plantations, diminishing tea exports by 93 per cent between 1981 and 1985. In 1985 tea production stopped completely. Without agricultural exports to earn foreign exchange, Mozambique was unable to pay for increasingly necessary imports of food, let alone consumer goods.

The two generations of Mozambicans born since 1960 have experienced levels of violence, social differentiation, impoverishment, and suffering that makes the late colonial era pale in comparison.[91] By the early 1990s the cost of Mozambique's continuing conflict was staggering: more than one and a half million of the country's less than sixteen million people were international refugees, approximately four million, like Leia, were internally displaced by the conflict, and between one and three million deaths were attributed to the violence and deprivation of continuing conflict.[92] The combined cost of lost productivity since the early 1980s was conservatively estimated at $18 billion in a country whose gross domestic product in 1990 was estimated at only $1.2 billion.[93] By the early 1990s Mozambique had become the world's poorest, most devastated country: more than 90 per cent of its population lived below the poverty line, and 60 per cent of those lived in absolute poverty.[94]

Mozambicans experienced this poverty, devastation and conflict unevenly. Some regions were engulfed in almost chronic violence, while in other areas people like Leia remained relatively safe until the late 1980s. Northern Mozambique bore the brunt of the independence conflict in the 1960s, while southern Mozambique remained quiet. Twenty years later, however, the pattern was different: more than a quarter of the population in Zambezia province and a fifth of Niassa province fled the conflict, while only about 5 per cent of the populations of Nampula and Cabo Delgado left. More than a third of Inhambane's population and almost a quarter of Gaza's lived in refugee

90 Phyllis Johnson and David Martin (eds), *Frontline Southern Africa: Destructive Engagement*, Four Walls Eight Windows, New York, 1988, Introduction.
91 The literature documenting these conditions is extensive, but see, for example, Johnson and Martin (eds), *Frontline Southern Africa* n.3., p.467; Robert Gersony, 'Summary of Mozambican refugee accounts of principally conflict-related experience in Mozambique', U.S. Department of State, Washington, 1988.
92 Djene and Olivares, *Integrating Environmental Issues*, p.2, United Nations High Commission for Refugees [UNHCR]; *The State of the World's Refugees; The Challenge of Protection*, Penguin, London 1993, see p.108 for the estimate of three million dead.
93 Hanlon, *Who Calls the Shots?*, pp.5,265; Bertil Egerö, *Mozambique: A Dream Undone; The Political Economy of Democracy, 1975–1984*, Scandinavian Institute of African Studies, Uppsala, 1990.
94 The World Bank's *World Development Report*, Washington, 1990, p.178; United Nations and the Government of Mozambique, *Emergency Situation in Mozambique; Priority Requirements for the Period, 1990–1991*, United Nations Publication, New York, p.2.

settlements for fear of attack.[95] Mozambique's hundreds of thousands of land mines were seeded heavily along the Zimbabwe border and in central Manica and Sofala, whereas Niassa and Cabo Delgado provinces remained relatively mine-free.[96] Eventually, safe areas also felt war's impact as refugees consumed available resources, overwhelmed local service capacity and stretched accommodation beyond its limits.[97]

The tapestry of conflict drove more than half the population into the driest, sandiest, most flood-prone lowland areas. The capital city's overall population grew at about 5 per cent annually while more than 90 per cent of the country's potentially cultivable lands in the higher, healthier, better-watered, and more fertile areas went untilled, unplanted and unharvested.[98] Conflict undermined and skewed resource management nationally. Large areas of mangrove ecosystems, that provided the necessary environment for the country's essential prawn and shrimp harvest, were destroyed from Inhambane and Zambezia to Nampula by displaced people desperate for wood fuel. Meanwhile, security concerns have constrained Mozambique's ability to develop its potentially productive forests for timber production.[99]

Agriculture contributed about half of Mozambique's gross domestic product and 80 per cent of its export earnings but, by the 1990s, less than 7 per cent of the country's potentially cultivable lands was in production.[100] The government's hastily conceived strategies to encourage greater production and marketing in the wake of drought, floods or security crises sometimes had the opposite effect.[101] The food shortages aggravated malnutrition, and reversed the progress Mozambique made toward reducing rates of infant mortality in the early years of independence. By the early 1990s Mozambique had the second highest rate of infant mortality in the world and was dependent upon international aid for 90 per cent of the cereals available to feed its population.[102] Clearly, Frelimo's plans, whatever their merits, could not be effectively implemented in the face of widespread violence, and again, when nearly half of the entire population lived in absolute poverty, the margin for error was treacherously narrow.

DEBT, PRIVATISATION AND PEACE

Samora Machel directly confronted Mozambique's crisis in 1984. Without international assistance, Mozambique could no longer stand up to South African aggression. The president humbled himself and his country by signing a 'good

95 Djene and Olivares, *Integrating Environmental Issues*, p.2.
96 Human Rights Watch Arms Project [HRW], *Landmines in Mozambique*, New York, 1994, pp.1,14.
97 *Ibid.*, pp.1,14.
98 Dejene and Olivares, *Integrating Environmental Issues*, p.1.
99 *Ibid.*, pp.7–15.
100 *Ibid.*, pp.4–5.
101 Marshall and Roesch, 'The "Green Zones"', pp.244–50.
102 UN and Government of Mozambique, *Emergency Situation*, p.2.

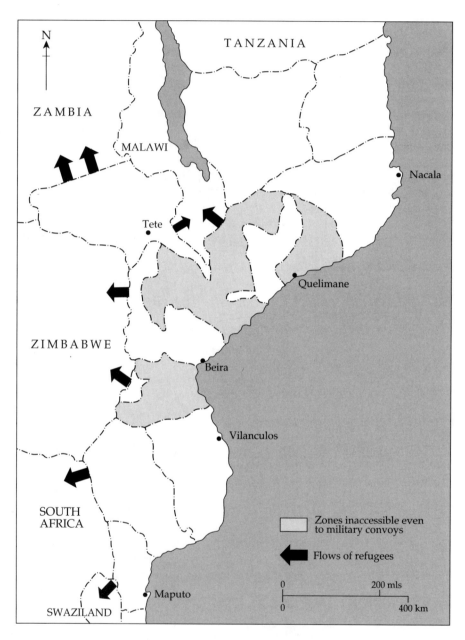

Map 9.2 Patterns of military and civilian access, Mozambique, early 1990
After Joseph Hanlon, *Mozambique, Who Calls the Shots?*, James Currey and Indiana
University Press, London and Bloomington, 1991.

neighbour' agreement, the Nkomati Accord, with South African President, P. W. Botha. Machel thus severely compromised the country's stalwart anti-apartheid status and its alliance with the African National Congress. In exchange it received South Africa's commitment to stop its extensive support for Renamo. The strategy did not work. South African military and intelligence forces continued to train, supply and support Renamo.

Machel then turned to the United States for support. His visit to Washington in 1985 marked the beginning of a rapprochement with the west that was enhanced after Machel's death in a suspicious plane crash in 1986. When Joaquim Chissano succeeded to the presidency, he struck a deal with the World Bank and the International Monetary Fund (IMF) that allowed Mozambique to restructure its mounting debt. As part of the deal Mozambique, like many other African nations, reluctantly agreed to implement a structural adjustment plan. The price of restructuring was revealed in the reforms promulgated through the Fifth and Sixth Party Congresses in 1989 and 1990. A new constitution, articulated in the Fifth Congress, reversed earlier policy by restoring rights in private property and private enterprise, and by instituting a multi-party political system with separation of powers, freedom of the press, speech, religion and association, the right to strike, respect for human rights and prohibition of the death penalty. The challenge was to sustain these rights beyond the printed page.

Shifts in national and international politics in the late 1980s and early 1990s finally brought negotiations among all parties to the conflict. Mozambique's membership in western-dominated financial institutions, the end of the Cold War and South Africa's dismantling of apartheid suggested that key players in the international community might be ready to start seriously promoting peace. A political settlement meant 'buying [Renamo] out of the bush' and into a peace settlement.[103] Renamo, which had been developed as a war machine by the Rhodesian and South African military, was now groomed by its international supporters for political participation.

Ironically, the record-breaking drought that struck southern Africa in the early 1990s may have made conditions so bad that people at the local level finally realised that war could not be sustained. Surviving social relationships became unhinged, and the resource base became utterly exhausted. Power-seekers on all sides turned to negotiation when the spoils of contention were completely spent. Peasants could not be terrified into handing over food they had not been able to produce. The head of Mozambique's leading humanitarian assistance programme observed, 'If we have another war in Mozambique, it is only to kill the people, because everything else is destroyed. Both sides already destroyed the country. There is nothing else to destroy except the people'.[104] A killer drought may have given life to a peace process.

103 Quote from former U.S. Under Secretary of State for Africa, Herman Cohen, at the Africa Orientation of Fulbright Scholars, Africa Orientation, Washington D.C., 7 June 1992.
104 Ernesto Pedro Martinho, secretary general of Caritas/Mozambique, quoted in USCR, *No Place Like Home*, p.9.

Jeanne Marie Penvenne

In mid-1992 the United Nations despatched a mission of 6,500 troops and a bevy of diplomats under the secretary-general's representative, Aldo Ajello. The goal was to keep the Frelimo and Renamo armies separate and to bring their warring leaders together.[105] Eventually, 'despite the United Nations, Renamo and Frelimo', peace was signed in Rome.[106] The Renamo leader, Afonso Dhlakama, repudiated any further armed conflict and the United Nations monitored a multi-party national election in 1994.[107] Joaquim Chissano of Frelimo won 53.3 per cent and Dhlakama 33.7 per cent. Frelimo also won 129 parliamentary seats to Renamo's 112, with a coalition of smaller parties taking 9 seats.[108]

GENDERED PERSPECTIVES

The textures and contradictions of thirty years' experience are complex. The challenge all Mozambicans faced trying to fashion a more equitable future for everyone was enormous. Some of the challenges and contradictions are reflected in Frelimo's economic and social policies relating to women. Frelimo was heralded in international circles as a model of pro-woman politics, but the historical record is more complex.[109] Samora Machel's famous statement, 'The liberation of women is a fundamental necessity for the Revolution, the guarantee of its continuity and the precondition for its victory', was more broadly quoted than was its subsequent clarification: 'To liberate herself, a woman must assume and creatively live the political line of Frelimo'.[110]

Women's roles in Mozambique's liberation struggle have generally been misrepresented and exaggerated.[111] Frelimo's original membership was all male. Women were first included around 1966, and then only in response to their strong lobby to participate in discussions that directly affected them. The experiment was short-lived. In 1966 the original women's group was purged and a women's detachment was appointed in its stead.[112] Several hundred women participated as combatants in Frelimo's military force of some 9,000–10,000. Both the political role of the women's detachment and women's role in food production and basic group reproduction were essential and not to be diminished in contrast with trousered young women carrying guns. Women and youth remained unrepresented or underrepresented in Frelimo's central

105 Diniz, 'Mozambique's 1994 General Elections', p.57; Alex Vines, *'No democracy without money': The Road to Peace in Mozambique*, Catholic Institute for International Relations, London, 1994; Schultz, 'The heritage of revolution', pp.117–19.
106 'Off the record' remark by a senior U.N. official quoted in Kenneth Wilson, 'The people's peace in Mozambique', *SAR*, March, 1994, p.22.
107 Vines, *'No Democracy without Money'*.
108 Diniz, 'Mozambique's 1994 general elections', pp.54–6.
109 Sheldon details myth and reality in 'Women and revolution', esp. pp.41–3; Stephanie Urdang, *And Still They Dance: War, Women and the Struggle for Change in Mozambique*, Monthly Review Press, New York, 1989.
110 Sheldon, 'Women and the revolution', pp.34,44.
111 *Ibid.*, esp. pp.41–3.
112 Henriksen, *Revolution and Counterrevolution*.

committee, assigned instead to separate women's and youth auxiliary branches: the *Organização da Mulher Moçambicana* and the *Organização da Juventude Moçambicana*. Ironically, both branches echoed the experience of Portugal's corporativist structures in that they implemented and interpreted government policy to their respective constituencies rather than articulating their constituent interests as policy-makers.

Many of Frelimo's initiatives in the first half decade of independence broadly benefited ordinary women, men and children. Immunisations, education, literacy campaigns and greater access to primary health care were undertaken in rural and urban areas, public places and workplaces. One striking result was that the infant mortality rate was halved within four years.[113] Yet, the impact of Frelimo's policies was always shaped by a person's specific location within the socio-economic, political and cultural configurations of their region and the impact could be mixed.

In matrilineal areas of the country, mature women wielded significant power as spiritual and ritual specialists but Frelimo's political stance against ethnic, religious or spiritual organisations that compromised its authority meant that such groups were attacked as 'obscurantism'. In some cases, therefore, Frelimo's campaigns against 'obscurantism' compromised women's status more than its pro-woman rhetoric improved their lot.[114] On the other hand, single, divorced or separated women, who were marginalised within the patrilineal social order of southern Mozambique gained some important advantages in communal villages and poor urban neighbourhoods where female-headed households predominated. In the towns of southern Mozambique, women whose husbands were often absent working in South Africa, lived in households with their sisters and maternal aunts. In this situation, their husband's lineage usually did not seek to assert authority over them.[115] Frelimo's developing system of popular justice served such women well. Their testimony was regularly and directly heard in family law cases and they were appointed as popular justices.[116]

Divorced or separated women who supported themselves and their children by working in the cashew-shelling factories of Maputo had a mixed, if basically positive view of life since independence. At the very least, they felt their personal status enhanced by the publicity they received from President Machel during the first decade of independence. They also eventually learned to exercise influence over their work experience through political channels. They were able to demand greater accountability within the factory through their party representatives.[117]

113 Isaacman and Isaacman, *Mozambique*.
114 Ruth Jacobson, 'Women's political participation: Mozambique's democratic transition' in *Gender and Development*, 3, 3 (Oct. 1995), pp.29–35.
115 Ana Maria Loforte, 'Migrantes e sua relação com o meio rural', *Trabalhos de Arqueologia e Antropologia* 4 (1987), pp.55–69.
116 Albie Sachs and Gita Honwana Welch, *Liberating the Law: Creating Popular Justice in Mozambique*, Zed Press, London, 1990.
117 'A luta dos trabalhadores na "Caju Industrial"', *Tempo* 405 (9 July 1978), pp.15–20.

That was not the case further north in Islamic and matrilineal areas. The cashew-shelling factory in Ilha de Moçambique, for example, did not employ a single woman.[118] With privatisation men will increasingly displace women because women are more apt to miss work to attend to sick family members or to recover from the birth of a child. Despite their ability to use Frelimo's political and legal channels to secure and advance their needs, cashew-shellers, like others dependent on wage labour in cities, were hard hit by the government's failed economic policies, food shortages, collapse of the agricultural supply networks and inflation linked to economic reforms. By 1993, many women complained that, 'in the old days we suffered, but we could eat – now we do not suffer, but we cannot afford to eat!'[119] In that year, if a retired cashew factory worker purchased nothing else with her monthly pension she could afford to buy a single loaf of ordinary bread for twenty-seven days every month. On the remaining three or four days she could not afford to eat.[120]

In the most critical areas and in the most general terms, Frelimo's governance from 1975 to 1995 did not serve women well. Mozambican women were overwhelmingly occupied in family farming, thus, Frelimo's broadly acknowledged neglect of the family farming sector in favour of large state farms had direct implications for women.[121] Despite Frelimo's characteristic willingness to reverse policy if it acknowledges a mistake, the neglect of women in family farming remains an important and largely unaddressed weakness. The single or divorced women employed on state farms or working in cooperatives, especially in the so-called Green Zones of southern Mozambique where women predominated in cooperative management, were better served by Frelimo's agrarian policies prior to the mid-1980s. The Green Zone cooperatives were developed around Maputo to supply fresh produce to the urban markets. Few of the cooperatives really flourished, but their role in women's political empowerment remains one of Frelimo's demonstrable achievements, as revealed by the vigorous political resistance the Green Zone women mounted to the threat of privatisation and a free market economy.[122] The perceived threat of privatisation and land sales was clearly stated by one woman:

> Big foreign companies may be able to produce much more than the peasants. But then what will become of us? These companies set their machines to work and they don't even need our labour. And they will produce things for export, not to feed the people.[123]

118 Cajú Industrial de Mocambique (CIM), Interview with Boaventura Mondlane and Elena Faustinho Machava of Sindicato National dos Trabalhadores de Cajú [SINTIC], 26 May 1993.
119 CIM, Laura Nhachunha Tsambe, 21 May 1993.
120 CIM. The average retiree's payment of 13,500 Meticais per month and the usual market price for bread at 500 Meticais per loaf in August 1993.
121 Bowen, 'Beyond reform'.
122 Sheldon, 'Women and revolution', pp.50–4.
123 Quoted in Bowen, 'Beyond reform', p.275.

Whether they labour on the farms or in the factories, Mozambican women are expected to help increase productivity without any diminution of their already disproportionate role in reproducing the labour force. The breakdown of state and market services exerted extreme pressure on water, fuel and food supplies. Women had to spend more time and energy daily acquiring the basic minimum their households needed to survive. The shift to private, capitalist investment in production is unlikely to ameliorate those burdens.

Frelimo's changing social policy was similarly gendered. As mentioned above, bridewealth, polygyny, and initiation rituals were derided in Frelimo's *Abaixo* choruses as oppressive and anti-modern. Each was also framed in terms of the oppression of women. Each was then subsequently contested and to some extent thwarted by men and women alike. Although Christians, Muslims and the elders of both patrilineal and matrilineal families who drew spiritual orientation from ancestors and spirits may have approached Frelimo's policies regarding women's sexuality, labour and offspring quite differently, they all resisted the whole concept of 'liberation'. In many ways the debates about bridewealth and polygyny in the Frelimo-controlled press echoed earlier debates in the newspapers run by mission stations and Mozambique's African petite bourgeoisie from the turn of the century to the close of the colonial era. Such issues are contested and complex.

When firmly confronted on issues relating to women, Frelimo back-peddled, first on its directives regarding bridewealth and, eventually, regarding polygyny. Many Mozambicans viewed bridewealth as an important aspect of social control and, like most social controls, it featured both sanctions and protections. Frelimo soon masked its reversal on bridewealth by referring to it simply as a 'gift' conferred at marriage in appreciation of the bride.[124]

Frelimo's women's organisation eventually deleted polygyny from their chorus of *abaixos* before abolishing *abaixos* altogether. Like bridewealth, polygyny was perceived as having both disadvantages and advantages.[125] It could be an advantage in households that depended upon female labour for extensive reproductive tasks to have many girls and women to carry out some of the heavier tasks in teams. Rural women worked together and often counted on co-wives for the most basic health and child care assistance. Urban and rural women pointed out that, 'Children are not like chickens, you cannot just give them out to the neighbours to feed'.[126] As directly interested parties, women were often important players in negotiations over wives and co-wives. By the late 1980s women's national leadership was prepared to concede that its earlier position on polygyny had been 'premature'.[127]

Women have not been proportionally represented in Frelimo leadership posts.[128] The only woman who ever served as a minister under Frelimo was

124 Penvenne, 'A luta continua', pp.129–30; Sachs and Welch, *Liberating the Law*.
125 Saul, 'Recolonization', p.61.
126 CIM, Interview with Rabeca Notiço, 24 May 1993.
127 Sheldon, 'Women and revolution', p.48.
128 *Ibid.*, p.43ff.

Graça Machel, wife of Samora Machel. She served as minister of education until she resigned in 1989. Salomé Moiane, long-time director of the women's organisation became deputy minister for foreign affairs two years later. Until 1989, however, Mozambican women had no direct voice, and no discernible role in the formulation of Frelimo policy. The widely publicised representational gains made by women within Frelimo in the early 1990s were the direct result of a policy shift mandated by the Central Committee when international agencies demanded that programmes consider the impact of policy on women.[129]

Frelimo determined at its Fifth Party Congress, held in August 1989, to broaden party appeal substantially and drop its Marxist-Leninist party designation. At the Sixth Party Congress in 1991 a woman, significantly a veteran of the women's detachment in the liberation struggle, was elected to the Political Bureau. With her election Mozambicans finally had a woman in the real hall of power. Frelimo had hitherto pursued women's interests as defined by the male leadership. Policy was also framed in a larger programme for transformation to a healthier, better educated, more productive society. The failures of initiatives revealed the extent to which the leadership, and the outside experts it consulted, failed to appreciate the complexity of Mozambique's socio-economic mesh. Policies that might be accepted without contest in southern Mozambique might have quite a different reception in the north. That was as true in 1975 as in 1995. There has never been anything straightforward about governing Mozambique in the name of its people.

CONCLUSION

During the first two decades of independence the Mozambican government struggled to overcome the strongly centralised, bureaucratic and authoritarian machinery of state it inherited from the Portuguese. The struggle was complicated by Frelimo's own tendency toward centralised, top-down control. It received much of its material, technical and military assistance between the early 1960s and the mid-1980s from Soviets who further encouraged Frelimo along that path. Threatened by hostile military forces in the region, emboldened by their hold on power, and facing the destruction and collapse of the country's productive and communications infrastructure, the leadership repeatedly tried to resolve complex, multi-layered problems by decree.

In closing, we return to Marcelino dos Santos. In 1990, when Mozambique was nearly at its nadir, he said: 'We admit that we made mistakes. But look at the quality of those errors. Were they fundamental mistakes, or did we fall short on secondary aspects?' Some of the mistakes, such as Operation Production, were indeed fundamental – but even that mistake was halted in less than a year, and frankly acknowledged as a mistake. Some mistakes, acknowledged or otherwise, caused irreparable damage in a very short period of time.

---

129 *Ibid.*, p.43ff, and Jacobson, 'Women's political participation'.

Who bears responsibility and who will pay the price for that damage? Dos Santos's point was that, in the context of increasing conflict that was broadly acknowledged to have been initially generated and subsequently fuelled by Rhodesia and South Africa, any mistake, fundamental or otherwise, took on new meaning. Much of what went wrong was out of the government's hands.

The economic sabotage wreaked upon Mozambique first by the fleeing settlers, then by the Rhodesians and their agents in Renamo, then by a South African-revived Renamo, and finally by Renamo as it took on a life of its own, increasingly stifled the range of options for state policy. Within the first few years of independence, major revenues from transport, migrant labour conventions, tourism and cash crops diminished drastically. Destruction of infrastructure and widespread insecurity curbed the government's power to recoup or redirect the situation. As the resource base weakened, the government's ability to provide goods, services, and protection diminished. International shifts in the Eastern bloc by the mid-1980s shut off Mozambique's principal fall-back. At the same time Renamo was 'stoked up' by the South Africans. With such a critical diminution of resources, and such an enhanced level of conflict, the government could not afford to make any mistake because the quality of any error would be magnified exponentially when experienced by those living on the edge.

Mozambique's economic free fall, Frelimo's move from crisis to near-collapse, and Renamo's holocaust were only held back from the brink by an upsurge in interest from western governments who were empowered to assert their concern through Frelimo's decision to join the World Bank and the IMF. However, the anonymous farmer who wondered what would become of her if big foreign companies forced her off her land was not alone in her concern. Privatisation and juggling a wide array of foreign government and non-government interests require important choices, and could result in errors whose costs will be borne by ordinary Mozambicans.

In November 1994, Mozambique carried the experiences and problems of its first twenty years of independence into a new chapter in its history. The government faced the challenge of implementing privatisation and democratisation without neglecting the rights and needs of those without money and influence. Since women are disproportionately represented among the deprived, the gendered nature of Mozambique's struggle will continue into the new era.

By the end of 1994, refugee repatriation was well under way, although more than a million Mozambicans had not yet made the trek back to rebuild their devastated local economies and societies. During the thirty years of conflict, each of the contending groups protected its bush bases and developed its offensive and defensive strategies through the extensive use of anti-personnel mines. The locations of these mines were often ill-mapped, unmapped or drawn on maps long since lost.[130] Bush paths in the agricultural areas of

130 Human Rights Watch Arms Project, *Landmines in Mozambique*, New York, 1994.

the central region were particularly hazardous: 'In a repatriation filled with uncertainties, one of the few certainties is that some refugees who managed to survive years of war, drought and crowded refugee camps will return home, step on a landmine and die'.[131]

None of the challenges that faced Mozambique in 1995, as it entered its twentieth year of independence, promised to be any more tractable than those of its past. Marcelino dos Santos's generation will pass from the political scene, but the struggle it waged will continue. Whether the ballot box will be adopted as an appropriate tool through which to accord legitimacy and wrest accountability from successive generations of leadership, and whether it will be an effective tool if adopted, has yet to be demonstrated. In the meantime, Frelimo's old slogan *A Luta Continua*! ('The Struggle Continues!') seems tried and true in comparison with the National Electoral Commission's slogan, '*No teu voto, o Futuro de Moçambique*' ('Mozambique's future rests with your vote').[132]

131 USCR, *No place like home*, p.27.
132 Jacobson, 'Women's political participation'; Diniz, 'Mozambique's 1994 General Elections', p.46ff; Mazula, *Moçambique; Eleições*.

266

CHAPTER 10

Images and themes in the nineties

DAVID BIRMINGHAM

The 1990s, like the 1960s, opened a new era in the history of Central Africa. Some long-running wars, as in Mozambique, ended. Some security forces, as in Malawi, lost their capacity to coerce people with fear as they had long done. The French-speaking countries held national conferences on democracy. In Zaire the great dictator was no longer seen as the essential custodian of order and security. In Angola peace was delayed by the war of 1992–4 but by 1997 hopes had revived. At an international level changes affecting Central Africa also began to take place in 1990. Beyond the Limpopo Nelson Mandela was released from gaol to orchestrate the reform of South Africa's hitherto undemocratic political system. In the industrial world forty years of Cold War came to an abrupt end; the Soviet Union virtually withdrew from Africa and the United States moderated some of its aggressive aspirations. As the superpowers retreated from Africa, the International Monetary Fund and the World Bank advanced with an intrusive authority that used the words of democracy but which lacked its legitimising accountability. Thus a new generation of neo-colonial institutions came to manipulate the financial politics of Central Africa and override the autonomy of nation-states.

In the 1990s the role of the state dwindled and some citizens were spurred to new initiatives which fostered a vibrant culture of self-reliance and survival. For others the economic agenda imposed by outside agencies led to poverty, dependency and insecurity. For a few a sudden burst of French-style democratic debate and multi-party elections provided an opportunity to flex political muscles and try out new ideas. For the rest the new democracy proved a false coinage which inspired hope but offered no redistribution of power or wealth. As a factor in people's lives demographic change, and notably urbanisation, became more influential than the ideological and political aspiration of the shrinking state. As floods of refugees swept across the north-eastern frontier from Rwanda and Burundi in the 1990s multinational agencies with humanitarian agendas attempted to take on privately some of the emergency functions which governments could no longer undertake.

As part of the change of the 1990s an economic ideology of privatisation spread across Central Africa. Banks dictated policy and voluntary bodies responded to famines or epidemics. In some respects the new dogmas of political economy represented a return to the early colonial period when public service was minimal and private enterprise was dominant. The initial colonisation of Central Africa by Britain, Belgium, France and Portugal had been left to the plundering care of private companies under charters of administration granted by metropolitan governments. Shareholders had extracted natural wealth and conscripted subject peoples on the lawless colonial frontiers, bringing darkness to the heart of Central Africa. As colonialism became more formalised the various colonial states took on a more traditional, though still far from benign, range of government responsibilities and in 1960 bequeathed their role to the successor republics. By the 1990s, however, many of the eleven independent republics of Central Africa were no longer able to provide even colonial levels of service. Foreign banks and agencies insisted that government revenue be used first and foremost to pay overseas debts and suggested that private initiative should once again replace public responsibility. Both planned and spontaneous change in Central Africa therefore mimicked fashionable western ideology as the state shrank. When law and order could no longer be guaranteed by the police, private security companies began to protect the assets of multinational companies and of privileged élites. When education was neglected by the state some ambitious parents financed private schools in order that their children might inherit the opportunities of the future. When inefficiency and pilferage destroyed the postal services independent carriers and satellite companies catered for the requirements of the very rich.

Strategies for survival took many forms in the 1990s. The most basic requirement was to supply a growing population with food. Local initiative was commonly in the hands of women: women farmers, women porters, women cooks, women brewers, women traders, women entrepreneurs, women money-lenders, women land-owners. The colonial-type economies continued to extract men from rural communities and send them to the mines and plantations, leaving women to manage not only the subsistence base of peasant society but also its market sector. Women with commercial acumen moved into the expanding towns of the postcolonial period and took responsibility for developing peri-urban farming and for supplying maize, cassava and vegetables to the city markets. In coastal areas women sometimes managed to recover their historic domination of the lucrative fish trade. Women also shouldered the heavy responsibility for cutting and carrying firewood from the countryside to the villages and even to the towns. As the towns spread into the countryside fuel became scarce and charcoal-burners living in the woods carried their charcoal to the cities. There it was used both in home kitchens and on roadside stalls where urban men bought ready-cooked food from businesswomen. Throughout most of Central Africa the food supply and the strategies for survival, were assisted by an ongoing symbiotic relationship between the towns and the provinces. This relationship was often based on networks of kinship which linked ethnically distinct urban enclaves to their ancestral home territories.

Society did not survive by bread alone, however, and the ever more exuberant Central African élite cultures evolved a demand for luxury goods as well as for basic foods. Old trading networks were revived and cross-border business flourished. Frontier towns and river ports became poles of opportunity where contraband goods that had escaped the customs and excise supervision of the dwindling state were ostentatiously displayed. As in precolonial times, textiles and clothing were the most valued items on display. Men patronised the best tailors and dressed themselves in the sharpest suits while women decked themselves and their daughters in gorgeous wax-print cloths and colourful headscarves. Extravagance and escapism were not only the preserve of the rich. Ordinary people also found ways of celebrating, despite adverse conditions of life. Football remained an almost universal passion among the people of Central Africa. In Luanda the carnival was a supreme popular occasion of competitive dancing and of the fine display of costumes. Next to clothing, the most conspicuous item of consumption was alcohol, ranging from locally bottled lager and home-brewed rum to the most expensive Scotch whisky. As in the production of food, women played a prominent part in the luxury trades and in the distribution of bootleg liquor. At the most immediate level women walked across the old colonial frontiers with contraband concealed under their voluminous robes. At the top end of the market, women wholesalers bought and sold bolts of textiles on a world scale, flying not only to Europe but to the Gulf states and the Americas. Informal domestic banking was as often in the hands of women as of men.

One of the most pervasive heritages of European rule in Africa had been standardised colonial currencies measured in francs, escudos and pounds. By the 1990s, however, significant distortions had taken place in the currency systems of the financial zones of Central Africa. The greatest apparent continuity was maintained in the former French colonies of equatorial Africa where the old colonial franc remained a multinational currency, controlled by Paris and used in the five autonomous territories. Under the fiscal domination of France the new republics of north-west Central Africa were unable to regulate their own money supply or to vary the exchange rates as a means of determining policies of their own. Worse still, the exchange rate could be, and in January 1994 actually was, unilaterally changed when it suited the interest of France so to do. Independence, as granted by de Gaulle in 1960, had not included fiscal independence. This continued French control contrasted sharply with the situation in south-east Central Africa where the individual territories of the old British Federation of Rhodesia and Nyasaland each adopted their own currency with their own autonomous central bank. As a result, modest levels of inflation could be adopted, either as a prudent policy or as an emergency measure in times of crisis. The best defended of these currencies, ironically, was that of Zimbabwe, which for fifteen years had been officially excluded from the world banking system during the regime of unilateral white rule.

269

In former Belgian and former Portuguese Central Africa the history of money was much more turbulent than in the ex-French or even ex-British zones. In Zaire hyperinflation became endemic and on one occasion the unit of currency was shorn of several zeros to make the counting of banknotes more manageable. Astute merchants who went in and out of Zaire with an eye for speculative opportunity used suitcases to carry their bundles of cash. The state president, Mobutu, was able to enhance his already substantial fortune by granting to himself the contract for printing currency notes. Presidential private initiative backfired, however, in the Kasai mining province where local politicians refused to accept a new national currency standard and managed to preserve a lower rate of inflation than the one which prevailed in the capital by continuing to use the old money. In Angola similarly acute inflation led housewives and market 'mammies' to seek alternative measures of value and exchange for their daily transactions. In precolonial Angola copper ingots and raffia squares had been the commodities with the most stable value which served as currency substitutes. In postcolonial Angola the aluminium can of beer became the most widely recognised yardstick of value and became a unit for measuring the worth of traded commodities. For small-scale transactions crates of beer-cans could be used as actual payment in lieu of cash, but in larger transactions bulk transport became difficult and alternative forms of money had to be adopted. The one that eventually became most widely used was the United States dollar bill. Since Angola's main export was oil, which was shipped to the United States, the exchange rate of the 'beer-can currency' shadowed the price of oil very precisely, even before dollars became a semi-legitimate means of payment.

The most dramatic change in fiscal practice in Central Africa concerned the methods which the informal economy used to make international payments. The most common 'currency' was diamonds. Throughout the colonial period diamond digging had been carefully controlled by the state through a network of private companies linked to the De Beers world consortium. After independence wild diamond-digging, unsupervised by members of the marketing cartel, spread widely. Diamonds were found throughout a geological belt that spread from Namibia through eastern Angola and western Zaire to the Central African Republic. Some of the finds were of gem quality but the majority, especially in the huge Zaire fields, were industrial stones. Unlike minerals such as copper or oil, surface diamonds could be mined and washed without heavy capital investment, or sophisticated technology, or a government licence, and could easily be smuggled. Lawlessness became endemic in the digging fields, as it had in the great diamond strikes of earlier centuries, but the market was dominated by well-armed entrepreneurs. In Angola it was the warlords of the opposition political party, UNITA, who gained the lion's share of the traffic. They were able to use diamonds as the currency with which to buy weapons for their long-running guerrilla war and to hire aircraft in which to fly supplies of ammunition and diesel oil to their shifting military camps in the Angolan interior. On the other side of the border, in Zaire, diamonds also became the alternative currency of large-scale business transactions and the source of wealth for semi-autonomous politicians who ruled nation-sized fiefs with little respect for state authority. Further north, in the Central African Republic, politicians had long been able to use their share of the diamond winnings to manipulate politics as far away as Paris. President Giscard D'Estaing had allegedly burnt his political fingers by accepting gifts of diamonds from Bokassa, the notorious 'emperor' of the 1970s, who had risen up from the ranks of the French colonial army.

In the 1990s all of Central Africa's presidents, and not only those few who, like Bokassa and his successors, had gained office by means of a military coup, needed to take great care in nurturing their relations with the military or other men with guns. Violence had become a constant reality in both social and political life. Bands of young robbers armed with cheap automatic weapons helped themselves when society neglected to provide them with opportunity or hope. At the political level the enemies of government were sometimes able, as in Chad, to protect their regional fiefs by military action. The most ubiquitous popular experience of violence, however, came from the presence of soldiers and paramilitary policemen on the streets of almost every country of Central Africa. People often preferred to melt into the crowd rather than seek protection or justice from the unpredictable custodians of order. Although nominally paid by the state, soldiers and policemen were often short of rations and wages, as in Zaire, and their foraging for food could turn to extortion and looting. In Angola, by contrast, the two rival armies were sometimes the least unreliable source of food and many young men spent long years as conscripts in preference to being hungry. When ordered to do so by battle-hardened veterans they fought pitched battles in the jacaranda-lined streets of Huambo, but in between engagements the boy-soldiers cadged cigarettes, whistled at girls, and challenged each other to a game of football across the wasted no-man's-land of civil war.

Although the role of the state declined in Central Africa during the 1990s, one must take care not to overexaggerate the weakness of government. Politicians continued to compete fiercely to win and retain state power. In Africa no enterprise commanded such lucrative resources as the state and those who had access to national wealth did not relinquish their position readily. When pressures from above and below forced them to do so, statesmen endeavoured to refurbish their image as leaders of their people by organising 'democracy conferences'. Some, as in Mozambique, were able to retain their hold on power in the 1990s by submitting themselves to elections in which they were freely and fairly returned to office. A few, as in Zambia, retired reasonably gracefully after being defeated by public ballot. Several others managed to manipulate the electoral choice and so give themselves a new, if suspect, presidential mandate.

The nation-states continued to build prestigious presidential palaces and to post diplomatic envoys to the world's capitals. Even the mobile warlords of Chad recognised a national territory, a national capital, and national assets

271

whose sale could be negotiated with foreigners. Where the state controlled deep-level mines or oil-wells, as in Zambia or Angola, the incentive to gain the political power to concentrate, or redistribute, wealth derived from mineral royalties was particularly strong. One of the less publicised forms of mining that attracted tight state supervision was the mining of uranium in Gabon. It was not, however, only in ex-French Gabon that the state remained in command of the economy. In ex-British Central Africa the nation-state whose government showed the greatest continuity with the colonial past was Zimbabwe. There civil servants continued to ensure that roads were paved, post offices staffed, children taught, and felons prosecuted. The colonial-style economy of capital-intensive farming provided exports that could still be taxed to finance the cost of state services. By the mid-1990s, however, the new politics of Zimbabwe had only been tested for fifteen years, after the long search for independence, and more radical adaptations of the old colonial systems were anticipated with various degrees of hope and fear.

One of the key forces for change in Central Africa that had little or nothing to do with the state, or with political choice, was demography and the structure and distribution of population. Central Africa always was, and still is, one of the least populated regions of the tropical world and has low demographic densities when compared to Ethiopia or Nigeria, let alone Bangladesh or the Caribbean islands. But the population of Central Africa is also very unevenly distributed so that the sparsely peopled forests of Congo, and the lightly inhabited savannas of Zambia, are counterbalanced by zones of dense occupation in the highland of Cameroun, on the plateau of Malawi, or around the twin cities of Kinshasa and Brazzaville. Demographic pressure has sometimes been acute. Human fertility rates were so high that they exceeded the comparably high infant mortality rates and created a demographic pattern in which about half the population of Central Africa was below the age of fifteen. Localised population growth and rapid population movement brought social crises, violence and even war. The most dramatic of these conflicts was the war of 1996 in Zaire which was triggered by the demographic and political crisis which spilled over from the Eastern African highlands of Rwanda.

In Rwanda the inexorable rise of population in a tiny, mountainous country had led to sharp competition over the few arable acres where staple crops of maize and banana could be grown and where export crops of coffee and tea could be harvested. A once-traditional élite of cattle herders, some of whom had become the semi-privileged middle class of the colonial period, had lost much of its political influence during the years of independence. In the 1990s, however, a growing population crisis had led to armed confrontation between the now much impoverished former élite, loosely identified by their opponents as the 'Tutsi', and the ruling majority, broadly referred to as the 'Hutu'. The 'Hutu' attempted, with some military help from France, to retain their power and their access to farmland. These efforts deteriorated, in 1994, into a systematic killing of any rivals who were seen as ethnically distinct. A genocidal massacre of village neighbours assumed to be descended from the

'Tutsi' took place across the 'kingdom of a thousand hills'. It did not, how-ever, prevent the return to power of men from the once-privileged minority who had spent a generation of exile in English-speaking East Africa and were now led by an American-trained general, Paul Kagame.

The Rwanda killings of 1994 were followed by the largest population stam-pede that Central Africa had ever seen. It was comparable in scale, and in its political impact, to the great Nigerian migrations of Igbo peoples in the mid-1960s. Hundreds of thousands of Rwandans abruptly left their homes to settle in huge plastic-covered refugee encampments in French-speaking Zaire. Their houses and farms were meanwhile taken over by their neighbours, under the protection of the English-speaking soldiers who had seized power. Two years later, however, the massive population flow was reversed. By November 1996 the Zaire government had lost control not only of the refugee camps, but also of the whole Kivu district of eastern Zaire in which the camps were located. Zaire rebels, led by politicians who had been in the political wilder-ness ever since Mobutu and his army had come to power thirty years earlier, took control of the east with discreet help from the new Rwanda government. By March 1997 their leader, Laurent Kabila, had captured Kisangani with apparent American connivance. The city associated with Lumumba's radical-ism of the 1960s was liberated as Mobutu's army and his Serbian mercenaries fled. The bend in the river was once more referred to as the bank of the Congo rather than of the Zaire. Meanwhile, most of the refugees were ordered home to Rwanda, though the military perpetrators of the 1994 mas-sacre fled west into the Zaire forest, along with Mobutu's disintegrating army, which France was unable to shore up. The returnees arrived home in the Rwanda hills to find them still crowded. In many cases their jobs, their houses and their farms were now occupied by others and a new demographically-driven crisis was in the making. Meanwhile Mobutu fell and Kabila took Kinshasa.

To the south of Rwanda another miniature kingdom-turned-republic, Burundi, also brought demographic and political turbulence down from the lakeside highlands of East Africa to the plains of Zaire. The scale of the refugee flows may not have been as large as those out of Rwanda, but the violence of local confrontation, whether class-based, historical, or driven by land-hunger, was no less murderous for being smaller in scale. Shocked wit-nesses drew parallels with Europe, where recent community blood-letting had disfigured Bosnia. In 1996 an army supported by many who defined themselves, or were defined by others, as 'Tutsi' seized power from a more broadly-based government and caused more refugees to spill out into Central Africa. Burundi's neighbours sealed the borders and placed its military rulers under an interdict of isolation and disapproval which did little to help the crowded population find new strategies for securing peace and prosperity.

Demographic pressure was not the only cause of large-scale population movement in Central Africa. Poverty and war also caused great migrations in sparsely peopled countries such as Mozambique. The scorched-earth policies of destabilisation orchestrated by colonial Rhodesia in the 1970s and white-ruled South Africa in the 1980s caused mass flight. The return to peace after the end of the Cold War, and after the democratisation of South Africa, permitted the return from exile of tens of thousands of cross-border refugees. Before they could return to farming, however, they had to call on experts from the world community to clear their millet and cassava fields which had been strewn with land mines. Throughout village Mozambique these anti-personnel weapons continued to maim children who went to the river for water and women who carried heavy bundles of firewood along wood-land paths. Even where farming had once more been made relatively safe by international teams of explosive experts, Mozambicans discovered that the old colonial realities of economic life had not changed. The way to earn money was not to improve the family farm but to send sons, and even some daughters, to the city, the plantations, or the century-old Transvaal mines. Migration continued to be a way of life, and a means of survival, even when population densities were very low.

The most destructive of Central Africa's wars, and the one which caused the most dramatic internal population flight, was the one which broke out in Angola in 1992. This war was different from any that had occurred before in Central Africa. Fighting with heavy artillery, with aircraft, and even with missiles had already occurred during the 1980s, but only in the remote and sparsely peopled south of Angola. The war of 1992–94, however, was a war that involved the starvation and destruction of whole cities. These cities had grown during the long years of guerrilla war when people escaped from the mine-infested countryside to seek refuge in the towns. A wholesale shift in population also brought people down from the highland to the more secure coastland. In 1992 this pattern of urbanisation and migration had a profound effect on Angola's first general election in which the towns and the coast voted predominantly for the MPLA government party, which won more than half of the parliamentary seats, while the villages and the highland voted predominantly for the UNITA opposition party, which won only a third of the seats. Rather than concede defeat, the UNITA leader, Savimbi, determined to destroy the government's urban base and win power by force of arms. The urban war was launched in the port cities of Luanda and Lobito by the government, which violently expelled the opposition and its military units. War then spread to the highland, where UNITA forces besieged government troops in the towns of Malange and Huambo. Each side built arsenals of heavy and sophisticated weapons on a scale not hitherto witnessed in Africa. Oil revenues and diamond sales were mortgaged to arms-dealers for years into the future. Towns, which had been havens in the old war, became deathtraps in the new war. The world community and its humanitarian agencies struggled to airlift food-aid to the victims. When a ceasefire was finally agreed in November 1994, millions of people were living in the ruined shells of Angola's cities. Huambo, once the 'New Lisbon' of Portugal's premier colony, resembled Berlin in 1945.

Cities and towns exerted their pull on nearly all the peoples of Central Africa, not merely those who lived in areas of chronic insecurity and fled there for safety. A striking case of rapid urbanisation was that of Congo, where more than half the country's population lived in the slums and suburbs of Brazzaville. Kinshasa grew tenfold after the end of Belgian colonial rule, while Yaoundé rose from a medium-sized administrative town to a capital city of over half a million people. Towns were places of commercial opportunity where men and women alike thronged the open-air markets. Young bachelors came to town in search of education, training and jobs. Town was also the place of avant-garde music, of sophisticated nightlife, of wheeling and dealing, and of escape from the moral supervision of clan elders. A new generation of children was born in the towns. Some were destined to a life of scavenging on the streets but others found opportunities denied to their country cousins. They also had a slightly better chance of surviving in town since health care had become notoriously weak in the rural provinces.

The early postcolonial period had brought some provision of modern health care, and some distribution of new medical drugs, but by the 1990s facilities were being starved of resources and disease remained a constant preoccupation for the peoples of Central Africa. Smallpox was apparently eradicated, but the incidence of malaria, the greatest of killers, rose when sanitation departments failed to maintain drainage systems, fumigate city streets, or eliminate new breeding grounds of mosquitoes. Tuberculosis also returned to weakened people who were not adequately nourished or immunised. When bridewealth and wedding costs rose beyond the reach of impoverished men and women, alternative patterns of sexual relationship put them at increasing risk from sexually transmitted diseases. Worse still, the virulent new AIDS virus took its toll of young adults, some of them miners returning from South Africa, where sexual outlets were commercial, or promiscuous, or homosexual. The low life expectancy for the middle-aged and the high infant mortality for the very young was tragically accentuated by a rising death rate among bread-winning adults whose immune systems had been destroyed.

In the growing cities of Central Africa a search for security led many to turn to new forms of religion. Folk from the countryside brought with them the old beliefs and practices which warded off evil and honoured the ancestors. Methods for eradicating witchcraft became important in mediating conflict in communities of unequal opportunity which were riddled with envy and where success was deemed to be procured by the occult. In addition to consulting diviners and magicians, established townsmen also worshipped in the independent churches where black priests and prophets had gained an extensive following during the late colonial and early independence years. By the 1990s, however, churches with mission roots and world links were in the ascendancy once more, their association with colonialism now forgotten. In addition to thriving Catholic and Protestant churches, new Pentecostal churches sustained active worshipping communities. In remote villages a new breed of missionaries brought not only travelling preachers but also flying nurses and doctors piloting light aircraft. Across the region from Cameroun to Malawi Catholic, Methodist and Anglican bishops took a leading role in the campaign for democracy. In Zaire, where Mobutu had tried but failed to crush the power of the church, a religious zeal informed the courageous voice of the democratic opposition in the 1990s. In Angola even Marxists turned to the superior power of the church and invited the pope to visit their country. Dos Santos, the Moscow-trained president, led his followers to a huge religious ceremony held in the national football stadium and received holy communion.

Religion may have been the most lasting legacy of empire in Central Africa, but commerce left its mark too. Before 1960 the epitome of the colonial relationship between Central Africa and the outside world had been the selling of raw materials at low cost in exchange for processed goods to which a high value had been added by European manufacturers. One of the aspirations of independence had been to create local industrial complexes which would free Africa's new nations from neo-colonial dependency on their trading partners. By the 1990s this dream had made but little progress. The list of exports which enabled Central Africa's governments to pay hard currency for foreign goods and services retained a thoroughly colonial appearance. In the north the dominant export remained coffee, with some cocoa and cotton. In the south the leading export crop was tobacco, with some sugar and tea. In the west the traditional export of tropical hardwoods continued to offer employment, though the profits were largely garnered by international logging companies. The timber-exporting countries of the Atlantic fringe were also the ones that became the oil-producing countries of Central Africa. Unlike the rest of the region, they benefited from the creation of the oil-exporting cartel OPEC. In the heart of the region dependency on the mining of copper and allied minerals remained as complete as ever it had been under the colonial regimes of Britain and Belgium. The mining of diamonds did escape from the traditional controls formerly imposed by South Africa and new cross-border trading conduits flew the stones via Lebanon to new international centres of cutting and polishing in India and Thailand. Other forms of mining, however, remained closely linked to the great industrial and financial complexes of South Africa.

In the second half of the twentieth century South Africa cast a long shadow across Central Africa. In 1960 there was an apparent political retreat as South Africa left the Commonwealth and created a beleaguered Afrikaner republic with a rigorous colonial style of racial segregation. Economically, however, South Africa continued to interact with its northern neighbours. In Zambia it supplied the managerial and technological expertise to keep the mechanised copper industry working. In Zaire it supplied frozen meat to feed Lubumbashi and the mining cities of Shaba province. South Africa discreetly built up trading partnerships with the French client states of Central Africa and enhanced its trade with France. It also became the close ally of Malawi and helped finance grandiose projects such as a prestigious new capital city at Lilongwe. South Africa's most complex relationship, however, was with the

Portuguese colonies. In Angola the Portuguese army apparently received advice and subsidised weapons to try to quell the nationalist revolution and prevent it from spilling across the Namibian border into South Africa's illegitimate dependency. Mozambique was even more closely linked to South Africa since it hired out nearly a quarter of a million low-paid workers to the South African mines. South Africa's most immediate and dependent neighbour, however, was Rhodesia. From 1965 to 1980 the country, which was ruled by a political party espousing concepts of racial supremacy not dissimilar to those of apartheid, was isolated from the world by economic sanctions and was dependent on South Africa for essential supplies of oil and raw materials and for strategic weapons with which to resist the black nationalist challenge.

In the 1980s the southern states of Central Africa were increasingly concerned at their dependency on imported South African goods. They tried to establish a Southern Africa development coordination committee, SADCC, to coordinate regional manufacturing strategies and reduce imports from South Africa. The national economies proved, however, not to be complementary to one another and the scope for exchange was very limited. No Central African country, with the partial exception of Zimbabwe, was even able to sustain processing and manufacturing plants that could supply its own needs, let alone those of its neighbours. In the case of Zimbabwe industrialisation had, ironically, expanded during the years of economic sanctions when industrial self-reliance and commercial dependence on South Africa were imposed upon the country. When the world boycott of Zimbabwe was lifted in 1980 South Africa was reluctant to relinquish the monopoly on trade and transport that had grown up during the years of isolation. Zimbabwe was compelled for another ten years to rely unwillingly on South Africa for its supplies of oil and for deep-sea harbours through which to export its tobacco.

The year 1990 was not only the year in which the Cold War ended but also the year in which South Africa was transformed. The roots of the change, and of the far-reaching consequences of reform for the contemporary history of Central Africa, are to be found in the last years of the 1980s. The transformation grew out of a confrontation between the South African military complex, which was close to government, and the South African industrial complex, which was increasingly reluctant to bear the heavy tax cost of repression at home and aggression abroad. The industrialists wanted peace, reform, and a domestic market of black consumers with rising purchasing power. The military men wanted weapons, promotions, and a spectacular victory against the allegedly Marxist government of Angola. They invaded Angola in 1988 but their campaign failed in the protracted battle for Cuito Cuanavale, where the South African army lost its support at home and its credibility abroad. As the Cold War came to an unexpected close, and the Soviet Union dissolved into its component parts, South Africa could no longer present its military adventures to its western allies as being the defence of Central Africa against Soviet imperialism. The South African army lost its hold on political power and withdrew from Angola and Mozambique. A new, civilian, generation of white politicians negotiated agreement with black nationalists for the gradual reform of South Africa's political system.

The election of Nelson Mandela to the presidency of South Africa brought a search for a new partnership between South Africa and its Central African neighbours. The new government still needed export revenue to finance its policies and the Central African market provided attractive options, albeit ones tinged with neo-colonial inequalities. Peaceful relations were restored with Mozambique, which even joined South Africa as a member of the hitherto largely English-speaking, ex-British, Commonwealth. Peace, however, was not the whole story. One of the most sophisticated industries that Mandela's government inherited was weapon manufacturing. Democratic South Africa therefore continued to sell guns, new and second-hand, to Central Africa. Many of these guns fell into the hands of villains or of rebels and intensified the already endemic violence that threatened the fabric of society and the stability of government. Military influence from the south went beyond the supply of equipment, however, and the old South African tradition of hiring out mercenaries to serve in Central Africa took on a new form. An organisation euphemistically named 'Executive Outcomes' rented out commandos to armies which could afford to pay for its military expertise. In a striking turn of fortune, South Africans who had previously supported UNITA while wearing government uniform, now supported Angola's MPLA army wearing mercenary uniform. Such military services increased the death-toll in Central Africa, rather than spreading the tradition of reconciliation that had begun to blossom inside South Africa itself. Yet the end of apartheid made South Africa the new haven of toleration and opportunity; refugees, political and economic, tried to make their way south. For Central Africans South Africa was now a role model rather than a threat.

While South Africa reassessed its relations with its northern neighbours in the 1990s, the rest of the world tried to turn its back on Central Africa. The Cold War and its accompanying 'wars by proxy' had ended. International neglect replaced international interference and brought new crises of stability and survival. The world was reluctant to broker a peace in Zaire in 1996 or even to feed people driven into the huge refugee camps. It became clear that 'humanitarian aid' was not politically neutral. Diplomatic and strategic interests which pitted France and America against one another in Zaire stalled attempts at concerted relief action for the victims of war. As the marginalisation of Africa grew, industrial nations turned away from a continent which had supplied their raw material on the cheap since the nineteenth century. Other 'third-world' regions with low-paid, partially skilled labour offered better prospects for investment and trade than did Africa with its low-level human skills, its crumbling infrastructure and its turbulent politics.

The one region of Central Africa that did remain of interest to the outside world after the withdrawal of the battling superpowers was the western fringe. It was there that oil prospecting and drilling continued to take place all the way from Lake Chad in the far north to Luanda on the south coast. One of the advantages of Central Africa's oil, from the point of view of refining companies and consuming nations, was that it was not politically controlled by the relatively powerful Muslim nations of the Middle East. Seven billion dollars' worth of oil, at United States prices, was not large in world terms but it was a useful margin of supply from a non-Muslim source. In 1995 half of Central Africa's exported oil was pumped from wells in Angola, a quarter from Gabon, and an eighth each from Cameroun and Congo. Oil revenue, however, was not generally ploughed back into economic development, productive investment, training and employment, or local services. The industry remained strictly limited to expatriate-dominated enclaves of extraction and the royalties were largely used by politicians for military expenditure, prestige building, and conspicuous consumption by urbanised élites. While Angola's people starved on the margins of the battlefields, its leaders drove BMW cars round the potholes of their suburbs. In Gabon half the national population moved from the neglected countryside into the booming city of Libreville, where many became accustomed to eating French bread, imported salad, and frozen beef in preference to local cassava dough with spinach and smoked fish. When oil prices dropped in the late 1980s the oil-exporting nations of Central Africa all found that they had overstretched themselves by indulging extravagant consumer tastes and accepting imprudent state loans.

Beyond the oil-rich coast of north-west Central Africa two off-shore island republics kept a close eye on the development of petroleum drilling. One was the former Portuguese plantation colony of São Tomé, which gained its independence in 1975. The politicians of the island were in close touch with those of Libreville, two hundred miles away. Some of the tiny middle-class élite of the island had spent the last colonial years, and indeed some of the independence years, in exile in Gabon. They naturally watched closely the rise of the Gabon oil industry, but at first had little success in their own endeavours at prospecting. The minute republic remained poor and dependent on a small-scale survival of cocoa and coffee production. The other island republic, Equatorial Guinea, was economically a little more successful. Although the plantation economy collapsed after Spain had granted self-governing autonomy and later full independence during the 1960s, the island and its on-shore enclave of Rio Muni, around the town of Bata and squeezed between Cameroun and Gabon, did find petroleum and drill wells. Despite the incompetent and often brutal mismanagement of the state, prospecting companies began to export small quantities of oil during the 1990s to supplement the income derived from logging on the mainland. But the island fell under the economic shadow of Gabon even more directly than did São Tomé. Large numbers of Equatorial Guineans migrated to Gabon to find work. The Spanish-speaking republic eventually joined the equatorial franc zone and became closely integrated into the French sphere of influence, somewhat to the chagrin of Spain. The dictatorial rulers of the island looked to other Spanish-related countries, first Cuba and later Morocco, to supply them with élite troops to staff their palace

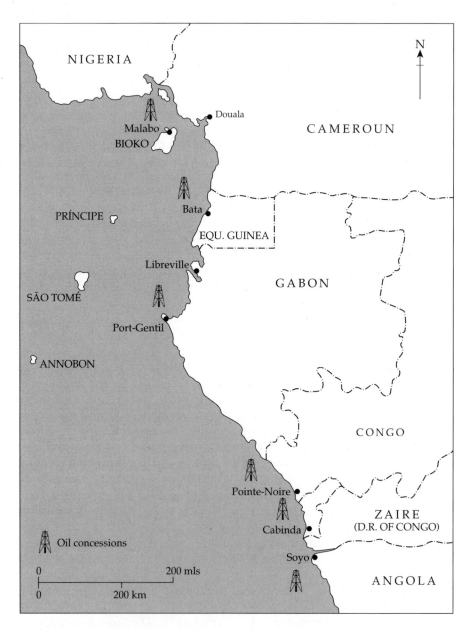

Map 10.1   North-west Central Africa: the oil producing coast

TABLE 10.1

CENTRAL AFRICAN INDICES C.1995

	Purchasing power per head ($)	People per doctor	Foreign debt as % of GDP	Main export	Main trade partners: Exports	Imports
Chad	710	33,000	64	cotton	Portugal	France
Cameroun	2,060	12,000	71	oil	France	France
Central African Republic	1,060	25,000	64	diamonds	Belgium	France
Gabon	?	2,000	80	oil	?	?
Congo	2,430	8,000	248	oil	USA	France
Zaire (D. R. Congo)	?	?	?	copper	Belgium	Belgium
Angola	?	14,000	182	oil	USA	Portugal
Zambia	1,170	11,000	231	copper	Japan	?
Malawi	780	50,000	91	tobacco	?	?
Zimbabwe	1,900	62,000(?)	78	tobacco	S.Africa	S.Africa
Mozambique	380	50,000	419	prawns	Portugal	France

Source: Roland Dallas, *The Economist Pocket Africa*, Hamish Hamilton, London, 1995.

guard. Economically, however, it was the link with Gabon which remained the dominant factor in the postcolonial history of the off-shore islands.

In the 1990s all eleven of the nations of Central Africa, even the four oil-producing states of the Atlantic seabord, had overstretched their international credit and were as dependent as ever they had been under colonialism on the commodity prices offered to them by foreign buyers. The Central African debt crisis had many local causes reflecting the collapse of copper prices, the demonisation of tobacco, the outlawing of ivory, the overproduction of coffee, the smuggling of diamonds, and the closing of cattle trails. When loan interest and capital payments had been settled, few countries had adequate budget revenue left to pay civil service salaries, let alone to buy chalk for schools or penicillin for hospitals. The monitoring of debt servicing was taken over by the International Monetary Fund, which insisted that each government cut the level of service it offered to its citizens and spend current revenue on debt repayment as a priority. For all the pious talk of 'aid' and 'development' mouthed by western governments, capital actually flowed from the poor world to the rich during the 1990s. The IMF had little means of monitoring the social and political consequences of its actions on the lives of local people, and seemed reluctant to take to task the western firms, politicians, diplomats and businessmen who had created the debt with often wholly inappropriate capital-intensive projects.

In the nineties life had to carry on in Central Africa and people found ingenious ways of coming to terms with insecurity. Although politicians became predators, and aid-donors behaved like loan-sharks, household routine

281

adapted to each new circumstance. Women were not only economic innovators but also the custodians of culture who ensured social renewal as political structures crumbled. One symbol of cultural survival and adaptation amidst the political transformations and the military insecurities of Central Africa was the annual carnival at Luanda in Angola. Carnivals at Luanda had been a means of coming to terms with often traumatic social, political and religious change for over three centuries. They enabled the powerless to mock the powerful in the structured security of established ritual. Early seventeenth-century carnivals had enabled Africans to come to terms with Catholicism and the canonisation of Saint Francis Xavier. Later carnivals had helped heal the traumatised victims of the slave trade by lampooning the slave masters. In the postcolonial wars carnival was an exuberant celebrating of survival against adversity, an allegorical and carefully ritualised display in which politicians could be mocked in relative safety. The ceremonial 'kings' of the rival dance groups supervised the election of wealthy carnival queens, auditioned the performances of champion drummers, and ordered costly foreign textiles to robe the dancers. Palm wine was tapped and cane-rum was distilled in anticipation of three days of blind celebration. Politicians were kept at arm's length. They would have liked the carnival to celebrate their prowess, but it did not. Instead carnival was a celebration of life in a war that seemed without end. It was a celebration of the identity in which people rejoiced, not a national identity, or even a city identity, but an identity with their neighbours and kinsfolk in the safest community they knew. It was a celebration of the limited freedom from fear which they could hold on to, a challenge to the awesome figures of authority. It was a celebration of youth in which grandmothers paraded the offspring of their daughters with pride and finery. It was a celebration of defiance before the uncomprehending bourgeoisie of a city bursting with class conflict. But above all it was a celebration of that historical tenacity and endurance which had enabled people throughout Central Africa to survive the colonial experience and live in a world beyond independence.

Sources and further reading

CHAD IN THE AGE OF THE WARLORDS

Over the last thirty years, Chad has been rather neglected by scholars. This is partly due to the civil war which drove out some of the French academics doing fieldwork in the country. The war also monopolised the attention of the few Chadian intellectuals who could have taken over their work. Given Chad's poor economy, working conditions were not favourable to scientific research.

Two general introductions to Chad's recent history are important: J. Chapelle, *Le Peuple Tchadien: ses Racines, sa Vie Quotidienne, et ses Combats*, L'Harmattan, Paris, 1980 and S. Decalo, *Historical Dictionary of Chad*, The Scarecrow Press, Metuchen, NJ, 1977.

The most comprehensive overviews of the Chad civil war are provided in two volumes by R. Buijtenhuijs, *Le Frolinat et les Révoltes Populaires du Tchad, 1965–1976*, Mouton, The Hague, 1978; and *Le Frolinat et les Guerres Civiles du Tchad (1977–1984)*, Karthala, Paris, 1987. See also S. C. Nolutshungu, *Limits of Anarchy: Intervention and State Formation in Chad*, University Press of Virginia, Charlottesville, 1996. This emphasises foreign interventions in the civil war. Other valuable sources in this field are: C. Bouquet, *Tchad: Genèse d'un Conflit*, L'Harmattan, Paris, 1982; A. Dadi, *Tchad, L'Etat Retrouvé*, L'Harmattan, Paris, 1987; and J.-P. Magnant, 'Tchad: crise de l'état ou crise de gouvernement?,' in J.-F. Médard (ed.), *Etats d'Afrique Noire: Formations, Mécanismes et Crise*, Karthala, Paris, 1991. Comprehensive studies in English have been written by V. Thompson and R. Adloff, *Conflict in Chad*, University of California Press, Berkeley, 1981, and M. P. Kelley, *A State in Disarray: Conditions of Chad's Survival*, Westview Press, Boulder CO, 1986. See also W. J. Foltz, 'Reconstructing the state of Chad' in I. W. Zartman (ed.), *Collapsed States: The Disintegration and Restoration of Legitimate Authority*, Lynne Rienner Publishers, Boulder CO, 1995. The only studies addressing the Frolinat experience at a local level are P. Doornbos, 'La révolution dérapée: la violence dans l'est du Tchad', *Politique Africaine*, 7 September 1982; and C. Pairault,

Retour au Pays d'Iro: Chronique d'un Village au Tchad, Karthala, Paris, 1994. The factionalist dimension of the civil war has been analysed very well by R. Lemarchand, 'Chad: the misadventures of the north–south dialectic', *African Studies Review* 29, 3 (September 1986). On this point see also S. Decalo, 'Chad: the roots of centre–periphery strife', *African Affairs*, 79, 317 (October 1980), and J.-L. Triaud, 'Le refus de l'état: l'exemple tchadien', *Esprit*, 100 (April 1985).

A good specialist on northern Chad is P. Hugot, 'Le vide politique du Tchad musulman', *Revue Française d'Études Politiques Africaines*, 163–164 (July–August 1979). B. Lanne is the only scholar who has paid attention to the specific experience of southern Chad during the chaotic period around 1980. See 'Le sud du Tchad dans la guerre civile (1979–1980)', *Politique Africaine*, 3 (September 1981); and 'Le sud, l'état et la révolution', *Politique Africaine*, 16 (December 1984), special issue of *Politique africaine* entirely devoted to Chadian affairs. Unfortunately, there are no studies of the survival strategies developed by civil society or, at the grass-roots level, social forces which responded to the corrosion of formal public institutions.

French interventions in Chad have been covered by two doctoral theses: N. Mouric, 'La politique tchadienne de la France sous Valéry Giscard d'Estaing (1974–1981): stratégie puissance et politique occidentale', Thèse de doctorat d'Histoire, Université Paris VII, 1989–90; and Y. Rabier, 'Politique internationale du conflit tchadien (1960–1990); guerre civile et système mondial', Thèse de doctorat en Science Politique, Paris, 1993.

Several authors have tackled the intricate problem of Libyan interferences in Chadian affairs: B. Lanne, *Tchad–Libye: la Querelle des Frontières*, Karthala, Paris, 1982. Lanne pays special attention to the Aouzou question which is also covered by A. Dadi, *Le Litige Frontalier avec la Libye: la Bande d'Aozou*, ARESAE, Paris, 1994; B. Neuberger, *Involvement, Invasion and Qadhafi's Withdrawal: Libya and Chad, 1969–1981*, Tel Aviv University Press, Tel Aviv, 1982; R. Otayek, 'La Libye face à la France au Tchad: qui perd gagne?', *Politique Africaine* 16 (December 1984); R. Lemarchand (ed.), *The Green and the Black: Qadhafi's Policies in Africa*, Indiana University Press, Bloomington IN, 1988 and J. Wright, *Libya, Chad and the Central Sahara*, Hurst, London, 1989.

The recent democratisation process has been described by R. Buijtenhuijs, *La Conférence Nationale Souveraine du Tchad: Un Essai d'Histoire Immédiate*, Karthala, Paris, 1993. Three articles are equally of interest in this field: J.-L. Triaud, 'Au Tchad: la démocratie introuvable', *Le Monde Diplomatique*, Feb. 1992; J.-P. Magnant, 'Le Tchad', in G. Conac (ed.), *L'Afrique en transition vers le pluralisme politique*, Economica, Paris, 1993; and V. Mandigui, 'Les vicissitudes de la transition démocratique tchadienne', *Revue Juridique et Politique* 49 (3 October–December 1995). For the 1996 elections, see R. Buijtenhuijs, 'Le Tchad est inclassable: le référendum constitutionnel du 31 mars 1996', *Politique africaine* 62 (June 1996) and by the same author '"On nous a volé nos voix!" Quelle démocratie pour le Tchad?', *Politique Africaine* 63 (October 1996).

For Islam in Chad there are three main sources: J.-P. Magnant (ed.), *L'Islam au Tchad*, Centre d'étude d'Afrique Noire, Bordeaux, 1992; H. Coudray, 'Chrétiens et musulmans au Tchad', *Islamochristiana* 18 (1992); and M. A. Doutoum, 'Processus de démocratisation et résurgence des sectes intégristes au Tchad (1991–1993)' in M. A. Doutoum, *Actualité Tchadienne*, 1991–1994, ARESEA and PMCT, Paris, 1994.

Chad's economy has been even less studied than its political evolution. Three sources nevertheless throw some light on the subject: G. N. Gatta, *Tchad: Guerre Civile et Desintégration de l'Etat*, Présence Africaine, Paris, 1985; *La Situation Économique et Financière au Tchad: Choix et Contraintes en Matière de Finances Publiques*, Bureau du Coordinateur Résident des Nations Unies, N'Djaména, March 1993; and *Marchés Tropicaux et Méditerranéens* 2347 (2 November 1990) which is a special issue on Chad's economic situation and performance.

Finally, one recent all-Chadian publication should be mentioned: *Tchad, 'Conflit Nord-Sud': Mythe ou Réalite?*, Sépia-Centre Culturel Al-Mouna, Paris, 1996.

CAMEROUN AND THE POLITICS OF PATRONAGE

Cameroun is, in comparison with other Central African countries, fairly well covered by scholarly work. Historians within Cameroun were mostly interested in precolonial and colonial history which seemed less controversial than contemporary studies. Given the political situation in Cameroun, political science was not prolific and most analyses of the political system were written by lawyers adopting a juridical perspective and emphasising constitutional developments. Critical assessments were published with a time-lag, such as Jean-Pierre Fogui, *L'Intégration Politique au Cameroun: Une Analyse Centre-Périphérie*, Librairie Générale de Droit et de Jurisprudence, Paris, 1990 (written in 1980), and Joseph-Marie Zang Atangana, *Les Forces Politiques au Cameroun Réunifié* 3 vols, L'Harmattan, Paris, 1990 (written in 1963). When in the 1990s it became more permissible to express critical ideas, Camerounian authors remained ironically and sadly absent from discussions since universities and publishing houses were in crisis.

The basic reference works are Mark DeLancey and Mbella Mokeba, *Historical Dictionary of the Republic of Cameroon*, 2nd edn., Scarecrow Press, Metuchen, NJ, 1990, and Kees Schilder, *State Formation, Religion and Land Tenure in Cameroon: A Bibliographical Survey*, African Studies Centre, Leiden, 1988. As a general introduction, focusing on the Ahidjo years, see Mark DeLancey, *Cameroon: Dependence and Independence*, Westview Press, Boulder, CO, 1989. Descriptive but well-informed is the work of the journalist Philippe Gaillard, *Le Cameroun* 2 vols, L'Harmattan, Paris, 1989, and also his biography of the first Cameroun president, *Ahmadou Ahidjo*, Jeune-Afrique, Paris, 1994.

Classical works on nation-building in the 1960s include Victor T. LeVine, *The Cameroons from Mandate to Independence*, University of California Press, Berkeley, 1964, and its update, *The Cameroon Federal Republic*, Cornell University

Press, Ithaca, N.Y., 1971. More theoretical works are Willard Johnson, *The Cameroon Federation*, Princeton University Press, Princeton, NJ, 1970 and a collection of articles in Ndiva Kofele-Kale (ed.), *An African Experiment in Nation Building: The Bilingual Cameroon Republic Since Reunification*, Westview Press, Boulder, CO, 1980. A brief, but encyclopaedic, description is delivered by Michel Prouzet, *Le Cameroun*, Librairie Général de Droit et de Jurisprudence, Paris, 1974, but by far the most influential work remains Jean-François Bayart, *l'État au Cameroun*, Presses de la Fondation Nationale des Sciences Politiques, Paris, 1979, which concentrates on political history and the state apparatus. Jean-François Médard, 'L'état sous-développé au Cameroun', *Année Africaine* (1977), highlights the neo-patrimonial character of Cameroun politics.

A political economy approach is adopted by Hans F. Illy, *Politik und Wirtschaft in Kamerun: Bedingungen, Ziele und Strategien der staatlichen Entwicklungspolitik*, Weltforum Verlag, Munich, 1976. Two important collections of articles in the same tradition are Michael G. Schatzberg and I. William Zartmann (eds), *The Political Economy of Cameroun*, Praeger, New York, 1986 and Peter Geehiere and Piet Konings (eds), *Conference on the Political Economy of Cameroon – Historical Perspectives, Proceedings/Contributions* 2 vols, Centre of African Studies, Leiden, 1989. These two collections cover the period up to the middle of the 1980s. A comprehensive study of the Biya years, until 1992, is Andreas Mehler, *Kamerun in der Ära Biya, Bedingungen erste Schritte und Blockaden einer demokratischen Transition*, Institut für Afrika-Kunde, Hamburg, 1993. Two issues of *Politique Africaine*, 22 (1986) and 62 (1996), contain important articles concerning Cameroun under Biya. The 1970s and 1980s are still poorly covered by scholarly work. They can also be understood through novels such as Mongo Beti, *Perpétua et l'Habitude du Malheur*, Buchet/Chastel, Paris, 1974; Bernard Nanga, *Les Chauves-Souris*, Présence Africaine, Paris, 1980, and Francis Beng Nyamnjoh, *Mind-Searching*, Kucena Damian, Awka, Nigeria, 1991. For a complete analysis of Cameroun literature see Richard Bjornson, *The African Quest for Freedom and Identity. Camerounian Writing and the National Experience*, Indiana University Press, Bloomington, IN, 1991.

Several works, some of pure hagiographic value, by Camerounians were written in the aftermath of the presidential succession from Ahidjo to Biya. The interesting account of Célestin Monga, *Cameroun. Quel avenir?*, Silex, Paris, 1986, and the sociological portrayal of the contemporary élites by Pierre Flambeau Ngayap, *Cameroun: Qui gouverne? De Ahidjo à Biya: L'Héritage et l'Enjeu*, L'Harmattan, Paris, 1983 are worth mentioning. Essays and polemics on the democratic transition of the 1990s are plentiful, but the main titles worth citing are Milton Krieger, 'Cameroun's democratic crossroads, 1990–9', *Journal of Modern African Studies* 32, 4 (1994); Maurice Kamto, 'Quelques réflexions sur la transition vers le pluralisme politique au Cameroun', in Gérard Conac (ed.), *L'Afrique en Transition vers le Pluralisme Politique*, Economica, Paris, 1993; Luc Sindjoun, 'La cour suprême, la compétition électorale et la continuité politique au Cameroun: la construction de la démocratisation passive', in *Afrique et Développement*, 19, 2 (1994); or Andreas Mehler, 'Kamerun: eine blockierte Demokratie', in Gunter Schubert and Rainer Tetzlaff (eds), *Die blockierten Demokratien der Dritten Welt*, forthcoming. The important aspect of press freedom is well summarised in Charles Manga Fombad, 'Freedom of expression in the Camerounian democratic transition', *Journal of Modern African Studies* 33, 2 (1995).

Specialised socio-anthropological literature generally has a regional focus. Outstanding studies have been published by Peter Geschiere, *Village Communities and the State: Changing Relations among the Maka of Southeastern Cameroon since the Colonial Conquest*, Kegan Paul, London, 1982, and *Sorcellerie et Politique en Afrique. La Viande des Autres*, Karthala, Paris, 1995, which deals essentially with Cameroun despite the general title. Articles on the south-west province by another social-anthropologist are to be found in Edwin Ardener, *Kingdom on Mount Cameroon: Studies in the History of the Cameroon Coast 1500–1970*, Berghahn Books, Providence, 1996. The same region is at the centre of Piet Konings, *Labour Resistance in Cameroon: Managerial Strategies and Labour Resistance in the Agro-Industrial Plantations of the Cameroon Development Corporation*, African Studies Centre, Leiden, 1993. For northern Cameroun interested readers can rely on Alain Beauvilain, *Nord-Cameroun: Crises et Peuplement* 2 vols, A. Beauvilain, Notre-Dame-de-Gravenchon, 1989, and Jean Boutrais et al., *Le Nord du Cameroun. Des hommes. Une Région*, Orstom, Paris, 1984. For the Meiganga region and the Gbaya people see Philip Burnham, *The Politics of Cultural Difference in Northern Cameroon*, Smithsonian Institution Press, Washington, D.C., 1996. There are several studies on the impact of Islam, including Kees Schilder, 'Etat et islamisation au Nord-Cameroun (1960–1982)', *Politique Africaine* 41 (1991). Another influential work on a much-discussed ethnic group by a Camerounian geographer is Jean-Louis Dongmo, *Le Dynamisme Bamiléké (Cameroun)* 2 vols, Centre d'édition et de production pour l'enseignement et la recherche, Yaoundé, 1980. A study highlighting modern forms of ethnicity is called Colletif 'Changer le Cameroun', *Le Cameroun Eclaté? Anthologie Commentée des Revendications Ethniques*, Editions C3, Yaoundé, 1992.

For economic developments and their link to politics see Nicolas van de Walle, 'The politics of non-reform in Cameroun', in *African Governance in the 1990s. Objectives, Resources, and Constraints*, Carter Center of Emory University, Atlanta; 1990, Nantang Jua, 'Cameroun: jump-starting an economic crisis', *Africa Insight* 21, 3 (1990) and Philippe Hugon, 'Sortir de la récession et préparer l'après-pétrole: le préalable politique', *Politique Africaine* 62 (1996). For a focus on state and parastatal enterprises see Paul-John Marc Tedga, *Entreprises Publiques, Etat et Crise au Cameroun*, L'Harmattan, Paris, 1990, and Nicolas van de Walle, 'The politics of public enterprise reform in Cameroun', in Barbara Grosh and Rwekaza S. Mukandala (eds), *State-Owned Enterprises in Africa*, Lynne Rienner, Boulder, CO, 1994. A sociological analysis of capitalist motivation in the Bamiléké ethos, and perceptions of success and ambition is Jean-Pierre Warnier, *L'Esprit d'Entreprise au Cameroun*, Karthala, Paris, 1993. On a wider scale, readers can find contributions to this subject in Peter Geschiere and Piet Konings (eds), *Itinéraires d'Accumulation au Cameroun*, Karthala, Paris, 1993.

The UPC uprising is best covered in Richard Joseph, *Radical Nationalism in Cameroun: Social Origins of the UPC Rebellion*, Clarendon Press, Oxford, 1977, and by Achille Mbembe, *La Naissance du Maquis dans le Sud-Cameroun (1920–60)*, Karthala, Paris, 1996, though both focus on the pre-independence period. The continuing impact of maquis ideas and the historical and mythical role of the UPC Leader, Um Nyobè, is outlined by Achille Mbembe, 'Pouvoirs des morts et langage des vivants: les errances de la mémoire nationaliste au Cameroun', *Politique Africaine* 22 (1986). For a short, clear description from the beginning to the 1990s see Abel Eyinga, *L'UPC: Une Révolution Manquée?*, Editions Chaka, Paris, 1991. Only very rarely do autobiographical approaches have the same value as Eyinga's writings. Several political autobiographies have been written since the beginning of the 1990s by former collaborators of Ahidjo, but they only explain small episodes of Cameroun history and are more revealing for what they do not tell than for their explicit thoughts.

COMPARISONS AND CONTRASTS IN EQUATORIAL AFRICA: GABON, CONGO AND THE CENTRAL AFRICAN REPUBLIC

Unstable political conditions, severe economic constraints and the rise of one-party states soon after independence all contributed to difficult research conditions in Gabon, Congo and the Central African Republic. Most published social science research is based on government documents or international agency reports and other sources available outside Central Africa. Local scholars work under extremely difficult material conditions with little support for research and publishing. For the Central African Republic, in particular, publications are thin. The coming of 'democratisation' in the 1990s did contribute to the opening up of the research environment but persistent insecurities that made travel within countries difficult continued to deter most foreign scholars from choosing to do their research in the former French Equatorial African countries. For Congo, two publications of the faculty at Marien Ngouabi University are worth noting, however: *Cahiers Congolais d'Anthropologie et d'Histoire* which publishes articles by local historians and anthropologists, and *Cahiers Congolais de l'Imaginaire* which mainly focuses on expressions of contemporary life conveyed in music and the visual arts. In Gabon, publications by local and foreign researchers appeared for several years while the *Centre Internationale de Civilisation Bantu* was active as a research centre. One publication was the journal *Muntu* which emphasised articles on history and culture. A report on the state of historical research in Gabon in 1993 and information on unpublished work available at institutions in Libreville can be found in Chris Gray, 'Who does historical research in Gabon: obstacles to the development of a scholarly tradition', *History in Africa* 21 (1994), pp.431–3.

For sources in English, the African Historical Dictionary series is a useful starting point. The bibliography and entries for Gabon are particularly comprehensive. The relevant volumes are: David E. Gardinier, *Historical Dictionary of Gabon*, Scarecrow Press, Metuchen, NJ, 2nd edn., 1994; Samuel Decalo, *Historical Dictionary of Congo*, Scarecrow Press, Metuchen, NJ, 2nd edn., 1996; and Pierre Kalck, *Historical Dictionary of the Central African Republic*, Scarecrow Press, Metuchen, NJ, 2nd edn., 1980. The bibliographical series published by Clio Press is also a good reference guide: David E. Gardinier, *Gabon*, World Bibliographical Series, no. 149, Clio Press, Oxford, 1992; Randall Fegley, *The Congo*, World Bibliographical Series, no. 162, Clio Press, Oxford, 1993; and Pierre Kalck, *The Central African Republic*, World Bibliographical Series, no. 152, Clio Press, Oxford, 1993. Also useful for Congo is the reference work with 3,400 titles compiled by Carlo Carozzi and Maurizio Tiepolo, *Congo-Brazzaville: Bibliografia Generale/Bibliographie Générale*, Edizioni Libreria Cortina, Turin, 1991. These scholars are part of an urban geography research centre based in Turin which has chosen Brazzaville for in-depth research. Roland Pourtier, *Le Gabon* 2 vols, L'Harmattan, Paris, 1989, has a comprehensive bibliography, especially on developments in the postcolonial period. Also, for general surveys, see M. Aicardi de Saint Paul, *Le Gabon: du Roi Denis à Omar Bongo*, Albatrosse, Paris, 1987; H. O. Neuhoff, *Le Gabon*, Internationes, Bonn, 1970, and James Barnes, *Gabon: Beyond the Colonial Legacy*, Westview Press, Boulder, CO, 1992. For the Central African Republic see Thomas O'Toole, *The Central African Republic: The Continent's Hidden Heart*, Westview Press, Boulder, CO, 1986.

Important journals with up-to-date information are *Africa Confidential*, *West Africa*, *Marchés Tropicaux et Méditerranéens*, *Jeune Afrique*, and *Politique Africaine*. The latter has emerged as a particularly important source in recent years, with a wide range of short articles written by specialists from several disciplines. It is particularly notable for the number of contributions by African scholars. Issues that specialise on various topics appear from time to time. For example, 31 (October 1988) focused on Congo, 43 (May 1991) featured 'Roads to democracy', and another, 61 (March 1996), focused on the state in Africa.

For early postcolonial political history, see H. Bertrand, *Le Congo: Formation Sociale et Mode de Développement Economique*, F. Maspero, Paris, 1975; John A. Ballard, 'Four states in equatorial Africa', in Gwendolen Carter (ed.), *National Unity and Regionalism in Eight African States*, Cornell University Press, Ithaca, NY, 1966, pp.321–35; Rémy Boutet, *Les Trois Glorieuses ou la Chute de Fulbert Youlou*, Editions Chaka, Dakar, 1990; and Brian Weinstein, 'Léon M'Ba: the ideology of dependence', *Genève-Afrique* 6, 1 (1967), pp.49–62. For an overview of postcolonial developments in Gabon, see also M. Aicardi de Saint-Paul, *Gabon: the Development of a Nation*, Routledge, London, 1989. On the Marxist period in Congo, see E. Wamba-Dia-Wemba, 'Attempted revolutionary politics in Congo-Brazzaville', in Peter Anyang 'Nyong (ed.), *Popular Struggle for Democracy in Africa*, The United Nations University, Tokyo, 1987. On the mobilisation of youth by the socialist party in the 1960s, see Pierre

Bonnafé, 'Une classe d'âge politique: la JMNR de la République du Congo-Brazzaville', *Cahiers d'Etudes Africaines* 8, 31 (1968), pp.327–66. Particularly striking and innovative in its analysis of the growth of political culture in Congo and Gabon after the Second World War and in the early years of independence is Florence Bernault, *Démocraties Ambiguës en Afrique Centrale: Congo-Brazzaville, Gabon, 1940–1965*, Karthala, Paris, 1996.

The National Conferences of the early 1990s were a catalyst for a considerable amount of writing concerning the conditions and process of 'democratisation'. The collection of essays *Political Reform in Francophone Africa*, Westview Press, Boulder, CO, 1997 was 'inspired' by this 'outburst of political reform' according to the co-editors, John F. Clark and David E. Gardinier. It contains useful surveys of individual countries, including chapters on Gabon, Congo and the Central African Republic. There are quite a few publications on the transition to democratic elections. These include: F. Weissman, *Election Présidentielle de 1992 au Congo: Entreprise Politique et Mobilisation Electorale*, Centre d'Etudes d'Afrique Noire, Université de Bordeaux, Bordeaux, 1993; T. Robinson, 'The National Conference phenomenon in francophone Africa', *Comparative Studies in Society and History* 36, 3 (July 1994), pp.575–610; F. Eboussi Boulaga, *Les Conférences Nationales en Afrique Noire: une Affaire à Suivre*, Karthala, Paris, 1993. For Gabon, see François Gaulme, 'Le Gabon à la recherche d'un nouvel ethos politique et social', *Politique Africaine* 43 (1991), pp.52–60, and, also by Gaulme, *Le Gabon et son Ombre*, Karthala, Paris, 1988.

The interrelationship of political change, social pressures, economic deprivation and religious belief has been the subject of some particularly interesting studies. Most concern developments in Congo where people have experienced dramatic change in the postcolonial years. The classic work of Martial Sinda, *Le Messianisme Congolais et ses Incidences Politiques*, Payot, Paris, 1972, on the rise and evolution of Matswaism is still essential reading on this topic. On religious responses to events surrounding the National Conference of 1992 in Congo, and the close relationships of religion and political culture, see the excellent article by Marc-Eric Gruénais, Florent Mouand Mbambi and Joseph Tonda, 'Messies, fétiches et lutte de pouvoirs entre les "grands hommes" du Congo démocratique', *Cahiers d'Etudes Africaines* 137, 35–1 (1995), pp.163–93; also, J. Tonda, 'Marxism et l'ombre des fétiches', *Politique Africaine* 31 (1988), pp.73–83; and the chapter on Congo in Paul Gifford (ed.), *The Christian Churches and the Democratisation of Africa*, Brill, Leiden, 1995.

The continued dominance of France in the affairs of the region and in those of francophone Africa in general is also the subject of several books and articles. These include: John Chipman, *French Power in Africa*, Blackwell, Oxford, 1989; Anton Andereggan, *France's Relationship with Subsaharan Africa*, Praeger, Westport, CN, 1994; Francis Terry McNamara, *France in Black Africa*, National Defence University, Washington, DC, 1989; Guy Martin, 'Francophone Africa in the context of franco–African relations in Africa', in John W. Harbeson and Donald Rothschild (eds), *Africa in World Politics: Post*

Cold-War Challenges, Westview Press, Boulder, CO, 2nd edn., 1995, pp.163–88. On France's continued economic and military influence, see Robin Luckman, 'French militarism in Africa', *Review of African Political Economy* 2, 5 (May 1982), pp.55–82; and Nicolas van de Walle, 'The decline of the franc zone: monetary politics in francophone Africa', *African Affairs* 90, 4 (1991), pp.383–405. An unusual and localised study of French influence in Gabon is Michael C. Reed, 'Gabon: a neocolonial enclave of enduring French interest', *Journal of Modern African Studies* 25, 2 (1987), pp.283–320. An important study of foreign economic intervention and its local impact is the classic work of Pierre-Philippe Rey, *Colonialisme, Néocolonialisme et Transition au Capitalisme: l'Exemple de la COMILOG au Congo-Brazzaville*, Maspero, Paris, 1971. For the early oil industry in Gabon, see two articles by J. Bouquerel, 'Le pétrole au Gabon', and 'Port-Gentil, centre economique du Gabon', in *Cahiers d'Outre-Mer* (April–June 1967), pp.186–197, and (July–September 1967), pp.247–274.

Compared to the quite impressive number of publications on political affairs and on foreign relations, rather less has been written for fields such as social history. Some areas of research which have been well-researched elsewhere, such as peasant movements or gender relations, have received little attention in equatorial Africa. However, a growing interest in urban life has led to several publications. The study of G. Lasserre, *Libreville: la Ville et sa Région*, Colin, Paris, 1958, is still useful. Brazzaville is particularly well-served by recent publications. Such an interest is appropriate, given that Congo is one of the most highly urbanised countries in Africa. Several books deal with the cultural life of the town after the Second World War. Two books from the mid-1990s deal with the cultural life, political culture and social formations of the town: Phyllis M. Martin, *Leisure and Society in Colonial Brazzaville*, Cambridge University Press, Cambridge, 1995, focuses on the colonial period but gives details of contemporary politicised ethnicity as well; Charles Didier Gondola's work, *Villes Miroirs: Migrations et Identités Urbaines à Kinshasa et Brazzaville, 1930–1970*, L'Harmattan, Paris, 1996, compares urbanisation and culture in Brazzaville and Kinshasa. Two other books are worth noting for their focus on fashion and music, essential elements in town life. These are by the sociologist, J.-D. Gondoulou, *Dandies à Bacongo: le Culte de l'Elégance dans la Société Congolaise Contemporaine*, L'Harmattan, Paris, 1989 and by Sylvain Bemba, *50 Ans de Musique du Congo-Zaire, 1920–1970*, Présence Africaine, Paris, 1984; and on the bars frequented by the élite, Henri Ossebi, 'Un quotidien en trompe l'oeil: bars et "nganda" à Brazzaville', *Politique Africaine* 31 (1988), pp.67–72. Still on Brazzaville, a fascinating collection of essays concerning a whole variety of subjects from popular culture to urban planning grew out of a conference on the town: *Journées d'Etudes sur Brazzaville, Actes du Colloque ORSTOM-Programme Santé et Urbanisation. Association des Géographes du Congo, 25–28 Avril 1986*, Brazzaville, Mission Française de Coopération et d'Action Culturelle, 1987.

ZAIRE: THE ANATOMY OF A FAILED STATE

For the first three decades of independence, a very extensive literature exists for Zaire, the Democratic Republic of Congo. By the later 1980s, as conditions within the country became more difficult, the rhythm of research slowed in tandem with the decline of the state. The large Zairian intellectual community struggled for survival within the country, and external scholars found it far more difficult to conduct research within Zaire.

No overall bibliography exists for the most recent period. For the first decade covered in this volume, the comprehensive bibliography compiled by Edouard Bustin, 'Congo-Kinshasa, guide bibliographique I' and 'II' in *Cahiers du CEDAF* 3 and 4 (1971), remains valuable. For subsequent events, particularly important serials are the *Cahiers du CEDAF*, and *Zaïre-Afrique*. For current information, the rapidly expanding resources of the World Wide Web deserve note; there are as well several Zaire lists on the Internet.

The 1960 'Congo crisis' gave rise to an immense literature. The most important single source is the series of yearbooks published by the *Centre de Recherche et d'Information Socio-Politiques* (CRISP) from 1959 to 1967. The most useful overall treatments of the turbulent transition and the First Republic years are Herbert Weiss, *Political Protest in the Congo*, Princeton University Press, Princeton, NJ, 1967; René Lemarchand, *Political Awakening in the Belgian Congo*, University of California Press, Berkeley, CA, 1964; Catherine Hoskins, *The Congo: A Chronology of Events, January 1960–December 1961*, Oxford University Press, London, 1962; Crawford Young, *Politics in the Congo*, Princeton University Press, Princeton, NJ, 1965, and Pierre de Vos, *La Décolonisation: Les Évènements du Congo de 1959 à 1967*, Editions ABC, Brussels, 1967.

The rebellions of 1964–65, whose lingering significance was highlighted by the eastern Kivu uprising in 1996, are exhaustively chronicled in Benoît Verhaegen, *Rébellions au Congo*, Centre de Recherche et d'Information Socio-Politiques, Brussels, 1966, 1969. See also Crawford Young, 'Rebellions and the Congo', in Robert I. Rotberg and Ali A. Mazrui (eds), *Protest and Power in Black Africa*, Oxford University Press, New York, 1970, pp.969–1011, and a recent collective reconsideration of these events by Catherine Coquery-Vidrovitch, Alain Forest and Herbert Weiss (eds), *Rébellions-Révolution au Zaïre 1963–1965* 2 vols, L'Harmattan, Paris, 1987.

The most important political figure of the First Republic was the martyred first premier, Patrice Lumumba. His role and political persona receive masterful treatment in Jean-Claude Willame, *Patrice Lumumba: la Crise Congolaise Revisité*, Karthala, Paris, 1990. Earlier works include Thomas Kanza, *The Rise and Fall of Patrice Lumumba: Conflict in the Congo*, R. Collings, London, 1982, and Jean Van Lierde, *La Pensée Politique de Patrice Lumumba*, Présence Africaine, Paris, 1963.

The crucial international dimension of the 'Congo crisis' has received extensive treatment. On the Katanga secession and its international prolongations, see Jules Gérard-Libois, *Sécession au Katanga*, Centre de Recherche et d'Information Socio-Politiques, Brussels, 1963, appearing in English translation as *Katanga Secession*, trans. Rebecca Young, University of Wisconsin Press, Madison, WI, 1966. On the United Nations' role, see Conor Cruise O'Brien, *To Katanga and Back: A UN Case History*, Hutchinson, London, 1962; Rajeshwar Dayal, *Mission for Hammarskjold: The Congo Crisis*, Princeton University Press, Princeton, NJ, 1976, and Indar Jit Rikhye, *Military Advisor to the Secretary General: U.N. Peacekeeping and the Congo Crisis*, Hurst, London, 1993. On American policy, see especially Stephen R. Weissman, *American Foreign Policy in the Congo*, Cornell University Press, Ithaca, NY, 1974; Richard D. Mahoney, *JFK: Ordeal in Africa*, Oxford University Press, New York, 1983, and Madeleine G. Kalb, *The Congo Cables: The Cold War in Africa from Eisenhower to Kennedy*, Macmillan, New York, 1982.

On the Mobutu era, a very large literature is available as well. Useful works include Crawford Young and Thomas Turner, *The Rise and Decline of the Zairian State*, University of Wisconsin Press, Madison, WI, 1985; two excellent volumes by Michael Schatzberg, *Politics and Class in Zaire: Bureaucracy, Business and Beer in Lisala*, Africana Pub. Co., New York, 1980, and *The Dialectics of Oppression in Zaire*, Indiana University Press, Bloomington, IN, 1988; Jean-Claude Willame, *Patrimonialism and Political Change in the Congo*, Stanford University Press, Stanford, CA, 1972; Jean Kestergat, *Du Congo de Lumumba au Zaire de Mobutu*, P. Legrain, Brussels, 1986; Jacques Vanderlinden (ed.), *Du Congo au Zaire 1960–1980: Essai d'un Bilan*, Centre de Recherche et d'Information Socio-Politiques, Brussels, 1980. For critical works by Zairian authors, see Cléophas Kamitatu, *La Grande Mystification du Congo-Kinshasa*, F. Maspero, Paris, 1971; Nzongola-Ntalaja (ed.), *The Crisis in Zaire: Myths and Realities*, Africa World Press, Trenton, NJ, 1986, and Monguya Mbenge (Daniel), *Histoire Secrète du Zaire*, Editions de l'Espérance, Brussels, 1977.

Useful sources which focus upon Mobutu Sese Seko himself include Sean Kelly, *America's Tyrant: The CIA and Mobutu of Zaire*, American University Press, Washington, DC, 1993; Nguza Karl-i-Bond, *Mobutu ou l'Incarnation du Mal Zairois*, R. Collings, London, 1982, and Emmanuel Dungia, *Mobutu et l'Argent du Zaire*, L'Harmattan, Paris, 1992. Corruption finds probing documentation in David J. Gould, *Bureaucratic Corruption and Underdevelopment in the Third World: The Case of Zaire*, Pergamon Press, New York, 1980. On the most recent period, useful works include Jean-Claude Willame, *L'Automne d'un Despotisme: Pouvoir, Argent et Obéissance dans le Zaire des Années Quatre-Vingt*, Karthala, Paris, 1992, and Colette Braekman, *Le Dinosaure: le Zaire de Mobutu*, Fayard, Paris, 1992.

On the economy, see Fernand Bézy et al., *Accumulation et Sous-Développement au Zaire 1960–1980*, Presses Universitaires de Louvain, Louvain-la-Neuve, 1981; Jean-Claude Willame, *Zaire: l'Epopée d'Inga: Chronique d'une Prédation Industrielle*, L'Harmattan, Paris, 1986; J. Winsome Leslie, *The World Bank and Structural Transformation in Developing Countries: The Case of Zaire*, Lynne Rienner, Boulder, CO, 1987, and Janet MacGaffey, *The Real Economy of Zaire:*

The Contribution of Smuggling and Other Unofficial Activities to National Wealth, University of Pennsylvania Press, Philadelphia, 1991.

ANGOLA: THE CHALLENGE OF STATEHOOD

Despite the abundance of literature, syntheses of Angolan history can only rely on a narrow base of original case studies. Angola has been the focus of a confrontation of words as well as of arms since the Second World War as Portuguese authors disputed history with nationalist writers, and as nationalist writers argued among themselves, while none judged it fit to encourage independent research. Politics, social history, and even historical facts, all become polemical and influence international authors. Even when ignoring the mass of deliberately biased material it is difficult for serious scholars to remain immune from the opposed reconstructions of Angolan history.

The period of late colonialism saw a notable development of research by the Portuguese on Angola. The bulk of the writing was still devoted to white settlement and the extractive economy but there was also a surge in studies on the colonised peoples although these only by colonial administrators. Nationalist writing, although short on data and high on polemic, also proliferated. Independent research by foreign academics was seriously handicapped by censorship in the colonial period and by lack of field access since independence. After 1974 the intellectual opening of Portugal led to the growth of research and eventually to renewed interest in Angola. Inside Angola, research both by Angolans and by foreigners remained limited as, unlike Frelimo in Mozambique, MPLA discouraged even sympathetic research, postponed the creation of a faculty of social science, and placed historical investigation in the hands of the party school of ideology rather than in those of a research institute. In 1984–86 Cubans and Angolans conducted a joint research project on the 'national question' but self-censorship prevented publication. Angolan academics were given little time and means for research. Some archival work was developed, but foreign academics continued to meet restriction as war prohibited access to the provinces. On the UNITA side of the national conflict the research situation was limited to partisan journalists on guided tours who were granted interviews with Savimbi.

The historiography of contemporary Angola is therefore still largely shortsighted and lacunary. Some of the texts are nevertheless illuminating, though not impartial. Academically, the *Revista International de Estudos Africanos* (Lisbon) and the journal *Lusotopie* (Bordeaux-Paris) are the main vehicles for specialist articles on Angola. Most detailed case studies on Angola are published in Portuguese, however, and only a few are listed in this guide to further reading. Others can be looked up in the bibliographies of the region cited below.

Useful syntheses include:
Thomas Collelo, *Angola: A Country Study*, USGPO, Washington, DC, 3rd edn, 1991; Conceição Neto, 'Contribuições a um debate sobre "as divisões

étnicas" em Angola', *Cadernos do Codesria*, Luanda, 2 (November 1991), pp.17–35; René Pélissier, 'Angola, Mozambique: des guerres interminables et leurs facteurs internes', *Hérodote* 46 (1987), pp.83–107; David Birmingham, *Frontline Nationalism in Angola and Mozambique*, James Currey, London, 1992; Susan H. Broadhead, *Historical Dictionary of Angola*, Scarecrow Press, Metuchen, NJ, 2nd edn., 1992.

Basic studies on the colonial period include:
René Pélissier, *La Colonie du Minotaure: Nationalisme et Révoltes en Angola, 1926–1961*, Ed. Pélissier, Orgeval, 1978; Franz-Wilhelm Heimer, *Der Entkolonisierungskonflikt in Angola*, Weltforum Verlag, Munich, 1969; Christine Messiant, '1961. l'Angola colonial, histoire et société, les prémisses du mouvement nationaliste', Doctoral thesis in sociology, EHESS, Paris, 1983; Gerald Bender, *Angola Under the Portuguese: the Myth and the Reality*, Heinemann, London, 1978; Gervase Clarence-Smith, *The Third Portuguese Empire, 1825–1975: a Study in Economic Imperialism*, Manchester University Press, Manchester, 1985; and 'Capital accumulation and class formation in Angola', in David Birmingham and Phyllis M. Martin (eds), *History of Central Africa*, Longman, Harlow, 1983, Vol.2, pp.163–99; Perry Anderson, *Le Portugal et la Fin de l'Ultra-Colonialisme*, Maspero, Paris, 1963; Henrique Guerra, *Angola. Estrutura Económica e Classes Sociais. Os Últimos Anos do Colonialismo Português em Angola*, Edições 70, Lisbon, 4th edn., 1979.

Case studies include:
Franz-Wilhelm Heimer (ed.), *Social Change in Angola*, Weltforum Verlag, Munich, 1973; Christine Messiant, 'Luanda 1945–1961: colonisés, société coloniale et engagement nationaliste', in M. Cahen (ed.), *Bourgs et Villes en Afrique Lusophone*, L'Harmattan, Paris, 1989, pp.125–99; Fernando A. Mourão, 'Continuidades e descontinuidades de um processo colonial através de uma leitura de Luanda', Thèse de livre docencia, University of São Paulo, 1992, forthcoming as a book.

On the nationalist movement and the colonial war the key texts include:
John Marcum, *The Angolan Revolution*, Vol.1: *The Anatomy of an Explosion, 1950–1962*, MIT Press, Cambridge, 1969, and Vol.2: *Exile Politics and Guerrilla Warfare, 1962–1976*, MIT Press, Cambridge, 1978. A new work on the MPLA is by J.-M. Mabeko Tali, 'Dissidences et pouvoir d'État: le MPLA face à lui-même (1962–1977)', Doctoral thesis, EHESS, Paris, 1996, which includes new documentation and gives an inside view of MPLA. There is also the work of Basil Davidson, *In the Eye of the Storm: Angola's People*, Longman, London, 1972; and the novel by Pepetela, *Mayombe*, Heinemann, Oxford, 1996.

On the *first years of independence and the political fermentation* the best sources are:
Franz-Wilhelm Heimer, *The Decolonisation Conflict in Angola, 1974–76*, IUHEI, Geneva, 1979; W. G. Clarence-Smith, 'Class structure and class struggles in

Angola in the 1970s', *Journal of Southern African Studies* 7, 1 (1980), review article, pp.109–26, Claude Gabriel, *Angola: Le Tournant Africain*, La Brèche, Paris, 1978; Michel Cahen, 'Syndicalisme urbain, luttes ouvrières et questions ethniques à Luanda: 1974–1977/1981', in M. Cahen, *Bourgs et Villes en Afrique Lusophone*, L'Harmattan, Paris, 1989, pp.200–69; R. Kapuscinski, *Another Day of Life*, Viking, New York, 1987, is a haunting eyewitness account of that period.

On *international intervention and policy*:
John Stockwell, *In Search of Enemies: a CIA Story*, Norton, New York, 1978; Pedro Pezarat Correia, *Descolonização de Angola: a Joia da Coroa do Império Português*, Editorial Inquérito, Lisbon, 1978; William Minter, *Apartheid's Contras: an Inquiry into the Roots of War in Angola and Mozambique*, Zed Press, London, 1994; Chester Crocker, *High Noon in Southern Africa: Making Peace in a Rough Environment*, Norton, New York, 1992.

On the *consolidation of MPLA*:
M. R. Baghavan, *Angola's Political Economy, 1975–1985*, Scandinavian Institute of African Studies, Uppsala, 1986; Michael Wolfers and Jane Bergerol, *Angola in the Frontline*, Zed Press, London, 1983, both Marxist sympathisers; David Birmingham, 'The twenty-seventh of May: an historical note on Angola's 1977 coup', *African Affairs* 77, 309 (1978), pp.554–64.

On *UNITA*:
Fred Bridgland, *Jonas Savimbi: a Key to Africa*, Mainstream, Edinburgh, 1986; Linda Heywood, 'Unita and ethnic nationalism in Angola', *Journal of Modern African Studies* 27, 1 (1989), pp.47–66; Sousa Jamba, *Patriots*, Viking, New York, 1990.

On the *economy*:
Tony Hodges, *Angola to the 1990s: the Potential for Recovery*, Economist Intelligence Unit, London, 1987, and *Angola to 2000: Prospects for Recovery*, Economist Intelligence Unit, London, 1993.

On the *evolution of the Angolan regime and society and the first peace process*:
Christine Messiant, 'Angola, les voies de l'ethnisation et de la décomposition. I. De la guerre à la paix (1975–1991): le conflit armé, les interventions internationales et le peuple angolais', *Lusotopie* (1994), pp.155–210, and 'Angola, les voies de l'ethnisation et de la décomposition. II. Transition à la démocratie ou marche à la guerre? L'épanouissement de deux partis armés (mai 1991–octobre 1992)', *Lusotopie* (1995), pp.181–212; Africa Watch, *Violations of the Laws of War by Both Sides*, Africa Watch, London, 1989; Africa Watch, *Angola: Civilians Devastated by 15-Year War*, Africa Watch, London, 1991; David Sogge (ed.), *Sustainable Peace: Angola's Recovery*, SARDC, Harare,

1992; J.-M. Mabeko Tali, 'La "chasse aux Zairois" à Luanda', *Politique Africaine* 57 (March 1995), pp.71–85; Margaret J. Anstee, *Orphans of the Cold War*, Macmillan, Basingstoke, 1996; 'Democratization in Angola', Seminar Proceedings, African Studies Centre, Leiden, 1993; Christine Messiant, 'Le retour à la guerre ou l'inavouable faillite d'une intervention internationale', *Afrique Politique*, Karthala, Paris, CEAN, Bordeaux, 1994.

On the *war of 1992–94*:
Fátima Roque, *Angola. Em Nome da Esperança. O Meu Depoimento*, Bertrand Editora, Venda Nova, 1993 (a UNITA version); Karl Maier, *Angola: Promises and Lies*, SERIF, London, 1996; 'L'Angola dans la guerre', special issue of *Politique Africaine* 57 (March 1995).

Since the *Lusaka Protocol*:
Human Rights Watch, *Angola: Arms Trade and Violations of the Laws of War Since the 1992 Elections*, HRW, New York, 1994; Human Rights Watch, *Angola: Between War and Peace, Arms Trade and Human Rights Abuses Since the Lusaka Protocol*, HRW, London, 1996.

On *churches and religion*:
Lawrence Henderson, *Angola: Five Centuries of Conflict*, Cornell University Press, Ithaca, NY, 1979; Emílio J. M. Carvalho, *A Igreja Africana no Centro da sua História*, ed. do autor, Luanda, 1995.

On *Cabinda*:
Phyllis M. Martin, 'The Cabinda connection', *African Affairs* 76 (1977), pp.47–59; João Baptista Lukombo, 'Uma problemática de sociologia política à luz de traçados fronteiriços', *Africana*, 15 (1995), pp.73–85.

EXPLOITATION AND NEGLECT: RURAL PRODUCERS AND THE STATE IN MALAWI AND ZAMBIA

Anyone wishing to trace the fortunes of rural postcolonial Zambia and Malawi must confront the problem of 'grey literature'. Much of the empirical data on rural households, their land-holdings and sources of income has been collected by a multitude of donor agencies, non-governmental organisations, and, increasingly, private consultants acting on behalf of the donors. Unfortunately, only a proportion of this work is ever written up in accessible form and made available to researchers in the countries concerned. The following brief guide to further reading refers to some of this 'grey literature', as well as to published sources.

The suspicion with which the Banda regime in Malawi regarded the activity of academics, particularly that of 'social scientists', left its mark. In comparison with the large volume of social science research produced in Zambia in the 1970s and 1980s, that on social and economic conditions in rural Malawi in the same period was limited, and often carried out in difficult circumstances. The change of government in Malawi brought a more positive attitude to the role of the researcher. In both Malawi and Zambia, however, economic crisis and budget cuts have had profound effects on the institutions of higher education, making it increasingly difficult for local scholars to fund and pursue their research.

There is a relatively rich literature on agricultural policy in Zambia in the first decade or so after independence. Early accounts include C. Lombard and A. H. C. Tweedie, *Agriculture in Zambia since Independence*, National Educational Company of Zambia, Lusaka, 1972; D. Dodge, *Agricultural Policy and Performance in Zambia*, Institute for International Studies, Berkeley, 1977, and the important work of Charles Elliott, including C. Elliott, 'Equity and growth: an unresolved conflict in Zambian development' in D. Ghai and S. Radwan (eds), *Agrarian Policies and Rural Poverty in Africa*, ILO, Geneva, 1983 and R. Roberta and C. Elliott, 'Constraints on agriculture' in C. Elliott (ed.), *Constraints on the Economic Development of Zambia*, Oxford University Press, London, 1971, pp.269–99. More recent, retrospective analyses of this period can be found in A. P. Wood and E. Shula, 'The state and agriculture in Zambia' in T. Mkandawire and N. Bourenane (eds), *The State and Agriculture in Africa*, CODESRIA, London, 1987, pp.272–317, and in S. Berry, *No Condition is Permanent: the Social Dynamics of Agrarian Change in Sub-Saharan Africa*, University of Wisconsin Press, Madison, WI, 1993. For early studies of the nature of rural poverty in post-independent Zambia see D. Honeybone and A. Marter (eds), *Poverty and Wealth in Rural Zambia*, Institute of African Studies, University of Zambia, Lusaka, 1979.

The politics of agricultural policy in the Banda regime in Malawi are analysed in J. Kydd and R. Christiansen, 'Structural change in Malawi since independence: consequences of a strategy based on large-scale agriculture', *World Development*, 10, 5 (1982), pp.355–75; J. Kydd, 'Malawi in the 1970s: development policies and economic change' in *Malawi: an Alternative Pattern of Development*, (Centre of African Studies, University of Edinburgh, Seminar Proceedings No.25, 1984), pp.293–381; R. Laslett, 'An account of Malawi's economy and economic policy in the 1970s' in *Malawi: an Alternative Pattern of Development*, pp.381–407; G. C. Z. Mhone, 'Agricultural and food policy in Malawi: a review', in T. Mkandawire and N. Bourenane (eds), *The State and Agriculture in Africa*, CODESRIA, London, 1987, pp.59–87.

For the consequences of structural adjustment policies and agricultural reform in Malawi in the 1980s and 1990s see D. J. Sahn, J. Arulpragasam and L. Merrid, *Policy Reform and Poverty in Malawi*, Cornell Food and Nutrition Policy Program, Ithaca, NY, Monograph No.7, 1991; J. Harrigan, 'Malawi: the impact of pricing policy on smallholder agriculture, 1971–1988', *Development Policy Review* 6 (1988), pp.415–33; B. Kaluwa, 'Malawi: private traders in food marketing' in J. Benyon (ed.), *Market Liberalisation in Eastern and Southern Africa*, Food Studies Group, Oxford, Working Paper No.6, 1992, pp.29–30;

K. M. Mtawale, 'Trade, price and market reform in Malawi', *Food Policy*, 18 (1993), pp.300–07; V. Scarborough, *Agricultural Policy Reforms under Structural Adjustment in Malawi*, Agricultural Development Unit, Wye College, Occasional Paper No.12, 1990.

The expansion of Malawi's tobacco estates in the 1970s and 1980s and the central role of tenant production are examined in S. Jaffee, R. Mkandawire and S. Bertoli, *The Migrant Smallholders: Tenant and Labourer Participation, Remuneration and Social Welfare within Malawi's Expanding Estate Sector*, IDA/Bunda College/US AID, Binghampton, 1991; R. Mkandawire, S. Jaffee and S. Bertoli, *Beyond Dualism: the Changing Face of the Leasehold Estate Sub-Sector of Malawi*, IDA/Bunda College/US AID, Binghampton, 1990; D. Sahn and J. Arulpragasam, *Development Through Dualism?: Land Tenure Policy and Poverty in Malawi*, Cornell Food and Nutrition Policy Program, Ithaca NY, Working Paper No.9, 1991; M. Vaughan and R. Mkandawire, *Report on Recent Developments in the Estate Sub-Sector of Malawi*, Government of Malawi and ODA, 1991; M. Nyanda, *The Labour Market in Malawi's Estate Sub-Sector*, Centre for Social Research, University of Malawi, Zomba, 1989.

For the debate on the relationship between the development of maize cash-cropping and prevalence of child malnutrition in rural Zambia see H. L. Moore and M. Vaughan, *Cutting Down Trees: Gender, Nutrition and Agricultural Change in the Northern Province of Zambia, 1890–1990*, James Currey, London, 1994, chapter 7; B. Sharpe, 'Nutrition and the commercialisation of agriculture in Northern Province' in A. P. Wood et al. (eds), *The Dynamics of Agricultural Policy and Reform in Zambia*, Iowa University Press, Ames, 1990, pp.583–603; S. Kumar, *Maize Policies and Nutrition in Zambia: a Case Study in Eastern Province*, IFPRI/NFNC/RDSB Project, Lusaka, 1985; C. Siandawazi, *Household Food Security and Nutrition in Zambia*, Institute of African Studies, University of Zambia, Lusaka, Working Paper No.3, 1992. The essentially extractive nature of much 1980s maize cash-cropping is discussed in L. M. Malambo, *Rural Food Security in Zambia*, Studien zur Integrierten Landlichen Entwicklung, Hamburg, 1988.

Views differ on the impact of refugees on the local economies of Malawi: A. Callamard, 'Refugees and local hosts: a study of trading interactions between Mozambican refugees and Malawian villagers in the district of Mwanza', *Journal of Refugee Studies*, 7 (1994), pp.39–61; L. Long et al., *The Local Impact of Mozambican Refugees in Malawi*, Study prepared for the US Embassy and US AID, Malawi, 1991; K. Wilson et al., *Food Provisioning amongst Mozambican Refugees in Malawi*, Report for the World Food Programme, Malawi, 1989.

Since the mid-1980s increasing numbers of Malawians and Zambians have fallen victim to HIV/AIDS. Both countries have simultaneously experienced a decline in health services due to budget cuts. See W. C. Chirwa, 'Malawian migrant labour and the politics of HIV/AIDS, 1985 to 1993' in J. Crush and W. James (eds), *Crossing Boundaries: Mine Migrancy in a Democratic South Africa*, IDASA, Cape Town, 1995; Y. Sliep, 'Malawi after Banda: building new bridges to the community', *AIDS Analysis Africa*, 5, 1 (1995) p.4; B. Schoepf,

'Women, AIDS and economic crisis in Central Africa', *Canadian Journal of African Studies*, 22, 3 (1988), pp.625–44. For continuities between community responses to the AIDS epidemic and the phenomenon of anti-witchcraft movements in Malawi and Zambia see P. Probst, 'The hybridity of Mchape', Paper presented at the 11th Satterwaite Colloquium on African Ritual and Religion, April 1996.

ZIMBABWE AND THE LONG SEARCH FOR INDEPENDENCE

Students of Zimbabwe are fortunate in possessing one of the best African country bibliographies, Deborah Potts' *Zimbabwe*, in the World Bibliographical Series, Clio Press, Oxford, 1993. Potts' bibliography is up-to-date, contains a select list of unpublished theses and dissertations, and has entries for History, Population, Religion, Social Conditions, Politics, Economy, Land, Finance, Media and many more.

There are two significant collections for the nationalist period and for the guerrilla war. One is Marion Doro's *Rhodesia/Zimbabwe. A Bibliographic Guide to the Nationalist Period*, G. K. Hall, Boston, 1984. Another is Goswin Baumhogger's six volume *The Struggle for Independence. Documents on the Recent Development of Zimbabwe (1975–1980)*, Institute of African Studies, Hamburg, 1984.

Much of the best research on Zimbabwe is represented by articles in the *Journal of Southern African Studies*, Carfax, Abingdon. Three special journal issues give testimony to the strength of Zimbabwean studies in a variety of fields. *Africa* published a special issue on Zimbabwe in 1983; this was also issued as a book, J. D. Y. Peel and T. O. Ranger (eds), *Past and Present in Zimbabwe*, Manchester University Press, Manchester, 1983. There has been a special 'Zimbabwe' issue of *Environment and History*, 1, 3 (October 1995). Most recent is the special issue on 'Religion in contemporary Zimbabwe' in the *Journal of Religion in Africa*, XXV, Fasc. 3 (August 1995).

There is no adequate general history of Zimbabwe. As its title suggests, Robert Blake's *A History of Rhodesia*, Eyre Methuen, London, 1977, is a study of white rule in Zimbabwe and ends with the Internal Settlement. David Beach's *The Shona and their Neighbours*, Blackwell, Oxford, 1994, largely deals with precolonial history but has a final chapter of twenty pages on 'Conquest, change and challenge, 1890–1990'. There is currently no account available of the experience of Ndebele-speakers over the last hundred years. Anthony Verrier's *The Road to Zimbabwe, 1890–1980*, Cape, London, 1986, is essentially an account of Britain's dealings with Rhodesia. Martin Meredith's *The Past is Another Country. Rhodesia, 1890 to 1979*, Deutsch, London, 1979, focuses on the African nationalist movements and the guerrilla war. So, too, does Canaan Banana (ed.), *Turmoil and Tenacity: Zimbabwe, 1890–1990*, College Press, Harare, 1989, though this also includes a valuable section on the first decade of Zimbabwe's independence.

Accounts of UDI, again largely from a British perspective, are James Barber, *Rhodesia. The Road to Rebellion*, Oxford University Press, Oxford, 1967; R. C. Good, *U.D.I. The International Politics of the Rhodesian Rebellion*, Faber and Faber, London, 1973; Elaine Windrich, *Britain and the Politics of Rhodesian Independence*, Croom Helm, London, 1978; Kenneth Young, *Rhodesia and Independence*, Eyre and Spottiswoode, London, 1967. The final settlement at Lancaster House is discussed in James Barber, et al., *From Rhodesia to Zimbabwe. Behind and Beyond Lancaster House*, Cass, London, 1980; J. Davidow, *A Peace in Southern Africa. The Lancaster House Conference on Rhodesia, 1979*, Westview Press, Boulder, CO, 1984; H. Wiseman and A. M. Taylor. *From Rhodesia to Zimbabwe. The Politics of Transition*, Pergamon, Oxford, 1981.

There are two autobiographies by nationalist leaders, Joshua Nkomo's *Nkomo. The Story of My Life*, Methuen, London, 1984, and Abel Muzorewa's *Rise Up and Walk*, Evans, London, 1978. Robert Mugabe has not published a book but a collection of his speeches is available, N. M. Shamuyarira and C. M. B. Utete (eds), *Our War of Liberation*, Mambo, Gweru, 1983. A controversial account of the death by bomb of ZANU's chairman, Herbert Chitepo, in March 1975, is David Martin and Phyllis Johnson, *The Chitepo Assassination*, ZPH, Harare, 1985. There have been few accounts by guerrillas or party activists. One exception is Andrew Nyathi, *Tomorrow is Built Today*, Anvil, Harare, 1990. *The Organiser. Story of Temba Moyo*, LSM Press, Richmond, 1974, is an account of an urban ZAPU activist who becomes a guerrilla. 'Temba Moyo' is in reality Dumiso Dabengwa, currently minister of home affairs. Two fascinating accounts by white Zimbabweans sympathetic to the nationalist cause are Judith Todd, *The Right to Say No*, Sidgwick and Jackson, London, 1972, and Patricia Chater, *Caught in the Crossfire*, ZPH, Harare, 1985. Two memoirs by whites who served in the Security Forces are Bruce Moore-King, *White Man Black War*, Baobab, Harare, 1988, and Peter Godwin, *Mukiwa*, Picador, London, 1996.

There is a large literature on the guerrilla war. Two recent edited assessments of the war and its consequences are Ngwabi Bhebe and Terence Ranger (eds), *Soldiers in Zimbabwe's Liberation War*, James Currey, London, 1995, and *Society in Zimbabwe's Liberation War*, James Currey, London, 1996. These volumes have been hailed by Zimbabwean reviewers as the first to give a balanced account of the war and to begin to explore its secret history. An account of the war from a ZANU perspective is David Martin and Phyllis Johnson, *The Struggle for Zimbabwe. The Chimurenga War*, ZPH, Harare, 1981. Military histories of the war are P. Moorcraft and P. McLaughlin, *Chimurenga: the War in Rhodesia, 1965–1980*, Galago, Alberton, 1985, and J. K. Cilliers, *Counter-Insurgency in Rhodesia*, Croom Helm, London, 1985. Accounts of Rhodesian Intelligence tactics during the war are H. Ellert, *Rhodesian Front War*, Mambo, Gweru, 1989, and K. Flower, *Serving Secretly: An Intelligence Chief on Record*, Murray, London, 1987.

Several books explore the experience of particular rural areas of Zimbabwe during the war. David Lan's *Guns and Rain: Guerrillas and Spirit Mediums in*

Zimbabwe, James Currey, London, 1985, deals with the war in the Dande Valley of north-east Zimbabwe; Terence Ranger's *Peasant Consciousness and Guerrilla War in Zimbabwe*, James Currey, London, 1985, focuses on Makoni District in eastern Zimbabwe. Norma Kriger's *Zimbabwe's Guerrilla War: Peasant Voices*, Cambridge University Press, Cambridge, 1992, which is critical of both Lan's and Ranger's interpretations, draws its data from Mutoko district in the north-east; Janice McLaughlin's *On The Frontline. Catholic Missions in Zimbabwe's Liberation War*, Baobab, Harare, 1996, also deals with eastern Zimbabwe and hence with ZANLA. A rare and very important study of experience of both the 1970s and 1980s in south-western Zimbabwe is Richard Werbner, *Tears of the Dead*, Edinburgh University Press, Edinburgh, 1991. Ngwabi Bhebe's *ZAPU and ZANU Guerrilla Warfare and the Evangelical Lutheran Church in Zimbabwe*, Mambo, Gweru, 1997, presents the first comparative assessment of ZIPRA and ZANLA and also the first account of the war in the Midlands. A valuable edited collection of testimonies by Zimbabwean women of their experiences during the war is Irene Staunton, *Mothers of the Revolution*, Baobab, Harare, 1990.

General accounts of white Rhodesian experiences in the war are David Caute, *Under the Skin: The Death of White Rhodesia*, Penguin, London, 1983 and P. Godwin and I. Hancock, *Rhodesians Never Die*, Oxford University Press, Oxford, 1993.

Accounts of relations between the churches and the Rhodesian and Zimbabwean states are Ian Linden, *The Catholic Church and the Struggle for Zimbabwe*, Longman, Harlow, 1980 and Carl Hallencreutz and Ambrose Moyo (eds), *Church and State in Zimbabwe*, Mambo, Gweru, 1988.

Significant treatments of the politics and economics of Mugabe's Zimbabwe are: Victor de Waal, *The Politics of Reconciliation. Zimbabwe's First Decade*, Hurst, London, 1990; John Hatchard, *Individual Freedoms and State Security: The Case of Zimbabwe*, Baobab, Harare, 1993; Jeffrey Herbst, *State Politics in Zimbabwe*, University of Zimbabwe, Harare, 1990; Ibbo Mandaza (ed.), *Zimbabwe. The Political Economy of Transition, 1980–1986*, CODESRIA, Dakar, 1986; Ibbo Mandaza and Lloyd Sachikonye, *The One-Party State and Democracy. The Zimbabwe Debate*, Sapes, Harare, 1991; Jonathan Moyo, *Voting for Democracy. Electoral Politics in Zimbabwe*, University of Zimbabwe, Harare, 1992; Colin Stoneman (ed.), *Zimbabwe's Inheritance*, Macmillan, London, 1981; Colin Stoneman (ed.), *Zimbabwe's Prospects*, Macmillan, London, 1988.

The continuity of agrarian expertise is documented in M. Drinkwater, *The State and Agrarian Change in Zimbabwe's Communal Areas*, Macmillan, London, 1991. The lives of women in the Communal Areas are fascinatingly illustrated in Ilse Noy, *The Art of the Weya Women*, Baobab, Harare, 1992. Women's experience in town is described in Terri Barnes and Everjoyce Win, *To Live a Better Life*, Baobab, Harare, 1992. Two important books on children are Pamela Reynolds, *Dance Civet Cat: Child Labour in the Zambezi Valley*, Baobab, Harare, 1991, and Pamela Reynolds, *Traditional Healers and Childhood in Zimbabwe*, Ohio University Press, Athens, 1996.

MOZAMBIQUE: A TAPESTRY OF CONFLICT

Lusophone and Francophone literature

Mozambican researchers have risen to the high standard set by Eduardo Mondlane. A generation of scholars, largely trained since independence, have developed an impressive body of scholarship on this historical period. Most of their work is published in Portuguese and is not widely available outside Mozambique. Since the emphasis here is on English-language literature, these works are not generally cited throughout the text, but they should be highlighted. The periodicals, monographs and collaborative essays published by the faculty of letters and associated research centres, archives and libraries of the Universidade Eduardo Mondlane contain much of the work produced by Mozambican historians and research scholars. These works reveal the lively spirit of inquiry that survived despite difficult conditions and the tragic deaths of successive research directors Ruth First and Aquino Bragança.

Arquivo Histórico de Moçambique publishes *Arquivo: Boletim do Arquivo Histórico de Moçambique* (Vol.1, 1987) and the important *Estudos* series, which includes excellent studies on the liberation struggle in Tete and Cabo Delgado. The Department of History published *História de Moçambique, Vol.3 – Moçambique no Auge do Colonialismo, 1930–1961*, Universidade Eduardo Mondlane, Maputo, 1993 and *Cadernos de História* (Vol.1, 1985). The Centro de Estudos Africanos publishes several periodicals including *Estudos Moçambicanos* (Vol.1, 1980) and *Boletim Informativo da Oficina de História: Não vamos Esquecer!* (Vol.1, 1986) as well as occasional monographs, joint studies and edited collections such as *Moçambique: 16 Anos de Historiografia: Focos, Problemas, Metodologias, Desafios para a Década de 90*, edited by Alexandrino José and Paula Maria Meneses, Colecção Painel Moçambicano, Maputo, 1992. The Arquivo do Património Cultural (ARPAC), a branch of the Ministry of Culture and Youth, has also published collections of documents and occasional papers.

The bibliographic survey compiled by Colin Darch with the assistance of Calisto Pacheleke, *Mozambique*, Clio Press, Oxford, 1987 provides an excellent overview of the national and foreign-produced literature up to the mid-eighties. David Hedges, who coordinated the third volume of *História de Moçambique*, will soon publish a monograph in both English and Portuguese covering this thirty-year period in full detail and historical depth. Finally, at least two electronic publications provide important information on Mozambique: NOTMOC – Notícias de Moçambique – a subscriber news service available from notmoc@oceano.uem.mz and the *Internet Journal of African Studies* available from http://www.brad.ac.uk/research/ijas.

French and Portuguese literature from Europe is also important and incompletely cited here. Edições Afrontamento in Oporto regularly publishes literature, documents, historical studies and translations of interest to the history of Mozambique, as does the Lisbon-based scholarly journal *Revista Internacional de Estudos Africanos*, edited by Jill R. Dias. Fernando Jorge Cardoso's recent

303

Gestão e Desenvolvimento Rural: Moçambique no Contexto da África Sub-Sahariana, Fim de Século, Lisbon, 1995 provides useful and extensive detail. João Paulo Guerra's *Memória das Guerras Coloniais*, Afrontamento, Porto, 1994, is more manageable than José Freire Antúnes' massive *Guerras em Africa*, Círculo dos Leitores, Lisbon, 1995.

Francophone scholarship on Mozambique has emerged regularly in *Lusotopie: Enjeux Contemporains dans les Espaces Lusophones*, Centre d'Études d'Afrique Noire, Talenca, *Afrique Contemporaine* and *Politique Africaine*, esp. 29, (March 1988). The first issue of *Lusotopie*, coordinated by Michel Cahen, appeared in 1994. Two francophone works in particular have shaped scholarly discourse on Mozambique: Michel Cahen's *Mozambique: La Révolution Implosée*, L'Harmattan, Paris, 1987, and Christian Geffray's *La Cause des Armes aux Mozambique: Anthropologie d'une Guerre Civile*, Karthala, Paris, 1990. Cahen's analysis and bibliographic survey of relations between Portugal and Mozambique, 1965–85, published in *Afrique Contemporaine* 137 (1986) are also important. Gervase Clarence-Smith's article, 'The roots of the Mozambican counter-revolution', *Southern African Review of Books (SARoB)* (April/May 1989) pp.7–10, reviewing both Cahen and Geffray's articles in *Politique Africaine*, triggered a vigorous exchange in subsequent issues of *SARoB*. The conversation was picked up in *Southern Africa Report (SAR)*, published by Bridgette O'Laughlin in Toronto.

Anglophone literature

English-language historical overviews with important coverage of this period include: Landeg White and Leroy Vail, *Capitalism and Colonialism in Mozambique: A Study of Quelimane District*, University of Minnesota, Minneapolis, 1980; Malyn Newitt, *A History of Mozambique*, Indiana University Press, Bloomington, IN, 1995; Allen Isaacman and Barbara Isaacman, *Mozambique: From Colonialism to Revolution, 1900–1982*, Westview Press, Boulder, CO, 1983; W. G. Clarence-Smith, *The Third Portuguese Empire*, Manchester University Press, Manchester, 1985. David Birmingham's *Frontline Nationalism in Angola and Mozambique*, Africa World Press, Trenton, NJ, 1992 most closely parallels the period covered by this essay. *Southern Africa Report* has published a steady run of important papers on Mozambique from its inception to the present, as illustrated by M. Anne Pitcher's essay, 'Chiefs, companies and cotton: observations from rural Nampula', *SAR* 12, 1 (Nov. 1996), pp.26–30.

The development and experience of the armed struggle (1965–74) is detailed from a variety of perspectives in the following works: Eduardo Mondlane, *The Struggle for Mozambique* (introduced by John Saul, biographical sketch by Herbert Shore), Zed Press, London, 1983; Thomas Henriksen, *Revolution and Counterrevolution: Mozambique's War of Independence, 1964–1974*, Greenwood Press, Westport, CN, 1983; Edward A. Alpers, 'The role of culture in the liberation of Mozambique', *Ufahamu* 12, 3 (1983), pp.143–87; John Paul, *Mozambique: Memoirs of a Revolution*, Penguin, London, 1975; Adrian

Hastings, *Wiriyamo*, Orbis, New York, 1974; 'Torture, massacre and destruction in Mozambique', *Objective: Justice; Quarterly Magazine Covering United Nations Activity Against Apartheid, Racial Discrimination and Colonialism*, Special Supplement, 1 (Sept. 1973).

Academic surveys of this period include Barry Munslow, *Mozambique: The Revolution and its Origins*, Longman, Harlow, 1983; Edward A. Alpers, 'The struggle for socialism in Mozambique, 1960–1972', in C. G. Rosberg and T. M. Callaghy (eds), *Socialism in Sub-Saharan Africa: a New Assessment*, Berkeley Institute of International Studies, 1979 pp.267–95; Walter C. Opello Jr., 'Pluralism and elite conflict in an independence movement: FRELIMO in the 1960s', 2, 1 (Oct. 1975) pp.66–82. The following are collections of speeches, documents and guides with limited introductions and overviews: Aquino de Bragança and Immanuel Wallerstein (eds), *The African Liberation Reader* 3 vols, Zed Press, London, 1982; Ronald H. Chilcote, *Emerging Nationalism in Portuguese Africa: A Bibliography of Documentary Ephemera through 1965*, Hoover Institution, Stanford, 1969; and Chilcote, *Emerging Nationalism in Portuguese Africa: Documents*, Hoover Institution, Stanford, 1972: Samora Machel, *Mozambique: Sowing the Seeds of Revolution*, MAGIC, London, 1975.

Ndabaningi Sithole's treatment is distinguished for its insight and irony, *Frelimo Militant: The Story of Ingwane from Mozambique, an Ordinary, yet Extraordinary, Man, Awakened* . . . Transafrica, Nairobi, 1977. By the early eighties the literature began to reflect the deepening crisis in Mozambique: John Saul (ed.), *A Difficult Road: The Transition to Socialism in Mozambique*, Monthly Review Press, New York, 1985; Stephanie Urdang, *And Still They Dance: Women, Destabilization and the Struggle for Change in Mozambique*, Monthly Review Press, New York, 1989; Bertil Egerö, *Mozambique: A Dream Undone: The Political Economy of Democracy, 1975–1984*, Scandinavian Institute of African Studies, Uppsala, 1990; Iain Christie, *Machel of Mozambique*, Zimbabwe Publishing House, Harare, 1988.

English-language literature on agriculture, land and the privatisation controversy includes: Merle Bowen, 'Peasant agriculture in Mozambique: the case of Chokwe, Gaza province', *Canadian Journal of African Studies*, 23, 3 (1989), pp.355–80, and 'Beyond reform: adjustment and political power in contemporary Mozambique', in *Journal of Modern African Studies*, 30, 2 (1992), pp.25–79; Otto Roesch, 'Rural Mozambique since the Frelimo Party Fourth Congress; the situation in the Baixo Limpopo', in *Review of African Political Economy*, 41 (Sept. 1988), pp.73–91; 'Renamo and the peasantry in Southern Mozambique: a view from Gaza', in *Canadian Journal of African Studies*, 26, 3 (1992); Kenneth Hermele, *Land Struggles and Social Differentiation in Southern Mozambique: A Case Study of the Chokwe, Limpopo 1950–1987*, Scandinavian Institute of African Studies, Uppsala, 1988; M. Anne Pitcher, 'Conflict and cooperation: gendered roles and responsibilities within cotton households in northern Mozambique', *African Studies Review (ASR)* 39, 3 (Dec. 1996), pp.1–32; Pitcher, 'Recreating colonialism or reconstructing the state? privatization and politics in Mozambique', *JSAS* 22, 1 (1996), pp.49–74; John S. Saul,

Recolonization and Resistance: Southern Africa in the 1990s, Africa World Press, Trenton, 1993. The complex issues around land are raised in Gregory Myers, 'Comparative rights, competitive claims: land access in post-war Mozambique', *JSAS* 20, 4 (1994), pp.603–32; Harry G. West and Gregory W. Myers, 'A piece of land and a land of peace? state farm divestiture in Mozambique', *JMAS* 34 (1996), pp.27–51; *Mozambique Peace Process Bulletin* issue 17 (November 1996): part 2, 'Land law sets precedents for debate', by Joseph Hanlon.

Joseph Hanlon's work on recent Mozambican history merits a shelf of its own. He explores the complexity of Mozambique's national, regional and international situations with a command of detail and sources from interviews and unpublished papers to reports by the World Bank and Human Rights Watch: Joseph Hanlon, *Mozambique: The Revolution under Fire*, Zed Press, London, 1984; *Beggar Your Neighbors: Apartheid Power in Southern Africa*, Indiana University Press, Bloomington, IN, 1986; *Mozambique: Who Calls the Shots?*, Indiana University Press, Bloomington, IN, 1991; *Peace Without Profit: How Adjustment Blocks Rebuilding in Mozambique*, Heinemann, Portsmouth, NH, 1997.

William Finnegan's, *A Complicated War: The Harrowing of Mozambique*, University of California, Berkeley, 1992 conveys the perspective of a fresh, yet sensitive, outside observer. To some extent Finnegan does for Mozambique what Joseph Lelyveld did for South Africa in *Move Your Shadow: South Africa, Black and White*, Times Books, New York, 1985: he made the tragedies, ironies and complexities of the situation accessible to the American public. Essays by Kenneth Maxwell, Gillian Gunn, Carlos Gaspar and Richard J. Bloomfield in Bloomfield (ed.), *Regional Conflict and U.S. Policy: Angola and Mozambique*, Reference Publications, Inc., Algonac, 1988, help place Mozambique's experience in an international context chilled by the Cold War. See also Allen F. Isaacman, 'Mozambique: tugging at the chains of dependency', in Gerald Bender (ed.), *African Crisis Areas and U.S. Foreign Policy*, University of California, Berkeley, 1985, pp.129–57.

William Minter and Alex Vines both write extensively about Renamo and regional conflict: William Minter, *Apartheid's Contras: An Inquiry into the Roots of War in Angola and Mozambique*, Zed Books, Atlantic Highlands, 1994; Vines, *RENAMO: Terrorism in Mozambique*, Indiana University Press, Bloomington, IN, 1991. See also K. B. Wilson's 'Cults of violence and counter-violence in Mozambique', *JSAS*, 18, 3 (Sept. 1992), pp.527–82; Tom Young, 'The MNR/RENAMO: External and Internal Dynamics', *African Affairs*, 89, 357 (Oct. 1990), pp.491–509; Margaret Hall, 'The Mozambican National Resistance Movement (RENAMO): a study in the destruction of an African country', *Africa*, 60, 1 (1990), pp.39–68.

Perspectives on contemporary issues in Mozambique are raised in the following: João Bernardo Honwana, 'Establishing democractic defense forces in Mozambique: a case study', in H.-J. Spanger and P. Vale (eds), *Bridges to the Future: prospects for Peace and Security in Southern Africa*, Westview Press, Boulder, CO, 1995; John S. Saul, *Recolonization and Resistance: Southern Africa in the 1990s*, Africa World Press, Trenton, NJ, 1993. The peace process is detailed in Brazão Mazula et al., *Moçambique: Eleições Democracia e Desenvolvimento*, A. Embaixado, Maputo, 1995 and Alex Vines, *'No Democracy Without Money': The Road to Peace in Mozambique, 1982–1992*, Catholic Institute for International Relations, London, 1994; Kathleen Sheldon, 'Women and Revolution in Mozambique: A Luta Continua' in Mary Ann Tétreault (ed.), *Women and Revolution in Africa, Asia and the New World*, University of South Carolina Press, Columbia, SC, 1994; K. B. Wilson, 'Refugees and returnees as social agents – the case of the Jehovah's Witness from Milange', and K. B. Wilson with J. Nunes, 'Repatriation to Mozambique – refugee initiative and agency planning in Milange District 1988–1991', both in Tim Allen and Hubert Morsink (eds), *When Refugees Go Home: African Experiences*, Africa World Press, Trenton, NJ, 1994.

Finally, the following confirm that the struggle continues in Mozambique: Rachel Waterman, *Up from the Ashes*, Oxfam, Oxford, 1996 and Patricia Flederman (ed.), *Despite the Odds: A collection of Case Studies on Development Projects in Mozambique*, UNICEF, Maputo, 1993.

Acknowledgements

The editors wish to thank the Nuffield Foundation for a grant which enabled them, the eight authors, and an international team of discussants to analyse previously circulated copies of this research at a workshop held in Saint Antony's College, Oxford, on 2–5 July 1996. They are very grateful to Professor Terence Ranger who hosted the workshop and to Dr Phyllis Ferguson who undertook the administrative preparation. They would also like to thank all those who participated for their critical advice.

Phyllis Martin wishes to thank Indiana University for research support and Joanna Ochsner for her assistance in compiling tables and checking bibliographies.

Robert Buijtenhuijs is grateful for the research support which he received from the African Studies Centre, Leiden, Netherlands. He also wishes to thank Andreas Mehler and Elikia M'Bokolo for the comments they sent on his draft chapter since he was in Chad at the time of the workshop.

Crawford Young expresses his appreciation to Michael Schatzberg, Jean-Luc Vellut and Bogumil Jewsiewicki for their comments on a draft of his chapter. He also acknowledges the work of the Cartographic Laboratory at the University of Wisconsin on his maps.

Christine Messiant particularly wishes to acknowledge the critical comments of the editors and their rewriting and translation skills.

Megan Vaughan wishes to thank Sharon Molteno for her invaluable help in preparing her chapter.

Jeanne Penvenne thanks the Tufts University History Department, the Tufts Faculty Research Awards Committee and the American Council of Learned Societies for bibliographical and travel assistance. Bibliographical material was supplied by Anafidelia Tavares, Sol Gittleman, Gerald Gill, Benigna Zimba, Eric Allina, Teresa Cruz e Silva, Olga Iglésias Neves, Norman R. Bennett, David Hedges, Antónia Sopa, Jocelyn Alexander, Joann McGregor, Robin Palmer, Anne Pitcher and Leroy Vail. Special thanks are due to Kathleen

Sheldon, Sherilynn Young, Anne Pitcher and the Oxford workshop for excellent critiques.

David Birmingham gratefully received assistance from the University of Kent, from the secretarial staff of the History School, and from Elizabeth Birmingham who drafted most of the maps.

Index

315